# Snowshoeing
# Colorado

# Snowshoeing Colorado

Claire Walter

Fulcrum Publishing
Golden, Colorado

Library of Congress Cataloging-in-Publication Data

Walter, Claire.
    Snowshoeing Colorado / Claire Walter.
      p.   cm.
    Includes bibliographical references and index.
    ISBN 1-55591-403-9 (pbk.)
    1. Snowshoes and snowshoeing—Colorado—Guidebooks.   2. Trails—
Colorado—Guidebooks.   3. Colorado—Guidebooks.   I. Title.
GV853.W35   1998
917.8804'33—dc21                                            98–29071
                                                               CIP

Printed in the United States of America
0  9  8  7  6  5  4  3  2  1

Fulcrum Publishing
350 Indiana Street, Suite 350
Golden, Colorado 80401-5093
(800) 992-2908 • (303) 277-1623
website: www.fulcrum-books.com • e-mail: fulcrum@fulcrum-books.com

# Contents

# Preface

My snowshoeing history resembles many other people's—perhaps yours. I first tried snowshoes some years ago, on a visit to California's Yosemite National Park, on a ranger's recommendation for exploring the Mariposa Grove of giant sequoias. The snowshoes were the old wooden variety—probably too big, and definitely too heavy, for my height and weight—the kind that should have been retired to become decorative objects over someone's fireplace. The wet snow kept wadding up under my boot soles and hardening until I felt as if I were walking with baseballs under my arches. I rolled along like the proverbial drunken sailor until I could hardly stand up. Periodically, I'd have to stop, unstrap the snowshoes, chip away at the rock-hard clumps and saddle up again for the next leg of the hike.

At first, I longed for the familiarity of cross-country skis on the descent into the grove, but even then I grudgingly acknowledged the advantages of snowshoes, frustrations and all. It was nice not to think about snagging long skis on the underbrush. It was liberating to stomp off by myself without worrying about sinking knee-deep into the snow. It was fun to take little detours to see another tree from another angle, just getting far enough from the group to be awed by the arboreal majesty. Yet, in their own way, the snowshoes inspired as much humility as the sequoias. My gait was ducklike, and my energy expenditure certainly excessive, but because I was in such a special place, I was willing to waddle and chip and scrape snow until I ran out of steam, which was right about the time the naturalist trip ended. Even in my discomfort, I knew snowshoes had great potential, if someone would only perfect them.

And darned if that hasn't happened. Technology has taken hold of this ancient form of snow travel and turned it into a beguiling winter recreational activity. Today's snowshoes have all the benefits of the traditional wooden ones but without the drawbacks. Current models are lightweight, the bindings are easier to use and talons underfoot minimize sliding on slopes. Although some hardcore traditionalists still use them, the tennis-racquet-like snowshoes that frustrated me in Yosemite have fallen out of favor.

Back home in Colorado, my snowshoe epiphany came on a summer hike. A few years ago, my husband and I planned a late-June hike to

Playing on snowshoes at Cathedral Lake in late June—
an epiphany for the author. *Photo by Ral Sandberg.*

Cathedral Lake near Aspen. When we heard about the heavy snowpack remaining near the lake, we strapped borrowed snowshoes to our packs and began hiking. We felt silly, in the 90-degree heat, with the tools of winter flopping along behind us. Then, as we got close to the lake, several hikers on their way down remarked, "You'll be really glad you brought those. There's still a lot of snow up there, and it's soft." And we were glad. The snowshoes allowed us to frolic on the snow surface while other hikers were post-holing the final quarter mile. We fooled around like kids with new toys, then clomped off to the far side of the lake for a picnic in splendid isolation, even on a summer Sunday when we shared the trail with many other hikers. Since then, I've come to love the freedom and ease of snowshoeing. And, yes, it's fun and good exercise too.

## About This Book

Writing a where-to guide for Colorado snowshoers is a daunting task, because when there's snow on the ground, you can go just about anywhere on snowshoes. Indeed, one of the sport's greatest pleasures is its versatility. *Snowshoeing Colorado* is a trail guide—and more. It starts as a basic resource for the new snowshoer and veteran, followed by descriptions of some of the best, most accessible and varied trails, as well as guided snowshoe tours, snowshoe races and sources for equipment and further information of equal interest to new and experienced snowshoers. Traditional wood frame snowshoes and contemporary lightweight models are different, but assume that issues of equipment and technique in this book refer to modern snowshoes. This book concentrates on representative snowshoeing routes within day-trip distance of Front Range population centers, as well as a sampling of trails at and very near major resorts. I've narrowed it down by selecting, in some of the state's most popular and accessible recreation areas, an easy trail, several moderate ones and perhaps a challenging one.

# How Trails Are Described

Each trail description begins with some important statistics: starting elevation, highest elevation, elevation difference (including gains and losses due to undulations in the route) for the length described, and distance (one way or loop). Starting elevation, measured at the trailhead, and highest point should be pretty straightforward, but even expert sources frequently conflict. For example, Bierstadt Lake, one of the most popular year-round hiking destinations in Rocky Mountain National Park, is shown at 9,320 feet on the park's own Bear Lake Area winter map and at 9,416 feet on the U.S. Geological Survey's 7.5 Minute topographic map. Kent and Donna Dannen's *Rocky Mountain Hiking Trails* uses the USGS figure, while Dave Muller's equally carefully researched *Colorado Mountain Ski Tours and Hikes* uses 9,430 feet. The two altimeters in our family have each indicated different elevations (different from each other and from those listed above) each time we've hiked to this beautiful lake, and when you go, yours probably will show yet another number. So we've done our best, but consider these numbers guidelines and not gospel.

Elevation gain and trail length are even more elusive to pin down, because undulations in the trail make measurements difficult. Additionally, variations between summer and winter versions of the same route sometimes modify its length, and snowshoers often bushwhack and shortcut a standard route. One-way distances are the maximum length, in miles, for the routes described. Obviously, they must be doubled for an out-and-back round-trip. They can be shortened, and in many cases, the prime route description is followed by a few words on possible extensions for strong, fast snowshoers.

"Difficulty" is subjective. In this book, "Easy" means a route that is wide, flat and has very little elevation change. "Challenging" refers to a route that has one long or several shorter steep sections, is a long route, is at high elevation or exhibits a combination of these factors. "Moderate" is everything in between. I have purposely avoided giving hiking times, because time is based on a number of factors. It takes longer to cover the same distance and elevation gain when breaking trail than it does on packed-down snow, and conditioning, skill level and experience factor in also. A well-conditioned runner and a parent with a small child cover the same distance in very different times.

# Of Skiers, Snow Slides and Other Matters

Many of the trails are on public lands, mostly managed by the U.S. Forest Service. The routes are open to the public for recreational use, and you can find many of them described in numerous hiking and backcountry ski guides. Because cross-country skiing became popular before snowshoeing took off, and because snowshoers and skiers share the same trails, skiing and awareness of skiing and other uses are often mentioned in this book. Also, snowshoeing is such a multifaceted activity that this book attempts to be more than just a trail guide, also covering snowshoeing venues beyond the trails on public lands. Therefore, snowshoeing opportunities at cross-country ski centers and Alpine areas are included, as are guided snowshoe tours and annual races.

Forest Service and National Park rangers who are familiar with each area have been asked to confirm distances, elevations and such and also to provide their take on avalanche hazard for these routes. When the danger level is described as "None," it means that there are no slopes anyplace nearby where snow could slide. "Low" means that such problems are very unlikely. "Moderate" is just that, implying that the route is probably safe in low-hazard situations, while "High" means stay away unless hazards are reported *and* you are experienced in the winter backcountry. For information on obtaining timely avalanche reports, see Appendix E, page 297.

In addition, this book is defined as much by what it is not as by what it is. It is not intended as an in-depth book on snowshoeing equipment or technique, nor is it meant to be a guide to the deep backcountry, nor is it a primer on cold-weather camping or winter survival, nor is it a training manual for serious snowshoe racers. Other authors have covered these subjects in depth. Although these topics are valid and are occasionally touched on where appropriate here, they go beyond the scope of this book.

Claire Walter
Boulder, Colorado
July 1998

# Acknowledgments

In preparation for writing this book during the winter of 1997–1998, I racked up many miles on snowshoes and more on my car's odometer. I've traveled around Colorado to snowshoe on National Park and National Forest trails; on cross-country trails lovingly tended by volunteers; on professionally maintained trails at for-profit Nordic centers and guest ranches, and up and down ski trails at Alpine areas. I've gone alone, I've followed guides and I've shared trails with friends. I have many people to thank for making the research such a pleasure.

Professionals—snowshoeing guides, racers and others—who have given of their time and shared their insights to help make this book as good as it is include Katey Buster in Aspen, Terry DuBeau in Salida, Dave Felkley in Nederland, Jana Hlavaty at Keystone, Jean Pavillard and Mary Pavillard-Cain in Crested Butte, Robb Reece at Powderhorn and Grand Mesa, Erik Skarvan in Aspen, Tom Sobal in Leadville, Karen Walker in Telluride, Rebecca Lemburg Weiss in Aspen, Cathy Young in Crested Butte and the "guest wranglers" at dude ranches that I visited in my winter travels. Representatives of snowshoe companies, cross-country centers, Alpine ski resorts, resort associations and chambers of commerce helped me round out this book, and also supplied the finest photographs. Mike's Camera of Boulder gave me permission to use the information on "Photography in the Snow" from the store's customer newsletter. My appreciation also extends to my friends, Jim Boeck and especially Janet Robertson, who critiqued chapters and shared their knowledge of and insights into trails with which they are very familiar, and to Rebecca Horowitz for research assistance.

I appreciate my patient snowshoeing companions, who were always willing to wait while I scribbled notes or took some photos, often of them. So thanks to Jim Boeck, Kathleen Brown, Laura Burke, Lee Fowler, Patti Hecht, Holly Johnson, Crimson Guido, Warren and Karen Ohlrich, Jeannie Patton and Vivian Wilson.

On behalf of us all who love the outdoors, thanks also go to the dedicated rangers in Colorado's National Forests and National Parks who devote themselves to nurturing our special backcountry. In particular, I direct my appreciation to those who took the time to go over the manuscript to help me get my facts straight.

My deepest gratitude goes to my husband, Ral Sandberg, who joined in as many trips as his schedule permitted. He also contributed many photographs to this book, and poured over maps and instruments to track elevations and distances and make it as accurate as possible.

And of course, appreciation flows to Alison Auch and Daniel Forrest-Bank, my editors at Fulcrum Publishing, who have now shepherded another of my works from concept to completion; to Patty Maher who saw it through the book-production process and to Bill Spahr who designed the book.

# Introduction

Snowshoes are the sport utility vehicles of the winter backcountry. They can take you virtually anywhere there's snow. These big webbed feet that attach to your smaller ones provide hassle-free access to the white world, limited mainly by your level of fitness, your experience in the backcountry, your liking for marked trails at a ski-touring center and your feelings about guided touring versus the quiet companionship of just a good friend or two. It's a tranquil activity, yet it can be a sociable one. Snowshoeing with a group of amiable companions is not just a winter pleasure, but a safety measure as well.

Other than the snowshoes themselves, you probably already own all the equipment and clothing you'll need. Quite literally, if you can walk, you can snowshoe. The learning curve is minimal, the pleasures are virtually instant and the chances for injury are far less than for most other outdoor activities. It's a multigenerational sport, one which parents can do with their children, and adults can do with their own parents.

Snowshoeing is so hot that it's cool. Why? It's practically custom-made for baby boomers, no longer in the flower of youth, who find it a low-key, easy way to enjoy winter, bond with nature and get whatever degree of exercise they desire. It is winter's answer to walking and hiking, which are arguably America's most popular outdoor leisure activities, and it is equally popular with ultra-fit runners, who use it for winter training. In short, it is an activity that crosses boundaries of age, fitness level, outdoor experience and personal ambition.

You can follow a well-marked trail at a cross-country or Alpine ski center, or amble along a hiking trail or even a local park path dozing under a blanket of white, where it's impossible to get lost or confused. You can roam around in the confined area of a snowed-in campground to get the feel of snowshoeing, or wander down a snow-covered logging or mining road that may be closed to vehicles in winter or that at least has minimal traffic. You can enjoy snowshoeing as a family, or join a guided naturalist tour to learn about the seemingly somnolent winter world. You can slot snowshoe running into the most ardent fitness program. Or you can bundle up for a snowshoe walk under a full moon, which can be an incredibly romantic experience, even if you and your special someone are snowshoeing with a group and are not alone.

## Roots and New Growth

Snowshoeing is at once the newest snowsport and one of the oldest. Snowshoes' origins are shrouded in the misty days of prehistory and distant places. The year 4000 B.C. is an oft-quoted guesstimate for the existence of the earliest ones. Some archaeologists believe the first snowshoes were lashed together circles or ovals of wood, bark or rawhide. Others believe that they were solid slabs of wood. They probably were first made in central Asia. It is conceivable—in fact, very likely—that the people who long ago crossed the Bering land bridge to North America did so on snowshoes.

Over the centuries, snowshoes were refined. They are used by the native peoples of the Arctic region, those early North Americans whose ancestors came to this continent on rudimentary snowshoes. Their descendants moved south into the Great Plains as well as into the forested but still snowy zones we know as the North Woods, where they still needed over-snow transportation. They developed finely crafted wood frame models, often of ash with rawhide webbing, and added crossbars for lateral stability. They also developed long-tailed models as an improvement over the simple oval for tracking straight and tinkered with the part that actually holds the foot onto the snowshoe.

After this slow evolution, during which wooden models were steadily improved, the late twentieth century has witnessed a true revolution in snowshoe design. Dramatic technical advances—lightweight, easy-to-use aluminum frame snowshoes, functional footwear and versatile winter outerwear—have turned a quaint, quirky Paul Bunyan–esque activity that was primarily functional into a fast-growing recreational activity. Unprecedented numbers of snowshoers have established their place in the backcountry, on trails and elsewhere in the snowbelt. Snowshoe sales have, not surprisingly, skyrocketed. Many Colorado winter trails now see more snowshoers than skiers.

# THE BASICS

# Getting Started

Snowshoeing is so technically simple that just about all you have to do is decide to try it, and then go out and do it. You can amble, stride, jog or run on snowshoes. This sport doesn't involve much more than putting one foot in front of the other. "Learning" to snowshoe is as simple as getting used to having gear on your feet that sort of flops up and down while you walk. Fifty paces on the flat, and you're a snowshoer. Fifteen minutes later and you've got some experience under your belt. After an hour on a few inches of snow and varied terrain, you might call yourself an expert.

The preparation is as straightforward as the activity. Dress for winter in warm, breathable layers that you can don or shed as body heat and weather dictate. Put on warm socks (wool, silk/wool or fleece), waterproof footwear (Sorel-type boots, Gore-Tex hiking boots or the new generation of footwear especially designed for snowshoeing) and a pair of gaiters. Snugly strap on a pair of lightweight snowshoes, and take ski poles for stability and balance. And, oh yes, slather on some sunscreen, because the combination of sun and snow can bring more than just the rosy glow of the outdoors to your cheeks, and protect your precious eyes with UV-filtering sunglasses or goggles. Grab a daypack and a water bottle, and off you go.

Outdoor, hiking and ski retail stores all over Colorado rent snowshoes for a very modest amount of money, usually $10 or less per day, which normally can be applied to the purchase if you decide to buy a pair. You'll find many of these outlets listed in Appendix D (page 285). Putting on snowshoes isn't much more complicated than getting into a car and fastening the seatbelt, and someone at the rental shop will even show you how to do it. Subsequent chapters of this book cover equipment, clothing and technique in more detail, but here are the quick-and-dirty basics of snowshoeing.

## Starting Off on the Right Foot

There is actually no "wrong foot" in snowshoeing, but you may feel more comfortable beginning with a little lesson, or you may want to tap into snowshoeing's sociable side from the start. All sorts of outdoor clubs, social organizations from singles' to seniors' clubs, recreation centers and adult education programs are putting snowshoeing on their winter calendars. It has become a staple with the esteemed **Colorado Mountain Club,** which now has 150 or more snowshoeing trips on its winter schedule for their members. Snowshoeing increasingly is finding its way into local snow festivals. All of these are discussed in the following chapters. Sporting goods stores that sell and rent snowshoes also often put on clinics, workshops or slide shows on the subject. Check local newspapers for listings of snowshoeing activities.

Organized trips are popping up all over Colorado. Rocky Mountain National Park rangers lead free weekend snowshoe hikes from late December through the end of March. For details, see the Rocky Mountain National Park–East chapter (page 49) and Rocky Mountain National Park–West chapter (page 209). Snowshoeing guides based at mountain resorts lead excursions on quiet trails within the confines of the lift-served ski area or nearby and cater to resort guests. Naturalist-guides pass on their knowledge about winter ecology in the mountains and show clients how to identify animal tracks in the snow. Hiking and climbing guides have found a winter niche, customizing snowshoe tours for any level of fitness, from timid novices to veterans who want to learn about winter camping and mountaineering. Some even offer avalanche safety courses.

First-time snowshoer gearing up for a guided tour at Telluride. *Photo courtesy Telluride Ski and Mountain Resort.*

Winter Trails Day held in mid- to late February at locations all over the snowbelt provides newcomers with a free introduction to the sport via use of demo equipment and instruction, often in a festive atmosphere. When it debuted in 1997 with very little fanfare, more than 2,000 people showed up at community parks, nature centers and public lands whose recreation trails are used for snowshoeing. You can call the **American Hiking Society** toll-free at **(888) SNO-HIKE**, check www.snowlink.com or keep your eyes open for Winter Trails Day promotional material alerting you to where and when it will take place.

A major issue for skiers and snowshoers is trail etiquette, especially in areas close to Colorado's Front Range population centers, and when they are not accustomed to each other's sports, conflicts often arise. In most places, snowshoers and cross-country skiers share the same trails. At established cross-country centers, a set of parallel, ski-width "classical tracks" is mechanically etched into the snow for skiers to follow. These areas generally ask snowshoers to stay on the "skating lanes," which are wide, trackless trails. Some Nordic ski areas offer designated snowshoeing trails, while others prohibit snowshoeing entirely to prevent conflict. In the backcountry, the first skiers to break trail set tracks in new snow. They often do this at great effort, especially on the uphill, expecting the reward of a fast downhill run on the return. They get *very* upset when snowshoers have walked on their tracks. Leave No Trace, a

Snowshoes to provide floatation on snow and winter-worthy boots are all the gear needed for snowshoeing. Poles are optional—but popular. *Photo by Alan Becker/ Redfeather Snowshoes.*

national organization dedicated to promoting ethical use of the wilderness, is developing winter guidelines that will probably address trail etiquette issues. For more information on trail courtesies, see the Technique chapter (page 23).

# Equipment Basics

The typical modern snowshoe consists of a lightweight aluminum frame with a platform made of a durable, forgiving fabric for flotation on the snow, a binding that affixes your foot to the snowshoe and a mechanism that allows the foot to move in a natural, free-heel stride, so that your gait is close to your normal walking or running motion. Snowshoes also have metal talons (also called crampons or claws) on the bottom for traction. Snowshoes come with integrated bindings, so take a few moments to adjust the binding or strapping system to your footwear of choice (see pages 10 and 13) and learn how the buckle system works. The shop where you rent or buy will help you with this. See the Equipment chapter (page 9) for more on selecting snowshoes and accessories.

# Clothing Basics

Dress in layers and be prepared to shed or add layers if you heat up or cool down or if the weather changes abruptly, as it often does in Colorado's high country. Thermal underwear, windproof pants, an insulating layer of synthetic fleece or wool and a windproof and water-repellent shell jacket are the basic components of a layering system. Some snowshoers like to add a vest, or use a vest instead of a long-sleeved pullover, sweater or shirt as the insulating jacket. A hat and a pair of warm gloves complete the basic outfit. If you are going for a short snowshoe at an established resort center, you can be casual with the number of layers and options you take along. However, if you are going out for several hours and particularly into the backcountry, never assume that the weather will be as good when you are out there as when you get out of your car. Being prepared for worse—often far worse—weather than at the beginning of your excursion isn't just a good idea. It can save your life. For more on apparel, see the Clothing chapter (page 19).

# Packing the Pack

A daypack or waist pack isn't "equipment" in the sense of snowshoes and poles, nor is it "clothing" in any sense even though you wear it. Nor is it an accessory, but rather a necessity. The size of your pack depends on how much you're carrying. For a short hike in a controlled situation such as a cross-country or Alpine ski area or on a guided tour, a waist pack with an extra layer of clothing, sunscreen and water will probably do. If you're going out for several hours away from support services, prepare as you would for mountain hiking. Plan on toting a daypack stocked with extra layers of clothing, extra socks, water and food (snacks, lunch and perhaps a couple of energy bars), plus basic emergency gear (a small first aid kit, waterproof matches and/or flashlight, a pocket knife, a whistle for emergencies, chemically activated hand and foot warmers and, of course, proper navigation aids). For more on the whats and whys of what you'll need, see the Backcountry Cautions chapter (page 30).

# How Far? How Fast?

When you begin planning your first snowshoe outing, how do you select a trail to match your stamina and ability? Experience is the best way, but if you don't have a lot of backcountry experience, you can tap into the knowledge of someone who has. If you are new to winter walking or hiking, you can sign up for an introductory program at an outdoor store or recreation center, which often will include a class excursion. You can take a guided beginner tour led by a ranger or professional guide. Making your first snowshoe excursion at a cross-country center with marked trails, facilities and patrollers is not a bad idea, especially if you are not an experienced summer hiker.

If you want to go on your own, start with one of the easy routes in this book or, if you are more ambitious, select an out-and-back trail so that you can turn around when you need to. Altitude, dry air and the unaccustomed weight on your feet can affect you. Until you have some mileage under your snowshoes, be conservative in estimating your energy and limitations.

However, if you are an experienced summer hiker, you will probably know the impact of variations in terrain, weather and other factors. For instance, you already know that you cannot make the same time or keep the same pace in the mountains as you do in town. Four miles an hour is considered a good, solid walking pace on dry pavement. Two miles an hour on a trail with up to a 1,000-foot elevation gain is a respectable hiking pace. Leadville-based snowshoe racer Tom Sobal believes that a fit snowshoer who is used to his or her equipment will go 25 percent slower than on bare ground "under the best conditions," which is to say snow that is hard packed and fast. Add the element of soft snow, which is kind to your joints but cuts your speed, and your pace will be slower. In addition, breaking trail is slower and requires far more energy than snowshoeing on a packed route.

The upshot of all these variables is: Don't be disappointed if you are only hiking 1.5 to 2 miles an hour on snowshoes and, more important, plan your itinerary accordingly. Unless you are a runner, a 6- or 7-mile tour could easily take the better part of a day. Also remember the obvious: Mid-winter days are short, so you will probably start out later and lose light and heat far earlier than you would in summer.

When you are ready for your first snowshoe outing, plan to go with at least one other person or in a group. Remember that a group's pace is only as fast as its slowest member. Underestimating your snowshoeing pace is wiser than overestimating it until you've been out a few times and know how accurate your estimates are. When selecting a backcountry trail take into account your fitness and energy, as well as that of your companions. Then factor in trail length, elevation, snow conditions and weather. If you plan on a loop trail, you are committed to the whole route once you have passed the halfway point. An out-and-back trail gives you the option of turning around whenever you wish, but remember that you have to double the distance to return to the trailhead.

Snowshoeing is an individual yet a very sociable activity, not just for companionship, but also for safety. Again, a guided hike is not a bad idea for your snowshoeing inaugural, especially if are going alone. Later, as you become more experienced, be sure to tell someone reliable of your plans if you do hike alone, and check in with him or her upon your safe return.

## Technique Basics

Snowshoeing technique is essentially as easy as walking. On flat ground, or on a slope that is mild to moderate, all you have to do is to put one foot in front of the other and go. The greatest adjustment you'll have to make to your gait is to walk with your feet a bit wider apart than normal so that you don't step on your own snowshoes or kick the frame of your forward foot as your back one passes it. If the snow is hard packed and sloping, pressing the talons firmly into the snow with each step will give you traction and prevent backsliding. Snowshoes will not keep you on top of soft snow. In fresh powder, which is where snowshoes really shine, the surface will shift some and compress under your weight, and you'll feel as if you were walking on feather-light sand, if you can imagine such a thing.

When you are descending, keep your weight over your heels as much as possible. The talons provide traction, so if the snow is firm or the slope is steep, be sure that they are biting firmly into the surface. If the snow is deep and the slope is steep (though not dangerously so, please), you might want to play at glissading. Take long, gliding strides—sort of a downhill lope—and keep the snowshoe toes up out of the snow. You will find this exhilarating. For hints on snowshoeing on more advanced terrain or in other conditions, see the Technique chapter (page 23).

## The Fitness Dividend

Snowshoeing at any level is good for your body. At its most fundamental, this low-impact activity also boasts an injury rate so low that injuries are not even an issue. Spills tend to be gentle, and because every step and stride is different, muscles and joints are not even susceptible to the kind of overuse or repetitive-motion problems that plague participants in such other sports as running, tennis and mogul skiing. In fact, as soon as suitable equipment became commonly available, serious runners discovered snowshoeing to be outstanding winter training for their summer sport.

## Snowshoeing Checklist

### Equipment and Accessories

- Snowshoes
- Boots
- Warm socks
- Gaiters
- Poles (optional)

### Clothing and Accessories

- Base layer (polypropylene top, tights)
- Insulating layer (fleece or insulated long-sleeved top or vest)
- Outer layer (waterproof, breathable jacket or shell)
- Hat (headband optional)
- Gloves
- Neck gaiter

### Other Necessities for the Trail

- Pack
- Water (between 1 pint per hour and 1 quart per outing, per person)
- Food (including more than you think you'll need, energy bars and, on cold days, a Thermos of hot tea or soup)
- Trail map
- Compass
- Sunglasses
- Sunscreen
- First aid kit
- Waterproof matches and/or lighter
- Pocket knife
- Whistle
- Flashlight
- Extra socks
- Chemically activated hand and boot warmers
- Watch

### Extras for the Backcountry

- Navigational aid
- Avalanche beacon
- Ice ax
- Shovel
- Wire pocket saw

- Fire starter
- Bivouac sack, space blanket or emergency shelter
- More spare clothing, food and water

Some people hit the trail at full speed. *Photo by Alan Becker/Redfeather Snowshoes.*

# Hit the Trail

Once you've outfitted yourself with gear and duds and have gone on a couple of group snowshoe hikes—perhaps even have played around on your snowshoes in a park near your home—you'll want to get out and explore the backcountry on your own. You probably have some summer hiking experience, when following a well-trod trail is easy. Still, you may wonder what clues you can use in winter to prevent you from getting lost when everything is white, and even familiar territory looks different.

Fortunately, others often will have blazed a trail for you, literally and figuratively. You will be able to follow the tracks of snowshoers and skiers who have preceded you. On well-traveled trails, even new snow does not usually obliterate established paths. However, on public lands, you can follow permanent trail markers, called blazes, which are more reliable than someone else's tracks. Summer four-wheel-drive roads are wide swaths cut through forest that you will find easy to follow, even in winter. If the road is also open to snowmobiles in winter, you will see orange diamond markers affixed at intervals to trees along the route. Any route prohibited to snowmobilers is marked by blue diamond markers. When a trail crosses an open area, these blue markers may be attached to poles stuck into the snow. Summer and winter trails may go to the same destinations, but they do not always follow the same route. A summer trail might cross an area that is a winter avalanche hazard zone, or a winter trail might cross an area that in summer is a marsh or a streambed. The rest of Part I summarizes what you need to know to get started, but the chapters that follow in Parts II through V summarize some of Colorado's best snowshoeing trails. It's time to put the pieces of the snowshoeing puzzle together and enjoy them too.

# Equipment

Snowshoes, waterproof boots and perhaps poles are all the gear you'll need to become a snowshoer. Snowshoes come fully assembled with integral bindings that can be adjusted easily to fit your boot and traction devices underfoot. At the end of the 1990s, a pair of snowshoes ranged in price from about $100 to $250, and kids' snowshoes started at even lower prices. Modern snowshoes are virtually indestructible, so you'll probably have whatever you buy for a long time. Recognizing, however, that someone out there always manages to break the unbreakable, most models carry generous warranties. (For information on snowshoe equipment suppliers, see Appendix D, page 285.)

## Snowshoes in the Old Days

Traditional snowshoes, those wood frame numbers with a webbing or lacing of rawhide or other material to provide flotation over the snow, have been around for a long time. Purists still use the old-style shoes, especially for deep powder, but the great majority of participants are now on modern, aluminum alloy frame models. There's a lot of terminology related to traditional snowshoes that you probably won't need much, unless you find yourself gravitating toward the shapes and materials that are snowshoeing's heritage. Whether you ultimately go with the old or not, the following guide at least will clue you in to what others might be talking about. There are four basic designs of traditional snowshoes, and some styles have at least two names.

The Yukon, Alaskan or Pickerel snowshoe is oblong, usually between 4 and 5 feet long, and has turned up toes and long tails for tracking and stability. These snowshoes were developed for use in deep, heavy snow, especially over nonmountainous, open terrain, yet they are also well suited to descending steep slopes when the snow is soft.

The Algonquin, beavertail, Maine, Michigan or Huron snowshoe is a foot or two shorter but a couple of inches wider than the Yukon design. These snowshoes also have long tails, but less radically turned-up toes. They became most popular with Eastern snowshoers because they are good for hill ascents.

The Ojibwa snowshoe was designed in central Canada, where deep snow blanketed wide-open tracts. This snowshoe is characterized by a pointed, turned-up toe and long tail. An Ojibwa snowshoe can be as small as 9 by 36 inches or as beefy as 12 inches wide by 50 or 60 inches long. While most wooden snowshoe frames are made of one curved piece of wood, the Ojibwa is made of two that are affixed together at both the heel and the toe.

Finally, the bearpaw snowshoe is a short, wide and fairly flat oval suitable for dense underbrush and relatively even ground. Originally, they ranged from 14 by 36 inches to 12 by 30 inches, with the most common later being the modified model called the Green Mountain bearpaw at about 10 by 36 inches. They are good for kicking steps in the snow during steep ascents. Some later modifications incorporated a tail design to help them track and a nose lift to clear deep snow, as well as size adjustments that made them suitable for travel through underbrush and thickets.

Webbing or lacing, originally of rawhide and later of synthetic materials, provided flotation and kept the snowshoer from sinking far into the snow. Whatever the webbing material, the result resembled the strings of a tennis racquet. There were about as many kinds of traditional bindings as there were traditional snowshoes, but few users these days need to know a Western binding from a wet noodle binding. The most basic binding for these traditional models consists of two straps, one over the toe or instep and one behind the heel.

What made these snowshoe/binding combinations functional, and what is still important in modern bindings, is a design that enables the foot to move freely and naturally while walking. A binding that pivoted around a toe cord and toe hole that made room for the boot to move through the plane of the snowshoe enabled the foot to flex fully during the stride. This became standard for traditional snowshoes, and eventually rudimentary underfoot traction devices were also incorporated, even though the crossbars and rawhide or other lacing automatically provided fairly good traction on all but ice.

# Modern Snowshoes and Bindings

Modern snowshoes trace their roots back to the 1950s, with the development of the first aluminum frame models in the Pacific Northwest. In fact, for a time they were called (by those who noticed them) Western snowshoes. They limped along as an oddity among oddities until the 1970s, when they slowly began gathering fans. Smaller than even the most compact wood frame shoe, but with an assertively upturned toe and a solid, synthetic decking material in place of lacing or webbing, this type of early modern snowshoe was found to be lighter in weight, more maneuverable and more durable than wood ones. A metal pivot rod replaced the old toe cord, and more sophisticated bindings of nylon and/or plastic and built-in talons (also called cleats or claws) for traction have become standard over the years.

Just as wooden snowshoes evolved, so have the newer metal ones, with choices of size, material, frame shape, binding design and other components. By the end of the 1980s, the shift in design and materials was well under way, providing a launching platform for the rocketlike rise of snowshoeing in the 1990s. Snowshoes continue to change. Contemporary models with compact streamlined shapes enable the snowshoer to stand normally and stride as if not wearing the big shoes. Asymmetrical snowshoes come in mirror image right and left, like street shoes or ski boots. Symmetrical models differ only in the placement of the binding. The buckle is supposed to go on the outside of the foot, but that is not gospel, and some less flexible people find it easier to fasten the binding (or harness) when it is on the inside.

The advent of aluminum, and later aluminum alloy, snowshoes revolutionized the sport. Components include integrated bindings, a pivot mechanism and talons to grip the snow. *Photo courtesy Redfeather Snowshoes/ Peak Exposure.*

To adjust your snowshoes, place the ball of your foot, in the boot you will wear for snowshoeing, over the pivot point and then fit the toe or front part of the binding to your boot size. It might be some kind of heavy-duty nylon strapping system or a lace-up design, and straps, snap buckles or a ratchet mechanism is generally used to tighten the binding around your forefoot. With most binding types, once the toe is adjusted, you can just slip your boot in and out without having to readjust each time. Fasten the binding by tightening the heel strap. Step-in bindings compatible with cross-country boots and specialized bindings designed for snowboarding boots are also available from some makers. Other snowshoe models are collapsible for carrying and storing ease.

In addition to modern materials and easier fastening, today's binding is hinged around a rod that serves the same purpose as the old toe cord. The "free rotation" design allows the greatest range of motion, up to 90 degrees, and is popular for mountain snowshoeing up steep slopes. The "fixed" design limits rotation to 45 degrees, which keeps the snowshoe deck closer to the boot sole and offers more control. The "rotating" design is just that, a system that rotates freely and fully. You can also find snowshoe/binding combinations with special design features, such as a rigid plate that fits under the entire boot sole to provide additional stability, or built-in heel lifts for climbing steep slopes.

Injection-molded plastic snowshoes, which first became popular in Europe, are also gaining adherents in North America. Made of heavy-duty, lightweight plastics called copolymers, these snowshoes combine the frame and deck in one piece. Otherwise, they are similar to aluminum frame designs, with toe holes, bindings and some sort of pivot system.

## First Ladies

Crescent Moon became the first company to market a snowshoe specifically to women with the introduction of the Permagrin 13 model for the 1998–1999 season. The aircraft aluminum frame tapers into an exaggerated teardrop shape to accommodate the shorter stride. The snowshoe is 8 inches wide and 24 inches long, and weighs just 2 pounds, 10 ounces per pair, which is just a bit beefier than the company's performance running snowshoe.

One feature available with some of these shoes is a clip-on extender that provides additional carrying surface area and therefore better flotation in deep snow.

## Size Matters

Size is important, as it relates both to function and to weight. Today's snowshoes come not just in different shapes but also in different sizes for different purposes. While it is clear that, all other things being equal, a small shoe isn't enough for deep powder (it will sink), and that a large shoe is excessive on packed terrain, experts say that what really matters is weight. I have heard various comparisons, ranging from "1 pound on the foot is like 3 pounds on the back" to "1 pound on the foot is like more than 5 pounds on the back," so don't buy more snowshoe than you'll need for the conditions that you are most likely to encounter most of the time.

The most appropriate snowshoe size for you is a combination of your body weight, the snow conditions you are likely to encounter and the use you will make of them. The smallest snowshoes (about 6 by 16 or 17 inches) are designed for children. Slightly larger snowshoes, say about 6 by 21 inches, are best for mountain or trail running (or walking) on packed snow, especially by women and lightweight youths. These models weigh about 2 pounds per pair. Medium-size snowshoes (about 8 by 24 or 9 by 25 inches) weighing between 2.5 and 4 pounds per pair, are the golden mean. These multipurpose snowshoes are suitable for most adults to use under most conditions, including recreational day hikes on packed snow, broken trail, settled snow or fresh powder over a firm base.

The largest commonly available snowshoes (9 by 34 or 10 by 36 inches) are designed for a strong, large man carrying a heavy pack in deep snow, and may weigh 5 pounds or more. Specialized snowshoes complete the spectrum on each end: small children's snowshoes on the low-performance end and models designed for mountaineering or expeditions on the high-performance end. Manufacturers all print catalogs describing their models, including dimensions, weight and material specifications, as well as a chart for recommended sizes.

# Feet First

The single most common question that beginners ask is, "What should I wear on my feet?" Footwear, in this case the combination of boots and socks, needs to be warm and keep moisture out. Because snowshoe bindings are infinitely adjustable, you can wear pretty much what you want on your feet. For recreational snowshoeing, you can use traditional Sorel-type insulated and waterproof winter boots, waterproof hiking boots, water-resistant overshoes or even cross-country ski boots. When you get into the sport, you might consider the new specialized snowshoe boots that have appeared on the market, which feature extra insulation and waterproofing.

The most popular footwear for new snowshoers is what they are used to. In Colorado, where many people hike, waterproof hiking boots that are lined with Gore-Tex and/or treated with a waterproofing spray are a common choice. Runners often just use their running shoes, but get protection from the cold and moisture from Neoprene, either socks worn under their shoes or winter cycling booties over

## Heat for the Feet

"Waterproof and insulated" is the theme that runs through the snowshoeing footwear scene. Boots can be waterproof either because the material, like rubber, is inherently so or because it is a coated or laminated nylon or leather. Seal Skinz are waterproof socks made of a DuPont material. A Gore-Tex liner also waterproofs a boot. For some casual snowshoers, water-resistant boots are enough, and serious runners do use just regular running shoes with Neoprene socks, booties or spats for insulation. Other insulations that you might see are generics such as wool felt, wool fleece, acrylic pile fleece or polyester fleece, or such brand-name materials as Thermolite, Thinsulate, ThermoPlus or Zylex.

In addition to warm socks, insulated boots and/or spats, chemically activated heat packets, sold in ski and sporting goods stores, are great for snowshoers with chronically cold feet (usually women). Take them out of the cellophane wrapper, shake briefly and insert them into the boot toes before putting the boots on. The heat packs emit warmth in the confined space and help keep feet comfortable for hours.

them. If you prefer not to invest in specialized footwear, you can follow the same strategy, and if you have cross-country skiing boots that you're fond of, you can seek out snowshoes with multisport bindings (see below). Theoretically, telemark boots would also work, but they tend to be heavier than most snowshoers like.

With the sport's boom, boots designed specifically for snowshoeing are now on the market. Tecnica made the first, the Snow Paw, which debuted with all the characteristics desirable for snowshoeing. This warm and waterproof boot has been engineered for extra control on climbs, sidehill traverses and steep ascents and is also compatible with snowshoe binding systems. The distinctive feature that makes it a snowshoeing

While snowshoers generally use poles, and backcountry snowshoers virtually always do, people who run on snowshoes often find poles extraneous. *Photo courtesy Tubbs Snowshoe Company.*

boot, rather than a winter boot also suitable for snowshoeing, is the removable Pressure Distribution Plate. Nicknamed PDP, this insert in a pocket on top of the tongue disperses the pressure exerted by the boot's conventional laces and by extra leather to make the boot more comfortable. Also, it has a Velcro power strap to help hold the heel down in the boot and to alleviate instep discomfort.

Sorels and similar insulated boots are a category of cold weather footgear that snowshoers have long found suitable. Sorel itself, in fact, now offers the Active Performance Collection of lightweight boots, including models designed specifically for women. The Sorel Quest is a speed-lace boot with a nylon storm collar to eliminate the need for gaiters, a full-bellows tongue and a comfort rating to -40° Fahrenheit—the first snowshoe-specific product from a company that was founded in 1907.

Other new types of winter boots, some derived from Eskimo mukluks, are also appearing on the scene. For instance, Taiga makes an ultra-warm and ultra-lightweight high Polartec pull-on boot that is waterproofed and snugs on with a drawstring cuff and toestrap. N.E.O.S. makes a new generation of warm, weather-resistant and moderately priced overshoes that you can pull on over conventional running shoes. Salomon's Winter-X is a lace-up cold weather hiking boot that is insulated, waterproof and well cushioned, and has a small metal loop just below the laces to accommodate a gaiter hook. If these companies are successful with their snowshoe-friendly boots, others will surely follow.

## To Pole or Not to Pole

Ski poles are optional. Some snowshoers won't leave home without them, while others wouldn't be caught dead with them. This is a matter of personal taste and style. When you use ski poles, you swing your arms naturally—right foot/left arm, left foot/right arm—just as if you were walking. And when you are on a packed-snow trail, it will feel much like walking or cross-country skiing. By planting your pole ahead of you at each stride, you increase the cardiovascular benefit, add stability and reduce fatigue.

Another benefit of poles is that you can use them to knock off snow that clumps onto the talons under certain conditions, usually on warm days when new snow has fallen on a layer of packed snow. Just lift your foot, bang your pole against the frame, and the snow should fall off. If that doesn't work, you can use the pole tip to chip snow off the metal.

For snowshoeing only on packed trails, especially at a Nordic area, regular cross-country poles are enough to help you maintain rhythm while you walk. If you're planning to head mostly into the backcountry, a pair of heavy-duty mountaineering poles is what you'll need. Best are adjustable poles, whose shafts can be lengthened or shortened with just a twist. You can adjust these poles for the type of terrain (uphill, downhill or flat) and the snow depth that you encounter on any hike. Backcountry poles usually have large-diameter baskets for deep powder, and many models also can be coupled together to use as avalanche probes if needed. These benefits notwithstanding, most snowshoe runners do not use poles at all.

## Snowshoe Equipment Accessories

Gearheads unite. Even though snow-shoeing is a simple sport, special-purpose accessories have sprouted up all over to make snowshoeing easier, more fun or more convenient. They include:

- Add-on crampons that snap onto snowshoes to provide additional traction on ice, sidehills or steep downhills.
- A carrying bag, designed to protect your snowshoes during travel, and to protect other objects from being damaged by the talons.
- Heel lifts to keep your heel from extending down to the snow on steep climbs, therefore preventing the calf muscles from over-stretching, fatiguing and ultimately aching. They are made for extended climbs and are especially favored by upward-bound runners who train or race up ski trails. Made of a lightweight material such as molded polyethylene, they are designed to be easily attached to, or removed from, snowshoes.
- Multisport bindings, developed for cross-training. Such bindings accept three-pin, Nordic norm or hard-shell mountaineering boots for telemarkers, cross-country skiers or winter expeditions, respectively, as well as snowboarding boots for those legions of backcountry riders who must hike uphill for their turns. The bindings that take cross-country footwear are especially welcome in Nordic centers' rental programs.
- Snowboard packs, daypacks for backcountry riders that accommodate snowboards while snowshoeing uphill and snowshoes and poles while snowboarding downhill.

- Spats, small gaiters made of Neoprene or other synthetics, that snug around the foot to keep the ankles dry and also provide extra warmth.
- Talon covers, used for protection when storing or transporting snowshoes, even in a suitcase with clothing and other possessions.
- A small can of silicon spray, to be spritzed onto the talons to keep snow from clumping on them. This tends to occur on warm days when a couple of inches of fresh snow have fallen on packed snow.

# Other Gear You'll Need—Or Want

As simple as snowshoeing is, all sorts of accessory gadgetry can appeal to the most ardent gearhead, and enhance the snowshoe experience as well. Whether your "map" is as low-tech as a folded sheet of paper with a sketch on it or as high-tech as satellite-dependent GPS instruments, you need to know where you are and where you're going. Beyond that, various other tools and toys appeal to snowshoers.

## Personal Protection

If it's sunny, as it often is, you'll need to protect the parts of you that are most likely not to be covered by clothing, that is, your face and eyes, perhaps your ears and the back of your neck also. High SPF sunscreen and sunglasses affording ultraviolet protection are absolutely crucial in Colorado's winter outdoor environment. Apply sunscreen liberally, and reapply it during your snowshoeing day, especially if you are perspiring. For more on this topic, see the Backcountry Cautions chapter (page 30).

## Maps and Other Essential Navigation Aids

Unless you are very familiar with your route as it appears in winter, or are with a guide or someone else you can trust to be very familiar with your route as it appears in winter, venturing out without a map is silly at best and treacherous at worst. Routes may seem distinctive at first, but when you get into a crunch situation, especially in changing weather conditions and visibility, one trail through a forest of conifers and/or aspens may look a lot like another trail through similar trees.

If you are snowshoeing at a developed cross-country center, the area's patrol normally will ski each trail at day's end to make sure that no one is left out on the network, perhaps injured or simply lost. Nevertheless, all Nordic centers provide free trail maps, and you should take one and consult it. The U.S. Forest Service puts out maps of public lands under its jurisdiction showing roads, rivers, bridges and other landmarks, and commercial mapmakers such as Trails Illustrated issue maps designed for recreational use.

However, for the backcountry, the most useful map is the United States Geological Survey (USGS) 7.5-minute topographic map for the area. These maps, which are 1:24,000 scale, depict and identify paved and unpaved roads, trails, rivers, streams, summits, ridges, towns, townsites and mines. Each one also includes contour lines to indicate elevations, compass direction and declination and other pertinent information for route finding. A compass and an altimeter are also useful navigation aids, and if you know how to use them in concert with the appropriate map, getting lost is much less likely.

## Optional Instruments

The gizmos described below are not required, certainly not by casual recreational snowshoers, but they are nifty to have, especially for gadget fanatics.

Multifunction sport watches do more than tell time. Common features include an altimeter (and the ability to calculate vertical feet of your ascent or descent), a stopwatch, a thermometer, a barometer and more. Avocet Vertech launched this category of habit-forming instrument, which provides instant answers to, "How long have we been out?" "How far have we come up?" and other compelling questions that hikers tend to ask each other. The Kestrel 2000 is a handheld instrument that measures and calculates temperature, wind speed and wind chill.

If you plan extensive backcountry travel in risky regions located in avalanche-prone or high-hazard areas—perhaps snowshoeing to high slopes to snowboard or telemark—an avalanche transmitter or transceiver (also called a tracker) can speed rescue and possibly save your life if you are buried in a slide. A transceiver both emits and receives signals and is preferable for groups going out independently, who are responsible for their own searches. A transmitter only sends signals and is often used for guided groups, where the guides, who are trained in such matters, do the searching and the clients are asked to stay out of the way. Arva, Backcountry Access, Ortovox, Pieps, Ramer and Skadi all make state-of-the-art, high-frequency transceivers. Backcountry Access and Ramer are both based in Boulder, Colorado. Most instruments transmit on one frequency but are able to receive on several, but check before you go out into potentially hazardous terrain, because compatibility between the transmitting and receiving instruments is critical. Many mountaineering stores rent these devices.

More pinpoint precise than a compass/map/altimeter combination is a Global Positioning System (GPS) receiver, a device that allows one to find one's position anywhere on earth with incredible accuracy by receiving and interpreting satellite signals. It is the ultimate route-finding tool. These expensive instruments are not just useful for winter sports, but also for hiking, open-water sailing and even road trips in unpopulated areas. For information on GPS units, look for manufacturers such as Garmin International, Magellan Systems and Trimble Navigation.

Finally, if you have a lightweight cellular telephone, you can take it with you to use in case you are lost or someone in your party is injured or is caught in an avalanche. Cell phone coverage in the mountains, especially in tight valleys, is not 100 percent, but it is improving all the time. In an emergency, a call to 911 will be relayed to the appropriate county sheriff's office, which is responsible for organizing search-and-rescue operations in Colorado. Remember that your cell phone is battery operated and should be kept inside your jacket.

## Photography in the Snow

Whether you're aiming for high art or fond memories, you'll very likely want to take a camera with you on your snowshoeing excursions. A point-and-shoot camera is lighter weight than a conventional single-lens reflex camera, and unless you are taking high-action shots of snowshoe racing, it is a convenient type to take along. Otherwise, the good SLR that you probably already own provides great versatility in adjusting the settings to compensate for all that meter-fooling white. Still, taking good photographs in the snow can be tricky.

A popular saying is "what you see is what you get." Unfortunately, WYSIWYG does not apply to snow photography. Large areas of snow, or any white material, confuse light meters, causing photos to be underexposed. Color negative film (i.e., print film) has a great deal of latitude and is therefore more forgiving when the camera automatically adjusts for the film speed and cannot be changed, and some poorly exposed negatives can be corrected in printing.

Slide film, however, must be exposed properly in order to yield expected results. Light meters assume that a scene is medium (18 percent) gray. While this works for most situations, it will cause inaccurate exposures in scenes that contain lots of black and white. In the case of snow, the light meter will set an exposure that will render the snow gray (underexposed) rather than the white your eye sees. To compensate, you must overexpose the film by approximately 1.5 stops. If your camera has manual controls, meter normally and then either open the aperture (f-stop) by 1.5 stops or slow down your shutter speed by 1.5 stops. If you are using a camera with automatic or program exposure mode and the camera has an exposure compensation setting, adjust it to +1.5. This will automatically overexpose the meter reading by 1.5 stops. (Remember to reset your compensation dial to 0 when done.)

Cold temperatures drain batteries quickly. Photographers should always carry extra batteries with them when dealing with prolonged exposure to cold temperatures. It is also useful to keep a camera inside a coat or pocket to lessen the impact of the cold on the batteries. However, moisture is one of the major causes of camera malfunction, and condensation can build up inside the garments when some type of strenuous activity is involved. If condensation or snow gets on the camera, wipe it dry with a towel or lint-free cloth if you need to, and remember those extra batteries, which are always the best insurance.

# Clothing

Snowshoeing does demand specialty equipment (i.e., snowshoes) and appropriate footwear. However, there is no such thing as snowshoeing clothing—at least not yet. "Snowshoewear" has not entered the sports vocabulary in the mode of swimwear, skiwear, tenniswear, golfwear or other "wears." And it very well might never do so, because, if you live in Colorado or vacation here and participate in outdoor activities in the mountains, you probably already own all the apparel you need.

Snowshoeing is winter's warmest sport. Your body steadily generates heat because you really chug on the uphills and also move your legs and arms on the downhills. No gliding or sliding is involved, so you will produce a lot of body heat while you snowshoe. The faster your pace, the less warmly you

Components are the name of the game when it comes to layering, a way of dressing that provides maximum flexibility for staying dry and comfortable. *Photo courtesy Lowe Alpine.*

need to dress for snowshoeing itself. In addition to the body heat you produce, which will mandate less clothing as you hike, you might have to adjust your clothing as the day warms up or cools down. The cold morning when you started out can warm up to a mild, sunny afternoon, or you might have to pass through a wind-whipped stretch. You can always take a garment off or unzip if you get too warm. But remember that you also need to be prepared for wind, the onset of foul weather or, in the case of a backcountry excursion, the fact that you might be slower than you expect and not return as early or directly as you planned. There is one solution to all of these possibilities: layering. Layering has been refined to a high art by outdoor activewear manufacturers.

## Layering 101

Such standbys as wool, down and cotton, which were once state of the outdoor art, have been replaced by high-tech, high-performance synthetic fabrics and insulations that can be combined into a clothing system that you will be able to tailor to the conditions of the moment. The purpose of a layering system is to keep you warm and dry. The principles behind staying warm are to wick perspiration away from your skin, insulate your body from the cold and keep rain and snow from penetrating. Not counting your normal underwear, three layers make up the modern winter outerwear system. Numerous manufacturers utilize a variety of brand-name and private label high-tech synthetic materials to accomplish this. When you are out snowshoeing, you can wear one, two or all three layers in combinations that suit your energy expenditure, the air temperature, the wind and any precipitation.

## The Fundamentals

The first layer, the one you'll wear next to your skin, is usually known as the base layer or sometimes the wicking layer, which (by whatever name) is the long underwear layer. It usually consists of  polypropylene tops and bottoms. This miracle fiber is woven into underwear that actually draws perspiration vapor from your body and transports it away from the skin. Manufacturers frequently offer it in three weights: lightweight, medium-weight and heavy- or expedition-weight. Tops usually come in crew or zip-turtleneck styles. The latter design tends to be more practical, because you can zip it up at the neck when you're cold and unzip to ventilate as you get warm.

The second or middle layer, which is usually called the mid-layer of the insulating layer, has two functions. It keeps moving the moisture away from your body and also provides insulation against the cold. Synthetic polyester fleece, pioneered by Polartec, has become the mid-layer of choice, because it is comfortable, warm, inexpensive, easy to care for and quick-drying, yet retains its insulating properties even when it is wet. Like today's longjohns, fleece is also produced in a variety of weights. Long-sleeved and vest styles are available in a variety of zip-front and pullover styles, and if you are environmentally concerned, note that some fleece, notably Patagonia's Synchilla, is made of recycled materials. You can wear one mid-layer garment, two or none.

The top, shell or outer layer must permit vapor to vent away from your skin, yet protect you from wind, rain and snow. Gore-Tex was the first of the so-called waterproof, breathable fabrics, and now there are many on the market. As important as the fabric is the finishing of the garment. If you will be going out in heavy winter weather, look for such features as sealed seams, an integrated hood, underarm zippers for ventilation and perhaps reinforcement in such high-wear areas as the shoulders, where the pack straps can rub against the garment. If you keep to a slow and leisurely pace with frequent stops, that outer layer should be fairly substantial. If you are a runner and will be sustaining a high level of physical exertion, a lightweight shell will do.

In a nutshell, the most versatile and functional outfit for most snowshoers is a polypro first layer, a fleece mid-layer and a waterproof, breathable shell jacket on top, and stretch fleece tights and wind- and waterproof shell on the bottom. That shell pant is an important garment, because snowshoes tend to kick snow up behind you. If you aren't wearing element-fighting pants, you'll find yourself with snow-covered thighs and backside. Fleece, which attracts snow, doesn't make a good material for snowshoeing pants despite its other excellent qualities.

## The Extras

Other garments, while not essential to "Layering 101," are versatile and nice to have. If you select a long-sleeved insulating top as a basic, consider a vest as an alternative (and vice versa). A vest will keep your torso warm and yet offers a great deal of mobility to your arms, whether you are walking with poles or running and pumping your arms aggressively. Vests can be made of fleece or nylon (or other synthetic material) insu-

The base layer is the foundation, wicking perspiration from the skin, while the mid-layer provides warmth. *Photo courtesy Lowe Alpine.*

lated with down or some sort of fiberfill. They can be used on top of the middle layer on a clement day or between the mid-layer and the outer layer when it's really cold. Many active outerwear manufacturers offer "systems" that consist of a jacket—that is, the third or outer layer—with a zip-in vest. Depending on the temperature, wind and activity level, these two components can be worn together or separately. Another brand-name fleece item, called Windstopper, consists of a fleece bonded with a wind-resistant material that offers the warmth of fleece and yet blocks the wind.

# Necessary Accessories

A hat is essential in the Colorado winter, because some 40 percent of body heat is lost from the head. Everyone has a favorite style: a traditional ski hat or toque for most conditions, a balaclava with ear protection and under-chin ties for very cold weather or a baseball cap or other brimmed headgear to shade the eyes and face on warm, sunny days. Toques and balaclavas are available in fleece, wool or synthetics, and in many colors and patterns. Baseball caps are made of—well, you know. A headband, also available in fleece, wool or a synthetic knit, is a nice, lightweight accessory to tuck into your pack for warm days when a little ear protection is all you need.

Being appropriately dressed for winter activities and prepared for conditions that could change from driving snow to brilliant sun are the keys to a comfortable and safe snowshoe hike. *Photo courtesy Tubbs Snowshoe Company.*

Like hats, gloves are made of various materials and come in different weights to meet various weather conditions. Lightweight cross-country gloves are fine for warm days; heavy-duty insulated expedition mitts are necessary to prevent frosty fingertips when it's cold. Glove liners or overmitts can add an additional layer of necessary warmth and protection when it's frigid.

Experienced snow-shoers know that gaiters are good. There are two kinds: the ones that fasten over your pant legs and boot tops to keep powder snow from seeping down to your ankles and feet, and the tubular version of stretch fleece or knit that keeps snow and wind from blowing down your neck. The former are called simply "gaiters" and are generally available in outdoor stores. They come in two lengths, one that reaches to just below the knee and is suitable for deep snow, and one that reaches the ankle and is meant just to keep snow out of your boot tops. They are neither an equipment accessory nor an article of clothing, but combine characteristics of both. The second type is known as a "neck gaiter" and is more common in ski shops.

While sunglasses with ultraviolet protection, water bottles, sunscreen and a pack are not really clothing accessories, they are truly necessities, so I take every opportunity to mention them.

# Technique

One of the wonderful ironies about the first steps of snowshoeing is that it takes practically as long to string the descriptive words together and imprint them in your mind as it does simply to try the sport. The trial is easy and the errors are few. Calling this chapter "Instruction" would be an exaggeration, yet a few tips are appropriate. The tips that follow are suitable for modern aluminum frame snowshoes. Traditional wood frame models call for specific techniques for special conditions, which are detailed in several excellent technical books now on the market (see Appendix B, page 281). Once you are comfortable on your snowshoes, follow your inclination and your heart, and use them for your own purposes.

## The First Steps

Basic snowshoeing is the winter answer to walking or light hiking, and the easiest way to get started is to find a level patch of ground or a flat trail and simply begin to move forward. Because snowshoes are bigger than hiking boots, the main accommodation you'll be making is to adjust your gait to the difference in size—especially with symmetrical snowshoes. To get the feeling of the snowshoes, simply start to walk naturally and rhythmically. As you do, you'll discover that you need to clear the leg, foot and snowshoe that is on the ground as you move your other foot forward. You can do this by lengthening your stride and, if you need to, widening your stance a little.

If you hear and feel the frames clunking together as you put one foot in front of the other, you'll know that your feet are too close together. Tweaking your natural movements to clear up this little glitch does not take long. Simply widen your stance a little more and move your "passing" foot forward in a slight arc to clear the "standing" foot. Soon, you'll no longer hear or feel one shoe frame hitting against the other. You may initially feel as if you are waddling, but that sensation will pass quickly and the rhythm and motion of snowshoeing will soon come easily. That's about all the technique you'll need on packed trails and well-settled snow.

Swing your arms naturally—right foot/left arm, left foot/right arm— just as if you were walking. Most recreational snowshoers now use ski poles for balance and stability when walking or hiking. Using poles makes snowshoeing resemble cross-country skiing, minus the glide. Also, think of snowshoes as vehicles with several forward gears (strolling, determined hiking pace or running) but no reverse gear. In other words, remember that snowshoes are designed to enable you to move forward.

Even though snowshoeing comes easily, be aware that your energy expenditure is greater than when you walk on dry ground. The positive side of this is that you get stronger and fitter and use more calories. The downside is that you cannot cover as much distance and you may tire more quickly. The extra energy goes to having the weight of winter boots, gaiters and snowshoes on your feet. Other factors affecting your energy use include your own weight, the depth of the snow and the size of snowshoes you are using.

Nordic skiers work hard to break trail after a snowfall. It is discourteous, insensitive and even inflammatory for snowshoers to trample ski tracks (above). New trail etiquette calls for snowshoeing beside ski tracks (below). *Photos by Ral Sandberg.*

# Snowshoeing the Soft ...

Snowshoes really shine in fresh powder, but don't expect to walk solidly on the surface. Snowshoes are not life vests for the feet. Even though the deck or platform provides flotation, you will sink as the snow surface shifts and the powder compresses under your weight. The softer the snow, the more you'll sink, but you will never find yourself crotch-deep in deep powder as you would if you were floundering around without snowshoes. Once you get used to drifting along in the deep, it is a fine feeling. You'll have the sense of walking on feather-light sand, if you can imagine such a thing.

When the snow is really soft and really deep, you can minimize sinking and maximize flotation by a motion that snowshoers call "stomping." Place your foot firmly on the snow surface and pause for a moment to compact it before putting your weight on it. Other techniques for deep powder are more fun. You can either lift the front of your snowshoe out of the snow or submarine it under the snow. If you lift, the toe pivot system will cause the snowshoe's deck to slant backward and the loose fluff will slide off the back. If the snow is not only deep but also soft, you might find it easier simply to tunnel or submarine your snowshoes through the snow. The snowshoes will stay fairly level, though you won't see them on the surface. Sometimes, when you look down as you walk like this, you will have the amusing sense of watching two gophers preceding your own feet.

Breaking trail takes more energy than following in someone else's wake. One of the reasons beginning snowshoers enjoy guided hikes is that the guide is always in front, breaking trail and sparing clients this energy-sapping chore. However, when you are hiking in a group and the snow is soft, the custom is for everyone to take a turn breaking trail and to follow the leader in single file. When you are leading, remember to stay off any cross-country tracks. If there are no other tracks, make yours along the side of the trail, so that any skiers who follow will have ample room. (The other side of the equation is that skiers who get to new powder first should also make their tracks on one side of the trail so that snowshoers have room.)

## ... and the Steep

The preferred technique for climbing in soft snow is a little like "stomping" up an incline. First, kick the front of the snowshoe horizontally into snow to compact it into a "step" with each step you take and then weight the snowshoe. When you are ascending a steep slope this way, you climb up a snowy "staircase" of steplike platforms. The major adjustment you have to make while climbing is to lengthen your step so that you are putting your snowshoe down on new snow. If the slope is really steep, you may even have to lift your knee quite high, even raising your foot so that the snowshoe's tail points up. If your steps are too small, each indentation that you have already made in the snow will undermine the next step above it. However, before you get too concerned about this, remember that the routes described in this book normally are not steep enough to require such step building, though you may use it for off-trail exploration.

Snowshoes are not really intended for traversing across a slope. Unlike metal-edged skis, which are designed to grip when the user moves across a steep slope, snowshoe "edges" aren't edges but tubes. In addition, the heel-free bindings that make them so easy to go forward on tend to contort when the side of the snowshoe is pressured. If you are trail hiking, the technique described below is not a skill you'll use often, because marked trails don't normally traverse a slope. However, if you're bushwhacking in the backcountry, you may find yourself having to do this.

Though snowshoeing fundamentals are as elementary as walking, a few tricks make climbing, descending or traversing a slope easier. *Photo courtesy Tubbs Snowshoe Company.*

For those times when you need to traverse a slope, snowshoers have developed a technique that resembles the same principle as climbing up a steep incline with soft snow. As you traverse, kick the uphill edge of the snowshoe into the slope to create a platform that is horizontal or nearly so. Because snowshoes are designed for going up and down hills, you have to adjust your technique somewhat to cross a hill. (Remember, never cross a steep slope in avalanche country.)

When descending, bend your knees a little and shift your weight back slightly to ride the back section of the snowshoe downhill. It won't be a steady slide like skiing, but you will feel some slippage with each step, especially in soft snow. Metal heel cleats underfoot will help you to keep your weight back, to maintain control. For stability, you must pressure your snowshoes to engage the cleats and shift your weight aggressively on the uphill side to edge the side of the snowshoe frame into the snow. Although it may seem instinctive to do so on the steeps, avoid the temptation to lean back into the hill. You'll also find poles especially useful, both in maintaining your balance and to provide a sense of security.

This book focuses on easy to moderate trails, but if you get into serious backcountry snowshoeing, you'll begin to learn or develop maneuvers for handling very steep ascents and descents, major traverses and different snow conditions. Again, check Appendix B (page 281) for books that cover advanced techniques or sign up for a backcountry course and learn these advanced techniques correctly.

## Getting Up

Everyone falls now and then. Tumbling into snow is gentler than on solid ground, but getting up from packed snow is similar to getting up from the ground. If you fall in deep snow, a companion's hand provides the best assistance. If you have fallen on a slope, have your companion stand below you to help pull you up. If no one is around, you can pull yourself up on a branch if one is handy (taking care not to fall into a tree well in the process). If no branch is within reach, remove your pack if it's heavy and affects your balance. Either cross your poles or put your pack down on the snow on your uphill side, brace yourself lightly on it, and push yourself up with your arms.

## Backcountry Ethics

Avoiding ski tracks is good trail etiquette, but in the great scheme of things, it is ephemeral and trivial. More important and enduring is to adopt practices that do not damage the natural or cultural heritage of the backcountry. Leave No Trace, a nationwide campaign for wise and respectful use of the backcountry, has developed ethics guidelines. Many of their guidelines reflect common sense and practices that should be self-evident, but reviewing them never hurts.

First, if you pack it in, pack it out. That means don't litter. Take all food wrappers, tissues, banana and orange peels, apple cores and other refuse with you and dispose of this trash properly. Birds or small animals will snap up crumbs that you might drop, but do not intentionally leave larger amounts of food for animals. It is not a kindness to habituate wildlife to "people food." A plastic bag makes a good receptacle for all trash.

Second, do not deface, destroy or damage trees or other flora, or structures, whether historic or still in use. You may think it clever or romantic to carve your initials somewhere, but this backcountry graffiti can be harmful to trees and disrespectful to property owners. Similarly, be aware of and respectful of private property.

Third, make use of any available toilet facilities before you hit the trail. If you need to relieve yourself during the hike, do so in an unobtrusive, off-trail spot that is at least 100 yards from a stream or lake. Cover waste with snow, and burn or pack out toilet tissue. (A small plastic zip-up bag is useful to have along for this.)

## Fitness Factors

You may wonder how anything as tranquil as snowshoeing can really help your physical conditioning, but it does. This low-tech, low-impact activity is also an endurance sport that provides steady muscle motion and cardiovascular conditioning, burning 25 percent more calories than simply walking on firm ground. Snowshoeing will not feel strenuous to the well-conditioned hiker or runner, and it provides a fitness benefit to everyone. Insulated boots and hiking boots plus even the lightest snowshoes add weight beyond running shoes or other common athletic footwear, so every step takes a little more energy and goes a little farther toward building muscle than walking on dry ground.

Depending on your body weight, you can burn 350 to 550 calories per hour if you just walk on snowshoes at a good clip on packed snow

## Etiquette on Multi-Use Trails

Cross-country skiers have been plying Colorado's trails for years, and some of them tend to view the hordes of snowshoers who have joined them with shock, dismay and anger. Some skiers simply don't want to share, feeling the trails are their own private places, while others are only put off by what they view as snowshoers' lack of consideration when they walk on carefully laid ski tracks. Often, the issue comes down to awareness about trail etiquette, usually on the part of new snowshoers who are not also skiers.

Following are the basic winter trail manners, both regarding sharing trails with other users and general use of the backcountry:

- If you are breaking trail through new snow, walk or hike along the side of the trail to leave room for skiers. (Savvy skiers are also learning to put their tracks on the side to leave room for snowshoers.)

- If you are snowshoeing in a group, don't spread yourselves across the entire trail, but leave a generous lane for skiers.

- If you see a set of ski tracks etched in the snow, don't step on them. Walk alongside them. The biggest single issue skiers have with snowshoers is trampled ski tracks.

- Yield to faster skiers or snowshoers who are coming up behind you on flat trails. On hilly trails, it is a matter of safety as well as courtesy to yield to downhill-bound ski traffic. Skiers do move quickly.

- Step quickly to the side of the trail if someone behind you yells "Track!" If you are the speedster, remember that "Track!" is the commonly accepted alert on the trail.

- Step off the trail, or to the side of a wide road, when taking a break. Don't block traffic with your body or your poles.

- When making a pit stop, use an outhouse if one is accessible. (There are facilities available on some busy trailheads and some are also often left unlocked at campgrounds that are closed in winter.) If none is available, make your stop off-trail, but also well away from streambeds. Kick new snow over the yellow snow you've created. Burn used toilet tissue or carry a small plastic bag and pack it out with you.

- Obey trail signs and policies regarding dogs (their yellow snow and, especially, their droppings are particularly unpleasant on trails).

- Obey directional signs, whenever they exist, such as on some loop trails.

- Respect private property, which often adjoins public access routes.

and flat terrain. Use poles and add hills, and your caloric expenditure is 670 to 1,000 calories per hour. During aggressive ascents up a steep powder slope or running an 8-minute mile, the calorie expenditure can be 700 to 1,000 calories an hour (see below).

Especially when you are climbing, you will not only be consuming calories, but also toning your body. Think of the muscles you'll use. You'll be working your hip flexors and extensors, hamstrings, quadriceps and calf muscles and, when you use poles, also the triceps and shoulders. This low-tech, low-impact activity is an endurance sport that provides steady muscle motion and cardiovascular conditioning.

# Running on Snowshoes

To add a really dynamite fitness element, you can snowshoe up a mountain. Because it is an endurance activity, snowshoeing, even up long, novice trails, is really good exercise. By planting your pole ahead of you at each stride, you not only add stability, but you also increase the sport's inherent cardiovascular benefit and reduce fatigue. And if you jog or run up, you've got yourself a gonzo workout. Snowshoeing can be a great cross-training tool or an end unto itself. Some people want a way to stay in shape during the winter, in preparation for the warm-weather running season. (Others run in summer to keep fit for winter.) Snowshoe races, for serious competitors and recreational runners alike, dot the calendar. Whichever is the chicken and whichever is the egg, running on snowshoes—especially uphill at Colorado's elevations—is just about as aerobic as a sport can get.

In chicken-and-egg fashion, some snowshoers run because they enjoy the activity and even like the challenge of racing. Others are runners who snowshoe as a winter cross-training activity. *Photo courtesy Louis Garneau Sports.*

Running uphill on snowshoes has taken on a cult status in some ski resorts. You often see snowshoers charging up steep slopes in the morning, even before the lifts are operating. Most Colorado ski areas are built on U.S. Forest Service land, which is public land, your land. The lift ticket is just that: proof of payment for riding the lifts, not an admission charge to be on the hill. Therefore, snowshoers are technically permitted on the slopes. Some ski areas discourage snowshoers during lift operation hours, or funnel upward-bound snowshoers to specific trails in the interest of safety, while others welcome them to the ski runs at any time. Good sense dictates that you stay along the edge of the trail when you are snowshoeing it with downhill skiers and snowboarders.

# Backcountry Cautions

This book is about the sheer joy, the health benefits and the thrill of a fast-growing winter outdoor activity. But sometimes the winter environment can become a tad too thrilling, especially in Colorado, where high altitude and fickle weather are part of mountain reality. While most snowshoers derive pleasure without pain from this sport, it would be remiss not to alert you to the unpredictability and hazards of winter in the outdoors. This chapter is not intended to make you nervous or imply that every snowshoe excursion is perilous (most, by far, are not), but winter in the high country cannot be trivialized either. The best preparation is knowledge and awareness, and many of the precautions snowshoers and other winter outdoor recreationists should take are quite simple. At the very least, heeding these cautions can minimize discomfort; at the most, it can save a life.

Elements common to the Colorado outdoor experience, regardless of the time of year, include being conscious of the altitude, drinking enough water to avoid dehydration and carrying a map and other aids to orient yourself—and knowing how to use them. You're unlikely to get lost at a ski-touring center or on a well-traveled, well-marked route system on public lands, but it's always a good idea to be able to use a map, altimeter and compass. In the backcountry, this "good idea" is imperative. Other potential problems are seasonal. Winter in the outdoors can mean cold, and you need to know something about frostbite prevention. Because avalanches are a potential hazard in the winter backcountry, prudent snowshoers need to learn to avoid slide situations and still know what to do if they or their companions are caught.

## Altitude Adjustment

Colorado's soaring mountains, wedged between the high plains in the east and canyon country to the west, give it the highest average elevation of any of the 50 states. Colorado residents, especially those who live in mountain communities, are acclimatized, but flatlanders sometimes suffer some degree of altitude sickness. It can strike at elevations of 8,000 feet or higher, where air pressure is lower and there is less oxygen than close to sea level. Medical experts estimate that as many as 25 percent of out-of-state visitors suffer at least mild symptoms of altitude sickness, including headaches, sleeplessness, dizziness and nausea. Even Front Range citizens are not immune, although they can generally go higher before symptoms hit.

Altitude sickness is unrelated to age or physical condition. Many people think that they are coming down with a cold, or perhaps have jet lag or a hangover. Symptoms usual disappear after three to five days, when the body has acclimatized, but that can take a big chunk out of the average trip. Preventative measures include drinking plenty of water, avoiding alcohol and cutting down on caffeine and, if possible, spending a night or two at a relatively lower elevation (e.g., Denver, Colorado Springs, Fort Collins, Boulder) before heading for the high country.

The most strident forms of altitude sickness are the stuff of high Himalayan or arduous Andean treks. Cerebral edema (a swelling of the brain) and pulmonary edema (fluid filling the lungs), the most severe forms of mountain sickness, can be fatal. Fortunately, they are relatively rare conditions, especially at the elevations common for snowshoeing excursions in Colorado.

Snowshoes make the deep backcountry accessible, but expeditions into terrain like the Maroon Bells require equipment for extreme conditions, and skills from route-finding to avalanche safety, as well. *Photo courtesy Tubbs Snowshoe Company.*

## What You'll Need: Essentials and Extras

Anytime you go out on snowshoes, you'll need to outfit yourself properly, not just for comfort, but for safety. At the risk of reiterating advice, keep the following in mind. For normal recreational snowshoeing on marked, avalanche-free routes, you'll need:

- Snowshoes
- Poles (optional)
- Waterproof boots
- Layered clothing
- Gaiters
- Gloves
- Water
- Sunscreen

For an excursion of a few hours at a marked, patrolled area such as a cross-country center or Alpine ski area, you can generally make do with a fanny pack with:

- An extra layer of clothing, especially for your torso, such as a vest or windshell
- The area's free map for that trail
- An energy bar

For a longer snowshoe hike on a backcountry or wilderness trail, your daypack should also contain:

- Pocket knife (Swiss army knife or similar)
- Topographic and/or winter trail map
- Compass and an altimeter
- Small first aid kit
- Dry socks
- Waterproof matches
- Small, chemically activated heat packs to keep hands and feet warm
- Food, such as a sandwich, fruit, trail mix and additional energy bars, plus a Thermos containing hot soup, hot chocolate or hot tea

For a trek farther into the backcountry, add the following to your pack:

- Enough warm and waterproof clothing for stormy weather or an emergency
- Avalanche beacon or transceiver
- Shovel
- Poles or avalanche probe
- Cup and candle (to melt snow for water)
- Extra food
- Pad to sit on
- Bivouac gear (if you are going on a long excursion deep into the backcountry, especially on a little-traveled route and/or during the week)

# Defense Against Dehydration

Dehydration can cause fatigue, headaches, nausea and muscle cramps. This is the simplest of all dangerous conditions to avoid. There are three ways to combat dehydration: drink, drink, drink. Water is the prevention, and water is the cure. Drink water in quantities that may seem prodigious, until you start snowshoeing hard. You can take part of that replenishment as hot herbal tea, fruit juice and sports drinks, which will not only keep you hydrated but will replenish your mineral stores. Avoid coffee, caffeinated tea, cola and other caffeine-laced soft drinks and alcohol, which are diuretics that hasten fluid loss. When you are hiking on a hot summer day, you may feel thirsty, and if you hike a lot, you know that you should be drinking before thirst sets in. You might not get that parched signal when snowshoeing, but exercising in the cold, dry outdoors also causes water loss from perspiration and respiration. The bottom line is to drink before you start hiking, drink frequently during your hike and rehydrate afterward.

A water bottle in a holster attached to the waist belt of your pack is convenient, because you can just reach for it frequently as you hike, and a Camelbak or other hydration system is even better. Hydration systems are becoming popular even with winter hikers. A hydration system resembles a small, narrow backpack or lumbar pack with a bladder to hold water, connected to a flexible tube and a mouthpiece so that you can sip as you snowshoe.

Outdoor stores carry insulated Camelbaks, insulated holsters, insulated water bottle covers or even insulated bottles for winter use. You can also keep water from freezing quickly by putting the bottle into the holster upside down—with the top on tight, of course. Keep your spare water bottle in the middle of your pack, where your extra clothing will protect it from the cold.

The big question is: How much water? An adult can require a minimum of 1.5 to 2 quarts per day while exercising minimally in a dry climate. Climbing uphill, carrying a heavy pack, running or fast hiking quickly increases those water requirements. Figure on at least a quart of water per person for a moderate snowshoe hike; a pint or more per person, per hour for a longer, more challenging one; and a quart or more per person, per hour when running or climbing on steep, prolonged uphills—and then bring along a big extra bottle.

## Emergency Kit

No one wants to get caught out overnight. No one really expects to get caught out overnight. But every winter, someone does. Headlines report a missing person or group in the high country. The media detail the rescue efforts. The ending is either a happy tale of survival or a tragic one of death. To maximize your chances of surviving with the least possible discomfort and damage should the unwished-for or unexpected happen, always carry basic emergency supplies on your backcountry excursions. Your pack should contain:

- Lightweight space blanket to wrap around you during an emergency bivouac, trapping in your body heat and providing a measure of insulation from the snow and cold air.

- Extra food

- Extra clothing, including warm hat, socks and gloves, mittens and/or glove liners

- Flashlight and/or headlamp with extra batteries

- Waterproof matches and/or a disposable cigarette lighter

- Whistle

# Fighting Frostbite and Hypothermia

It can get very cold very fast in the mountains. Frostbite and hypothermia are possibilities for the unprepared—or underprepared—snowshoer. Equipping yourself properly with suitable clothing, socks and gloves is the best prevention. See Feet First on page 13 of the Equipment chapter and the Clothing chapter, which begins on page 19, for guidance.

Frostbite is cold-caused tissue damage, which is painful at the least and permanently damaging in the worst case. Fingers, toes and exposed

## Wicked Wind Chill

You might have a thermometer to check the temperature when you're snowshoeing (those little plastic zipper fobs are popular), but you probably won't have an anemometer to measure the wind speed. Nevertheless, if you are planning to travel in the high country in winter, it is instructive and humbling to know what the combination of wind and cold can feel like. Traveling through high-altitude open areas in midwinter can expose you to some wicked weather. Wind chill is a formula developed by Antarctic scientists around 1940 to define "coldness." The formula calculates what various temperatures feel like when combined with winds of various wind speeds. To use the following table, find the closest temperature on the top and the wind speed along the left side. The wind chill, or equivalent temperature, will be where they meet on the table.

### Wind Chill Factor Chart

#### TEMPERATURE

| Calm | 50 | 40 | 30 | 20 | 10 | 0 | -10 | -20 | -30 | -40 | -50 |
|---|---|---|---|---|---|---|---|---|---|---|---|
| 5 | 48 | 37 | 27 | 16 | 6 | -5 | -15 | -26 | -36 | -47 | -57 |
| 10 | 40 | 28 | 16 | 4 | -9 | -24 | -33 | -46 | -58 | -70 | -83 |
| 15 | 36 | 22 | 9 | -5 | -18 | -32 | -45 | -58 | -72 | -85 | -99 |
| 20 | 32 | 18 | 4 | -10 | -25 | -39 | -53 | -67 | -82 | -96 | -110 |
| 25 | 30 | 16 | 0 | -15 | -29 | -44 | -59 | -74 | -88 | -104 | -118 |
| 30 | 28 | 13 | -2 | -18 | -33 | -48 | -63 | -79 | -94 | -109 | -125 |
| 35 | 27 | 11 | -4 | -20 | -35 | -51 | -67 | -82 | -98 | -113 | -129 |
| 40 | 26 | 10 | -6 | -21 | -37 | -53 | -69 | -85 | -100 | -116 | -132 |

portions of the face (tip of the nose, cheekbones and ears) are the most susceptible. Tingling can be the first sign that you need to take precautions. If your toes are affected, you can loosen your boots, change quickly to dry socks and/or put small heat packs into your boot toes. If your fingertips are feeling funny, heat packs again might help. So will warmer gloves, glove liners (or overmitts) and hand warmers inside your gloves. When tingling becomes stinging pain and numbness and white patches appear on the skin, frostbite has begun to set in, and it's important to get off the trail and indoors as quickly as possible. Warm the afflicted part rapidly in warm water.

Hypothermia is a drop in the body's core temperature that results when the body loses heat faster than it can produce it. Being very underdressed or clad in cold, wet clothing will most likely lead to hypothermia. Shivering, goose bumps and a lack of coordination, even when performing simple tasks, are signs of this condition. The first response is to protect the victim from additional heat loss by getting him or her out of the wind, changing from wet to dry clothing and adding extra layers of clothing. Warm liquids and food also help, as do hot-water bottles (which are hardly likely to be available on the trail). Winter first aid courses include instruction on what to do for both frostbite and hypothermia.

# Avalanches

"Avalanche" is more than just the name of Colorado's National Hockey League franchise. It's one of nature's more ferocious phenomena and a real threat in the backcountry. The Colorado Avalanche Information Center receives reports of some 2,000 slides annually, but that is just a small fraction of those that occur. An average of 22 people die in avalanches in the United States every year. Colorado—with the highest average altitude, a dry climate that exacerbates slide potential and a large population of backcountry users—is the number one state in terms of avalanche fatalities. Most are backcountry skiers, snowboarders and snowmobilers, but one woman was killed in a snowslide from the roof of her Vail home.

While this section describes some cautions to exercise if you have to travel in avalanche territory, a book cannot take the place of proper training, experience gained over time and, especially, good judgment. This book focuses primarily on marked routes with no or low avalanche potential, but snowshoes are so versatile that the temptation to go off-route is great. Backcountry skiers and snowboarders use snowshoes to access areas where slide potential is great, and even occasional snowshoers can be lured by the temptation of exploring the next ridge, the next valley, the next slope. Even recreational snowshoers on the most benign routes would do well to have rudimentary avalanche knowledge. If you plan on snowshoeing in avalanche country, take an avalanche safety course, go on a few guided tours and learn from your guides' experience or simply turn back rather than risk a hazardous area.

People heading into the risky high country should travel in groups, and everyone should carry an avalanche transceiver or beacon, a shovel and a probe pole, and know how to use them all. Also, it is important to know how to read avalanche terrain. Open slopes angled at more than 30 degrees are the most likely to slide. Slides can occur when the snow is unstable (including in the early season when cover is thin) or when freeze-thaw-snowfall cycles have caused instability between snow layers.

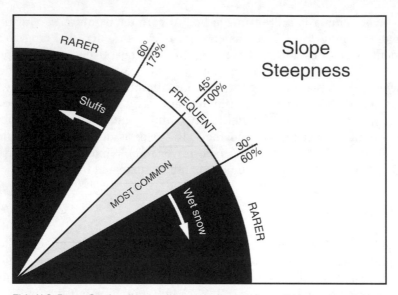

This U.S. Forest Service diagram illustrates slopes where slides can be most expected to occur, as well as those that are safer.

Eighty percent of avalanches occur during or just after major snowstorms, when deep, loose snow or overhanging cornices break from the force of gravity. That also means that 20 percent happen at other times. Skiers and snowshoers crossing an unstable slope, or snowmobilers cutting across an open area, can trigger avalanches. The first avalanche fatality of 1997–1998 was a snowshoer, also an experienced backcountry skier, who initiated a slide on Guanella Pass in an area not known by locals to have released previously. Although the safest part of the snow season is generally spring when the snow has settled and stabilized, two snowshoers were injured—one critically—during a slide in Pump House Gulch near Berthoud Pass in mid-April 1998.

The bottom line is that if you are using snowshoes to access the mountain danger zones of open slopes and wild weather, you should be especially slide-savvy. To minimize the risk, take known precautions. First, check the avalanche report. It is available by phone from the **Colorado Avalanche Information Center** and on several websites (see Appendix E, page 297), from local Forest Service offices or county sheriff's departments and at some sporting goods and outdoor shops in the mountains, and it is broadcast daily on some mountain town radio stations.

If you find yourself in an area where there is even a suspicion of avalanche hazard, know some basic principles. It is generally safer to cross an open area at the top rather than in the middle of the slope. It is also far safer to climb or descend a mountain on a ridge or along the edge of a slope, near trees or rocks, than in the middle. It is safer to move

## Avalanche Awareness

- Avalanches are most common on slopes of 30 to 45 degrees, but large avalanches can occur on slopes ranging from 25 to 60 degrees (on steeper slopes, snow normally slides off during the snowfall).

- Generally, avalanches occur over and over in the same areas, so watch for avalanche paths. Look for pushed-over small trees and trees with limbs broken off. Avoid steep, open gullies and slopes.

- If you see new avalanches, suspect dangerous conditions. Beware when snowballs or "cartwheels" roll down the slope.

- Dangerous slab avalanches are more likely to occur on convex slopes. Lee slopes are generally more dangerous than windward slopes.

- Snow on north-facing slopes is more likely to slide in mid-winter, while south-facing slopes are more dangerous in the spring and/or on sunny days.

- About 80 percent of avalanches occur during or shortly after storms, because loose, dry snow slides easily. Be alert to dangerous conditions if a foot or more of new snow has accumulated. Snow falling at a rate of one inch per hour or more increases avalanche danger.

- Snow persists in an unstable condition under cold temperatures. It settles and stabilizes rapidly when temperatures are near or just above freezing. However, rapid changes in weather conditions can cause snow-pack adjustments. Storms starting with low temperatures and dry snow followed by rising temperatures are more likely to cause avalanches.

- If snow sounds hollow, particularly on leeward slopes, this is a sign of dangerous slab avalanche conditions. Also, if cracks run throughout the snow and those cracks run, that is an indication that slab avalanche danger is high.

- The safest route is along the wide mountain ridge tops, slightly on the windward side and away from cornices. The next safest route is in a valley, far from the bottom of steep slopes.

through the trees or along the edge of the forest than through an open area. If you must cross an open slope, proceed one at a time instead of in a tight group. If you are moving along the valley floor, steer clear of evident avalanche paths. You can sometimes tell where snow has run by the broken snow chunks at the bottom of a gully. If you must cross below an avalanche path, do so one at a time, quickly and gingerly.

In the unlikely event that you are caught in an avalanche, try to grab a tree or a rock and hold on. If you are knocked down, try to "swim" with the avalanche to stay at the surface. Most avalanche deaths actually result from suffocation, so if you are buried, immediately try to clear as large an air pocket as you can in front of your face (and pull a neck gaiter, scarf or collar up over your nose and mouth). Try to stick one arm up (if you can determine where "up" is). You have no time to lose, because avalanched snow sets up as soon as it stops moving. If you are with someone who has been buried, first mark the place where you last saw the victim, quickly use your avalanche probe (see poles in the Equipment chapter, page 14) to locate the victim and then dig as quickly as possible. Precious minutes count.

## Sun Protection

The higher the altitude, the stronger the sun you will encounter while snowshoeing. Protecting yourself against powerful ultraviolet rays is not a secret. Use waterproof, high-SPF sunscreen (SPF 15 or more), applied liberally and, especially in the spring when the sun is high and hot, wear a brimmed hat. Remember also to protect your eyes with sunglasses that provide 100 percent UV filtration.

# FRONT RANGE

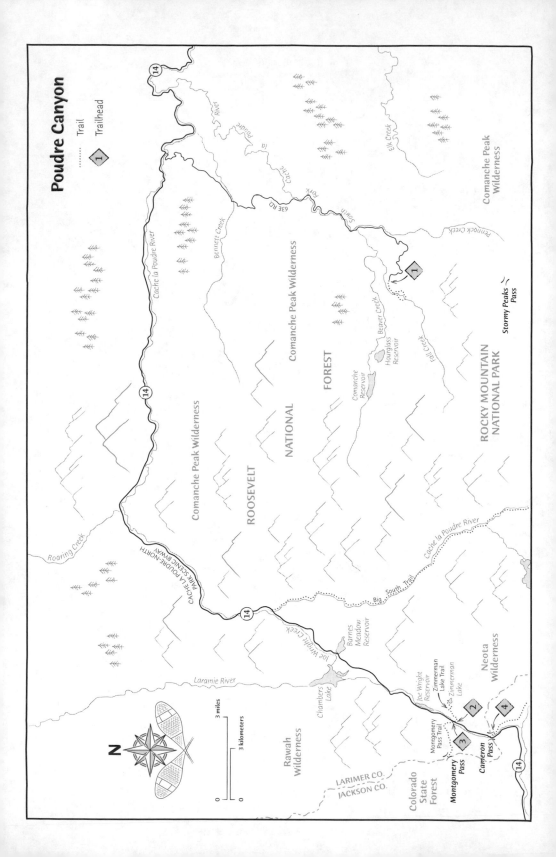

# Poudre Canyon

The Cache la Poudre River tumbles out of Rocky Mountain National Park and flows northeastward for about 25 miles before making a sharp turn to the east toward Fort Collins. It was Colorado's first designated Wild and Scenic River and is the Front Range's last remaining free-flowing river. It has carved a canyon that is sometimes deep, often dramatic and always exciting. The drive through the spectacular canyon cut by this roiling river is an attraction unto itself at any time of year, but it is also a great prelude to some excellent and usually uncrowded snowshoeing routes.

As you enter the canyon from the east, you will start in a near-desert and end up in the montane zone. The vegetation changes dramatically as the highway climbs, becoming less arid and more forested with beautiful conifers. The drive is 50-odd miles from the bottom of the canyon to the snow zone and 10,278-foot Cameron Pass,

Nokhu Crags, a Cameron Pass area landmark. *Photo by Ral Sandberg.*

where winter starts as early as October and lasts until May or June. In fact, only in 1979 was Highway 14 paved so that state crews could plow the road. Until then, the road was closed in winter, as Trail Ridge Road in Rocky Mountain National Park and several other high routes still are.

Especially in its lower sections, Poudre Canyon is sprinkled with small riverside resorts, campgrounds and picnic areas. You'll also pass trailheads here and there, many leading to places suitable for snowshoeing after a snowstorm. The entire route is bracketed by grandiose wilderness areas whose boundaries, in many cases, are close to the road. The first is the modestly sized Cache la Poudre Wilderness, which nestles along the canyon's lower section. Farther up, the Neota, Never Summer and Comanche Peak Wilderness areas lie more or less between Poudre Canyon and Rocky Mountain National Park, south of the highway. The highway eventually abandons the Cache la Poudre River for Joe Wright Creek, a tributary. You'll find winter trailheads every few miles along the upper canyon, providing abundant backcountry opportunities and reliable snow. The huge Rawah Wilderness stretches northward from Cameron Pass. Portions of the adjacent Colorado State Forest are on each side of the highway as it enters the vast and remote valley called North Park.

For tourist information, contact **Fort Collins Convention & Visitors Bureau, 420 South Howes Street, Fort Collins, CO 80533; (800) 274-FORT** or **(970) 482-5821.**

### Getting There
Colorado 14, which parallels the river, is a spectacular drive from the semiarid and scrubby lower canyon, where snow seems to melt as soon as it falls, to the high country of long winters. To get to Poudre Canyon, take U.S. 287 about 10 miles north of Fort Collins to a tiny speck on the map called Ted's Place. The turnoff to Colorado 14 is well marked. As you drive westward and "upstream," the scenery ping-pongs between narrow clefts through soaring rock walls to wider spots. Designated a Scenic and Historic Byway, this is a worthy excursion even if not heading for the excellent snowshoeing routes.

### Maps
USGS 7.5 Minute, Clark Peak, Chambers Lake
Trails Illustrated #112, Poudre River and Cameron Pass
USFS Roosevelt National Forest
Front Range Ski Trails, George J. Maurer, Inc.

# Pingree Park

Fans of this secluded area believe it to be inherently scenic enough to qualify as part of nearby Rocky Mountain National Park. That will probably never happen, because the access road is flanked by stretches of private land on which homes have been built, as well as Colorado State University's forest research facility at the end of the road. This area hit the headlines in 1994 when a 1,275-acre forest fire charred much of it. But much as the infamous Yellowstone fire six years earlier created an opportunity for natural rejuvenation, so did this one. Snowshoeing here in the dead of winter presents an opportunity to view the stark and dramatic beauty of burnt trees standing like sculpted black sentinels against the pure white snow.

The Pingree Park Road is on the left (south) side of Colorado 14, a scenic 25.7 miles from Ted's Place. Cross the bridge and continue on the unpaved road, bearing left at the fork at 4.2 miles. The road is generally well plowed for about 11.5 miles, the end of the final residential area. From there on, it is maintained only intermittently and therefore is often barely accessible with a four-wheel-drive vehicle, preferably one with high clearance. Consider the Tom Bennett Campground access sign, 16.4 miles from the main highway, to be the end of the road and the winter trailhead.

# 1. Pingree Park Road

| | |
|---|---|
| Starting elevation: | 8,960 feet |
| Highest elevation: | 9,040 feet |
| Elevation difference: | 80 feet |
| Distance: | 0.6 mile (one way) |
| Difficulty: | Easy |
| Avalanche hazard: | None |

Pingree Park is a generous valley carved by the South Fork of the Cache la Poudre River. The short, snow-shoeable portion of the road dead-ends near the head of the valley, site of the old Koenig Ranch. It might seem like a lot of effort to drive so far on a dicey road for a modest and easy snowshoe such as the one from the end of the plowed section and a summer parking area, but on a bright, sunny day, the view and the ecology lesson make it all worth-while. Park along the side of the road at the end of the plowed part and begin snowshoeing straight ahead (west) along the road. The CSU Cen-

An easy snowshoe walk in Pingree Park provides a lesson in ecology. The route skirts a 1994 burn area, and signs of regeneration are evident even in winter. *Photo by Ral Sandberg.*

ter is off-limits, so stay on the road as it bends to the left, following a fence for the entire distance. The forest fire came right up to the CSU facility, and the line between the burn area and the unscathed portion is right at the road. You'll feel a sense of power at having the fire line so close and so clear. There's also a real majesty to the panoramic view of the Stormy Peaks that appears as you approach the bend in the road. It is on your right as you snowshoe toward the summer parking area.

## If You Want a Longer Hike

To add both distance and challenge, begin climbing the Stormy Peaks Trail from the summer trailhead at the end of the Pingree Park Road. The trail parallels and climbs on a glacial moraine above the south fork of the Cache la Poudre River, which at this point is a modest stream. Although the summer trail continues for 5 miles and gains over 2,600 feet in elevation as it climbs above the timberline, then drops down into a remote corner of Rocky Mountain National Park, following it even for only a couple of miles through the trees and onto the ridge is a worthwhile winter excursion.

# Cameron Pass

This 10,276-foot pass is not the highest of Colorado's major mountain pass roads, but it is the most northerly. Drivers find it as hairy as the more frequently traveled passes, and recreationalists find it as attractive as any. The Nokhu Crags is a distinctive landmark, but the scenery all around is gorgeous. The highway actually snakes through a narrow corridor, with the Rocky Mountain National Park boundary directly on one side and the tip of the Colorado State Forest on the other. Colorado 14 is the only highway into the splendid, isolated expanse of North Park, one of Colorado's great mountain basins, formed by the peaks of the Continental Divide to the south and west and the Medicine Bow range to the east.

## 2. Zimmerman Lake

| | |
|---|---|
| Starting elevation: | 10,020 feet |
| Highest elevation: | 10,500 feet |
| Elevation difference: | 480 feet |
| Distance: | 1.1 miles (one way) |
| Difficulty: | Moderate |
| Avalanche hazard: | Low |

Some snowshoers consider Zimmerman Lake a suitable destination, while others add mileage by circling the lake. *Photo by Ral Sandberg.*

The capacious Zimmerman Lake parking lot is on the left side of the highway, approximately 58 miles up Poudre Canyon toward Cameron Pass. The trailhead is close to the upper end of the parking lot, but snowshoers and skiers familiar with the route tend to shortcut to the trail from their cars. Mercifully, it's just a few steps from the breezy parking area to the dense and sheltering conifers.

At the outset, the trail heads basically east, climbing somewhat steeply but very steadily. It is marked with periodic blue diamond blazes, but you won't need to refer to these because it was cut as a service road and is thus wide and very easy to follow. Also, it easily accommodates both upbound snowshoe and ski traffic, as well as fast-moving skiers coming back down. Occasional clearings offer fine vistas. After a major hairpin turn comes one of the better views, toward the cirque between Diamond Peaks and Montgomery Pass, and then the trail becomes less steep. The curves are milder too. The main trail comes in at the southwestern end of the lake, a lovely little jewel with fine views of a stark, glacial ridge.

## If You Want a Longer Hike

If you're game for a longer tour, you can branch off at a wooden sign to the right, roughly halfway to the lake, to circle the lake in a counterclockwise direction and rejoin the main trail close to the lake, or you can also stay on the main trail and circle the lake clockwise, a total hike of 3.1 miles.

# 3. Montgomery Pass

| | |
|---|---|
| Starting elevation: | 10,020 feet |
| Highest elevation: | 11,000 feet |
| Elevation difference: | 980 feet |
| Distance: | 1.7 miles (one way) |
| Difficulty: | Challenging |
| Avalanche hazard: | Low on lower trail; moderate in open areas on upper trail |

This route, which starts across the highway from the Zimmerman Lake trailhead and parking area, is suitable only for stronger snowshoers. Designated as a summer jeep trail, it is both narrower and far steeper than the Zimmerman Lake Trail, even though it's just 0.6 mile longer. You'll appreciate your snowshoes' grippiness as you pass skiers herringboning on the ascent, but because the trail is narrow, you'll want to stay alert for skiers coming back down. (Snowshoeing up and skiing down is also an option for skiers who aren't afraid of speed.)

At first the trail follows Montgomery Creek and climbs aggressively northward, initially through a clear area before it enters the trees. After a major curve, its direction is basically toward the west. A small clearing after 1.5 miles presents you with several options. Skiers and snowboarders heading for high powderfields often take a route to the left (southwest). Most

Routes at and near Cameron Pass offer variety, scenery and proximity to Fort Collins. *Photo by Ral Sandberg.*

snowshoers prefer to stay the course, passing a blue diamond marker and continuing toward the pass. Nearly 480 feet higher than Cameron

Pass, Montgomery Pass is actually above the treeline, and wind conditions can be daunting. It is therefore reasonable to turn around at this clearing, because the main route traverses an often windy open area and the top can be both avalanche-prone and windy. If you do make it to the top, take in the views of North Park, the flat whiteness of frozen North Michigan Reservoir and the surrounding snowy summits. Then, if you like, you can switch to your boards for a rollicking ride back to the trailhead.

## 4. Upper Michigan Ditch

| | |
|---|---|
| Starting elevation: | 10,280 feet |
| Highest elevation: | 10,320 feet |
| Elevation difference: | 40 feet |
| Distance: | 1.3 miles (one way) |
| Difficulty: | Easy |
| Avalanche hazard: | Low |

Snowshoeing along Upper Michigan Ditch with the Nokhu Crags in the background. *Photo by Ral Sandberg.*

This tour is excellent if you are new to snowshoeing, uncertain about the altitude, toting a baby in a pack or towing a toddler in a pulk. From the parking lot at the top of Cameron Pass, cross the highway to the gate on the Upper Michigan Ditch service road. The flat trail quickly enters the Colorado State Forest just before the self-service fee station. The calm, frozen surface of the irrigation ditch is on your left, and if you squint your eyes and crank up your imagination, you can almost visualize Hans Brinker gliding along on the ice—except, of course, that nothing in Holland approaches the elevation of the steep slope on the other side of the ditch.

Intermittently, through breaks in the tall trees, you will get wonderful views of the Nokhu Crags to the right of the trail. After a wide bend at about 0.6 mile, the trail reaches the Upper Michigan River drainage, a wide valley with open views. Continue another 0.6 (still mild) mile to several buildings remaining from the ditch's construction era. If you are attracted by the flat, easy trail, you'll find this to be a good turnaround point, but you can also continue another third of a mile to a fork in the trail, which provides a second good turnaround for most snowshoers.

## If You Want a Longer Hike

If you are curious about what lies ahead or are hardier than this mild road requires, you can continue. The left fork leads steeply to American Lakes (called Michigan Lakes in some books and on some maps), about 2.2 miles farther in. The right fork continues gently to Lake Agnes, a mild route but not necessarily a safe one, for it does cross some avalanche areas. The total length of the ditch is 4 miles, from Lake Agnes back toward Cameron Pass. Its 1,200-foot elevation difference puts it in a very different league from the tame first section.

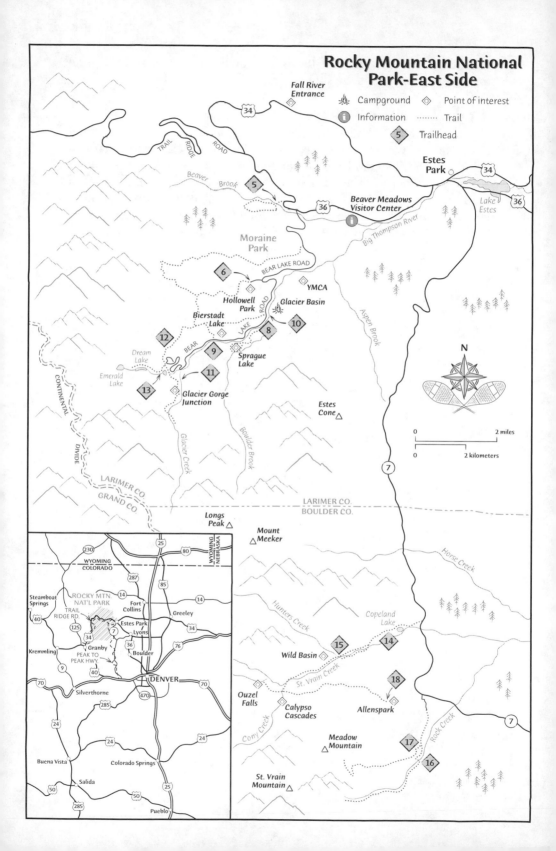

# Rocky Mountain National Park-East Side

☼ Campground ◇ Point of interest
ⓘ Information ⋯⋯ Trail
5 Trailhead

Fall River Entrance

Estes Park

Beaver Meadows Visitor Center

Lake Estes

Moraine Park

YMCA

Hollowell Park

Glacier Basin

Bierstadt Lake

Dream Lake

Sprague Lake

Emerald Lake

Glacier Gorge Junction

Estes Cone

CONTINENTAL DIVIDE

LARIMER CO.
GRAND CO.

LARIMER CO.
BOULDER CO.

Longs Peak

Mount Meeker

Copeland Lake

Wild Basin

Ouzel Falls

Calypso Cascades

Allenspark

Meadow Mountain

St. Vrain Mountain

WYOMING
COLORADO

ROCKY MTN. NAT'L PARK
TRAIL RIDGE RD.

Steamboat Springs

Fort Collins

Greeley

Kremmling

Granby
PEAK TO PEAK HWY.

Estes Park
Lyons

Boulder

Silverthorne

DENVER

Buena Vista

Colorado Springs

Salida

Pueblo

0          2 miles
0          2 kilometers

N

# Rocky Mountain National Park—East Side

Rocky Mountain National Park perches like a crown atop America's splendid national park system. This matchless high-Alpine environment is renowned for a magnificent landscape of craggy summits, glacier-carved valleys, sheer granite cliffs, perpetual snowfields, crystalline lakes, high cirques and stretches of tundra. One-third of the park's 414 square miles is treeless tundra, the greatest expanse in the lower 48 states, but none of the tundra, and only the fringes of the park, are easily accessible in winter. The park was the 21st place on earth to be named by the United Nations as a World Biosphere Reserve to showcase and protect its natural wonders. There are now more than 220 such reserves, but the park's early designation is a fitting testimonial to its internationally recognized distinction.

Even though the park claims no single signature feature, such as Yellowstone's Old Faithful or Yosemite's Halfdome, some three million people a year are drawn to its dramatic beauty. About 90 percent of these visitors experience Rocky Mountain National Park's splendor merely as drive-through tourists, and just a small fraction of them see it when there's snow on the ground. The last major prewinter attraction is in autumn, when the park's massive elk herd descends from the high country for the mating ritual known as "bugling season," so named after the bull elks' mournful sounds. Herds of tourists migrate to the park to see and hear these great beasts.

Trail Ridge Road is a 48-mile-long strip of asphalt, roughly following an old Ute Indian trail that threads through the breathtakingly beautiful heart of the park and across the Continental Divide. It connects the towns of Estes Park on the east and Grand Lake on the west. Not only is it one of the world's most scenic driving routes, it is also the nation's highest continuous paved road—and the highest unplowed road as well, closed to traffic by November and generally reopening around Memorial Day. When Trail Ridge Road is snowed in, the park is without its major attraction to sightseeing drivers. Winter is a season of quiet in the park, and both Estes Park and Grand Lake doze. It is a precious time, when virtually all the park's visitors are active outdoorsfolk.

Not only do both towns slumber, but there are virtually two separate parks, and therefore two different snowshoeing destinations. On the park's dramatic east side, you'll find many trails along the Bear Lake Road. Also, the Wild Basin area in the southeastern corner offers fine snowshoeing. So do numerous west side trails (see the Rocky Mountain National Park—West Side chapter, page 209). If you need advance information, call Park headquarters at **(970) 586-1206.** Remember that Rocky

### Getting There

From Denver, take Interstate 25 north. Take Exit 217 and drive west on U.S. 36 through Boulder and Lyons, continuing up North St. Vrain Canyon and into Estes Park. (From Denver, an alternative is to take Interstate 25 north to Exit 243 and follow Route 66 west to Lyons, where it merges with U.S. 36 to Estes Park.)

There are two entrances from Estes Park (east) into the main section of Rocky Mountain National Park. The Beaver Lake entrance station accesses Bear Lake Road, where you will find most of the good snowshoeing trails. To reach it, stay on U.S. 36, which makes a left turn at the second traffic light just as you enter downtown Estes Park. It becomes the main commercial street. Follow it through town and then make a left and then a right, following the U.S. 36 signs to the Beaver Meadows entrance and fee station. A few hundred yards inside the park boundary is the Beaver Meadows Visitors Center, where you can get maps and specific information on good snowshoeing trails and snow conditions. Bear Lake Road is on your left (south), 0.25 mile after the fee station.

The Fall River entrance accesses the Horseshoe and Hidden Valley areas. As you approach Estes Park, drive straight through the intersection at the second traffic light, which puts you on U.S. 34. You will pass the Stanley Hotel on your right. Continue on this road to the Fall River entrance and fee station. There is no visitors center at this entrance.

### Maps

USGS 7.5 Minute, Allenspark, Longs Peak and McHenry's Peak
Trails Illustrated #200, Rocky Mountain National Park
USFS Roosevelt National Forest
Front Range Ski Trails, George J. Maurer, Inc.
Rocky Mountain National Park maps (free at the entrance station and visitors center)

Mountain National Park is a fee area (currently $10 per car or $20 annually), and also that dogs are prohibited.

Estes Park is a true summer tourist center. It drops into a quaint and charming slumber when the aspen trees have dropped their golden leaves, the prime elk viewing season has passed and snow closes Trail Ridge Road. Some restaurants, shops and lodgings shut down as well, but many others operate fully or simply curtail their hours during the winter. For tourist information, contact Estes Park Chamber Resort Association, 500 Big Thompson Avenue, Estes Park, CO 80517; (800) 443-7837 or (970) 586-4431.

## Ranger Tours

Rocky Mountain National Park rangers lead weekend guided excursions for two levels of snowshoer: two-hour walks, currently beginning at

12:30 P.M. on Saturdays, for novices, and four-hour intermediate tours, currently beginning at 10:30 A.M., for those with some snow-shoeing experience. (This schedule could change in future years.) Both are interpretive, and the beginner version also covers some basic snowshoeing tips, including advice for sharing trails with other users. While these tours are free, reservations are required and are taken only the week before the desired date. Call immediately, for they fill up quickly. Participants must be at least 12 years old for the four-hour tour and 8 years old for the two-hour tour. No rental equipment is available in the park, but sporting goods shops in Estes Park rent gear. For tour reservations or information, call **(970) 586-1223.**

## Estes Park Center/YMCA

For a congenial, easy-on-the-exchequer place to stay, especially for a family or small group, it's hard to beat the Estes Park Center/YMCA. It lies just east of the Glacier Basin area and is a short drive to the Beaver Meadows entrance to Rocky Mountain National Park. Located southwest of town, it provides doorstep snowshoeing, when snow cover permits. The Y complex has economical cabins of all sizes with kitchen facilities, and spacious rooms in five lodges. All rent at low-season rates from November 1 through May 31, and meal plans are available. Other facilities include food service (including sack lunches if you want to take along trail food); an indoor swimming pool; a workout room with Nautilus equipment, weights, stairclimbers, stationary bikes and more; and a program center where snowshoe rentals are available. **Estes Park Center/YMCA, 2515 Tunnel Road, Estes Park, CO 80511; (800) 777-YMCA, (970) 586-3341 or (303) 448-1615 (Denver line); (970) 586-4444 (Loveland/Fort Collins line); www.ymcarockies.org.**

## 5. Beaver Meadows

| | |
|---|---|
| Starting elevation: | 8,300 feet |
| Highest elevation: | 8,440 feet |
| Elevation difference: | 140 feet |
| Distance: | 3.0 miles (loop) |
| Difficulty: | Easy to moderate |
| Avalanche hazard: | None |

Park rangers promote Beaver Meadows as a "winter hike," but after a snowfall, this huge open area of rolling meadowlands makes an excellent, accessible and easy snowshoe tour too. It is a comfortable drive for people who don't want to tackle Bear Lake Road's many twists and turns in the snow. Beaver Meadows is an undulating valley punctuated by

The gorgeous glaciated valleys of Rocky Mountain National Park are easily accessible from Bear Lake Road on the east side of the park. *Photo by Ral Sandberg.*

ponderosa pines and favored by some of the park's massive elk herd. However, ground coverage is iffy, and occasionally nonexistent, if seasonal snows have been sparse.

From the Beaver Meadows entrance to the park, pass the Bear Lake Road turnoff and continue another 0.5 mile to the parking pullout on the left. This area contains a web of unpaved summer routes, some used by horseback outfitters. Start your hike along a summer road that angles northwestward above the meadows, along the north side of willow-lined Beaver Brook. After about 0.8 mile, you will come to a fork. It is possible to cross the meadows and shorten the hike when there is good snow cover, but to make the entire loop, stay straight on a summer pack trail toward Deer Ridge, whose aspen-covered flanks often harbor deer and elk in winter. At the westernmost point of this route, about 1.5 miles from the trailhead (and just after crossing Beaver Brook), the trail makes a sharp hairpin bend to the left and goes southeast. After another 0.3 mile, turn left at the trail junction and continue east. As you descend into the flat meadows, it's about 1.2 miles east to the trailhead.

# Bear Lake Road

The generous size of the Bear Lake parking area, and the overflow lots that you'll pass on your way in, bear inanimate but eloquent witness to the popularity of this section of the park in the summer. Little wonder, for the views of the soaring summits with scooped-out bowls on their glaciated flanks, small remnant glaciers that continue their geological task to this day, and pristine mountain lakes within easy hiking distance of the parking areas are matchless in their appeal. In winter, however, lofty Longs Peak (at 14,255 feet, the highest mountain on the Front Range) presides over a less trafficked but no less beautiful area. The Bear Lake trails, at the end of the road, offer the most consistent snow cover on the park's east side. Some of the lower trails, including those around Sprague Lake, are not so predictable. One caveat is that the Bear Lake area, even at the parking lot, can be raked by fierce winds, so if you pick a route, be flexible and have a backup plan.

# 6. Hollowell Park

| | |
|---|---|
| Starting elevation: | 8,390 feet |
| Highest elevation: | 9,000 feet |
| Elevation difference: | 610 feet |
| Distance: | 1.8 miles (one way) |
| Difficulty: | Easy to moderate |
| Avalanche hazard: | None |

This mellow saucer, part of the larger Glacier Basin, was logged both by humans and by beavers, which continue to work Mill Creek. To reach the trailhead, go 3.5 miles past the turnoff onto Bear Lake Road and turn right to the parking area, a few hundred feet down the road. Hollowell Park ("park" being a Western synonym for "valley") shows nature in action. As the trail runs west toward Mill Creek Basin, it passes through open areas, where bushes poke out of the snow and there are stands of aspen and lodgepole pines that have grown since those long-ago logging days. For a pleasant but undemanding hike, turn around at the junction to the Mill Creek Basin Trail and return the way you came.

## If You Want a Longer Hike

This is the most basic Hollowell Park snowshoeing route, but you can also make several longer, more challenging excursions. One is to continue another 0.6 mile along a glacial moraine to the junction with a smaller trail to Bierstadt Lake. This trail branches to the left, continuing to the lake about 0.4 mile farther on. The lake offers grandiose views of Flattop Mountain, Hallett Peak and Longs Peak to the south, and it is possible to circle the lake on snowshoes. If you want to explore the network of trails around Bierstadt Lake, take a map and compass, because the area can be confusing, especially in winter when the lake is frozen and the snow cover hides rocks and other landmarks.

You can also combine Bear Lake and Bierstadt Lake, or Bierstadt Lake and Hollowell Park, as a one-way hike with a car shuttle. From Bierstadt Lake, it's 1.5 steep, twisting miles to the Bierstadt Lake trailhead along Bear Lake (see Bierstadt Lake from Bear Lake Road, below). Another option in this trail-laced section of the park, with a car shuttle plus stamina, is a longer route southwestward from the Bear Lake parking lot all the way to Hollowell Park, which measures out to 4 miles, with a 250-foot elevation gain but a 1,380-foot descent. If you want real exercise, snowshoe from Hollowell Park to Bear Lake, which, considering the elevation gain, cannot be considered a casual excursion.

## 7. Bierstadt Lake from Bear Lake

| | |
|---|---|
| Starting elevation: | 9,480 feet |
| Highest elevation: | 9,770 feet (along the trail) |
| Lowest elevation: | 9,430 feet (at Bierstadt Lake) |
| Elevation difference: | 290 feet up (to high point); 340 feet down (to Bierstadt Lake) |
| Distance: | 1.8 miles (one way) |
| Difficulty: | Moderate |
| Avalanche hazard: | Low |

This has long been one of the park's most popular cross-country skiing routes, and it is gaining favor as a snowshoers' choice too. No wonder. It is accessible, easy to follow, beautiful and a satisfying workout. From the huge, paved parking lot at the end of Bear Lake Road (see page 52), skirt the east shore of Bear Lake and take the trail that climbs to the northeast. The very first part, which ascends the Bierstadt Moraine, is the most—in fact, only—challenging part of the hike. Although the ascent may feel steep, the trail is wide and very well used and well packed, so conditions are usually very good. Just when you might feel that you are running out of steam, the route follows the gently undulating trail for a little bit over a mile down toward the lake. The nicely wooded trail opens up periodically to display a succession of mountain portraits and panoramas, an ever-changing exhibit as you proceed on your hike. When you reach Bierstadt Lake, you can snowshoe around it, and return the way you came.

### If You Want a Longer Hike

You can make a car shuttle of the trip and continue down to the Bierstadt Lake trailhead along Bear Lake Road or on to Hollowell Park (see separate route descriptions above), where a second vehicle must be left.

## 8. Sprague Lake from Glacier Basin Parking Area

| | |
|---|---|
| Starting elevation: | 8,620 feet |
| Highest elevation: | 8,740 feet |
| Lowest elevation: | 8,570 feet (crossing Glacier Creek) |
| Elevation difference: | 170 feet difference between highest and lowest elevations, with gentle ups and downs |
| Distance: | 3.3 miles (loop) |
| Difficulty: | Moderate |
| Avalanche hazard: | None to low |

Sprague Lake offers some excellent trails and opportunities to explore meadows, beaver ponds and woods. The trails are rather flat, so this is a fine area if you're not up to, or not inclined for, much challenge, or have small children along. Snow cover at the shoreline can be sparse, and crossing Sprague Lake is not recommended, even if the ice does appear solid. You have several choices for snowshoeing here.

If you want some distance and some elevation change to your hike, take Bear Lake Road and, after 5.3 miles, turn right into the Glacier Basin parking area (this is also the summer shuttle bus parking area). Cross the Bear Lake Road and then the Glacier Creek bridge to the summer campground and picnic area. Of the three marked trails that lead out from here, the westernmost is the most direct path to Sprague Lake. (The two on the southeastern end loop around south of the lake to access the main winter route to Glacier Gorge Junction but can be combined to make a loop.) The main trail, which is considered the Sprague Lake Trail, cuts across an open meadow, offering fine views of McHenry's Peak, Powell Peak and Taylor Peak. The Sprague Lake Trail makes a loop of about 3 miles, and you can do it in either direction. You need to make your choice at a fork on the west side of the open area: The left option passes through a summer campground and into dense trees, passes to the south of the lake and doubles back well beyond it, while the right leads directly to the lake.

You can also approach Sprague Lake by two shorter and easier ways. From the Bear Lake Road, the easiest option of all is via a short spur road on the left, about 0.3 mile beyond the Glacier Basin parking area. It leads to the northwestern end of the lake with minimal elevation change. It is a lovely and gentle snowshoe stroll that even the youngest child can manage, even when coupled with a circuit of the lake's little nature trail.

For a little more than this most modest walk, but less than the 3-mile round-trip from the Glacier Basin parking area, you can take a short connector trail that is actually the beginning of the Boulder Brook Trail. It is across Bear Lake Road from the Bierstadt Lake trailhead. It is easy to follow, angling toward the southeast and soon crossing the main ski trail. When it does this, bear left (east) and take the left of the two marked ski trails to the lake.

This web of unplowed roads, marked ski trails and summer hiking trails essentially parallels both the creek and Bear Lake Road, and in addition to the Sprague Lake Trail circuit, they can be combined into several other short, appealing loops. The woods open into what in summer is a somewhat marshy area, but in winter you can shoe among the willows and watch the unfolding panorama of Emerald Mountain, Giant Track Mountain, Rams Horn and Lily Mountain from various sections.

## If You Want a Longer Hike

The Sprague Lake area provides many other opportunities for exploration as well as longer routes. For example, from the Boulder Brook/Sprague Lake Trail intersection, it is another 2.4 miles to Glacier Gorge Junction.

## 9. Bierstadt Lake from Bear Lake Road

| | |
|---|---|
| Starting elevation: | 8,900 feet |
| Highest elevation: | 9,430 feet |
| Elevation difference: | 530 feet |
| Distance: | 1 mile (one way) |
| Difficulty: | Moderate to challenging |
| Avalanche hazard: | None |

This trail, which begins on the right side of Bear Lake Road, 6.4 miles beyond Beaver Meadows, is short, direct and challenging. It is too steep for most skiers, both on the climb and descent, so snowshoers tend to have it to themselves. Because it faces south, it's also a good choice on a chilly day, but if the chill has followed a warm, dry spell, there are places where the snow might be spotty. This route is ideal if you want to climb and descend instead of meander, but you can also combine it into a car shuttle excursion with Hollowell Park, Glacier Basin, Bear Lake or other options not covered in this guide. A winter trail map, available at the visitors center, can provide some suggestions.

From the trailhead, follow the clearly marked trail up a series of switchbacks that climb stiffly and steadily up the Bierstadt Moraine's south slope. The trail loops along a wonderful aspen forest, regrowth from a turn-of-the-century fire, and then enters a deeper, primarily lodgepole forest that surrounds the lake. When you reach the intersection with the Bear Lake Trail, which comes in from the left (west), you are getting near the lake. Bear right (east) at that intersection and you'll soon reach the lake.

## 10. Bierstadt Lake from Glacier Basin Parking Area

| | |
|---|---|
| Starting elevation: | 8,620 feet |
| Highest elevation: | 9,430 feet |
| Elevation difference: | 810 feet |
| Distance: | 1.5 miles (one way) |
| Difficulty: | Moderate |
| Avalanche hazard: | None |

From a trailhead at the west end of the large Glacier Basin parking area, 6.4 miles past Beaver Meadows, you can ascend steadily along a moderately steep trail to Bierstadt Lake. This trail climbs the east end of the Bierstadt Moraine. This is the pretty and well-forested eastern end of the Glacier Basin-Bierstadt Lake-Bear Lake route.

# 11. Mills Lake

| | |
|---|---|
| Starting elevation: | 9,240 feet |
| Highest elevation: | 9,940 feet |
| Elevation difference: | 700 feet |
| Distance: | 2.5 miles (one way) |
| Difficulty: | Moderate |
| Avalanche hazard: | Low to moderate |

Take Bear Lake Road to the Glacier Gorge Junction, and park at the small, triangular parking area in the crook of a hairpin turn 8.5 miles from Beaver Meadows. Cross the road and start walking southwest to the Glacier Gorge Junction trailhead sign. At the fork, bear left (south), cross a bridge over Chaos Creek at the next fork, then bear right (southeast). For beginning snowshoers or the unacclimatized, follow the summer trail signs to shimmering Alberta Falls, on your left about 0.6 mile from the trailhead, which is a nice destination in itself.

Rocky Mountain National Park offers a web of outstanding winter trails. *Photo by Ral Sandberg.*

The trail beyond is generally well used in winter, and is wide and clear to follow. It heads south/southwest, crossing Chaos Creek, passing a grove of stunted aspen trees, snow-covered beaver ponds and a bushy area of low-slung willows before going into the forest. About 1 mile from the trailhead, the trail forks (you will bear right) and curves to the right (west). After another 0.3 mile, you will come to a well-marked, four-way intersection. The right trail heads toward Lake Haiyaha, the one straight ahead to the Loch and the left one, which you want, to Mills Lake. Your main landmark is a geologic protrusion called Glacier Knobs on your right. The trail parallels Glacier Creek and bends to the left, and for 0.6 mile from the four-way trail junction, you will pass though a deep forest of fir and spruce and up two steep sections along Glacier Falls and thence through large boulders to Mills Lake. The dramatic views include Longs Peak's north face and a granite formation known as the Spearhead. Return the way you came.

## If You Want a Longer Hike

If you wish to continue farther, pass along the eastern shore of Mills Lake for the short climb to Jewel Lake. However, if you have visions of reaching Lake Haiyaha, which seems so close from the four-way trail junction, save them for next summer. Not only is the Lake Haiyaha Trail difficult to follow in winter, but sections of it are extremely avalanche-prone.

## 12. Bear Lake

| | |
|---|---|
| Starting elevation: | 9,440 feet |
| Highest elevation: | 9,490 feet |
| Elevation difference: | 50 feet |
| Distance: | 0.6 mile (loop) |
| Difficulty: | Easy |
| Avalanche hazard: | None |

A circumnavigation of Bear Lake is ideal for beginning snowshoers or small children making their first excursion. The lake is as lovely as it is accessible, located literally steps from the parking lot. (In fact, it is often more steps from one's car to the trailhead than from the trailhead to the lake.) It is possible to circle the lake in either direction.

## 13. Nymph, Dream and Emerald Lakes

| | |
|---|---|
| Starting elevation: | 9,440 feet |
| Highest elevation: | Nymph Lake, 9,700 feet; |
| | Dream Lake, 9,900 feet; |
| | Emerald Lake, 10,075 feet |
| Elevation difference: | Nymph Lake, 260 feet; |
| | Dream Lake, 460 feet; |
| | Emerald Lake, 635 feet |
| Distance: | 0.5 mile to Nymph Lake; |
| | 1.1 miles to Dream Lake; |
| | 1.8 miles to Emerald Lake (one way) |
| Difficulty: | Moderate |
| Avalanche hazard: | Low |

This daisy chain of three lovely mountain lakes nestled in snow-shrouded basins makes a wonderful snowshoe excursion. It is possible to tailor the length and challenge of the hike by taking in one, two or all three of these lakes. From the main trailhead at the Bear Lake parking area, pass the information signs and bear left, soon taking a substantial trail to the right (west) where the main wide route drops down into Glacier Gorge Junction. The route as far as Nymph Lake is straightforward, but if you want to go farther, there are some tricky spots to avoid, such as the slide paths between Nymph and Dream Lakes. Snowshoers and skiers who have come before you often will have pioneered the route. Experienced winter travelers in this section of the park tend to stay close to the streambed or even on the frozen stream itself. If you have any doubts about the route, check at the visitors center or information station at the Bear Lake parking lot before starting your hike.

The trail ascends gently through the pine forest, then steepens as it ascends a knoll at Nymph Lake, just 0.5 mile and 260 vertical feet from the trailhead. By itself, this is quite an easy excursion into a lovely little valley that offers good views of Flattop Mountain and Hallett Peak, providing a visual taste of what this part of Rocky Mountain National Park is all about. This is a fine destination, even without continuing to the two other lakes.

However, if you do wish to go on, the trail curves around along the north side of Nymph Lake, deviating from the summer trail for the next leg to Dream Lake, 1.3 miles and 385 vertical feet beyond. To continue on the winter route, go to the northwest end of the lake and find a route through a dense forest of lodgepole pines. Usually there will be tracks to follow. If there aren't, turn back, because this trail is unmarked and crosses some slide areas. The trees open up here and there to provide occasional

The route to Nymph, Emerald and Dream Lakes improves with elevation—and snow conditions tend to get better too. *Photo by Ral Sandberg,*

views of Longs Peak. To avoid the avalanche paths, be sure to follow the trail that jogs to the south and then back up to the north before "straightening out" and heading west again as it climbs up to Dream Lake, 1.1 miles and 460 vertical feet from the trailhead. If the Hallett and Flattop views seem good from Nymph Lake, they are great from Dream Lake. To continue to Emerald Lake, pass on the north side of Dream Lake and cross the lake to edge along the south side of a deep valley called Tyndall Gorge. When you get to a large boulder field, cross over to the north side of the gorge for the final leg to the lake, 1.8 miles and 635 vertical feet from the trailhead. From any of these three lakes, return the way you came.

# Wild Basin

While summer sightseers from all over the world drive over Trail Ridge Road and up to Bear Lake, Wild Basin is primarily visited by hikers and other backcountry users. It is tucked into Rocky Mountain National Park's southeast corner, with a seasonal ranger station that is closed in winter and no other facilities for casual tourists. Wild Basin is given over more to backcountry users. In winter, much of the access road itself becomes part of a network of 88 excellent miles of backcountry routes. Some of these are arduous and head into areas of known avalanche activity, but several offer first-rate snowshoeing.

## Getting There

From Estes Park, take Colorado 7 south for 13 miles. Turn right at the well-marked road to the Sandbeach Lake and Wild Basin trailheads. The road is normally plowed beyond the west end of Copeland Lake. The winter parking area and trailhead are just before the road crosses the North St. Vrain River, roughly 1.5 miles before the Wild Basin summer parking area and trailhead.

## 14. Wild Basin Road

| | |
|---|---|
| Starting elevation: | 8,320 feet |
| Highest elevation: | 8,500 feet |
| Elevation difference: | 180 feet |
| Distance: | 1.5 miles (one way) from road closure to ranger station |
| Difficulty: | Easy |
| Avalanche hazard: | None |

To access anything beyond the Wild Basin summer parking area requires this gentle walk of about a mile and a half to get to the next set of trailheads. Experienced snowshoers get it over with as soon as possible, but this wide road through the trees is easy to follow and makes a fine out-and-back route for beginners, those unaccustomed to the altitude, children or anyone with a little one in a pulk or a backpack.

## 15. Calypso Cascades and Ouzel Falls

| | |
|---|---|
| Starting elevation: | 8,320 feet (8,500 feet at the Wild Basin Ranger Station) |
| Highest elevation: | Calypso Cascades, 9,200 feet; Ouzel Falls, 9,450 feet |
| Elevation difference: | 880 feet to Calypso Cascades; 1,130 feet to Ouzel Falls |
| Distance: | 3.5 miles to Calypso Cascades; 4.2 miles to Ouzel Falls (one way) |
| Difficulty: | Moderate to Calypso Cascades; challenging to Ouzel Falls |
| Avalanche hazard: | Low to Calypso Cascades; moderate in burn area |

Start by snowshoeing along the Wild Basin Road from the winter parking area to the summer parking area at the Wild Basin picnic area and ranger station. The official Wild Basin trailhead at the summer parking area is well marked. Begin your hike by crossing over the Hunters Creek Bridge and head steadily southwestward on the Thunder Lake Trail, which passes through a sheltered valley. The ascent here is gradual, steepening after the Sandbeach Creek crossing, about 0.8 mile from the Wild Basin trailhead. Two miles from the trailhead, the route becomes a little steeper and then makes two sharp switchbacks before a bridge over Ouzel Creek that provides a view of Calypso Cascade's icy waterfalls.

If you have more energy—and if the snow is not too deep for comfortable snowshoeing and the avalanche report is favorable—you can continue on to Ouzel Falls through some of the park's most dramatic acreage. After Calypso Cascades, the trail parallels the North St. Vrain River. It steepens and climbs to a dramatic moonscape of trees charred in a massive forest fire in 1978. To the right (northwest) are Longs Peak and Mt. Meeker. About a mile after the burn area you reach another bridge, and on the left are the huge granite rock walls that channel the stream into the valley you've just ascended. The Allenspark trailhead (see below) provides an alternative route to Calypso Cascades and Ouzel Falls that eliminates the slog up the Wild Basin Road.

# Allenspark Area

This small community, originally a mining camp and later a colony of summer homes, nestles up against Roosevelt National Forest just southeast of Rocky Mountain National Park. There are still plenty of seasonal log cabins and wood cottages to give Allenspark and neighboring Ferncliff a rustic look and, with the abundance of horses in barns and corrals, a rural flavor. It is astonishing to find such a remote country ambience just 32 miles from busy Boulder. In summer, when the population skyrockets from 800 or so to more than 3,000, there's a bit of a buzz, but in winter this area slumbers. Four-wheel-drive roads become excellent and little-trafficked winter recreation trails. Snowshoers, skiers and even snowmobilers share them. Crowds are absent and conflict remains rare.

## Getting There

From Lyons, take Colorado 7 toward Estes Park. Turn off the highway to the left at the well-marked intersection with the road to Ferncliff. Proceed 1 mile to an unpaved road and turn left. (This is actually East Ski Road—at this writing, the road sign was missing.) Turn left again at the T-junction with Ski Road. Snow conditions and your vehicle will determine how far you can drive. If you can, drive as far as the sign for Rock Creek and St. Vrain Mountain. Alternatively, drive 1.4 miles on the Ferncliff-Allenspark road and turn left directly onto Ski Road, an unpaved, winding road that narrows to one lane for a short distance. You can also follow Colorado 7 (Peak to Peak Highway) south 18.6 miles from Estes Park. Bear right at the road to Allenspark and Ferncliff, turn right after 0.2 mile onto Ski Road (County Road 107) and then proceed as described above.

## 16. Rock Creek Trail

| | |
|---|---|
| Starting elevation: | Approximately 8,580 feet<br>(1.4 miles below former ski area) |
| Highest elevation: | 10,600 feet |
| Elevation difference: | 2,020 feet gain; 20 feet of loss |
| Distance: | 3.1 miles one way (1.4 miles to the former ski area, plus 1.7 miles above ski area) |
| Difficulty: | Moderate to challenging |
| Avalanche hazard: | Low |

This route has a "movable trailhead," and your starting elevation depends on the snow depth, the condition of the road, your vehicle and your experience in, and appetite for, snow driving. The road is not plowed past the last residence, about 0.3 mile before the Rock Creek/St. Vrain Mountain Trail sign, which must be considered the winter trailhead. Sometimes, you can drive as far as the sign, where you will find a few side-of-the-road spots to park. In any case, snowshoe left (southwest) at the fork in the road, following the branch that parallels Rock Creek. In low-snow years, you may be able to drive this stretch, perhaps to the hairpin turn just beyond the ghost of the long-abandoned Rock Creek Ski Area, which provides a wide pullout/turnaround area with enough space to park a couple of vehicles.

Except after new snow, the lower portion of the Rock Creek Trail can be uneven, with deep tire ruts, snow chunks and some icy sections, which provides less than pleasant shoeing conditions but really makes you appreciate the versatility of snowshoes. After about a mile, you'll probably find conditions much improved: powder after a snowfall and a soft, packed surface days after a storm. The road climbs consistently up the valley with steep pine-covered hills on both sides, but you can also occasionally see Meadow Mountain and St. Vrain Mountain to the west and north. After about 1.7 miles, the route steepens and twists into a series of switchbacks, and the snow gets smoother, a good turn-around spot.

### If You Want a Longer Hike
Several summer trails and logging roads branch off from the main Rock Creek route, and you might see tracks made by snowshoers and skiers who have explored some of these options. At 2.4 miles, for example, you

will reach a major junction with the Rock Creek Saddle Trail to Peaceful Valley, 1.8 miles away. As you approach the end of the Rock Creek Trail, the trees are more widely spaced, evidence of previous traffic is less and the view opens. This out-and-back route enables you to turn around whenever you wish, but if you go the distance to a high bowl 3.1 miles and over 2,000 vertical feet from the trailhead, the elevation gain alone makes it a very challenging snowshoe hike.

If, and only if, you have excellent stamina, your off-trail ability is strong and weather and snow conditions are prime, you can also continue beyond the most-used section of the route to the East Ridge of St. Vrain Mountain. This little-traveled, 1.5-mile route curves first northwest, then north, then northeast, to connect the Rock Creek Trail to St. Vrain Mountain Trail. The grade is moderate, but there is nothing else easy about it. It is high and exposed to wind, making for difficult route finding, packing the snow into concrete hardness and requiring good endurance for breaking trail. It is definitely not for casual users.

## 17. St. Vrain Mountain Trail

| | |
|---|---|
| Starting elevation: | 8,580 feet |
| Highest elevation: | 11,200 feet |
| Elevation difference: | 2,620 feet |
| Distance: | 3.5 miles (one way) |
| Difficulty: | Challenging |
| Avalanche hazard: | Low below the Meadow Mountain Bowl; high above it |

The St. Vrain Mountain Trail can be jokingly considered as the Rock Creek Trail's evil twin: longer, steeper, more challenging and generally much windier. Access to this trail is the same as for Rock Creek, except that you bear right at the Rock Creek/St. Vrain Mountain sign when on foot or, if snow is sparse, continue another 0.5 mile to a summer parking area. Whether you are driving or snowshoeing, the route starts with a climb right after the sign, and it doesn't ever really moderate. After a few tight bends in the road close to the trailhead, the route changes after about half a mile from a summer road to a summer hiking trail, marked with an Indian Peaks Wilderness sign.

This straightforward climb continues almost due west for nearly a mile, entering Rocky Mountain National Park. The route becomes steeper and virtually makes a 90-degree turn to the left (south) where the trees begin to thin. The snow conditions mirror Rock Creek Trail's: possibly ugly near the bottom, improving in the midsection and silky on the less traveled upper portions. The trail then it makes another sharp turn, nearly a switchback, to the right (northwest), across the head of a large basin. If you are snowshoeing after a snowstorm or any time that avalanche hazards are reported in this region, it is imperative to turn around below the bowl.

## 18. Calypso Cascades and Ouzel Falls

| | |
|---|---|
| Starting elevation: | 8,640 feet (approximate elevation of water treatment plant) |
| Highest elevation: | 9,700 feet (along the trail) |
| Elevation difference: | 1,060-foot gain (to high point); 500-foot loss (to Calypso Cascades) |
| Distance: | 3.7 miles (one way) to Calypso Cascades; 4.4 miles to Ouzel Falls |
| Difficulty: | Challenging |
| Avalanche hazard: | Low, except for the burn area, where it is moderate to high |

To avoid the trudge up Wild Basin Road, you can opt for the longer but also more interesting trail from Allenspark. To reach the trailhead, take Colorado 7 to the Allenspark turnoff, continue 0.1 mile to the post office and drive west on Triple Creek Road. The road is usually plowed to the Allenspark water treatment plant, a short distance from the trailhead. Park and begin snowshoeing by proceeding right to the trailhead. The route starts up the unplowed road to the northwest. After the last house, you will come to the Rocky Mountain National Park boundary, where the wide road turns into a trail. It mounts a ridge that separates the Allenspark area from Wild Basin and the North St. Vrain drainage. An immediate reward is an approximately 1.5-mile descent into Wild Basin, which seems like a gift until you remember that you will need to climb it on the way back.

The trail is never crowded (in fact, you often will see no tracks at all). It is marked with diamond tabs on the trees, and both snow and weather are known to be variable. Snowshoes are useful for the varying snow conditions, which often range from deep snow in drift zones to almost nothing on bare (or near-bare) stretches of trail. This area can be very windy, but it does offer great views of Longs Peak and Mt. Meeker.

If avalanche conditions are not favorable, enjoy the route just as far as this overlook, then return the way you came. If the snowpack is reported stable, go left (west) at this junction and continue up the trail past a couple of switchbacks and to Calypso Cascades, where the trail merges with the main trail system. You can also continue through the burn area to Ouzel Falls (above) as long as snow conditions are reported to be stable. It is, of course, feasible to do this as a car shuttle with a return to Wild Basin, which would eliminate the 1.5-mile uphill climb back to the ridge above Allenspark.

# Brainard Lake

If there's a more popular place for snowshoeing and Nordic skiing than the Brainard Lake Recreation Area, I certainly haven't found it. Located less than an hour's drive from Boulder and not much farther from Denver, this outdoor playground is virtually in the backyard of the largest metropolitan area within a 600-mile radius. On busy winter weekends, it sometimes seems as if all two million people in greater Denver converge on Brainard Lake.

In the warm months, it is possible to drive to, around and beyond the lake, and many people do so for RV or car camping, fishing, hiking or simply sightseeing. Although the lake and its immediate surroundings accommodate this variety of recreational activities, it is also the prime gateway to the backcountry trails that lace Indian Peaks Wilderness. In winter, Brainard Lake freezes into a thick sheet of flat, windswept ice enfolded in the Indian Peaks' panoramic embrace. This magnificent basin displays one of Colorado's most spectacular mountain vistas, with Kiowa, Niwot Ridge, Navajo, Apache, Pawnee and Audubon splayed across the western horizon. The Indian Peaks are more than just a pretty face. They form the Continental Divide, which is the spine of the North American continent and here is at about its easternmost point in Colorado.

Only the first 2.6 miles of Brainard Lake Road—as far as Red Rock Lake—are plowed, in effect expanding the wilderness seasonally. Most but not all the winter trails from this seasonal closure lead to Brainard Lake. Blue diamond blazes affixed to the trees mark many of the most popular routes, but only until they reach the wilderness boundary. Hardcore backcountry enthusiasts use Brainard Lake as a gateway to the high mountains for ski touring, winter camping and backcountry telemarking and snowboarding. But this wilderness area is not to be trifled with. It is avalanche territory, so good sense dictates that anyone venturing into the high country be well equipped as well as knowledgeable about snow safety and avalanche hazards. Snowshoes, increasingly, are the devices on which people reach the deep backcountry and the high peaks, but most recreational snowshoers and skiers don't go beyond the immediate Brainard Lake area, which is what I've concentrated on here.

No snowmobiles or other vehicles are permitted beyond the Red Rock Lake closure. The barrier even makes the unplowed road into part of the trail system. Depending on how one measures, there are 30 or so miles of well-marked, well-used winter trails in and around Brainard Lake. Dog regulations have changed over the years. Pooches are currently prohibited on ski trails from the Red Rock Lake parking area to Brainard Lake, but are permitted on the Brainard Lake Road, Lefthand Reservoir Road and both North and South Sourdough Trails. Dogs are required to be leashed in the Indian Peaks Wilderness year-round.

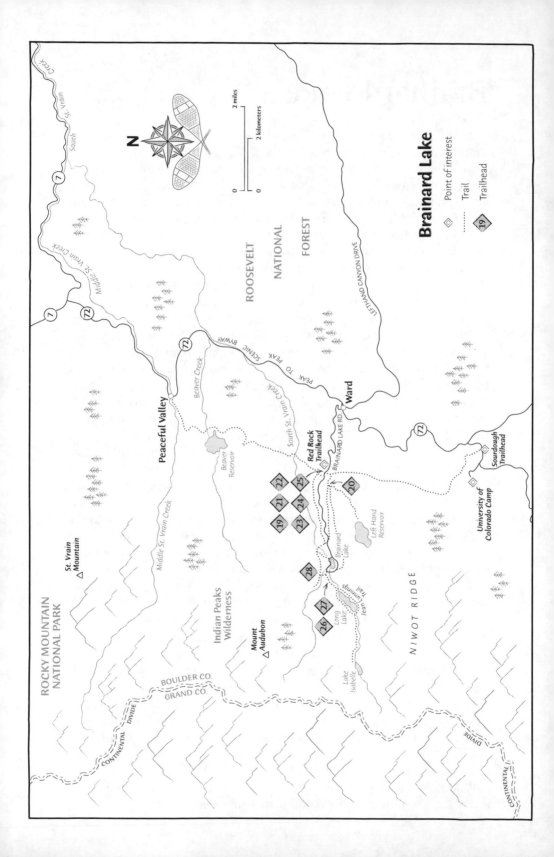

ROCKY MOUNTAIN
NATIONAL PARK

St. Vrain
△ Mountain

Indian Peaks
Wilderness

Mount
△ Audubon

BOULDER CO.
GRAND CO.

CONTINENTAL DIVIDE

CONTINENTAL DIVIDE

Peaceful Valley

Beaver Creek

Beaver
Reservoir

Middle St. Vrain Creek

South St. Vrain Creek

PEAK TO PEAK SCENIC BYWAY

Ward

Red Rock
Trailhead

BRAINARD LAKE RD.

Brainard
Lake

Left Hand
Reservoir

Long Lake

Lake Isabelle

Jean Lunning Trail

NIWOT RIDGE

LEFTHAND CANYON DRIVE

ROOSEVELT

NATIONAL

FOREST

University of
Colorado Camp

Sourdough
Trailhead

St. Vrain Creek

South St. Vrain Creek

Middle St. Vrain Creek

7

7

72

72

72

19

21

22

23

24

25

20

28

27

26

N

2 miles

2 kilometers

0

0

## Brainard Lake

◇ Point of interest

······· Trail

◆ Trailhead
19

### Getting There
To reach the Brainard Lake Recreation Area, follow Colorado 72 (Peak to Peak Highway) 12 miles north from Nederland and hook a hard left onto the well-marked Brainard Lake Recreation Area Road. (An option from Boulder is to take Broadway north to Lee Hill Road, then west up Lefthand Canyon through Ward to Colorado 72 and a nearly immediate left to the Brainard Lake Road.) The Brainard Lake Road is plowed for 2.6 miles from the turnoff, where you will find a barrier gate and several trailheads. The Red Rock Lake trailhead parking area is not adequate for weekend and holiday hordes, so unless you arrive really early, be prepared to park along the road, perhaps quite far down the road from the trailheads. Also, unless policies change and the parking area is expanded, be sure to pull completely off the road. In 1997–1998, the county sheriff began to ticket cars parked on the pavement.

### Maps
USGS 7.5 Minute, Ward
Trails Illustrated #102, Indian Peaks, Gold Hill
USFS Roosevelt National Forest
Front Range Ski Trails, George J. Maurer, Inc.
Colorado Mountain Club Ski Trail Map, Brainard Lake

The trails starting at, or near, the road seasonal closure were laid out over the years by Colorado Mountain Club volunteers for ski touring. Many make excellent snowshoeing routes too, and snowshoers are now legion at Brainard Lake. To accommodate them as well as to give the skiers more room, two new snowshoe-specific trails were being developed at this writing. This heavy use by snowshoers and skiers requires accommodation, tolerance and close attention to winter trail etiquette (see the Technique chapter, page 23).

## CMC Brainard Cabin
Since 1928, the Colorado Mountain Club's Boulder Group has maintained the Brainard Cabin, located at 10,425 feet near the Mitchell and Long Lake summer parking lots. Though it is quite near the trail, the cabin nestles in a discreet hollow, so look for the signs. Volunteer hosts welcome all winter backcountry users on most weekend days with a warm fire and hot chocolate. (Because they are volunteers, however, don't count on it.) If you might be heading to the west end of Brainard Lake, why not tuck a couple of dollar bills into your pocket to drop into the donation cup to help defray the cost of cabin upkeep? It is a wonderful spot to rest, have a snack, even warm your lunch on the stove and trade tips and tales with other snowshoers and skiers. CMC members may also use the cabin for overnights. The cabin accommodates up to 12 people

overnight. It is stocked with basic necessities, but guests must provide their own sleeping bags, food and flashlights. For overnight reservations (at least one CMC member per party), call **(303) 441-2436**.

### Active 2 Adventures

Front Range outdoor enthusiasts can tap into a combination of easy snowshoeing and easy socializing via Active 2 Adventures. Snowshoeing involves scheduled weekend or moonlight guided snowshoe hikes (and cross-country ski tours) on some of the most popular trails around Brainard Lake and environs. Socializing involves gathering around the woodstove at the Old Depot in Ward, where members enjoy hot drinks and snacks in the congenial atmosphere of a historic old railroad station. The ambiance is reminiscent of an old-time ski lodge, with a lunch area for brown-baggers, rest rooms (indoors!) and a place to change into dry clothes before driving home. Annual membership fees are $40 per family and $25 per individual at this writing, which is modest for weekend access to a mountain getaway. Rental snowshoes and telescoping poles are also stocked at the Old Depot. Active 2 Adventures, 3540 West 100th Place, Westminster, CO 80030; (303) 469-2070 or (800) 292-4169; www.activeadventures.com/.

# Trailheads at Red Rock Lake

## 19. Brainard Lake Road

| | |
|---|---|
| Starting elevation: | 10,060 feet |
| Highest elevation: | 10,330 feet |
| Elevation difference: | 270 feet |
| Distance: | 2.2 miles (one way, to the outlet bridge) |
| Difficulty: | Easy |
| Avalanche hazard: | None |

This is the easiest route in this area, of interest mainly to beginning snowshoers or anyone trying to make time on a level surface to Brainard Lake. It's useful when you want to reach some of the trails beyond as quickly as possible, or as a fast return if it's late or you're tired and not expecting great conditions. It is the (mostly) snow-covered paved road that leads west from the road barrier.

Portions of the road may be snow-free, which means you'll have to go off-trail. Therefore, you might find yourself shoeing along the road shoulder or to the edge of the woods, or perhaps even removing your snowshoes for a bit and just walking. Just because you hike up the Brainard

Lake Road doesn't mean that you have to go back the same way. This chapter details various options for returning to the trailhead.

## 20. Lefthand Reservoir Road

| | |
|---|---|
| Starting elevation: | 10,060 feet |
| Highest elevation: | 10,640 feet |
| Elevation difference: | 580 feet |
| Distance: | 1.8 miles (one way) |
| Difficulty: | Moderate |
| Avalanche hazard: | None |

About 100 yards before (east of) the barrier gate at the end of the plowed section of the Brainard Lake Road, you will see on your left (south) another metal gate. This gate blocks off the service road to Lefthand Reservoir. This route extends southwestward and is one of the most pleasant winter tours in the Brainard area. Starting from the Lefthand Ski Trail sign, you will find the route to be wide enough to accommodate both snowshoers and skiers, and it is consequently popular with both. It is also a good choice for a night tour on a clear night with a full moon.

This route's challenge comes at the beginning. The very first part of the road is the most heavily traveled, since it also accesses the South Sourdough, CMC South and Little Raven Trails. The early part also features the steepest sections, some of which are infamous because they often become windblown and dry. This comes as a surprise to first-timers on this otherwise well-covered, snow-packed route. Once you've made it past the steep section and the weekend traffic, it levels off into a gentle cruise until you get to the last third of a mile or so, where snow cover can again become sparse.

The Lefthand Creek bridge at 0.8 mile is one of the route's landmarks, as is the nearby junction with the Little Raven Trail. After that there is one more steep part, then the rest of the road is just a nice grade toward the reservoir. As you approach the lake, you will pass an old 21. quarry on the left, but it might be difficult to spot under snow. Still, you'll know when you're near the quarry, because around that point you may find that the wind picks up just as the scenery improves. Niwot Ridge stretches straight ahead, behind the reservoir, flanked by such Indian Peaks as Kiowa, Arikaree, Navajo, Apache, Shoshoni and Pawnee. It's worth a bit of bushwhacking just off-trail to avoid the bare spots in order to enjoy these views. The earthen berm that contains the water is dead ahead at the end of the road, though some people make a loop around the reservoir to enjoy the scenery and click off some more mileage.

## 21. Brainard Snowshoeing Trails

Family snowshoeing at Gold Lake Mountain Resort, within sight of the beautiful Indian Peaks. *Photo courtesy Gold Lake Mountain Resort.*

Brainard Lake boasts two new dedicated snowshoeing trails to diffuse two winter recreational activities and defuse the conflicts between cross-country skiers and snowshoers. Trail planning and tree pruning began in 1998, and one or both trails were expected to be flagged and snow-shoeable by 1998–1999. With snowshoer trails accessible from the Red Rock Lake trailhead, the Forest Service is expected to designate Little Raven as a skier-only trail and to make skier-only use of CMC South voluntary, at least in the beginning. Check future regulations, which could change.

In designing these trails, consideration was given not only to physically separating snowshoers and skiers in this busy and popular area, but also to separating them visually. Along most of the snowshoe and ski routes, trail users will not be able to see each other. Both trails, which were unnamed at this writing, begin together at the CMC South trailhead. After about 20 yards, the snowshoeing route veers off to the west, roughly paralleling the CMC South Trail. About 100 yards before Red Rock Lake, it crosses the CMC Trail and continues to the lake, where there are fine views of the Indian Peaks. There, the routes divide.

The shorter route, a loop of about 1.5 miles, bends right (north) along Red Rock Lake's east shore, then curves to the right. It comes out on the Brainard Lake Road close to the Waldrop trailhead. At Red Rock Lake, the longer route, which is about 4 miles one way, bears left (west) and continues along the south shore. It parallels the CMC South Trail to the Brainard Lake Cut-Off, where it bends right (north) across an open meadow to the Brainard Lake Road.

Snowshoers head west on the road for about roughly 150 yards and then pick up the trail again at a marked place on the north side of the road. The trail bears left (northwest) to the large clearing ,which everyone calls "the big meadow." It angles off to the west, again paralleling Brainard Lake Road, and ascends on a long, gradual uphill to a creek crossing just below the automobile bridge at the bottom (east end) of the lake. It continues for about another mile to the CMC Brainard Cabin.

## 22. CMC South Trail

| | |
|---|---|
| Starting elevation: | 10,060 feet |
| Highest elevation: | 10,380 feet |
| Elevation difference: | 320 feet, but many small rises and drops |
| Distance: | 2.5 miles (one way, to the west end of Brainard Lake) |
| Difficulty: | Moderate |
| Avalanche hazard: | None |

The CMC South Trail was cut as a ski-touring trail in the 1970s by volunteers from the Colorado Mountain Club's Boulder Group, and it is arguably the single most popular trail in the most popular Front Range system. From a trailhead that also starts at the Red Rock Lake winter closure, it parallels (but is rarely in sight of) the unplowed vehicular road to Brainard Lake and therefore has a winter sense of wilderness, albeit a heavily used wilderness. With the development of a snowshoeing-only option to the CMC South Trail, snowshoeing use will certainly diminish and may eventually be prohibited on this trail.

Begin south of the road, as if going to the Lefthand Reservoir Road. You will see the well-marked CMC South Trail almost immediately on your right (west). This is the first of two CMC South trailheads (the second is farther along the Lefthand Reservoir Road, also to the right). Take this trail west into the woods, ascending a short, somewhat steep section. It quickly levels out, and you'll soon fall into an easy rhythm on the narrow, well-contoured trail, which from then on plays like a symphony of mostly tame ascents, little drops and flat sections. Because of heavy use, this is an area where snowshoers should be particularly careful not to tramp the fresh ski tracks after a snowfall. Once the weekend snowshoeing and skiing masses arrive, however, this courtesy becomes irrelevant, because the trail soon turns into a single trough. The main challenge then becomes dealing with people. Snowshoers and skiers of different speeds and ability levels leapfrog along the trail, with snowshoers moving well on the uphill and fast skiers dusting everyone on the descents.

CMC South undulates prettily through the woods, which open periodically into small clearings and larger meadows, occasionally with views. At about 2 miles is a view down to the right toward Brainard Lake. You then pass several old chimneys, signaling that you are abreast of the western end of the lake, a good spot for a rest stop or turnaround. The trail actually continues a short distance to the road, which goes completely around the lake.

## If You Want a Longer Hike

If you want to continue to Brainard Lake, take the cutoff down a short, sharp descent to another open meadow and continue northwestward to the unplowed road along the western end of the lake to make a loop (see below) via the Waldrop Trail. Note that Little Raven, which is also accessible here, is now a skier-only trail.

# 23. Waldrop (CMC North) Trail

| | |
|---|---|
| Starting elevation: | 10,060 feet |
| Highest elevation: | 10,450 feet |
| Elevation difference: | 390 feet, with some additional descents and climbs |
| Distance: | 2.8 miles (one way, to the Mitchell Lake parking area road) |
| Difficulty: | Moderate |
| Avalanche hazard: | None |

The CMC North Trail was one of the first ski trails cut by the Colorado Mountain Club. It was renamed officially to honor CMC-er Harry Waldrop, who was killed in a kayaking accident on the Arkansas River. You may find references to either trail name on various maps and in different guidebooks. This companion to the CMC South Trail is slightly longer and has more ups and downs, which themselves are longer and steeper than anything you'll find on the South Trail.

The trailhead is near a large sign on the right (north), about 300 yards beyond the Red Rock parking area. The trail extends westward along the north side of the Brainard Lake Road. It starts with a long downhill, then undulates through the dense woods. After one long, steady climb, you will reach a section that includes several shorter descents, a few minor ascents and several meadow crossings, some of which are usually wind scoured. After the South St. Vrain Creek crossing, you first reach a T-intersection that is the junction with the South St. Vrain Trail and then a junction with the Brainard Lake Cut-Off Trail, which veers sharply to the left (south). This is a good place to turn around, take the cutoff that leads to the eastern end of Brainard Lake or continue to make a circuit around the lake (see Brainard Lake Loop, page 73).

## If You Want a Longer Hike

You can continue on the Waldrop Trail, which joins the St. Vrain Trail and after about 0.5 mile breaks away again at a marked trail junction. The left (south) branch is the Waldrop Trail, which continues on, passing the CMC Brainard Cabin just before reaching the road to the Mitchell Lake parking area.

## 22–23. Brainard Lake Loop

| | |
|---|---|
| Starting elevation: | 10,060 feet |
| Highest elevation: | 10,450 feet |
| Elevation difference: | 800 feet, inlcuding ups and downs |
| Distance: | 7 miles (loop) |
| Difficulty: | Moderate |
| Avalanche hazard: | None |

You can make a loop by combining the South CMC and North CMC
(Waldrop) with a connecting route along two unplowed roads, one around
Brainard Lake and one to the Mitchell Lake summer trailhead. It is possible to do the loop in either direction, but clockwise seems to be best for
most snowshoers. To do it in this direction, take the CMC South all the
way to the west end of Brainard Lake (passing the old chimneys, and
dropping down to the road around the west end of the lake). Continue
northwest along the road around the western end. Pass the lakeside Niwot
Mountain Picnic Area to a left fork, which is marked with a Mitchell
Lake sign. Proceed up this road past the Waldrop Trail and CMC Brainard
Cabin signs to a second Waldrop Trail sign, where you go right (east)
along the South St. Vrain Trail. After about 0.7 mile (including crossing
an open, windblown meadow, followed by a wooded area), you come to
another Waldrop Trail sign, where you must take a right to follow the
Waldrop Trail eastward. Along the 0.7-mile stretch, you will pass two
right forks (which may or may not be obvious), one leading back to the
CMC Brainard Cabin and the other leading to the Brainard Lake Road.
Stay left at each of these junctions if you want to stay on the Waldrop
Trail all the way back to the Red Rock parking area.

## 24. Sourdough Trail, South Section

| | |
|---|---|
| Starting elevation: | 10,060 feet (Red Rock Lake trailhead) |
| Highest elevation: | 10,340 feet |
| Elevation difference: | 280-foot gain; 1,120-foot loss (to Rainbow Lakes Road) |
| Distance: | 5.5 miles (one way) |
| Difficulty: | Moderate to challenging southbound; challenging northbound |
| Avalanche hazard: | None |

## 25. Sourdough Trail, North Section

| | |
|---|---|
| Starting elevation: | 10,060 feet (Red Rock Lake trailhead) |
| Highest elevation: | 10,060 feet |
| Elevation difference: | 900-foot loss (to Beaver Creek Road); 1,520-foot loss (to Camp Dick)—(all one way) |
| Distance: | 5.9 miles (Beaver Reservoir Road); 7.8 miles (Camp Dick) minus 2 miles if shortcut is used |
| Difficulty: | Moderate to challenging northbound; challenging southbound |
| Avalanche hazard: | None |

The Sourdough Trail roughly parallels the Peak to Peak Highway (Colorado 72) between Rainbow Lakes Road and Peaceful Valley, with the Brainard Lake Road interrupting the continuity of the trail. This interruption provides vehicle access to the middle, making it a feasible snowshoe tour for most people. (Trail runners, of course, delight in swallowing Sourdough whole.) You can snowshoe out and back on either section, turning around wherever it suits you, but a car shuttle is necessary to do either the north or south segment one way. If you are in the mood for a real workout, you can start at the Rainbow Lake Road trailhead and proceed north or start at Peaceful Valley and then proceed south, to the Red Rock Lake trailhead, where you've left the second vehicle. However, because the Red Rock Lake trailhead is almost the high point, it's easier and more congenial for many snowshoers to start there and go north or south. The north section can also be split up into two sections: Red Rock Lake trailhead to Beaver Reservoir Road and Beaver Reservoir Road to Camp Dick, near Peaceful Valley

The Sourdough Trail's three main trailheads, as well as the auxiliary connectors, are all accessible from side roads off the Peak to Peak Highway. To snowshoe South Sourdough from the south, drive north from Nederland for 7 miles (or south from Ward 5 miles), and turn west (left from Nederland, right from Ward) onto Rainbow Lake Road, an unpaved road prominently labeled "University of Colorado Research Station." The trailhead is 0.4 mile from the turnoff. Off-road parking is limited, but Red Rock–sized crowds never develop.

To come into North Sourdough's midsection, you start from the Beaver Reservoir Road trailhead, also off the Peak to Peak Highway, 14.5 miles north of Nederland or 2.5 miles north of the Brainard Lake Road. Turn left on the road to Camp Tahosa. The South St. Vrain trailhead is on your left, but continue 2 miles on an unpaved road to Beaver Reservoir.

The Sourdough Trail crosses this road about 0.2 mile below the lake. The northernmost access to North Sourdough is at Peaceful Valley, nearly 19 miles north of Nederland or 5.8 miles north of the Brainard Lake Road. Park at the wide intersection to the Camp Dick Road, which is unplowed in winter and is therefore part of the snowshoeing and ski-touring trail. The northern section of the trail and its connectors form a complicated network, so you definitely want a good map and probably a compass too.

Both sections offer nice ups and downs through the woods and over several large meadows and small clearings before the final descent to Rainbow Lakes Road or Camp Dick. Although the Sourdough Trail is relatively straightforward, be aware of trail junctions and tricky spots. The trail junctions are well marked, but if you are breaking trail in new snow, small, deceiving clearings can tug you off-route. Watch for the blue trail markers. Northbound from the Brainard Lake Road (i.e., the Red Rock Lake trailhead), you can either stay on the main trail or take a shortcut via a short stretch of the South St. Vrain Trail and the Church Camp Cutoff Trail. To use the shortcut, turn right (east) on the South St. Vrain Trail. After 0.2 mile, follow the shortcut that branches left (north) and intercept the Sourdough Trail. The shortcut eliminates 2 miles of the Sourdough Trail. When you rejoin the main trail, bear right (north).

If you want to visit the Stapp Lakes area, take Stapp Lakes Trail, which branches from the Sourdough Trail 4.5 miles (2.5 miles if you take the shortcut) north of the Red Rock Lake trailhead. The Sourdough Trail intercepts the Beaver Reservoir Road after about 5.9 miles (3.9 miles with the shortcut), which you can follow west to the reservoir. If you are heading to Peaceful Valley, continue northward on the Sourdough Trail another 2 miles to Camp Dick. Note that the descent into the Middle St. Vrain Valley and Camp Dick is steep. Be alert for skiers coming down behind you.

To explore the various snowed-over four-wheel-drive roads and short connecting trails integrated with portions of longer trails, study a good trail and topo map and plot other out-and-back routes with a loop in the middle. Because most of this trail system is in the woods, it is tree sheltered, and the snow is usually good. Beaver Reservoir is where you're mostly like to encounter wind. Another alternative is to take the South St. Vrain Trail directly to Tahosa Bridge near the Peak to Peak Highway, a steady 3-mile downhill. After leaving the Red Rock Lake Trailhead, go 1.1 miles, then turn right (east) on the South St. Vrain Trail and follow it to the Tahosa Bridge.

South Sourdough doesn't offer as many ancillary trails, but it is an extremely pleasant ramble through the forest. The trailhead at the Red Rock Lake parking area is about 50 yards east of the Lefthand Reservoir route. Pass the Little Raven Trail junction and continue in a south/southeasterly direction through woods and open meadows. There is one large, sharp hairpin turn at a bridge crossing at about 4 miles. About a mile farther on, following the junction with Niwot Ridge Road, the Sourdough Trail turns east, steepens and develops switchbacks before terminating 1.5 miles later at the Rainbow Lakes Road. Some of the roads near the University of Colorado Research Station are also accessible to snowmobiles.

# Trailheads Beyond Brainard Lake

Long Lake, Lake Isabelle and Mitchell Lake are the Indian Peaks Wilderness's three most accessible high-Alpine lakes. In the heart of winter, when you can't drive beyond the road barrier, they might seem to be epic snowshoeing destinations, because you have to get there and back from the road closure. The distances given below are from either the Long Lake or Mitchell Lake trailheads, so you will need to add about 6 miles (i.e., about 3 miles each way) to the distances given here when the Brainard Lake Road is closed at Red Rock Lake. Early in fall, when there's been some snow but before the main road is closed, and especially in spring, when the road has been plowed out but there's still deep snowpack in the forest, these three routes provide beguiling and much shorter snowshoe hikes in themselves.

These three lakes are not only relatively easy to reach (on snowshoes, accessed as described above from the west end of Brainard Lake), but they are excellent examples of high mountain lakes. Portions of the routes, particularly the drainage between Lake Isabelle and the bottom of the valley, are in normal avalanche zones, therefore demanding caution and respect. Still, snowshoeing these lower portions of these trails, surrounded by the wilderness that is also a watershed, provides some insight into the importance of water to semiarid Colorado.

The South St. Vrain drainage begins at Isabelle Glacier. Glacial melt water, plus runoff from Navajo Peak, Apache Peak and Shoshone Peak, flows into Lake Isabelle and then to Long Lake and Brainard Lake. Mitchell Lake is the lowest in a chain that drains off lofty Mt. Audubon, Paiute Peak and Mt. Toll, and it also drains into Brainard Lake. Brainard Lake's water flows into South St. Vrain Creek. The Indian Peaks Wilderness boundary lies west of Brainard Lake, so these are true—not just seasonal—wilderness routes.

# 26. Long Lake/Jean Lunning Trail

| | |
|---|---|
| Starting elevation: | 10,500 feet (Long Lake summer parking lot trailhead) |
| Highest elevation: | 10,640 feet |
| Elevation difference: | 140 feet |
| Distance: | 3 miles (loop from Long Lake summer parking lot) |
| Difficulty: | Easy to moderate |
| Avalanche hazard: | None |

It is possible to circle Long Lake in either direction, but counterclockwise is best, because there is more traffic to Isabelle Lake via the Pawnee Pass Trail, making the route easier to follow in that direction. The trail, also called the Long Lake Ski Trail, is narrow, threading through dense conifer woods, so the snow lingers and lingers. In fact, you can often combine snowshoeing and barebooting until July.

From the Long Lake/Lake Isabelle/Pawnee Pass trailhead, follow the snowed-over South St. Vrain Creek bed 0.3 mile to the northeastern end of Long Lake. At the Isabelle/Pawnee Pass sign, bear right through the woods and sporadic clearings. Continue along the obvious trail paralleling the north shore. Each open spot provides a wonderful view as you snowshoe. (In winter, the ice will easily hold your weight, but crossing it rarely seems worth the risk, especially very early or very late in the season.)

Roughly 1.3 miles from the trailhead is the junction with the Lake Isabelle/Pawnee Pass Trail, which in winter is the main trail. To circle the lake, however, bear left and continue on the Jean Lunning Trail, which is not as heavily used, so your map and even a compass might come in handy if you're confused. At the head of the lake, the trail is well above lake level and quite a distance from it, so don't be surprised by not seeing its flat, frozen surface. Then, beyond the head of the lake, the trail bends back in a northeast direction, paralleling the south shore. The trail is closer to the lower portion of the lake than to its head, so when the views begin to open up consistently and improve, you'll know that you are nearing the end. The Jean Lunning Trail reconnects first with the Niwot Cut-Off (sometimes called the Long Lake Cut-Off) and then with the main trail. The latter, back to the Long Lake summer parking lot, is easier by far. You can also do this trail clockwise.

## 27. Lake Isabelle

| | |
|---|---|
| Starting elevation: | 10,500 feet (Long Lake summer parking lot trailhead) |
| Highest elevation: | 10,930 feet |
| Elevation difference: | 430 feet |
| Distance: | 2 miles (one way, from the Long Lake summer parking lot); 10 miles (round-trip from Red Rock Lake trailhead) |
| Difficulty: | Moderate to challenging |
| Avalanche hazard: | Some, at the lower section of a side valley just before the lake; serious in the high bowls above Lake Isabelle |

From the Long Lake summer parking area, follow the Lake Isabelle/Pawnee Pass Trail along the lake's northern shore. (This is also called the Long Lake Ski Trail.) At the trail junction, take the right fork and begin climbing toward Lake Isabelle. The trees thin, the slope becomes steeper and the route switchbacks to a steplike rocky knob. You can get around it by snowshoeing to the right (north). Be sure to stay in the trees and avoid the clear avalanche path. At the top of this rocky section, bear left to Lake Isabelle. Set near timberline, this lake is a shimmering jewel in the precious setting of the Indian Peaks.

## If You Want a Longer Hike

Hardy backcountry touring skiers and snowboarders often continue above Lake Isabelle, but this is serious avalanche country and not recommended for recreational snowshoeing.

## 28. Mitchell Lake

| | |
|---|---|
| Starting elevation: | 10,450 feet (from Mitchell Lake summer parking lot) |
| Highest elevation: | 10,735 feet (Mitchell Lake) |
| Elevation difference: | 285 feet |
| Distance: | 1.1 miles one way (from Mitchell Lake summer parking lot); 9.5 miles round-trip (from Red Rock trailhead) |
| Difficulty: | Easy to moderate (from Mitchell Lake); moderate to challenging (from Red Rock) |
| Avalanche hazard: | None to Mitchell Lake; moderate on the continuation to Blue Lake; high above Blue Lake |

Take your choice of routes from the Red Rock trailhead to the CMC Brainard Cabin, where you might overnight or stop to warm up if you're making a long day of it. If you take this trail, you will probably leave most other people behind, for this is a far less traveled winter route. However, it is beautiful, the snow conditions are generally good and it offers wonderful views, especially of Mt. Audubon's impressive slopes just to the north.

After leaving the cabin, continue straight up the road toward Mitchell Lake. (A trail to the right accesses the Beaver Creek Trail.) The Mitchell Lake route passes through a dense Engelmann spruce forest, interspersed with occasional clearings. You will first reach Little Mitchell Lake, which in winter resembles just a large clearing. Continue over a small knoll, which is often wind scoured, until you reach Mitchell Lake at about 0.8 mile. Most people end their excursion here and return to the Red Rock trailhead, but it is also possible to continue around the lake.

### If You Want a Longer Hike

From the far end of Mitchell Lake, the trail continues another 1.3 miles to Blue Lake. This section is far more challenging and even less frequently traveled in winter, not surprising given the usual conditions, which include both strong winds and several slide sections. Therefore, this trail is best avoided whenever there are avalanche hazard conditions and unless you are knowledgeable about snow safety.

## *Gold Lake Mountain Resort*

This secluded mountain hideaway, located at 9,000 feet, features 17 delightful cottages tucked amid the pine trees. Each is furnished differently and exudes the quirky charm that comes from combining attic-treasure antiques, southwestern art, puffy down comforters and new gas stoves for cozy warmth. The spacious bathrooms are decorated as imaginatively as the rooms. Holidays are busy, even in winter, but the resort offers reasonably priced off-season specials throughout the winter except for such peak times as Thanksgiving, Christmas, New Year's and Presidents' weekend.

Gold Lake, one of a number of large and small lakes in and near the Indian Peaks. *Photo courtesy Gold Lake Mountain Resort.*

The small on-site spa offers massages and beauty treatments. The four hot tubs at the edge of the private 35-acre lake are romantic and ethereal (teepees for changing clothes in comfort, a luxury factor that cannot be dismissed). You can skate on the lake, snowshoe around the property or drive up to the nearby Brainard Lake Road. In addition, Alice's Restaurant is one of Greater Boulder's best dining spots, combining a rustically stylish atmosphere with creative cuisine. Karel's Bad Tavern, adjacent to the restaurant, is a congenial spot for an après-snowshoe cocktail or for lighter, less formal fare from the bar menu. **Gold Lake Mountain Resort, 3371 Gold Lake Road, Ward, CO 80481; (800) 450-3544 or (303) 459-3544.**

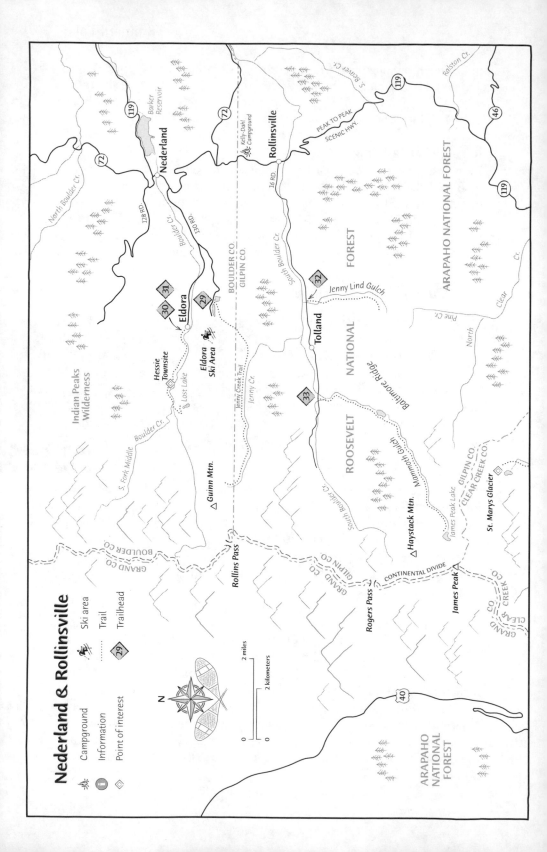

# Nederland & Rollinsville

Campground

Information

◇ Point of interest

Ski area

⋯⋯ Trail

◈ 29 Trailhead

N

2 miles

2 kilometers

0

0

Indian Peaks Wilderness

North Boulder Cr.

119

Barker Reservoir

Nederland

72

119

72

Boulder Cr.

128 RD.

130 RD.

◈ 30 31 ◇ Eldora

◈ 29

Hessie Townsite

Lost Lake

Eldora Ski Area

S. Fork Middle Boulder Cr.

△ Guinn Mtn.

BOULDER CO. GILPIN CO.

Jenny Creek Trail

Jenny Cr.

Kelly-Dahl Campground

Rollinsville

16 RD.

S. Beaver Cr.

Ralston Cr.

46

PEAK TO PEAK SCENIC HWY.

119

ARAPAHO NATIONAL FOREST

Clear Cr.

FOREST

◇ 32

Jenny Lind Gulch

South Boulder Cr.

Tolland

NATIONAL

Baltimore Ridge

◇ 33

ROOSEVELT

Mammoth Gulch

South Boulder Cr.

△ Haystack Mtn.

James Peak Lake

GILPIN CO. CLEAR CREEK CO.

St. Marys Glacier

North Clear Cr.

Pine Cr.

Rollins Pass

GRAND CO. BOULDER CO.

GRAND CO. GILPIN CO.

Rogers Pass

CONTINENTAL DIVIDE

△ James Peak

GRAND CO. CLEAR CREEK CO.

40

ARAPAHO NATIONAL FOREST

# Nederland and Rollinsville

To some people, Nederland is a western suburb of Boulder. To others, it's a laid-back mountain town with mining in its past and recreation in its present. In truth, it's a little of both. Nederland is a short commute from Boulder, yet the center of town, with board sidewalks and false-front, frontier-flavored, Victorian-era stores, could hardly seem less suburban, and the high peaks that form the Continental Divide are visible to the west. No matter where they work or what they do, Nederlanders understandably think of themselves as mountain people, rugged types who love the outdoors.

Boulder Canyon is a rock-rimmed link between Boulder and Nederland, which puts the mountain town within commuting distance of the city, and there's even an RTD public bus connection. Yet Nederland's winters are harsher, colder and snowier than Boulder's. Eldora Mountain Resort, a mid-sized Alpine and Nordic ski area just 3 miles from town, was one of the first in Colorado to welcome snowshoers. And if Nederland is a Boulder suburb, then little Eldora must be considered a Nederland suburb, and Rollinsville, perhaps, an exurb. These small mountain hamlets, rather than Nederland itself, are the gateways to some of the worthiest snowshoeing trails along the Front Range.

For tourist information, contact **Boulder Chamber of Commerce, 2440 Pearl Street, Boulder, CO 80302; (303) 442-1044.**

## Getting There

From Boulder, take Colorado 119 (Boulder Canyon) west for 17 miles to the center of Nederland. Go left (south) at the rotary, and drive out of town on a continuation of Colorado 119 (Peak to Peak Highway). For Eldora, turn right (west) onto Boulder County Road 130. The well-marked Eldora Mountain Resort access road forks to the left after 1.4 miles. The ski area is 4.2 miles farther. To get to any of the other Eldora area trails, continue on the main road through the village of Eldora to the end of the plowed area, just before the old Hessie town site and 3.9 miles from the Peak to Peak Highway turnoff. For the trails west of Rollinsville, continue south on Highway 119 for 4.4 miles from Nederland and turn right at the road to Tolland and East Portal, which is Gilpin County Road 16. Be aware that while this unpaved road is plowed, it has traditionally wind-drifted sections between Tolland and East Portal. From Denver, you can take U.S. 6 west through Clear Creek Canyon, drive through Black Hawk on Colorado 119 and, after 14.2 miles, make a left turn onto the road toward East Portal. For the Eldora trails, stay on Highway 119 until you almost reach Nederland and then turn left on Boulder County Road 130.

---

**Maps**
USGS 7.5 Minute, Nederland, East Portal
Trails Illustrated #102, Indian Peaks, Gold Hill
USFS Roosevelt National Forest
Front Range Ski Trails, George J. Maurer, Inc.
Colorado Mountain Club Ski Trail Map, Brainard Lake

---

# Eldora Trails

The settlement of Eldora is so quaint a mountain hamlet that it makes Nederland appear urban. Small log cabins, a sprinkling of vacation homes, a couple of long-shuttered mercantiles and one intersection that someone decided merits a four-way stop sign characterize Eldora. It is tucked into a tight valley carved by Middle Boulder Creek, from which there are views up toward the Alpine ski runs of Eldora Mountain Resort's Corona Bowl. The ski area also welcomes snowboarders.

## 29. Jenny Creek Trail

| | |
|---|---|
| Starting elevation: | 9,340 feet |
| Highest elevation: | 10,720 feet |
| Elevation difference: | 1,380 feet (plus 250-foot loss which must be regained) |
| Distance: | 4.8 miles (one way) |
| Difficulty: | Challenging |
| Avalanche hazard: | Low |

You can reach this popular trail by RTD bus, which comes up Boulder Canyon, through Nederland and directly to the Eldora ski area several times a day, but you'll probably drive. Park in the first ski area lot you'll reach. Although the trailhead is at the ski area, the trail is on Forest Service land and is free. Dogs are not permitted. Several old roads and pack trails criss-cross each other, but the Jenny Creek Trail is clearly marked at places that might be confusing. In addition to the customary blue-diamond ski trail markers, numerous signs direct you along the correct route. Whether they say "Jenny Creek Access Trail," "Jenny Creek Ski Trail" or Jenny Creek Trail," it's all the same route. The trail alternately heads to the south and west. At times, it is quite close to Eldora's Alpine ski runs. Parts are an old road of considerable width, while other parts are narrower and demand more caution, especially on weekends when it gets crowded with skiers who may be screaming past you on the descents.

From the parking area, ascend up the left side of the Ho-Hum beginner ski slope. At the top, pause for a moment for a fine view of South Arapaho Peak. Pass behind the chairlift for just a few yards, and enter the trees at a blue and white "Forest Access" sign. Climb briefly up a moderately steep hill where you can again glimpse South Arapaho, down into a small gully and then up another fairly long

The trail sign at Jenny Creek. *Photo by Ral Sandberg.*

hill. At the end of the second uphill, the trail comes to a T-intersection with a wide road. The large sign indicates clearly that the Eldora ski area is to the right, and the Eldora Snowshoe Trail and the Jenny Creek Trail are to the left. The Jenny Creek Trail bears west and drops gradually 250 feet toward Jenny Creek, which is on the left (south) at the bottom of the drainage.

After an old sign in a clearing, the trail begins a series of gentle ascents and flats. You will come to two trail junctions in rapid succession. Two branches of the Guinn Mountain Trail spur off to the right (northwest). The Jenny Creek Trail contours around the south side of Guinn Mountain. About 3 miles from the trailhead, it forks to the left at two small trail junctions. Many people elect to turn around somewhere in this vicinity—if not earlier, for the trail steepens considerably, crosses the creek bed and continues for nearly 2 more miles. To continue, stay on the north side of the creek. Following a steep climb, the trail ends in a cirque and Yankee Doodle Lake.

## *Eldora Nordic Center*

This Nordic center, which shares a base with the Alpine ski area, has two designated snowshoeing trails. You can use them for a modest trail fee. Eldora does not permit snowshoers on cross-country ski trails. (The Jenny Lake Creek Trail, discussed above, is free.) One snowshoeing trail, unnamed at this writing, skirts the perimeter of the Alpine ski area, climbing 1,400 vertical feet in 2 miles. It starts at the base area and arcs up to Corona Lookout, the ski area's highest point. This is a challenging trail, so you'll really appreciate the summit lodge for its snack bar as much as for the drop-dead views of the Indian Peaks. A second, gentler snowshoeing route climbs about 800 feet in 3 miles to the Tennessee Mountain Cabin, a hut that can be rented through the ski area for overnights. The Nordic Center also rents snowshoes and puts on the annual

Eldora Snowshoe Festival, normally in late February, which features demo snowshoes, tours, race clinics and more. For more information, contact the **Eldora Nordic Center, P.O. Box 1697, Nederland, CO 80466; (888) 235-3672** or **(303) 440-8700, Ext. 212.**

The Eldora Winter Triathlon, which features winter sports but takes place in spring (early April), comprises a top-to-bottom giant slalom race, a 3.5-kilometer snowshoe race and a 5-kilometer cross-country ski race. (Pacesetter and seven-time Ironman Triathlon champ Ray Browning lives in Nederland.) Categories are male and female aged 19 and under, 20 to 29, 30 to 39, 40 to 49, 50 to 59 and 60-plus. Information is available by phoning the **Nordic Center, (303) 440-8700, Ext. 212,** or writing **Eldora Winter Triathlon, P.O. Box 1697, Nederland, CO 80466.**

## Bigfoot Snowshoe Tours

The irrepressible Dave Felkley is a snowshoeing enthusiast and passionate lover of the winter trails around his adopted hometown of Nederland. He conducts day and moonlight excursions on private land, places that you simply aren't permitted to access on your own. Given the weekend crowds at some of the more popular Front Range routes, this is a real benefit. Specialty programs include nature tours, photography tours, wine-and-cheese tours and picnic tours. Felkley has his own favorite itineraries, which he tweaks to customize for his clients. He is an amiable and knowledgeable guide. Snowshoes and poles are included if needed. Information and reservations through **Bigfoot Snowshoe Tours, P.O. Box 1010, Nederland, CO 80466; (303) 258-3157.**

## 30. Hessie Road

| | |
|---|---|
| Starting elevation: | 8,820 feet |
| Highest elevation: | 9,030 feet |
| Elevation difference: | 210 feet |
| Distance: | 1.3 miles (one way) |
| Difficulty: | Easy |
| Avalanche hazard: | None |

The Hessie town site is the starting point for numerous summer hikes into the southern portion of the Indian Peaks Wilderness. In winter, it can be a destination in itself for new snowshoers. To get there, drive through Nederland toward Eldora, as above, but instead of bearing left to the ski area, take the right fork through the center of Eldora. Continue 3.9 miles from the turnoff from Highway 119 to the end of the plowed section and park.

Snowshoe over a large snowbank that always accumulates here and stay on the wide, unplowed road for about 0.75 mile. At the well-marked junction with the Fourth of July Road, continue straight (west) for another 0.3 mile to the Hessie town site. (This section of the road, just after the junction, drops into a minor dip in this old mining road and can get really icy, but you can easily avoid the worst of it by staying up on the snowy bank.) Hessie was attractively set in a wide open, but sometimes windblown, basin that now serves as the main summer parking area. However, in winter, it feels like an open field that you pass through.

Continue across the open area and go another 0.2 mile through a stand of tall conifers to the footbridge over the North Fork of Middle Boulder Creek. This is the trailhead for a number of summer routes and longer, more challenging winter trails. If you want to keep your walk short and easy, turn around at the bridge and retrace your route back. You can also continue across the bridge and hike a while longer on the flat road, before it starts to climb (see Lost Lake, below).

# 31. Lost Lake

| | |
|---|---|
| Starting elevation: | 8,820 feet |
| Highest elevation: | 9,770 feet |
| Elevation difference: | 950 feet |
| Distance: | 2.8 miles (one way) |
| Difficulty: | Moderate to challenging |
| Avalanche hazard: | None |

The first half of this route is the nearly level road to Hessie (above), and the second half is anything but level as it climbs, sometimes quite steeply, gaining more than 800 feet, with some 100 feet of it during the final one-half. (On their descent, skiers pick up a real head of steam here, so stay on the side as you are going up or coming down.) Follow the Hessie Road, as above, but cross the footbridge. Stay on the road, which soon begins climbing steadily and contours up an aspen-dotted hillside. There is one large switchback and several smaller curves, in addition to views across the valley to Eldora Mountain Resort's Corona Bowl ski trails.

The route to Lost Lake continues on the road, which crosses another footbridge over the creek. You then will tackle one of the road's steeper pitches. Just when you might have run out of steam, the trail levels again. Pass the junction with the Jasper Lake and Devil's Thumb Trails, 1.1 miles from the footbridge. At the next fork, bear left (south) toward the lake, which is tucked into the northern side of Bryan Mountain. The trail makes one big hairpin as you climb through a steep rocky gully toward Lost Lake. Return the way you came.

# Rollinsville

No trails actually start in Rollinsville, but this speck of a settlement along the railroad tracks is the gateway to the web of old roads and tight trails spoking out from the South Boulder Creek Valley. The road dead-ends at East Portal, where Amtrak and other trains still cross beneath the Continental Divide through the Moffat Tunnel. Trailheads to some good winter trails are accessible from the large parking area just beside East Portal and the tracks, but getting there can be a challenge. West of Tolland, ground blizzards often obscure parts of the road, and chronic snow-deposition areas make road conditions unpredictable. A high-clearance four-wheel-drive vehicle is recommended for winter access to the East Portal trails. Other trailheads closer to Rollinsville avoid that last snowy stretch of road.

## Front Range Mountain Guides

This guide service customizes half- or full-day immersion tours, designed for newcomers to snowshoeing who want the basics, ranging from advice on gear to a guided introductory excursion on appropriate terrain. Guide Bill Morris uses Boulder Open Space when there's enough snow, as well as public trails west of the city and also 140 acres of private land in the Rollinsville area. Longer hikes, including overnights that include an introduction to winter camping, are also available. **Front Range Mountain Guides, P.O. Box 17294, Boulder, CO 80308; (303) 666-5523.**

## 32. Jenny Lind Gulch

| | |
|---|---|
| Starting elevation: | 8,800 feet |
| Highest elevation: | 9,800 feet |
| Elevation difference: | 1,000 feet |
| Distance: | 2.2 miles (one way) |
| Difficulty: | Moderate to challenging |
| Avalanche hazard: | Low |

The trailhead for this well-used route is on the left, 3.9 miles west of the turnoff from the highway. The parking pullout area is modest, and on weekends, cars line the road before and after the trailhead. Jenny Lind Gulch was named after the Swedish singing sensation who toured the United States in the mid–nineteenth century, to great acclaim. It is a suitable name for a trail that is so popular with Front Range skiers and snowshoers, it rivals the Brainard Lake area for weekend density and popularity. But while Brainard Lake snowshoers and skiers disperse among several trails, Jenny Lind Gulch is just one route, and a congested one at that. Snowshoers have a real advantage on the long, constant uphill, where skiers often must resort to herringboning or putting on climbing skins. Skiers, however, have the benefit of a long, fast downhill run on the return. This, of course, means that you need to be aware of fast-moving skiers when you are on this trail. If you are looking for a place to combine snowshoeing up-

The Jenny Lind Gulch Trail leads through sparkling aspen groves. *Photo by Ral Sandberg.*

hill with skiing back down, this is an ideal route to do it.

From the gated trailhead, snowshoe south, ignoring the obvious road to the left and a more subtle trail to the right shortly after the trailhead. (Both lead to private land.) After 0.2 mile, the trail crosses Jenny Lind Creek, which will be on your left for the remainder of the hike. This trail is wonderfully sheltered in the trees even on blustery, windy days. It threads through an impressive forest composed primarily of Engelmann spruce and ponderosa pine. There are few views, but a nice sense of being sheltered. After about 1 mile, the trail opens up into a basin, where solid woods are replaced by a mix of open areas and stands of trees, now with occasional views of Colorado Mountain to the southwest. The trail then drops slightly and butts up against a steep hillside. Telemark skiers keep going to reach the open slopes higher on Colorado Mountain, but this is a good spot for snowshoers to turn back for the return by the same route.

## 33. Mammoth Gulch

| | |
|---|---|
| Starting elevation: | 8,920 feet |
| Highest elevation: | 9,640 feet |
| Elevation difference: | 720 feet |
| Distance: | 2.25 miles (one way) |
| Difficulty: | Moderate |
| Avalanche hazard: | Low |

One way to get away from the crowd of Jenny Lind fans is to snowshoe up Mammoth Gulch Road. Drive past the Jenny Lind Gulch trailhead and through Tolland to unplowed Forest Service Road 176, just 0.1 mile after this tiny settlement. Simply pull over at the intersection and begin snowshoeing up the road, which angles off to the left (southwest). This route starts as a rather steep ascent of the end of Baltimore Ridge. The

## Laura's Bakery

The low-slung red building, on your right just before the rotary as you enter Nederland from Boulder Canyon, is a classic stop for a morning jump start or a post-hike treat of bagels, brownies, barges or other wonderful breads and pastries. Snowshoe hiking guide Dave Felkley once had a part-time job baking here when it was called Bob's Mountain Bakery. For a time it was Rene's, and now it's Laura's. The atmosphere is still casual, the baked goods exceptional and the winter hours somewhat random. If the "open" sign is hanging out, stop in for some of the best oven-fresh yummies on the Front Range.

snow is often windpacked or crusty here, which discourages skiers and thins out any crowd that might develop. However, the compensation is fine views back down toward the hamlet of Tolland and the open, blown expanse of the valley called South Boulder Park.

The road hugs the hillside, so after the initial climb, you'll be on a gentler grade as you continue around the ridge, ultimately bearing south and into a broad basin. As it climbs, the road also draws closer to the valley and Mammoth Creek below. Don't be distracted by various road and side-trail junctions, but rather stay on the obvious main route. At 1.6 miles, the Baltimore Road branches off to the left. Turn around here and look north to South Arapaho Peak, 10 miles away yet visible on clear days.

Clear or not, you will be able to look down on Mammoth Gulch, the ghost town of Apex and the snow-covered surfaces first of Teller Lake and then Mammoth Creek Reservoir below on the right (north). Much evidence of mining can be seen in the gulch and on the mountainsides. The Giant's Ladder railroad cut leading to Rollins Pass is clearly visible on the other side of the South Boulder Creek Valley, but the natural splendor of 13,294-foot James Peak at the head of the valley you're hiking is what really draws the eye. This is a good place to turn around.

### If You Want a Longer Hike

If you decide to explore a bit, note that the right fork again splits into two roads, the rightmost of which descends to the reservoir. The left fork is the continuation of the Baltimore Road, which enters the trees and climbs again for a total of nearly 5 miles and some 900 vertical feet from Tolland to the Mammoth Mine. A 3- to-4-mile round-trip usually suffices as a snowshoeing hike here. In addition, the avalanche potential in run-out zones increases as the road skirts the steep hillside.

# Idaho Springs and Georgetown

For the thousands of daily travelers on Interstate 70, Idaho Springs and Georgetown are no more than names on exit signs or, at best, places to stop to fill the tank or grab a quick bite to eat. But these delightful and historic towns are worth visiting. Both of these towns' heydays came during Colorado's first gold rush, even though Colorado's first gold nuggets were not found in either of them. (That honor belongs to what is now Denver, where gold was found in 1858.)

Squaw Mountain, south of Idaho Springs, offers super-scenic snowshoeing in close proximity to metro Denver. *Photo by Ral Sandberg.*

A prospector named Green Russell panned over $20,000 in what came to be called Russell Gulch near the present Idaho Springs in 1859, the same year that a placer mining operation began in the present Georgetown.

Today, these are engaging little communities that hunker in narrow valleys, walled in by the steep mountains. Their locations make them gateways to recreational opportunities all year round. Hikers know this area for its quartet of nearby fourteeners: Mt. Evans southwest of Idaho Springs, Mt. Bierstadt just to the west of Evans but accessible via Georgetown and Guanella Pass, and Grays and Torreys, which are normally climbed together, astride the Continental Divide a few miles southwest of Georgetown off Intestate 70's Bakerville exit. Not only the fourteeners but lesser mountains hereabouts are steep and radical, so pay special attention to the cautions about avalanches in general as well as in specific trail descriptions.

Some excellent nearby snowshoeing routes are also extremely accessible from the Front Range. Because Idaho Springs and Georgetown are also at relatively low elevations, you'll find these trails in the mountains and canyons above rather close to the core of the communities. Convenience to metro Denver has its price, for some of these routes can get crowded, especially on weekends. Topography also gains the upper hand. Many of the summer trails, which might look tempting for winter use, climb steeply into high, open basins with avalanche potential, so special care is needed when venturing out. Trails not so near to Interstate 70 are often safer than the close-in ones. The Forest Service's Clear Creek Ranger Station, just off I-70's Exit 240, is open daily except holidays,

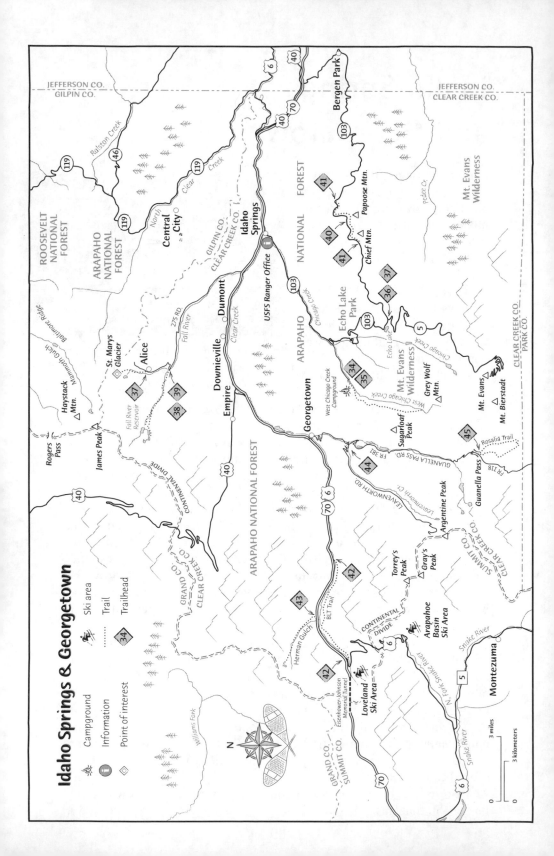

# Idaho Springs & Georgetown

Campground
Information
Point of interest
Ski area
Trail
Trailhead

and given the terrain and potential hazards, it is wise to stop there for route suggestions and current snow condition information.

For tourist information, contact the **Idaho Springs Visitor Information Center, P.O. Box 97, Idaho Springs, CO 80452; (303) 567-4382,** and **Georgetown Promotion Commission, P.O. Box 426, Georgetown, CO 80444; (800) 472-8230.**

### Getting There

From Denver, drive west on Interstate 70. Idaho Springs is 32 miles and Georgetown, 46 miles. Directions to snowshoeing trailheads vary and are included with each of the trail descriptions below, but the Squaw Mountain area, while physically close to Idaho Springs, is reached from Bergen Park.

### Maps

For USGS maps, see individual trail descriptions
Trails Illustrated #104, Idaho Springs and Loveland Pass
USFS Arapaho National Forest
Eagle Eye Maps, Nederland-Georgetown Cross-Country Skier's Map
(formerly Trails Illustrated)

# Idaho Springs

Idaho Springs is a long, skinny town wedged between Interstate 70 and the daunting mountains that separate it from Central City. What you see from the highway is an unassuming stretch of parking lots behind Miner Street, which is the main drag. If you take the time to get off the highway and actually drive along Miner, you will find charming downtown and quaint residential neighborhoods nearby. The east end of town, off I-70's Exit 241, features a strip of budget motels.

## 34. Lake Edith Road

| | |
|---|---|
| Starting elevation: | 9,350 feet |
| Highest elevation: | 9,950 feet |
| Elevation difference: | 600 feet |
| Distance: | 1.3 miles (one way) |
| Difficulty: | Moderate |
| Avalanche hazard: | None |
| Map: | USGS 7.5 Minute, Georgetown |

Get off Interstate 70 at Exit 240 (Idaho Springs and Mt. Evans) and drive south on Colorado 103. At the first switchback, about 6.5 miles from the

Interstate, turn right onto unpaved West Chicago Creek Road for about 2.5 miles. The route begins at the end of the plowed section. Begin snowshoeing roughly 0.8 mile along the road, which has one dramatic hairpin turn on its ascent to a summer campground. When you reach the campground gate, you will see on your right (west) a metal post marked 1881E. The Lake Edith Road is to the right of this post. This road is clear and easy to follow as it climbs steadily along the side of the ridge for 0.4 mile through a lovely aspen forest. It ends at a large clear area and a wooden, Western-style gate marked "Lake Edith," which leads to a private compound. Return the way you came.

## 35. Hell's Hole Trail

| | |
|---|---|
| Starting elevation: | 9,350 feet |
| Highest elevation: | 11,200 feet (at Hell's Hole) |
| Elevation difference: | 1,850 feet |
| Distance: | 4.5 miles (one way) |
| Difficulty: | Challenging |
| Avalanche hazard: | Low |
| Map: | USGS 7.5 Minute, Georgetown |

Drive to the end of the plowed section of West Chicago Creek Road and hike to the campground as described above. Continue 0.25 mile to the trailhead for the Hell's Hole Trail, which is at the southern end of the summer parking area adjacent to the campground. When others have preceded you, on skis or snowshoes, you can follow their tracks as they approach and enter the Mt. Evans Wilderness, but if snow has obscured their tracks, look for the blazes hacked into the bark of trees lining the route. The official blazes consist of one rectangle cut vertically into the bark with a smaller square cut just above it.

You will gain elevation quickly as you ascend through the forest in which conifers and aspens alternate as the dominant trees. The trail first follows fairly close to West Chicago Creek, into which several smaller creeks flow, and then climbs steeply up a ridge, with the creek below to the left, and Little Sugarloaf, a small forested peak, above to the right. About a mile from the Hell's Hole trailhead sign, you will come to a stand of aspens that arc strongly down toward the valley floor, perhaps the result of some powerful snow loading when they were saplings. When winter snows are deep, the trees seem to be growing sideways. Continue the fairly strenuous climb to the top of the ridge, where the grade becomes much gentler. As you follow the route almost due south, you will also get some tantalizing glimpses of the surrounding mountains—Sugarloaf, Gray Wolf and even Mt. Bierstadt— which play hide-and-seek behind the trees. The trail alternately passes open areas and forests, officially ending at about 11,200 feet in the bowl known as Hell's Hole. But for most snowshoers, the distance and significant elevation gain combine into something far more arduous than a comfortable day hike. Turn back whenever you wish and return the way you came.

## 36. Echo Lake

| | |
|---|---|
| Starting elevation: | 10,600 feet |
| Highest elevation: | 10,600 feet |
| Elevation difference: | Negligible |
| Distance: | 0.9 miles (loop) |
| Difficulty: | Easy |
| Avalanche hazard: | None |
| Map: | USGS 7.5 Minute, Mt. Evans |

From Interstate 70's Exit 242 (Idaho Springs and Mt. Evans), take Colorado 103 14 miles south and east to the Echo Lake parking area, near the bottom of the Mt. Evans Road. The parking area is on the south side of the highway, which winds up from Idaho Springs. You can snowshoe around Echo Lake in either direction along the well-used loop trail or explore several side trails and meadowed areas. The topography at the eastern end of the lake is fairly gentle, but the surroundings are wild because the lake is set against this huge mountain that rises from the western end.

### If You Want a Longer Hike
You can also snowshoe partway up the unplowed Mt. Evans Road, officially Colorado Highway 5, whose winter trailhead is southeast of the parking lot. It is North America's highest paved road, climbing nearly to the mountain's 14,264-foot summit. The safest distance, before reaching an avalanche area, is about 2.5 miles (one way) from the winter closure, with an elevation gain of roughly 750 feet.

## 37. St. Mary's Glacier

| | |
|---|---|
| Starting elevation: | 10,390 feet |
| Highest elevation: | 10,770 feet (foot of St. Mary's Glacier) |
| Elevation difference: | 380 feet |
| Distance: | 0.7 mile (one way) |
| Difficulty: | Moderate |
| Avalanche hazard: | Low to moderate |
| Map: | USGS 7.5 Minute, Empire |

Take I-70 to Exit 238, which is 2 miles west of Idaho Springs, turn right. Follow Fall River Road (Clear Creek County Road 275), a steep road winding northwestward for about 9 miles. This Fall River Road is, obviously, not the same Fall River Road that is on the east side of Rocky Mountain National Park. This one parallels the river of the same name that flows into Clear Creek. Bear right, passing the old mining town of Alice and the defunct St. Mary's Glacier ski area. Pull into a parking lot on the right. Cross the road to a chainlink fence and a sign at the trailhead. Ascend northwestward following a short but steep road and bear left at the wooden gate. The road climbs to frozen St. Mary's Lake, which is cupped in a small lake below the glacier. Note the stand of bristlecone pines around the lake. You can continue to the nearby base of the glacier itself, preferably around the right (north) side of the lake and then another short ascent. The glacier, a perpetual snowfield, ranks as a classic summer skiing and snowboarding site. These activities require a hike up (which is another good use for snowshoes).

### If You Want a Longer Hike

If you are game for a steeper winter climb, you can continue as far up the glacier as your energy and skill, but most of all safety, dictate. Only proceed if avalanche reports are favorable, for this is a known avalanche area, and people have been killed on the steep section above the glacier. The top of the glacier is at about 10,960 feet.

## 38. Fall River Reservoir Road

| | |
|---|---|
| Starting elevation: | 9,580 feet |
| Highest elevation: | 10,810 feet |
| Elevation difference: | 1,230 feet |
| Distance: | 3.0 miles (one way) |
| Difficulty: | Moderate to challenging |
| Avalanche hazard: | None |
| Map: | USGS 7.5 Minute, Empire |

Take I-70's Exit 238 as above and follow Fall River Road as if heading for St. Mary's Glacier, but pull into a parking area on the left side of the road but about 6.8 miles from the Interstate, at a sheer switchback. The route (Forest Service Road (1741), an obvious four-wheel road, follows Fall River northwest up the valley toward the Fall River Reservoir. You will find it to be a steady ascent, with just a couple of switchbacks at river crossings, the first early in the hike and the second about half-way to the reservoir. The lower part of the road is flanked by private property, so stay on course. The main road roughly follows the river and passes an old cabin, an old chimney and mining remnants, and about half-way up, it offers fine views of Mt. Bancroft and Perry Peak. It becomes markedly steeper just before the reservoir, so when you start pulling harder, you'll know the end is near. You can snowshoe as far as you like, backtracking on the return.

You won't want to go beyond the reservoir, because an avalanche area hangs north of it. In heavy slide years, this potentially could impact on the last stretch of the road, so it there is any question about danger, turn around then. The gateposts near the junction with the Chinn's Lake Road (see below) serves as a landmark for turning around with a very good safety margin.

## 39. Chinn's Lake Road

| | |
|---|---|
| Starting elevation: | 9,580 feet |
| Highest elevation: | 11,030 feet |
| Elevation difference: | 1,450 feet |
| Distance: | 3.2 miles (one way) |
| Difficulty: | Challenging |
| Avalanche hazard: | Moderate |
| Map: | USGS 7.5 Minute, Empire |

Start your snowshoe hike as above, but 2.2 miles from the winter trailhead, bear left onto the Chinn's Lake Road. The route veers to the west from Fall River Reservoir Road. It climbs steeply, especially the final mile, which gives snowshoers a real uphill advantage over cross-country skiers. If you like both snowshoeing and skiing, however, this is a good route for combining the two. Strap your skis to your pack and snowshoe up, and switch to skis for a fast ride back down, giving the snowshoes a ride. Just don't go all the way to the lake unless you're sure that the snow is reported to be stable. If conditions are right for continuing all the way to the lake, you will find yourself in a lovely basin with views toward Mt. Eva and Mt. Bancroft. A lakeside cabin makes a nice foreground feature for any photographs you might want to take, but do remember that the route does get into avalanche territory near the end.

## 40. Squaw Mountain

| | |
|---|---|
| Starting elevation: | 10,620 feet |
| Highest elevation: | 11,486 feet |
| Elevation difference: | 866 feet |
| Distance: | 1.9 miles (one way) |
| Difficulty: | Moderate |
| Avalanche hazard: | None |
| Map: | USGS 7.5 Minute, Squaw Pass, Idaho Springs |

This is one of the rare dominant summits in Colorado that is easily accessible on snowshoes, both because the trailhead is directly off a well-

The route to the top of Squaw Mountain offers oustanding vistas along the first stretch, soon after the trailhead. *Photo by Rals Sandberg.*

maintained, paved highway and because there is a wide, unplowed four-wheel drive road all the way to the top. It is not technically difficult, but the altitude makes it moderately challenging. Although Squaw Mountain is but 4 miles due south of Idaho Springs, there is no direct north-south road. The most sensible access from Denver and the Front Range is to take I-70 west to Evergreen Parkway. Continue straight through the traffic light at the bottom of the exit ramp and drive 3 miles to Squaw Pass Road (marked with a "To 103" sign) and turn right (west). Take this scenic and winding road 12.8 miles to a small, plowed-out parking area on the left. (As you pass about 11.5 miles from the intersection, note the ghost trails of the long-defunct Squaw Pass Ski Area, visible across a huge basin called Warren Gulch.)

From the parking area, begin snowshoeing up the unplowed Squaw Mountain Lookout Service Road (marked Forest Service Road 1921 on a small metal stake at the trailhead). The road's generous width, steady grade and constant uphill make it easy to establish a constant pace. You will immediately be rewarded for your choice of hikes with a grandiose panorama on your left: James Peak, the Indian Peaks and Longs Peak flare out like a peacock's tail. After about 0.3 mile, the Old Squaw Pass Road (see below), now also a recreational trail, crosses your route at an acute angle. Go straight and continue your steady ascent. The route heads southeast, with a few curves, including a hairpin after about another 0.3 mile, followed by a long straightaway at a somewhat steeper pitch. Now the views are on the right, and they are grand. Chief Mountain and Papoose Mountain, both over 11,000 feet, are just across the Metz Creek Valley, but the huge massif of 14,264-foot Mt. Evans dominates the landscape and can easily fill the frame of a telephoto lens.

The road then makes four quick switchbacks, which skiers must take straight but which you can shortcut by snowshoeing straight up through the woods. At the fifth switchback, you are at Squaw Mountain's 11,486-foot summit, right at timberline. It is the antithesis of a wilderness summit, with a forest of telecommunication towers bristling from the mountain's rounded top. A fire lookout perches on a mound of lichen-encrusted granite. Several auxiliary buildings, including a toilet (mercifully left unlocked in winter), are scattered about the summit. The sensational views, stretching from Longs Peak to Pikes Peak, make the hike worthwhile.

## 41. Old Squaw Pass Road

| | |
|---|---|
| Starting elevation: | 10,050 feet (eastern end) |
| Highest elevation: | 11,040 feet |
| Elevation difference: | 990 feet |
| Distance: | 3.8 miles (one way) |
| Difficulty: | Moderate |
| Avalanche hazard: | None |
| Maps: | USGS 7.5 Minute, Squaw Pass, Idaho Springs |

To reach the trailhead, follow the same route as for Squaw Mountain (see page 95), but stop at the parking area on the left side of the road at about 10 miles. Old Squaw Pass Road lies just south of and roughly parallel to the paved road—incidentally, the highest continuous road that is plowed for year-round use—that you drove up on. It is primarily an east-west route, but several generous curves that contour around Squaw Mountain, Papoose Mountain and Chief Mountain change the orientation for short stretches. In the middle is a north-south section. Whenever there are breaks in the conifers, you can count on excellent views.

Obviously, you can do an out-and-back hike, turning around anywhere you like and retracing your steps to the trailhead, but because the old road shadows the new—or vice versa—you have the option of a car shuttle. There are four additional marked connector trails from other parking pullouts, including the route to Squaw Mountain that crosses the Old Squaw Pass Road. The farthest pullout is 3.8 miles up Colorado 103 from the first one.

# Georgetown

Georgetown, the Clear Creek County seat, is as picture-perfect a Victorian town as you'll ever see. Gorgeous little houses, and some that are not so little, create a wonderful residential area surrounding a lovely downtown with nice shops, restaurants and cafes. Georgetown is also the gateway to Guanella Pass, which separates the Clear Creek/North Platte and Deer Creek/South Platte drainages.

## 42. Bakerville-Loveland Trail

| | |
|---|---|
| Starting elevation: | 9,780 feet (Bakerville) |
| Highest elevation: | 10,640 feet (Loveland Valley) |
| Elevation difference: | 860 feet |
| Distance: | 5 miles (one way) |

| Difficulty: | Easy to moderate |
|---|---|
| Avalanche hazard: | Low |
| Maps: | USGS 7.5 Minute, Loveland Pass, Grays Peak |

This is the Front Range's "stealth trail." The trees were cut and the trail was roughed in late 1996–1997. By the following winter, even without an official fanfare-filled opening (or even a full parking area and signage), it had been discovered by snowshoers and cross-country skiers seeking easy access and a good new trail. It follows Clear Creek, paralleling but satisfactorily remote from Interstate 70, between Bakerville (Exit 221) and the easternmost parking lot of Loveland Valley (Exit 216). A parking area and signs (and also rest rooms) will grace the eastern trailhead, which is located on the southwestern quadrant of the exit. Loveland Valley, with its food service and day lodge, already offers amenities and services aplenty. The trail will eventually be paved for four-season recreational use, but it will not be plowed, so snowshoeing will always be a winter option on this wide route. The trail runs south of Clear Creek, with a few planned year-round bridges and additional winter crossings. You can snowshoe this trail in either direction with a car shuttle or as an out-and-back route, turning around whenever you choose.

## 43. Herman Gulch

| Starting elevation: | 10,300 feet |
|---|---|
| Highest elevation: | 11,400 feet (treeline) |
| Elevation difference: | 1,100 feet (to treeline) |
| Distance: | 2.2 miles (one-way, to treeline) |
| Difficulty: | Challenging |
| Avalanche hazard: | Low to moderate in lower sections, but may be severe above 10,800 feet |
| Maps: | USGS 7.5 Minute, Loveland Pass, Grays Peak |

The trailhead for this popular year-round route is right off Interstate 70's nameless Exit 218, which is 1.9 miles west of Bakerville. Turn right to the large parking area. Its popularity is matched only by its slide potential in the higher, clear areas. Before you take this route, call the **Colorado Avalanche Information Center** (see Appendix E, page 297) to check conditions, and don't even consider anything but the lower, wooded portions of this route if there's a warning for the region.

Begin the hike by ascending an old, unpaved road that angles away from the trailhead, heading northwest on the left fork of a trail junction

(Watrous Gulch is the right fork). The Herman Gulch Trail parallels the creek of the same name. The first 0.40 mile is the toughest part, a short but dauntingly steep climb that can provide the additional challenge of avoiding fast-moving skiers as they descend. But the trail becomes more gentle as it passes through heavily wooded areas interspersed with clearings. After the slope eases, exercise normal precautions around the slide paths. When you approach a beautiful basin, take a look, but don't be tempted. It is time to turn back, because this is real avalanche territory. That beautiful basin will still be around for a summer hike, when you can go all the way up to Herman Lake.

# 44. Waldorf Mine Road

| | |
|---|---|
| Starting elevation: | 9,540 feet |
| Highest elevation: | 11,600 feet (at the Waldorf Mine) |
| Elevation difference: | 2,060 feet (to the Waldorf Mine) |
| Distance: | 1 mile (one way) for a moderate hike to 5.9 miles (one way) for a very difficult one |
| Difficulty: | Moderate for the first mile; moderate to challenging to Sidney Mine; challenging thereafter |
| Avalanche hazard: | Generally low, but some moderately hazardous sections |
| Map: | USGS 7.5 Minute, Grays Peak |

Get off I-70 at Exit 228 and work your way through the center of Georgetown, to the Guanella Pass Road (Clear Creek Country Road 118) for 2.5 miles to a parking pullout to the right, on the apex of the second big switchback. Forest Service Road 248 follows Leavenworth Gulch and is your route basically southwest. A number of old roads are tightly packed into the Gulch, so a good map is especially useful when you snowshoe here, especially after a storm has obliterated previous tracks.

The first mile bears little avalanche risk and makes a nice, short but moderately challenging hike due the first section's steepness. The first stretch climbs parallel the Guanella Pass Road and then bends to the right. The main road passes under a large power line and continues straight at the first intersection, but then begins a series of curves for about 2 miles before it straightens out again. After you cross the creek, the creekbed will be on your left, although as the gully narrows, you might not always spot it under a deep mantle of snow. Whenever you cross an avalanche path, do so one at a time and with great caution. For a quick, casual tour, the 1-mile mark is a good place to retrace your steps and return to the trailhead.

After the initial steep section, the route which intersperses relatively flat sections with occasional climbs. As long as the avalanche danger is low, you can continue as far as you like, returning by the same route, The Sidney Mine, about 3.5 miles from the trailhead, is a popular turn-around spot. The road ends the Waldorf Mine, which is etched onto the north side of Argentine Peak and into Colorado mining history. There is considerably avalanche activity right at the Waldorf Mine, so turn back before it if hazardous conditions have been reported.

## 45. Guanella Pass

| | |
|---|---|
| Starting elevation: | 11,700 feet |
| Highest elevation: | Varies |
| Lowest elevation: | Varies |
| Elevation difference: | Varies |
| Distance: | Varies |
| Difficulty: | Moderate to challenging |
| Avalanche hazard: | Moderate |
| Map: | USGS 7.5 Minute, Mt. Evans |

Because of its elevation and avalanche hazard, this is an area recommended only for spring, when the snowpack has stabilized and the weather is milder. The trailhead for 14,060-foot Mt. Bierstadt is right off the Guanella Pass Road, 10.7 miles south of Georgetown (and 5.3 miles north of Grant), which makes it a super-accessible fourteener. In summer, climbers must muck through a large, high-altitude marsh, known as "the willows" for the thick bushes that thrive there. In winter, the road is plowed and the mountain is just as accessible, but the wetlands are frozen and deep snow covers the willows in the large basin at Bierstadt's base. Navigating the willow maze, which doesn't seem quite so mazelike under a blanket of snow, is a kick on snowshoes, and you can also explore the great open areas on the mountain's lower flanks. (Bierstadt is also a popular winter climb, but the peak ascent itself does not begin quite as close to the parking area as does the trail up Quandary Peak; see the Summit County chapter, page 115.)

Another option is to follow Scott Gomer Creek, which flows through the basin and makes a fine winter excursion. Skiers blitz the 8.2-mile run all the way down into Geneva Park, a descent of more than 2,000 vertical feet, and often do this route as a car shuttle. On snowshoes, you'll probably have more fun just enjoying the upper sections of the creek above the treeline (remember, just when the snow has settled), then return to the parking area.

# 3

# CENTRAL COLORADO

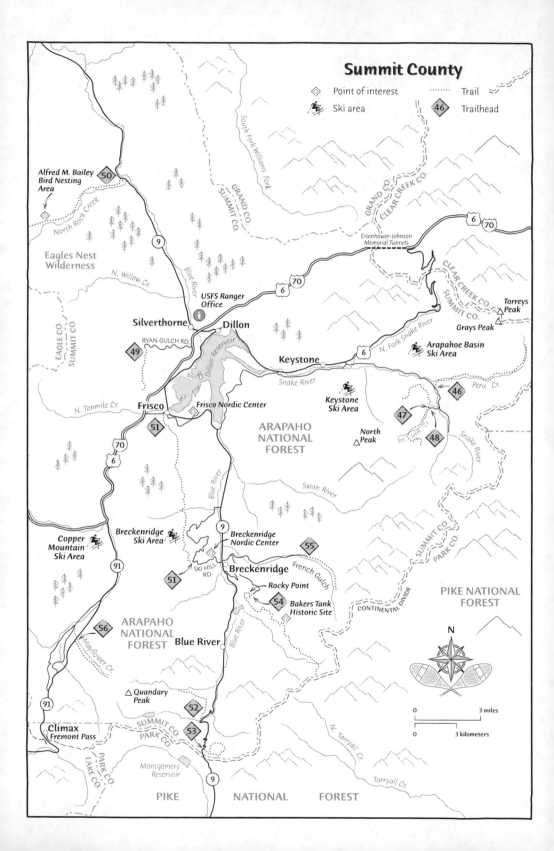

# Summit County

◇ Point of interest          ∴ Trail

⛷ Ski area          ◆ 46 Trailhead

Alfred M. Bailey Bird Nesting Area

◆ 50

North Rock Creek

GRAND CO.
SUMMIT CO.

South Fork Williams Fork

GRAND CO.
CLEAR CREEK CO.

6 70

Eisenhower-Johnson Memorial Tunnels

Eagles Nest Wilderness

9

N. Willow Cr.

Blue River

USFS Ranger Office ⓘ

CLEAR CREEK CO.
SUMMIT CO.

Torreys Peak △

Grays Peak △

Silverthorne          Dillon

RYAN GULCH RD.

EAGLE CO.
SUMMIT CO.

◆ 49

Dillon Reservoir

Keystone

6

N. Fork Snake River

⛷ Arapahoe Basin Ski Area

N. Tenmile Cr.

Frisco

◆ 51

Frisco Nordic Center ◇

Snake River

Keystone Ski Area ⛷

Peru Cr.

◆ 46

70

6

ARAPAHO NATIONAL FOREST

North Peak △

◆ 47

Sts. John Cr.

◆ 48

Snake River

Copper Mountain Ski Area ⛷

Breckenridge Ski Area ⛷

Blue River

9

Breckenridge Nordic Center ◇

◆ 55

Swan River

SUMMIT CO.
PARK CO.

91

◆ 51

SKI HILL RD.

Breckenridge

◇ Rocky Point

French Gulch

PIKE NATIONAL FOREST

ARAPAHO NATIONAL FOREST

◆ 56

Mayflower Cr.

Blue River          Blue River

◆ 54

Bakers Tank Historic Site ◇

CONTINENTAL DIVIDE

N

Quandary Peak △

◆ 52

91

Climax
Fremont Pass

SUMMIT CO.
PARK CO.

◆ 53

Montgomery Reservoir

N. Tarryall Cr.

0          3 miles

0          3 kilometers

PARK CO.
LAKE CO.

9

Tarryall Cr.

PIKE          NATIONAL          FOREST

# Summit County

Summit County is well named. This area of high peaks and deep valleys appeals equally to a growing population of locals who love the lofty lifestyle, to vacationers and to day-trippers, for it combines backcountry access, resort amenities and Front Range accessibility. There are four main towns (the historic county seat of Breckenridge, plus Silverthorne, Frisco and Dillon, which are basically new towns with a few old buildings) and two built-for-skiing, high-density resorts (Keystone and Copper Mountain). The county is undergoing a phenomenal building boom. Yesterday's open meadow is today's construction site and tomorrow's housing development. As you drive along Interstate 70, poised for a wilderness experience, you'll be assaulted by hot-and-cold-running fast-food chains, an outlet center that sprawls on both sides of the Interstate and even a Wal-Mart. It's suburbia in the mountains.

This isn't the first time this rugged region has boomed, as the old mine workings, old town sites and vast network of mining roads testify. What we now think of as wilderness valleys, even when they are not technically in protected wilderness areas, once housed tens of thousands of miners and merchants in some of Colorado's richest gold camps. When mining played out, most of the towns folded and many died. Summit County slumbered and has only reawakened in the last few decades because of the construction of Interstate 70 and the popularity of mountain recreation in both summer and winter.

Growth exploded into a new boom because of Summit County's proximity to Denver. Easy access to protected backcountry for year-round recreation is also responsible for an explosion in the year-round population, because many people really like to reside at the doorstep of the backcountry and there are now plenty of resort jobs to enable them to live there. But despite the quick suburbanization of some parts of the county, it is astonishing that the unvarnished backcountry is still close. A huge amount of Summit County is public land, and it is as wild as anyone could wish.

## Maps
For USGS maps, see individual trail descriptions
Trails Illustrated #108 Vail, Frisco, Dillon;
#109 Breckenridge, Tennessee Pass
USFS Arapaho National Forest, Dillon Ranger District
Eagle Eye Maps, Frisco-Breckenridge Cross-Country Skier's Map (formerly Trails Illustrated)

# Keystone and Montezuma

Located just below Loveland Pass and the Continental Divide is an area rich in mining history, now one of Colorado's premier ski and golf resorts. It is a massive ski resort that is still growing. Hotels, condominiums, private homes and developed recreation from golf courses to a man-made lake have filled up much of the Snake River Valley, and now the growth is mainly up toward Montezuma, a little old mining town trying to maintain its funky and laid-back ambience. For tourist information, contact **Keystone Resort, P.O. Box 38, Keystone, CO 80435; (970) 496-2316; www.snow.com.**

## Getting There

From Denver, take Interstate 70 west to the high country. One choice is to get off at Exit 216 (Loveland Pass) and drive over the 11,992-foot pass via U.S. 6 west. The well-marked Keystone Resort entrance is on your left as you come down from the pass. The other option is to follow I-70 through the Eisenhower Tunnel and get off at Exit 205 (Dillon and Silverthorne). Take U.S. 6 east for 7.7 miles, passing the first Keystone Resort entrance, to the second entrance at River Run. You can get to the well-marked Montezuma Road (Summit County Road 5) by passing the ski resort's parking lots.

## 46. Peru Creek

| | |
|---|---|
| Starting elevation: | 10,000 feet |
| Highest elevation: | 10,900 feet |
| Elevation difference: | 900 feet |
| Distance: | 3.6 miles (one way) |
| Difficulty: | Moderate to challenging |
| Avalanche hazard: | Low to moderate (route crosses some active avalanche paths) |
| Map: | USGS 7.5 Minute, Montezuma |

This is one of the prettiest and most popular winter trails in Summit County, starting in the woods and opening into a huge basin rimmed by gorgeous mountains. Take Montezuma Road 4.9 miles to a plowed parking area on the left. Begin snowshoeing north along Peru Creek Road, which soon curves to the east, contouring around a wooded hillside, and begins a long, steady but not steep ascent, passing several private houses. At 1 mile, you will pass below a slide area (carefully!), bear left and cross Peru Creek. Chihuahua Gulch forks off to the left, but the Peru Creek Trail continues straight back into the valley. A short, steep ascent brings you to some old mine structures, and within the next three-quarters of a mile or so, you will pass the intersections with the Lenawee Trail and then the Warden Road. About 3 miles from the trailhead is a fork in the trail. To continue, bear right and cross the creek into Cinnamon Gulch toward Pennsylvania Mine. The major avalanche area is beyond the mine, so do not under any circumstances go any farther. Turn around here, or any time earlier, and return the way you came.

## 47. Saints John

| | |
|---|---|
| Starting elevation: | 10,300 feet |
| Highest elevation: | 10,760 feet |
| Elevation difference: | 460 feet |
| Distance: | 1.3 miles (one way) |
| Difficulty: | Moderate |
| Avalanche hazard: | Low to Saints John; moderate beyond |
| Maps: | USGS 7.5 Minute, Montezuma, Keystone |

From the Keystone Resort, follow Montezuma Road 5.7 miles to the hamlet of Montezuma. Park on the right, at the intersection trailhead. The trail follows Summit County Road 275, an unplowed four-wheel-drive road that leads to the ghost town of Saints John. Colorado's first silver strike occurred here in 1863, and the town that grew around silver mining was named after St. John the Baptist and St. John the Evangelist (hence the plural of "saint"). It was destroyed in the 1880s by an avalanche that even a two-pack of patron saints could not prevent.

From the trailhead, the road first dips slightly as it crosses the Snake River, which here is a modest stream, and heads west, angling along the hillside with two quick switchbacks. At the fork with the trail to the Hunkidori Mine, bear left (southwest) along the Saints John Creek for the steady ascent to the town site. Return the way you came.

Saints John is an old mining camp that provides an excellent snowshoeing destination close to Keystone. *Photo by Claire Walter.*

### If You Want a Longer Hike

The road continues, following the creek for an additional 2.4 much steeper miles, making a huge hairpin turn to the Wild Irishman Mine, located on the side of Glacier Mountain at nearly 12,000 feet. This is above the timberline and includes passing areas of avalanche activity, so plan your trip according to snow conditions.

## 48. Hunkidori Mine

| | |
|---|---|
| Starting elevation: | 10,300 feet |
| Highest elevation: | 11,000 feet |
| Elevation difference: | 700 feet (plus 160-foot loss) |
| Distance: | 3 miles (one way) |
| Difficulty: | Moderate to challenging |
| Avalanche hazard: | Low until the mine; moderate at the mine |
| Maps: | USGS 7.5 Minute, Montezuma, Keystone |

Follow the same route for Hunkidori as for Saints John, but at the fork 0.25 mile from the trailhead, bear right (north), drop into a small drainage past some old mine structures and begin hiking north on a narrow trail through a tight valley. It contours around Bear Mountain, with small rises and drops on its generally gradual ascent for much of the distance to the mine. This trail is notable for its dense forest growth and exceptional loveliness. After 2 miles, the fun stops and the work starts, as the trail makes a sharp bend to the left and loops southwestward. It switchbacks a couple of times and also gets steeper as it nears the mine, which sits in a bowl carved out of the north side of Bear Mountain. The avalanche hazard is strongest near the top of this route, so turn back sooner if there is any chance of a slide.

## Keystone Resort

The Keystone Cross Country Center has one of Colorado's most comprehensive snowshoeing programs. Nordic director and former Olympian Jana Hlavaty is absolutely passionate about getting people into sports and outdoor activity, and she jumped on snowshoeing as an adjunct to her beloved cross-country skiing. The 12 miles of groomed ski trails are open to snowshoers, who are asked only to stay off the set tracks. In addition, Keystone's trails adjoin more than 35 miles of marked but ungroomed backcountry trails in the Arapaho National Forest. Some of the trails are in the Snake River Valley, while others are in the high country, which can be reached via enclosed gondola. Single-ride tickets are offered.

The Nordic center stocks dozens of pairs of rental snowshoes and also offers several guided tours. Schedules can change, but currently, nature walks are scheduled from 10 A.M. to noon on Mondays, Thursdays, Fridays and Saturdays, and moonlight tours vary according to the moon's schedule. Nature walks are gentle. Naturalist-guides introduce guests to the natural environment as well as the history of the resort. Moonlight tours, held on full-moon nights, include gondola rides to the top of Keystone's North Peak. This mid-level tour leads through rolling forested terrain and ridges above the timberline and ends with a hot drink in the beautiful Outpost lodge, located at 11,444 feet. Other guided tours include Peru Creek, Saints John and Deer Creek. For information about all programs and facilities, call the **Keystone Cross Country Center, (970) 496-4275.**

# Silverthorne

Silverthorne is one of Summit County's bedroom communities, housing locals and resort workers. Its Interstate 70 interchange is one of the state's brassiest, drawing travelers with its hodgepodge of neon signs, strip malls and fast-food outlets, standing out in brazen contrast to the surrounding mountains. It shares the Dillon exit off I-70 and is a gateway to the nearby backcountry.

## 49. Lily Pad Lake

| | |
|---|---|
| Starting elevation: | 9,720 feet |
| Highest elevation: | 9,920 feet |
| Elevation difference: | 200 feet |
| Distance: | 1.6 miles (one way) |
| Difficulty: | Easy |
| Avalanche hazard: | None |
| Map: | USGS 7.5 Minute, Frisco |

This short and easy hike is one of Colorado's easiest access points to a true wilderness trail, in a sense exemplifying Summit County today, as it enables you to pass easily from (the) Wildernest (subdivision) to the (Eagles Nest) Wilderness. Leashed dogs are permitted on this trail, which skirts the southern portion of the Gore Range.

Access is from the same Interstate 70 exit (Exit 205) that you use for Keystone. However, instead of driving south on U.S. 6, you go the other way, briefly heading north on Colorado 9, and then turn left almost immediately on Wildernest Road (a 7-Eleven is on the corner). Drive through the Wildernest development for 3.5 miles, then park in the cul-de-sac at the trailhead.

The trail goes south and slightly southwest. It begins with a minor climb past a water tank and then flattens almost immediately as it winds through a frozen wetland of beaver ponds and small lakes, framed in a forest of aspen and lodgepoles. Return the way you came.

## If You Want a Longer Hike

You can also make a short car shuttle by leaving a second vehicle closer to Frisco. Take Exit 203 (Frisco and Breckenridge) and turn right (if you are coming from the east). Turn right again, then bear left and cross a cattleguard to the plowed parking area near the Meadow Creek Trailhead, which leads into Eagles Nest Wilderness. Continue your hike past Lily Pad Lake, drop down to meet Meadow Creek and follow it to the trailhead and the second vehicle. The one-way distance is 4.5 miles and the elevation loss is about 600 feet from the lake.

# 50. North Rock Creek

| | |
|---|---|
| Starting elevation: | 9,180 feet |
| Highest elevation: | 10,180 feet (Boss Mine) |
| Elevation difference: | 1,000 feet |
| Distance: | 3.5 miles |
| Difficulty: | Moderate |
| Avalanche hazard: | None, except low to moderate in the upper meadow areas |
| Map: | USGS 7.5 Minute, Willow Lakes |

From Interstate 70's Exit 205, take Colorado 9 north for 7.3 miles to unpaved Rock Creek Road (Forest Service Road 1350) on the left, across from the Blue River Campground. The winter trailhead is about 1.3 miles from the highway turnoff. Begin snowshoeing south and then west along the unplowed continuation of the road along North Rock Creek, through a mixed forest of aspen and pine. The road passes some private property and then curves to the right (south) to the Arapaho National Forest boundary and the summer parking area and trailhead, about 1.7 miles from the start of the winter route.

Pass through a gate and continue hiking up the old Boss Mine Road. Roughly 0.3 mile from the summer trailhead, you will pass a junction with the Gore Range Trail and then enter the Alfred Bailey Bird Nesting Sanctuary, a warm-weather mecca for local ornithologists and birders. After crossing a flat area of snow-covered beaver ponds and wetlands for about another 0.6 mile, take the right fork. When you see the mounded tailings from the Boss, Josie and Thunderbolt Mines, you are at the end of this route. Mine equipment and buildings and fine views of Keller Mountain and the Gore Range cap this interesting hike. Return the way you came.

# Breckenridge and Frisco

Breckenridge is one of the most historic and neatest resort towns in Colorado. Well-preserved old buildings and newer infills coexist nicely in this bustling resort community in the Blue River Valley. The lifts of one of Colorado's largest ski areas, also named Breckenridge, stretch along three mountains, but the other mountains offer great locales for winter and summer hiking. For tourist information, contact the **Breckenridge Resort Chamber, P.O. Box 1909, Breckenridge, CO 80424; (800) 221-1091** or **(970) 453-2913.**

## Getting There

From Denver, take Interstate 70 west to Exit 201 (Frisco and Breckenridge). Turn left (south) onto Colorado 9 and drive 9 miles to Breckenridge. (The driving distance from Denver is 85 miles.) For Boreas Pass, continue south of town on Highway 9. From Colorado Springs, take U.S. 24 west into South Park. At Hartsel, bear right (northwest) on Colorado 9, which briefly joins U.S. 285 before turning left (northwest/north) at Fairplay, climbing over Hoosier Pass and dropping 10 miles down into Breckenridge. (The total driving distance from Colorado Springs is 125 miles.)

## 51. Peaks Trail

| | |
|---|---|
| Starting elevation: | 10,020 feet |
| Highest elevation: | 10,240 feet |
| Lowest elevation: | 9,100 feet |
| Elevation difference: | 220 feet, but many ups and downs |
| Distance: | 8.5 miles |
| Difficulty: | Moderate to challenging |
| Avalanche hazard: | Low |
| Map: | USGS 7.5 Minute, Breckenridge |

The Tenmile Range stretches along the west side of the Blue River between Frisco and Breckenridge. The three southernmost mountains—Peak 8, Peak 9 and Peak 10—comprise Breckenridge's lift-served ski area. Peaks 1 through 7 are backcountry, and the Peaks Trail skirts these mountains. The two ends are accessible by free Summit Stage buses, so instead of the traditional car shuttle, you could do the hike as a bus shuttle. Still, on snowshoes, 8.5 miles is a very, very long hike, so you may wish to do just a couple of miles from the south end of the trail and return the way you came.

The trail is marked with blue diamonds and is easy to follow. The best bet is to begin at the base of Peak 8, at the Breckenridge ski area. Drive up Ski Hill Road to Peak 8 past the parking lot and continue about

0.5 mile to a plowed area on the left side of the road to the Peaks Trail trailhead sign. Begin your northbound hike through a deep forest. The route crosses several creeks—Cucumber, South Barton, Middle Barton and North Barton—with steep little drops and climbs. The trail is marked and well used by skiers, so it is quite easy to follow. There are also a number of small clearings purposely cut by the Forest Service for wildlife habitat and also to make room for some smaller, younger trees to grow in the middle of the older, bigger ones. The intersection with Miner's Creek is at roughly the halfway point. The final descent is the steep section down into Frisco, which can get very hard-packed. That causes problems for some skiers, who in turn could cause problems for anyone else on the trail, and even snowshoers who, by this time, are generally bone-tired.

It is also possible to start the hike on the Frisco (north) end, but it involves a big climb right at the beginning, and few people do it that way. However, if you're a glutton for punishment and that's your choice, you'll find the trailhead by driving south on Colorado 9 to the parking area on the right, just before the road crosses Tenmile Creek. Cross the footbridge and walk east on the bike path to its intersection with the Peaks Trail at Second Street. There are two switchbacks on the south-bound climb, after which the trail is rather straightforward.

## Breckenridge Ski Area

At this writing, there were no formalized snowshoeing tours, programs or rentals right at the ski area, but there is a very good chance that there will be by winter 1998–1999.

One of Colorado's great multisport events is the **Imperial Challenge,** which takes place every April. Competitors start in downtown Breckenridge and ride their bikes to the Peak 8 base, carrying all their other sports gear. They then hike on snowshoes to the top of Imperial Bowl, at 12,998 feet, where they switch to skis or a snowboard and race back to the bottom. For details or registration forms, call **(970) 453-5000.**

## Breckenridge and Frisco Nordic Centers

These two cross-country centers are just a few miles apart, but they offer very different atmospheres and a different degree of snowshoeing. Both charge a trail fee and stock rental equipment. Both centers are along the free Summit Stage shuttle route, so no matter where you are in the county's resort belt, you can easily get to either. Many of the backcountry routes around Breckenridge include avalanche areas, so in periods of reported potential danger, or if you are unsure of the tricky outback, it is good to snowshoe in a controlled environment.

Snowshoeing is a major activity at the Frisco Nordic Center, located just off Colorado 9, 2 miles south of Frisco and 7 miles north of Breckenridge. It offers 20 kilometers (12.4 miles) of dedicated snowshoeing trails in addition to the 35 kilometers (about 23 miles) of groomed cross-country trails.

Late in the season, when the snow begins to soften and it is difficult to keep exposed tracks groomed up to serious Nordies' standards, the Frisco center switches some of the cross-country trails over to snowshoeing. The rolling terrain is known for its great views of Lake Dillon. The center also puts on half a dozen special events each year, including races, tours and equipment demos. **Frisco Nordic Center, P.O. Box 532, Frisco, CO 80443; (970) 668-0866.**

The Breckenridge Nordic Ski Center, which is located on the lower section of Peak 8, doesn't at this writing make a big deal of snowshoeing— but this could change. It has just a couple of miles of dedicated snowshoe trails, and its 35 kilometers (about 23 miles) of cross-country trails are always off-limits to snowshoers. **Breckenridge Nordic Ski Center, 1200 Ski Hill Road, Breckenridge, CO 80424; (970) 453-6855.**

Young children take easily to the fun and freedom of snowshoeing. *Photo courtesy Tubbs Snowshoe Company.*

The Frisco center is the site of the most prestigious annual Colorado Governor's Cup, a long-running cross-country ski race that now also has a 5-kilometer snowshoeing component. It takes place in late January or early February. For information or registration materials, contact the **Town of Frisco, P.O. Box 4100, Frisco, CO 80443; (800) 424-1554, www.colorado-fitness.org.** The Swift Skedaddle is an all-snowshoeing event held in early to mid-January at Breckenridge and in early to mid-March at Frisco. It consists of a 3-kilometer recreational run or walk and a 10-kilometer run. The organizer is a local ultrasports athlete named Dannelle Ballengee. Race details and registration are available from **Swift Skedaddle Snowshoe, P.O. Box 1590, Dillon, CO 80435; (970) 262-1603.**

## 52. McCullough Gulch

| | |
|---|---|
| Starting elevation: | 10,830 feet |
| Highest elevation: | 11,360 feet |
| Elevation difference: | 660 feet, plus 80 feet of loss |
| Distance: | 2.8 miles (one way) |
| Difficulty: | Moderate to challenging |
| Avalanche hazard: | Moderate; trail crosses some run-out zones |
| Map: | USGS 7.5 Minute, Breckenridge |

From Breckenridge, drive 5.5 miles south to Blue Lakes Road (Summit County Road 850). Turn right (northwest) and continue for 1 mile to McCullough Gulch Road (County Road 851) on the right. Park at the small plowed section. Begin snowshoeing north up the unplowed road, which climbs up along the high side of the valley. It bends to the left (west) and crosses a log bridge. At about 1.7 miles, your route intersects with another trail at the gulch's summer trailhead. Take the left fork, which actually means going straight, and continue before the final pull up to an old cabin 2.8 miles from the beginning of the hike. Look west for breathtaking views of Quandary Peak on the left and Pacific Peak on the right. Return by the same route.

## 53. Bemrose Ski Circus Road

| | |
|---|---|
| Starting elevation: | 11,560 feet |
| Highest elevation: | 11,600 feet |
| Elevation difference: | 40-foot difference between highest and lowest points (undulating road) |
| Distance: | 1 mile (one way) |
| Difficulty: | Easy |
| Avalanche hazard: | Low |
| Map: | USGS 7.5 Minute, Alma |

The Bemrose Mine, just below Hoosier Pass, lent its name to this network of ski routes in a high valley, which can be connected in mix-and-match fashion. The high-altitude route that skiers use to access the ski circus make for an unusual snowshoeing route, and you may be something of a curiosity in this unique little ski area. There are two parking areas and two trailheads, making a shuttle hike easy if you want to do that. A small parking area is at Summit County Road 670, 9 miles south of Breckenridge, and a larger one tops the Hoosier Pass summit, 2 miles farther to the south.

From the upper parking area on the right side of Colorado 9, cross the highway, climb a small embankment and begin hiking north along a water diversion ditch. This route adjoins private land for about 0.25 mile but is marked with blue diamonds and is easy to follow. Continue for about a mile to the first of several open areas and drainages toward Bemrose Creek. Watch telemarkers drop down, making graceful turns. Return the way you came.

### If You Want a Longer Hike
If you wish, continue another 1.3 miles to Bemrose Center.

# 54. Boreas Pass

| | |
|---|---|
| Starting elevation: | 10,340 feet |
| Highest elevation: | 10,680 feet (at Baker's Tank); 11,481 feet (at the Boreas Pass summit) |
| Elevation difference: | 340 feet (Baker's Tank); 1,141 feet (Boreas Pass summit) |
| Distance: | 3.1 miles (one way) to Baker's Tank; 6.4 miles (one way) to the Boreas Pass summit |
| Difficulty: | Moderate to Baker's Tank; challenging to the Boreas Pass summit |
| Avalanche hazard: | Moderate to high in some areas |
| Maps: | USGS 7.5 Minute, Breckenridge, Boreas Pass |

This route follows on old wagon road turned rail bed. The Denver, South Park and Pacific Railroad, once Breckenridge's lifeline, traveled this route. The grade is gentle, but other than that, it is full of caveats. It is long and therefore challenging. It is popular with skiers, who trudge up for the reward of zipping down. You need to stay out of their way. The final and most important drawback is that it crosses several avalanche run-outs, and because it tops out at a high elevation, this route, or at least its upper reaches, should only be attempted in good weather and low avalanche hazards. Having said all that, it is one of Breckenridge's signature routes. Nibbling at the beginning of the Boreas Pass Trail gives you been-there, done-that rights, making it to Baker's Tank and back is a good, solid itinerary for most recreational snowshoers and doing the whole thing is excellent conditioning for anyone using snowshoeing as a fitness tool.

Follow Colorado 9 south from Breckenridge. Turn left onto the Boreas Pass Road (Summit County Road 10) across from the U-Gas-Um station and drive to the end of the plowed section, about 3.5 miles from the highway. Views of the Blue River Valley and parts of the Tenmile Range greet you practically with your first step, and they just get better and better. The route passes through beautiful forests and exposed road cuts, showing people's determination to conquer nature by creating a pass-able route through challenging terrain.

You will reach Rocky Point about 0.4 mile from the trailhead, where the entire range is on display. Continue another 2.7 miles to Baker's Tank, where steam locomotives, especially designed for the tight curves and steady grades on this line, took on water. This is a good spot to turn around if you are not up for the entire tour. The 11,481-foot summit of Boreas Pass lies on the Continental Divide, another 3.3 miles ahead, which amounts to a formidable elevation gain and distance for most snowshoers. Whichever option you choose, return the way you came.

## 55. Sally Barber Mine

| | |
|---|---|
| Starting elevation: | 10,330 feet |
| Highest elevation: | 10,680 feet |
| Elevation difference: | 330 feet, plus 70 feet of loss |
| Distance: | 1.3 miles (one way) |
| Difficulty: | Easy to Moderate |
| Avalanche hazard: | None |
| Maps: | USGS 7.5 Minute, Boreas Pass, Breckenridge |

A short yet lovely trail, a whimsical name, an interesting and historic destination. What more can you ask of a snowshoeing route? From Frisco, drive 9.3 miles south on Colorado 9 and turn left (east) onto French Gulch Road (Summit County Road 450). From Breckenridge, take Main Street (Colorado 9) north and turn right (east) on Wellington Road, which curves before it intersects with French Gulch Road. Both routes go through many remnants of Breckenridge's mining history, including dredge piles left over from the "mechanical mines" that churned up local creeks in search of gold. The small plowed parking area is 3.9 miles from Highway 9.

Begin snowshoeing up French Gulch Road, and after a few hundred feet, take a sharp right onto County Road 440 toward the mine, respecting private property beside the trail. Cross the creek and follow the road southwest. You will gradually climb along the side of the hill until you reach the mine. The hike ends at the head frame of the Sally Barber Mine, which produced zinc in the late nineteenth and early twentieth centuries.

Jacque Peak is the fantastic backdrop for a Summit County snowshoeing excursion. *Photo by Ben Blankenberg/Copper Mountain Resort.*

# Copper Mountain

Of all the Colorado resorts, none will change so much during the time from when this book is being written to the time it is printed as Copper Mountain. This compact ski resort just off Interstate 70, on the east side of Vail Pass, has announced $400 million of village and facilities improvements over the next decade, beginning with the winter of 1998–1999. What this will mean in terms of snowshoeing terrain or programs at snowshoer-friendly Copper Mountain is still an unknown, but there is no reason to believe that the resort's attitude toward big-footers will change. For tourist information, contact **Copper Mountain, P.O. Box 3001, Copper Mountain, CO 80443; (800) 458-8386** or **(970) 968-2318; www.ski-copper.com.**

## Copper Mountain Resort

Snowshoers are permitted on all Alpine ski trails but must stay on the right both climbing and descending. The Copper Mountain Cross Country Center, located at Union Creek, permits snowshoers on the skating lanes of all 25 kilometers (about 15.5 miles) of groomed cross-country trails, but they are asked to stay off the classical tracks. A Nordic trail pass is necessary for all snowshoers except those using the trails to access backcountry routes. That trail pass is also good for one ride on the K-lift (ask the operator to slow it down or stop it for easy and safe unloading at the top). The cross-country center also offers daily guided tours, currently departing at 10:30 A.M. and 1:00 P.M., that are geared for the energy and interests of participants. Rates include rental snowshoes (available at the Union Creek rental shop) and one lift ride. You can also book guided gourmet snowshoe tours to Janet's Cabin up Guller Creek behind (west of) the ski area. For program details, call the **Cross Country Center, (970) 968-2318, Ext. 6342.**

Copper Mountain's Snowman Triathlon, first held in 1990, features citizen, masters and seniors categories, combining 5 kilometers each of

### A Snowshoeing Quandary for Fourteener Fanatics

If you've climbed some of Colorado's 54 fourteeners—those magical peaks whose summits crest at 14,000 feet or higher above sea level—and you're now into snowshoeing, you probably wonder if you can combine these two passions. The focus of this book is not on this kind of ascent, which is automatically into the Alpine zone of extreme wind and weather and requires a high level of skill, equipment and comfort at elevation. However, with that caveat, 14,265-foot Quandary Peak is a good choice. The trailhead is 8.2 miles from Breckenridge, via Colorado 9 over Hoosier Pass. You walk or snowshoe from the end of the plowed section of Forest Road 850 to the 10,900-foot summer trailhead. Snowshoe through the woods, past remnants of old mining activity, to the beginning of Quandary's East Ridge. Proceed on snowshoes as far as you can, and then continue hiking up the windblown ridge to the summit. The south side of the mountain is more like a cliff, so sheerly does it drop from this ridge. While climbers do not normally rope up here, real caution is required. (The east slopes, by contrast, are gentle enough to provide fine skiing.) Still, for most duffers in the game of winter fourteener ascents, staying on the exposed rock along the ridge top involves no avalanche danger and promises the safest hike.

cross-country skiing, on-snow mountain biking and snowshoeing and elite and team categories, with 10 kilometers in each of these events. There is also a 5-kilometer snowshoe race called the Snowman Stomp, held the same day. The events take place around the first weekend in March. For information or registration forms, call **(800) 458-8386, Ext. 7827** or **(970) 968-2318, Ext. 6342.**

## 56. Mayflower Gulch

| | |
|---|---|
| Starting elevation: | 10,940 feet |
| Highest elevation: | 11,520 feet |
| Elevation difference: | 580 feet |
| Distance: | 2.4 miles (one way) |
| Difficulty: | Moderate to challenging |
| Avalanche hazard: | Low in the lower gulch; moderate above timberline, especially near the sides of the valley |
| Map: | USGS 7.5 Minute, Copper Mountain |

A combination of elevation and steepness makes this a short but difficult snowshoe excursion, but the scenic beauty and physical challenge put it up in the pantheon of Summit County routes. In fact, it is just barely within the county. To get there from Denver, take Interstate 70 west to Copper Mountain (Exit 195) and drive south on Colorado 91 for 6.1 miles. A good-sized, plowed but unmarked parking lot is on your left.

Start snowshoeing up a road that parallels Mayflower Creek and climbs east/southeast toward Tucker Mountain. It passes through private property, so be sure to stay on the road. Staying on the main road, bear right at a fork just a few hundred yards from the trailhead and chug up the route's steep section. A mineshaft on your right signifies the 1-mile point from the start of the hike. It's a hard pull, but you will be rewarded for the climb by your descent into a grandiose basin, about 2 miles from the trailhead. The name Mayflower Amphitheater says it all, for it puts on a great and long-running show starring Mayflower Hill, Fletcher Mountain, Jacque Peak and other compelling mountains.

The basin also holds some remnants of the old Boston Mine and old cabins that you can explore. The gentle valley floor of this broad basin is safe; there is some avalanche hazard below the steeper slopes on the sides. Return by the same route, being especially careful to keep to the side of the trail so as not to be a target for fast-moving skiers on their way down.

# Vail and Beaver Creek

Vail is an island of luxury in the middle of a wild, mountainous sea. What started as a small ski development along Gore Creek in 1962 has grown into the largest ski resort in the United States— and one of the giants in the skiing world. Now promotionally called the Vail Valley, it is a long strip of resorts and nonresort towns stretching along Interstate 70, from the western side of Vail Pass all the way to the county seat at Eagle. Vail spawned a second complete ski resort, luxuri-

Thousands of snowshoers, touring skiers and snowmobilers arrange themselves around the vast expanses of Vail Pass Winter Recreation Area. *Photo courtesy Vail Mountain Resort.*

ous Beaver Creek, and also caused Avon to explode from a small crossroads at the head of the Eagle River Valley. Nowadays, golf rivals skiing as a recreational draw. As it already gobbled up old Avon, Greater Vail is also swallowing up the old railroad town of Minturn, plus ranch land as far west as Wolcott, which is quickly being developed into golf courses and golf communities. Each town has its own personality—these days created by designers, architects and resort conceptualizers—but much of it is very well thought out and well done.

Vail is Colorado's capital of resort-based snowshoeing. It developed the state's biggest and best on-mountain snowshoeing trail systems, with 28 miles of designated snowshoe trails at Vail and Beaver Creek. Guided tours of all sorts abound. These are user-friendly and safe ways of snowshoeing, not trivial in an area where backcountry access is dicey. Snowshoers are permitted on all the ski trails too, but these designated snowshoeing routes are better for most people than random wanderings around a huge ski mountain.

Vail Pass is the leading backcountry area for winter recreationists, but it does get crowded. Other trails on the vast tracts of public land that surround Vail, including the nearby Holy Cross and Eagles Nest Wilderness areas, are often remote, inaccessible in winter or susceptible to avalanches. Many Vail Valley guests who want to go off-campus sign on for guided tours, which may be as much as an hour's drive for more congenial backcountry terrain. Vail and Beaver Creek attract a moneyed crowd, and many of the resorts' guests are discovering snowshoeing and are willing to pay in order to play at it.

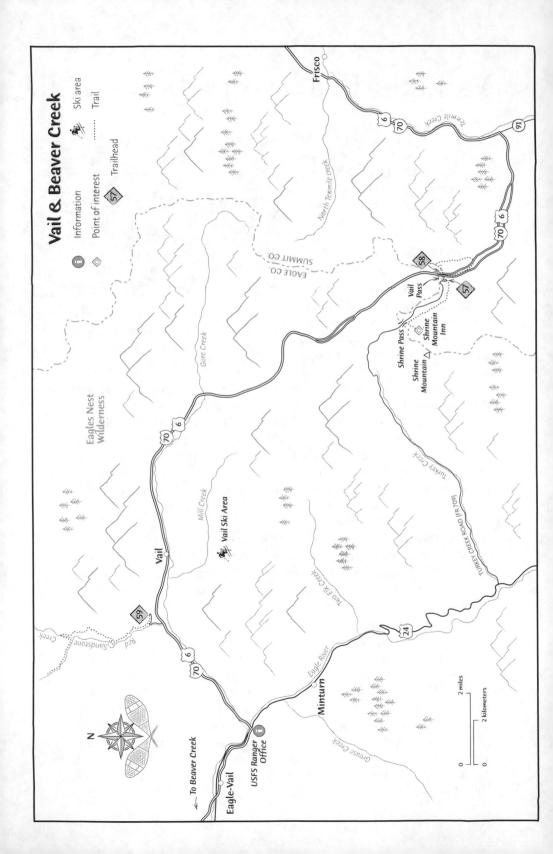

# Vail & Beaver Creek

Information ⓘ

Point of Interest ◇

Trailhead ⬦57

Ski area ⛷

Trail ·······

Eagles Nest Wilderness

Frisco

Tenmile Creek

North Tenmile creek

EAGLE CO
SUMMIT CO

Gore Creek

Vail Pass

Shrine Pass

Shrine Mountain △

◇ Shrine Mountain Inn

⬦58

⬦57

Vail

Mill Creek

⛷ Vail Ski Area

Turkey Creek

TURKEY CREEK ROAD (FR 709)

Two Elk Creek

⬦59

Red Sandstone Creek

Eagle-Vail

← To Beaver Creek

USFS Ranger Office ⓘ

Minturn

Eagle River

Grouse Creek

N

0        2 miles
0        2 kilometers

### Getting There

Vail is 110 miles west of Denver, directly off Interstate 70 (Exits 180, 176 and 173). Minturn is on U.S. 24, 2 miles south of I-70's Exit 171. Avon and Beaver Creek are just off I-70 at Exit 167.

### Maps

For USGS maps, see individual trail descriptions
Trails Illustrated #108, Vail, Frisco, Dillon
USFS White River National Forest
Eagle Eye Maps, Vail-Leadville Cross-Country Skier's Map (formerly Trails Illustrated)

# Vail

The town of Vail is a dream ski village, with the namesake Vail ski area stretching for miles above it. The ski area, which comprises 4,644 skiable acres, takes up so much space that there is no backcountry access and few getaway spots of any kind on the south side of Gore Creek. However, there are myriad snowshoeing opportunities, and the resort has even issued a separate snowshoeing map, the first in Colorado, and others face south and are vulnerable to snow-melt. Many of the summer hiking trails on the north side of the valley are simply too steep and slide-prone to be reasonable snowshoeing routes. The best routes are at the top of Vail Pass, but others are sprinkled around the fringes of the valley as well. For tourist information, contact the **Vail Resort Association, 100 East Meadow Drive, Vail, CO 81657; (970) 476-1000; www.vvtcb@vail.net.**

Looking back toward Copper Mountain from the Shrine Mountain Trail. *Photo by Claire Walter.*

## Vail Pass

The Vail Pass Winter Recreation Area is virtually a drive-in winter sports venue, whose main access is from a huge plowed parking area directly off Interstate 70 atop 10,666-foot Vail Pass. In fact, it has its own interchange, Exit 190, which puts it just 10 miles east of Vail. It is one of Colorado's finest, most accessible, most popular and most crowded areas for all manner of winter activities: 10 marked cross-country ski trails, most of which are suitable for snowshoers too, and 9 long snowmobile trails (a few have stretches of mixed use, but most segregate motorized and nonmotorized recreation), plus three backcountry huts. The cross-country/snowshoe trails are marked with blue diamonds, the snowmobile routes with orange diamonds.

The vast area encompasses a huge chunk of the White River National Forest and a small parcel of the adjacent Arapaho National Forest. Copper Mountain adjoins it on the southeast and Vail on the northwest, and the small town of Red Cliff nestles in a deep valley just west of the recreation area. In order to encourage backcountry enthusiasts to try less busy sites, the Forest Service inaugurated a fee system in 1997–1998 charging $2 per person midweek and $5 on weekends. At this writing, no decision had been made as to whether this would continue to be a fee area.

The Vail Pass altitude is both a curse and a blessing. It is one of the first places to get reliable snow in the late fall, and it often holds snow well into spring. When storms move through, the high elevation and vast, open terrain can translate to poor visibility and howling winds. However, on a blue sky, sun-kissed Colorado day, Vail Pass shines. In addition to snowshoeing the well-marked trails, most of which are far longer than the Shrine Pass Trail, you can pack a map and compass and play around virtually anywhere. You can explore the deep woods, find a secret spot and build a snow cave, glissade down powder slopes or use your snowshoes to get up and your snowboard to ride down. It is purely and simply a fantastic recreational treasure.

## 57. Shrine Pass Trail

| | |
|---|---|
| Starting elevation: | 10,600 feet |
| Highest elevation: | 11,020 feet |
| Elevation difference: | 420 feet |
| Distance: | 2.8 miles (one way) |
| Difficulty: | Moderate |
| Avalanche hazard: | None |
| Map: | USGS 7.5 Minute, Vail Pass |

This is one of the main thoroughfares atop Vail Pass. En route to the Shrine Mountain Inn, one of the most accessible and luxurious backcountry huts in Colorado, it passes through some of the most classic Vail Pass terrain: huge open bowls, gullies, deep forest areas and stands of widely spaced trees. Skiers zip along the Shrine Mountain Road en route to or from the inn or on a major loop in conjunction with other trails. Snowmobiles whiz alongside on the parallel Shrine Pass Road, which continues all the way down to Red Cliff.

An out-and-back hike to the inn is ideal for snowshoers. It's a straightforward, well-marked and well-traveled route that begins with a bit of a climb, with a switchback thrown in, out of the parking area and then contours along the side of Black Lakes Ridge for 2.5 miles. West Tenmile Creek Valley is down on your left (west), but given the expansiveness of the area, it's hard to tell whether the bottom of the valley is a little below you or far away.

Snowshoers en route to Shrine Mountain Inn, one of the most accessible backcountry huts. *Photo by Claire Walter.*

From its high point, the trail descends slightly, levels off and then makes a sharp bend to the right before reaching to the inn, 0.3 mile farther. If you want to plan an overnight at the hut, make reservations through the **10th Mountain Division Hut Association, (970) 925-5775.**

## 58. Corral Creek

| | |
|---|---|
| Starting elevation: | 10,459 feet |
| Highest elevation: | 11,000 feet |
| Lowest elevation: | 10,269 feet |
| Elevation difference: | 731 feet |
| Distance: | 5 miles (loop) |
| Difficulty: | Moderate |
| Avalanche hazard: | Low to moderate |
| Map: | USGS 7.5 Minute, Vail Pass |

From the main parking area for Vail Pass, cross over I-70 on the overpass to the marked trailheads on the other side of the service road. Begin your hike with a climb up an obvious ridge between the highway and the creek. Head northeast around the ridge, which tops out at nearly 11,000 feet, and begin snowshoeing down the other side, following the drainage and heading back toward Copper Mountain for about 1 mile. When the creek meets the Interstate, make a U-turn and begin ascending back toward the parking area on an old road that parallels the modern highway. This is an area favored by telemarkers who want to avoid the Vail Pass use fee. The open slope on the east side of Corral Creek can release in times of avalanche danger, but the old road close to Interstate 70 is a safety zone.

## 59. Red Sandstone Road

| | |
|---|---|
| Starting elevation: | 8,400 feet |
| Highest elevation: | 9,600 feet |
| Elevation difference: | 1,200 feet |
| Distance: | 5.5 miles (one way) |
| Difficulty: | Moderate to challenging |
| Avalanche hazard: | None |
| Map: | USGS 7.5 Minute, Vail West |

From Interstate 70's Exit 176, turn north and proceed on North Frontage Road about 1 mile to Red Sandstone Road (Forest Service Road 700). Turn right and drive about 0.5 mile to the end of the plowed section. Begin snowshoeing up this unplowed road a maximum of 6.5 miles north/northwest to the Lost Lake summer trailhead. The road has a southern exposure and may contain some bare patches, but when the cover is good, it offers as long, elevation-gaining and leg-stretching a snowshoe run or hike as you might wish. Go as far as you care to and return the way you came.

### If You Want a Longer Hike

It is hard to believe that many people—runners excepted—would find 6.5 miles and 1,200 vertical feet insufficient, but hardcore snow-shoers can add a 5-mile loop to Lost Lake and back via a return to a second trailhead that comes back into Forest Service Road 700 higher up and farther to the east.

Blue diamond markers affixed to trees or attached to poles mark ski and snowshoe routes on Vail Pass. *Photo by Claire Walter.*

## Vail Mountain

Snowshoeing is encouraged on designated trails at the Vail Cross Country Center at Golden Peak and Lionshead areas. Both also offer snowshoe rentals and guided nature tours. Snowshoers are welcome on the mountain but are asked to stay on the side of trails that they share with skiers. Golden Peak is best on stormy days, while the views from the top of Lionshead can't be beat on clear days.

If you want to take a snowshoe hike at Golden Peak, you can either do it the hard way, starting at the cross-country center at the 8,217-foot base and walking up Windisch Way and Mill Creek Road for a total of 3.1 miles, or you can buy a single-ride ticket for the Riva Bahn Express lift. You can ride to the top, at 9,740 feet, and snowshoe down, detouring on the 1.1-mile Mill Creek Loop if you like. Or you can get off at the midway unloading point and hike up or down.

If Lionshead appeals to you, buy a single-ride foot passenger ticket (good for a round-trip) on the Eagle Bahn gondola, which speeds passengers up to 10,350 feet. At this writing, the lift is free to nonskiers/non-snowboarders after 2:00 P.M. daily. For many people, the ride to the top station at Adventure Ridge is itself part of the adventure. Located high on a shoulder of Vail Mountain, this high-altitude theme park features many outdoor activities, including ice skating, snow tubing, snow biking and more. It also showcases three excellent and easy snow-shoeing loop trails. Top 'O the Mountain is a two-mile loop that ascends to 10,770 feet, Owl's Roost Trail skims across the mountain in a 0.75-mile loop and Eagle's View Trail is a one-miler. For details, contact the **Vail Activities Desk, P.O. Box 7, Vail, CO 81657; (970) 476-9090; www.snow.com.**

## Competitions and Special Events

Snowshoe races include the Vail Nordic Club Piney Ranch Duathlon, with cross-country skating and snowshoeing legs, held in late February, and the Gotthelf's/TAG Heuer Vail Mountain Uphill early in March. For details, call **(970) 845-0931.**

The annual Atlas Snowshoe Shuffle, benefiting breast cancer prevention, education and treatment, is the Vail Valley's biggest snowshoe event. It takes place early in April. There are a serious 10K race, competitive and noncompetitive 5K events and a 1-mile "family shuffle." For information and registration materials, contact the **Vail Valley Medical Center, 181 East Meadow Drive, Suite 100, Vail, CO 81657; (970) 845-9086** (Monday through Friday, 7:00 A.M. to 5:00 P.M.). Local snowshoe racer Mike Moher has been putting on the Snowshoe Shuffle Fitness Series, a four-week training session to prepare competitors for the event. For details or to sign up, call the **Beaver Creek Cross Country Center, (970) 845-5313.**

# Beaver Creek

If you like luxury and elegance, Beaver Creek is the resort for you. Access to Beaver Creek Village is limited to residents, overnight guests and the general public, who park in the valley near Avon and take the shuttle bus up to the main village and the lifts. The village sits in a high bowl, and the lifts climb higher still. The huge snowshoeing trail system winds around the mountains and through valleys. For tourist information, contact the **Avon/Beaver Creek Resort Association, 260 Beaver Creek Place, Avon, CO 81620; (970) 949-5189.**

## Beaver Creek Cross-Country Center

The Beaver Creek Cross-Country Center is located at the bottom of the Strawberry Park Express, but the trails actually fan out across two summits and three valleys. A dozen trails, ranging from long flat routes to short steep ones, with everything in between, total some 32 kilometers (nearly 20 miles). "Rustic" snowshoeing trails that are marked but not groomed resemble backcountry trails and are congenial for snowshoers, who may also use other Nordic trails but are asked to stay off the track. The trails atop McCoy Park, Colorado's only mountaintop cross-country and snowshoeing trail system, have the best reputation and offer the best views. Skiers and snowshoers reach them from Beaver Creek Village via the Strawberry Park Express chairlift, a modern, detachable chairlift that slows down each chair at the loading and unloading area. But other trails stretch from the golf clubhouse in the lower reaches of Beaver Creek Village to Arrowhead, a resort development several valleys away. Snowshoe rentals and guided tours are available at the cross-country center. For details, call **(970) 845-5313.**

## Snowshoe Tours

The Vail Valley offers more—and more luxurious—snowshoeing tours than anyplace else in Colorado.

### Vail Mountain and Beaver Creek Tours
Schedules, reservations policies, costs and other details can change, but at this writing Vail and Beaver Creek between them were putting on at least one and as many as five different snowshoeing tours every day. Saturday and Sunday are "slow" days, currently with just one tour each. Probably because Thursday is about the time vacationers are looking for a change of pace and a respite from the slopes, that day offers the fullest schedule: five different tours. Eagle's Nest Tours are offered at mid-day. Morning and afternoon nature tours leave from Golden Peak, Vail and Beaver Creek. Gourmet lunch tours are available at Golden Peak, Vail and Beaver Creek. Guided groups access come 40 trailheads throughout the Vail Valley. Many routes are within ski area boundaries, but some go into the surrounding White River National Forest. For details, call **(970) 845-5313.**

### Tours for Hotel Guests
The Vail Valley's resort hotels are unsurpassed in terms of luxury and service. Concierges can book any level of snowshoeing tour guests desire, but several properties put on their own programs exclusively, and we mean exclusively, for their own guests. The **Sonnenalp (800-654-8312 or 970-476-5656)**, boasting a location in the heart of Vail Village, offers charming, authentic Bavarian accommodations, three on-site spas and gourmet snowshoe tours (and other activities) arranged by the resort's knowledgeable activities staff. The **Hyatt Regency Beaver Creek (970-949-1234)** has developed a "nontour tour." The hotel's Snowshoe Package includes rental snowshoes, a ticket to ride the Strawberry Park Express

lift and a picnic lunch. It is the resort's largest hotel and features an excellent spa and the best swimming pool/outdoor hot tub complex in Beaver Creek.

The Lodge at Cordillera (800-548-2721 or 970-926-2200) is a small, exclusive lodge on a high mesa overlooking Edwards, near the western end of the Vail Valley. It serves as the centerpiece for a burgeoning development of luxury homes. The lodge boasts an excellent spa, a renowned restaurant and doorstep snowshoeing. Across the valley, additional snowshoeing routes lace around the links and surrounding forest from the Nordic center, which in summer is the golf clubhouse. Cordillera puts on renowned backcountry programs as well, including excellent gourmet picnic tours.

## Shrine Mountain Adventure

Guide Tom Wines leads outstanding hands-on naturalist tours into the backcountry not far from Vail. Full-day hikes include transportation, all equipment and a trailside picnic lunch. He'll do tours for as few as 2 people but no more than 12 (with two guides), so that everyone has a chance to learn about the forest and mountain winter environment. **Shrine Mountain Adventure, P.O. Box 4, Red Cliff, CO 81649; (800) 261-5364 or (970) 827-5363.**

## Paragon Guides

This is the mother of all guide services in and around the Vail Valley. Their specialty is multiday, hut-to-hut ski tours on the 10th Mountain Division system, but they can do snowshoeing tours of various kinds as well. **Paragon Guides, P.O. Box 130, Vail, CO 81658; (970) 926-5299.**

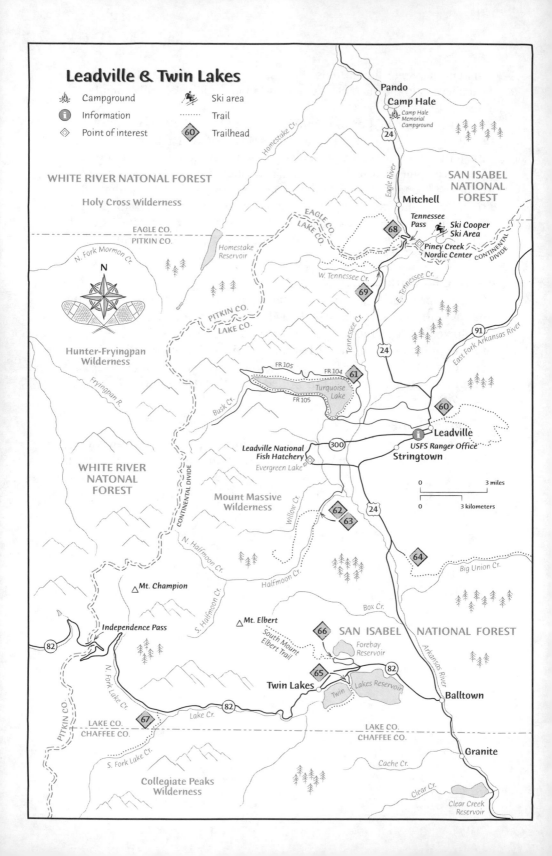

# Leadville & Twin Lakes

- ☼ Campground
- ⓘ Information
- ◇ Point of interest
- 🎿 Ski area
- ⋯ Trail
- 60 Trailhead

**WHITE RIVER NATIONAL FOREST**

Holy Cross Wilderness

Pando
Camp Hale
*Camp Hale Memorial Campground*
24

**SAN ISABEL NATIONAL FOREST**

Mitchell

Tennessee Pass
Ski Cooper Ski Area
Piney Creek Nordic Center
CONTINENTAL DIVIDE

EAGLE CO.
PITKIN CO.

EAGLE CO.
LAKE CO.

Homestake Reservoir

68

W. Tennessee Cr.
E. Tennessee Cr.

69

N

N. Fork Mormon Cr.

PITKIN CO.
LAKE CO.

91

East Fork Arkansas River

24

**Hunter-Fryingpan Wilderness**

Fryingpan R.

Busk Cr.

FR 105
FR 104
FR 105

Turquoise Lake

61

60

Leadville
ⓘ
USFS Ranger Office
Stringtown

Leadville National Fish Hatchery

300

**WHITE RIVER NATIONAL FOREST**

Evergreen Lake

**Mount Massive Wilderness**

Willow Cr.

CONTINENTAL DIVIDE

N. Halfmoon Cr.

S. Halfmoon Cr.

62
63

64

Halfmoon Cr.

Big Union Cr.

0 ————— 3 miles
0 ————— 3 kilometers

△ Mt. Champion

△ Mt. Elbert

Box Cr.

Independence Pass

82

N. Fork Lake Cr.

South Mount Elbert Trail

66

**SAN ISABEL NATIONAL FOREST**

Forebay Reservoir

65

82

Twin Lakes

Twin Lakes Reservoir

Balltown

67

Lake Cr.

PITKIN CO.
CHAFFEE CO.

LAKE CO.
CHAFFEE CO.

LAKE CO.
CHAFFEE CO.

82

S. Fork Lake Cr.

**Collegiate Peaks Wilderness**

Cache Cr.

Granite

Clear Cr.

Clear Creek Reservoir

Arkansas River

# Leadville and Twin Lakes

Leadville is the prototypical Colorado mountain town, a boom-and-bust community that was enriched by silver, gold, molybdenum, manganese and even turquoise hauled out of hundreds of surrounding mines. In 1880, it was Colorado's second-largest city. By the turn of the century, it had sunk into an economic abyss, a slump that continued as mine after mine shut down. The self-proclaimed "Cloud City" still reigns over the Rockies, but she has assumed the role of dowager queen. Her most glamorous years are behind her, but she still is a grand lady. She's got a wrinkle here and a sag there, with an overlay of funky charm. The main street, Harrison Avenue, is lined with historic buildings such as the Tabor Opera House, the Tabor Block, the Delaware Hotel and handsome storefronts. To the east and west are residential neighborhoods, whose whimsical, multihued Victorian buildings are reminiscent of San Francisco's Painted Ladies.

The heart of the city—at 10,152 feet, the highest in the United States—is a National Historic District. Even in winter, you can visit the National Museum of Mining, a treasure trove of memorabilia from a unique era in our past, and several house museums preserve the spirit of the boom days. Leadville has never forgotten its first millionaires, especially Horace Tabor, who went from rags to riches and back to rags. Tabor was a lowly merchant, a highfalutin silver baron, a U.S. senator and, finally, an impoverished postmaster. The stars of Leadville's true-life soap opera—Tabor, his stalwart first wife Augusta, whom he divorced, and his second wife, the winsome Baby Doe, who really did love him for richer and for poorer—still loom large on the local landscape.

And what a landscape it is. The Arkansas River headwaters are just to the north, and the state's loftiest summit stretches to the south. Colorado's two highest peaks, 14,443-foot Mt. Elbert and 14,421-foot Mt. Massive, are visible from many points around town. Hardcore mountaineers climb them year-round, starting these winter ascents on snowshoes as far as timberline and proceeding on boots from there. But even for those who would never dream of such an expedition, the high country is alluring. Winter starts early, sets in firmly and lasts well into spring, making Leadville a reliable snowshoe destination. You can snowshoe from the edge of town into a historic mining area, where dreams became fortunes, on wonderful backcountry routes and on groomed cross-country trails. Nearby Twin Lakes is a small resort that in winter is the end of the road, because Independence Pass to Aspen is unplowed.

Just to the north of Leadville, on the other side of Tennessee Pass, is Camp Hale, where the 10th Mountain Division trained. Camp Hale is a historic site in the midst of a spectacular mountain setting. The 10th,

## Getting There

From Denver, drive west on Interstate 70. Take the exit for Copper Mountain and Leadville (Exit 195) and drive south on Colorado 91 over Fremont Pass. Just north of Leadville, Colorado 91 merges into U.S. 24. From Grand Junction, take Interstate 70 east to the Minturn exit (Exit 171) and drive south for 25 miles over Tennessee Pass. From Colorado Springs, take U.S. 24 west through Buena Vista to Leadville. Leadville is 103 miles from Denver, 178 miles from Grand Junction and 129 miles from Colorado Springs. Twin Lakes is 22 miles southwest of Leadville. Take U.S. 24 south for 15 miles and turn right (west) on Colorado 82 for 7 miles to Twin Lakes Village.

## Maps

For USGS maps, see individual trail descriptions
Trails Illustrated #110, Leadville, Fairplay; #109 Breckenridge, Tennessee Pass
USFS San Isabel National Forest
Eagle Eye Maps, Vail-Leadville Cross-Country Skier's Map (formerly Trails Illustrated)
Leadville/Twin Lakes Cross-Country Skiing/Snowshoe Guide (available free at the Chamber of Commerce, sporting goods stores and other local sites)

America's only mountaineering and ski troop, distinguished itself in World War II. A solemn monument to the division sits atop Tennessee Pass at the entrance to Ski Cooper and the Piney Creek Nordic Center, and the 10th Mountain Hut System was created as a peacetime way to honor the men who learned to love the mountains during the war. For resort information, contact the **Greater Leadville Area Chamber of Commerce, 809 Harrison Avenue, P.O. Box 861, Leadville, CO 80461; (800) 933-3901** or **(719) 486-3901; www.colorado.com/leadville.** You can also get tourist information from **www.vtinet.com/14ernet.**

# Leadville

Not only is Leadville an authentic town with a colorful past, but it ranks as a hotbed of Colorado snowshoeing. Bill Perkins, the Johnny Appleseed of modern snowshoe design, lives in town, and Redfeather snowshoes, the first brand he founded, were long handmade in a small factory there. Tom Sobal, the Michael Jordan of snowshoe racers, and his wife Melissa Lee-Sobal, herself a renowned racer, call Leadville home. The local calendar is full of snowshoe races and events throughout the winter. Leadville and Twin Lakes offer an excellent winter escape. Lodging includes delightful B&Bs, budget motels and country inns, all at rates far lower than at those

Alpine ski resorts, and all offering easy access to snowshoeing trails. So committed is Leadville to snowshoeing that it became Colorado's first community to put out a winter trail map that specifically included snowshoers.

## 60. Mining District Loop

| | |
|---|---|
| Starting elevation: | 10,800 feet |
| Highest elevation: | 11,740 feet |
| Elevation difference: | 940 feet |
| Distance: | 7 miles (loop) |
| Difficulty: | Moderate to challenging |
| Avalanche hazard: | Low, but it is important to stay on the marked route, because shafts and other hazardous remnants of mining activity are just off-trail |
| Maps: | USGS 7.5 Minute, Leadville North, Climax, Mt. Sherman, Leadville South; Mining District Map, available free at the Chamber of Commerce and local businesses |

This route, which is called the Silver City Trail in some publications, is a hike through Leadville's mining history. Drive east on Seventh Street, passing the famous Matchless Mine, which launched the Tabor fortune, to a parking pullout at the end. The route follows old roadways and railroad grades through the fabled mining district. This is not an area of brightly painted houses or cute shops, but rather of the remnants of the working mines that made nineteenth-century Leadville the brightest star in Colorado. Look for the blue markers on the right side of the route; the orange markers indicate historic sites. It is imperative to follow the marked trail because of the old mine shafts and pits and other hazards. Snowmobiles also use this loop, another cause for caution.

From the trail junction, snowshoe southeastward, paralleling Lincoln Gulch. At the trailhead, take the left fork into Evans Gulch and cross South Evans Creek twice, winding through an area once known as Stumptown. At 0.6 to 0.7 mile, be sure to stay left of the mine shafts. This side loop first curves to the right, then to the left, then reconnects to the main route, which soon makes a swooping hairpin turn to the right. Two miles from the trailhead, it crosses Fifth Street and another parking area. From there, the Mining District Loop twists into a figure eight. Make a sharp left, which is a straight continuation of Fifth Street, and contour up the side of Breece Hill.

At the next trail intersection, you can either turn right to shorten the loop by about 1.5 miles and return to Fifth Street or you can continue straight to the route's highest point, 11,960 feet above sea level. If you choose the longest option, the route loops sharply around the head of Oro Gulch, where open pits on both sides require you to stay religiously on the trail. The downhill will take you back through the four-way inter-section, where you turn left to return to the Fifth Street pullout. Go straight to return to the Seventh Street parking area, going straight rather than right to repeat the Stumptown Loop.

## Colorado Mountain College Trails

Elsewhere in the state, "CMC" means Colorado Mountain Club. In high-country communities like Leadville, the initials stand for Colorado Moun-tain College. The Timberline Campus of this junior college perches on a hillside east of U.S. 24, just south of Leadville. One of its major fields of study is Ski Area Operations, and Nordic skiers and snowshoers are the lucky beneficiaries. The college owns 315 acres and leases an additional 400 acres, on which they groom 18 kilometers of unreplicated trail plus additional segments to create 1-, 3- and 5-kilometer loops—totaling roughly 15 miles of trails. Use of these trails is free. Snow-shoers are welcome to use the skating lanes, and in addition, local snowshoers have scouted out and informally maintain snowshoeing trails through the woods.

To reach the trailhead, drive south from town on U.S. 24 and turn left at the Colorado Mountain College sign. Drive up the hill, bear left twice and park near the trailhead, which is on the left. Free maps are available from the recep-tionist in the Administration Build-ing, but you don't really need a map to find your way back, because the entire trail system is a series of loops. The classic track is always set on the right, which creates an automatic orientation point.

Much of the trail system is atop a flat hill, so if you follow the Ex-ercise Loop, obvious because of the *parcours* exercise signs poking out of the snow, you will be on an easy trail. If you drop into Pawnee Gulch, you will have some uphill. If you

### Club Lead Snowshoe Races

The last weekend in January is annual Club Lead 5-K Plus Snowshoe Race, and a month later, the Diamond 5K and 15K races take place. Both start at Club Lead, Leadville's funkiest B&B, and thread through the mining district. The Janu-ary race, which attracts a field includ-ing everyone from recreational walkers to elite runners, can be as short as 5 kilometers (3.1 miles) or as long as 5 miles. Difficulty depends also on how challenging the course is and what the snow conditions are. The Diamond races are fixed in length and attract a more serious field. The course splits after 2.5 kilometers (about 1.5 miles), with the longer distance adding a 5-kilometer out-and-back segment and rejoining the short loop for a total of 15 kilometers. For registration information, contact **Club Lead, 500 East Seventh Street, Leadville, CO 80461; (719) 486-2202.**

## Mineral Belt Trail

What will potentially be Leadville's best and most popular recreational trail will be completed by the winter of 2000–2001. The Mineral Belt Trail is a 10.8-mile loop that circles beside U.S. 24, just below the Colorado Mountain College Timberline Campus, stretches deep into the mining area called California Gulch and returns back out to the highway again, where it will also intersect with downtown streets. Gold strikes made by disappointed prospectors who came to Colorado after the 1849 California gold rush created the foundation for Leadville's fame and inspired the deep valley's name. Old and new roads and railroad grades have been assembled into the Mineral Belt Trail. It is being paved for summer use by in-line skaters, wheelchair users, runners, joggers and walkers, and in winter will be maintained for snowshoers and cross-country skiers. At build-out, it will also incorporate sections of the Mining District Loop Trails.

go to the back end of the trail system, you can climb to Sunset Ridge, at 10,200 feet the highest point on the system. At this writing, none of the trails was labeled, but they may eventually be. The CMC trail system also links up with the developing Mineral Belt Trail (see above), which will put it in the recreational mainstream of central Colorado.

# 61. Turquoise Lake

| | |
|---|---|
| Starting elevation: | 9, 880 feet |
| Highest elevation: | 10,700 feet |
| Elevation difference: | 820 feet between trailhead and highest point, but entire loop has two significant ascents |
| Distance: | 14.3 miles (loop) |
| Difficulty: | Moderate to challenging (depending on distance) |
| Avalanche hazard: | None |
| Maps: | USGS 7.5 Minute, Leadville North, Homestake Reservoir |

To reach the Turquoise Lake winter trailhead, take Sixth West to the end and turn right on McWethy Road. Bear left and continue on Lake County Road 4 until you cross the railroad tracks. After 0.2 mile, the road splits into a three-pronged fork, where you bear right and continue 1.9 miles to the parking pullouts to the left and right side of the road just before

## Snowshoe Racing with Sobal

Tom Sobal, America's premier distance snowshoe racer and a Leadville resident, started two snowshoe competitions back in the winter of 1990–1991. Both have become Colorado classics for serious competitors and energetic recreational snowshoers alike, and this event was tied for second place with Piney Creek (see page 140) in *Rocky Mountain Sports'* 1998 readers' poll in the snowshoeing category. The Off-Track, Off-Beat 10K Snowshoe Race is generally held in the second weekend in December. The free-form route follows a windy and hilly unset, untracked and, as Sobal puts it, "unflat" 6.2-mile course between 9,670 and 9,900 feet. Men and women run separate but equal courses.

The annual 20-mile Turquoise Lake Snowshoe Run is far more serious, requiring excellent snowshoeing skills and endurance for the more than 2,600 feet of climbing to a high point of 11,370 feet. The "semipacked" course follows a large loop over, above and around Turquoise Lake. The route is scenic, but few competitors are there for the views. Racers are required to start with at least 20 ounces of water or other fluid and food. The race has a seven-hour time limit.

For both races, Sobal advises "knowing your ability, being water-wise and carrying extra food, water and clothing. Come totally prepared for the worst possible day and conditions, so that you can survive that and enjoy everything else. Bring warm, dry clothes to change into post-race to enjoy the feast." The feast comprises healthy and substantial dishes that participants may bring in lieu of the modest entry fee. Both events begin at the Sugar Loafin' Campground, west of Leadville. Pick up entry forms at snowshoe dealers, or send your request with a stamped, self-addressed envelope to **Tom Sobal, P.O. Box 251, Leadville, CO 80461.**

the Sugarloaf Dam at the south end of the reservoir. This popular and well-used route is a paved road that in winter is open to motorized and nonmotorized users. It is technically easy, but the sheer length makes it challenging for those who attempt the whole loop. Most recreational snowshoers won't do that, though runners who compete in local snowshoe races here think nothing of so long a jaunt over the snow. The lake is also known for its fine ice fishing, which gives snowshoers something to look at as they make their way around the shore, if they can wrench their eyes away from the panoramic Sawatch Range.

You can start out in either direction, go as far as you like and retrace your steps on the way back. To snowshoe clockwise, head north from the west end of the dam. The route begins to climb as it follows the southern shore of the lake, which has a somewhat elongated kidney shape. The route eventually leaves the lakeshore, climbing about 200 feet to its highest point on the south side of the lake, which is at the junction with the Hagerman Pass Road. Stay right at the junction, and drop down to the inlet, which you reach just after crossing Busk Creek. At this point, you are somewhat less than halfway around the lake. If you make it this far, you can decide whether to retrace your steps or to continue and complete the circuit.

If you continue clockwise, you will end up climbing to an elevation of 10,700 feet (even higher than the Hagerman Pass Road junction) after about another 2.5 miles. The trail is farther from the lake along the north shore than it is along the south shore. A highlight of this section is the Mosquito Overlook, which is popular as a summer picnic spot and offers a grand panorama in winter. Follow the trail along the ridge as it descends to the east, and then turns south passing boat ramps, campgrounds and picnic areas, on its route to the dam and the starting point.

# 62. Halfmoon Road

| | |
|---|---|
| Starting elevation: | 9,570 feet |
| Highest elevation: | 9,930 feet (Halfmoon Campground) |
| Elevation difference: | 360 feet |
| Distance: | 3.1 miles (one way) |
| Difficulty: | Moderate |
| Avalanche hazard: | None |
| Map: | USGS 7.5 Minute, Mt. Massive |

This route is special because it is in such a rarefied neighborhood. It heads toward Mt. Elbert and runs south of Mt. Massive, Colorado's two highest mountains. On clear days, the scenery is unsurpassed. To reach the trailhead, take U.S. 24 south of Leadville. Turn right (west) onto Colorado 300, then left (south) after 0.8 mile onto Lake County Road 160. Turn right after 1.2 miles onto County Road 110 at the sign pointing to the Halfmoon Campground. The road is plowed for almost another mile to the mouth of the Halfmoon Creek Valley, and the unplowed section is used for winter recreation, including snowmobiles. Parking can be tight on weekends, when vehicles—many with snowmobile trailers—vie for limited space at the trailhead of this well-used and popular route.

Halfmoon Road heads southwest for the entire distance, much of it through a broad valley floor. Only as you approach the campground, which is the destination of this hike, do you get close to a part of Mt. Massive, on the right. This wide road through a broad valley is technically easy. However, a round-trip of more than 6 miles, if you go all the way to the campground, as well as some early tricky spots, bump it up into the "moderate" category. If there are icy stretches or high winds, you are most likely to encounter them at the beginning of the route.

There are several spur routes and side trails, but the most distinctive fork comes at 0.5 mile from the start of the route, where you bear left to stay on the main road. Halfmoon Creek is on your left for the next 0.5 mile, during which you will pass several service buildings and cross a bridge as you continue toward Mt. Elbert. When the road enters the San Isabel National Forest, you will begin to see both orange and blue diamonds marking the trail for motorized and nonmotorized use. The campground is the main snowshoe destination of this fine route, although you can turn around at any point and retrace your steps back to the parking area.

# 63. Willow Creek Trail

| | |
|---|---|
| Starting elevation: | 9,570 feet |
| Highest elevation: | 10,580 feet |
| Elevation difference: | 1,010 feet |
| Distance: | 3.5 miles (one way) |
| Difficulty: | Moderate to challenging |
| Avalanche hazard: | None |
| Map: | USGS 7.5 Minute, Mt. Massive |

Access to this route is the same as for Halfmoon Road (see page 133). It is slightly longer and has more than twice the elevation gain of its neighbor. Because it enters the Mt. Massive Wilderness, snowmobiles are prohibited. Begin snowshoeing at the snow barrier, and at the fork after 0.5 mile, bear right (west). The initial mile, first along the often-windy portion of Halfmoon Road and then the lower part of the Willow Creek Trail, is very gentle.

After you pass an old ranch just short of a mile from the trailhead, the route begins to steepen and subtly curves south. It leads up along Willow Creek on Mt. Massive's southeast side and is easy to follow. The only questionable spot comes at about 1.5 miles, where you should continue snowshoeing up along the south side of the valley to remain on this trail rather than crossing the creek. The trail becomes more steep for the next mile, passing into the wilderness 2.25 miles from the trailhead. The junction with the Colorado Trail at 3.5 miles makes a suitable turnaround, but you may want to turn back sooner because the final 0.5 mile is the steepest.

## Sawatch Naturalists & Guides

Craig Schreiber is a landscape architect who used to be a full-time hiking and snowshoeing guide. He still guides on the side, especially in the winter, which is off-season for the landscape business. His knowledge of the Rocky Mountain environment is epic. **Sawatch Naturalists & Guides, 142 West Seventh Street, Leadville, CO 80461; (719) 486-1856.**

## Leadville National Fish Hatchery

Snowshoeing? At a fish hatchery? It seems improbable, but actually, it's quite wonderful. The historic Leadville National Fish Hatchery, operated by the U.S. Fish and Wildlife Service, was established in 1889. Fifteen trout tanks are housed in a complex of picturesque buildings located on vast, wooded acreage laced with summer work roads and trails, many within sight of mighty Mt. Massive. To reach the hatchery, drive south out of Leadville on U.S. 24. After 2 miles, turn right (west) onto Colorado 300 for about 2 miles more, to the well-marked parking area. The trailhead is to the left (south) of the main building, and trails fan out behind it. A pamphlet with a trail map can also be obtained at the hatchery. The network is complicated, so it's a good idea to consult the map frequently and also keep a sharp eye out for the blue markers that designate trails, except where the Kearney Park Loop enters the Mt. Massive Wilderness. In addition to ease of access and varied terrain, this system is even more appealing because it is entirely avalanche-free.

A mile-long beginner loop circles around some of the five little bodies of water called Evergreen Lakes, which are just steps from the hatchery buildings. Easy, flat and pretty, it is ideal for new snowshoers and small children. You can get in a little up and down on the Diversion Dam Loop, which measures 1.8 miles with 280 feet of elevation change. The climb and descent are concentrated in two short pitches, so it is more demanding than its modest numbers would indicate.

Two longer loops, which can be combined into one extralong one, follow summer hiking trails stretching westward from the trailhead. They can be hiked in either direction. The Highline Trail Loop is a 6-miler with 1,360 of elevation change, and the Kearney Park Trail is 5 miles with 1,050 feet of elevation change. Both of these loops involve using the Rock Creek Trail, paralleling a stream of the same name, either on the outbound or return leg, and a stretch of the Colorado Trail "across the top." Both include some steep sections. The hatchery is located at 9,650 feet.

### Leadville Plain, Leadville Fancy

To immerse yourself in a no-nonsense sporty atmosphere, book a bargain bunk at Club Lead. Operated by snowshoe race organizer Jay Jones, this is a B&B place where frills are nonexistent but the atmosphere is welcoming, rates are rockbottom and access to the Mining District Loop couldn't be easier. **Club Lead, 500 East Seventh Street, Leadville, CO 80461; (719) 486-2202.**

To plunge into luxury, try the Leadville Country Inn, arguably the finest of the town's selection of atmospheric B&Bs. This turreted landmark, on a quaint residential street just a few doors from Harrison Avenue, is an antique-filled inn known for the Clemmer family's fine hospitality, gorge-yourself gourmet breakfasts and an exceptionally romantic atmosphere. The nine rooms are located in the main house and the carriage house behind. One room has a copper soaking tub, another a whirlpool tub for two—and all have exceptional charm. An outdoor hot tub on the patio is just the ticket for soothing snowshoe-sore muscles. **Leadville Country Inn, 127 Easy Eighth Street, Leadville, CO 80461; (800) 748-2354 or (719) 486-2354.**

## 64. Weston Pass Road

| | |
|---|---|
| Starting elevation: | 9,670 feet |
| Highest elevation: | 10,980 feet |
| Elevation difference: | 1,310 feet |
| Distance: | 3.8 miles (one way) |
| Difficulty: | Moderate to challenging |
| Avalanche hazard: | Low to moderate |
| Map: | USGS 7.5 Minute, Leadville South |

To reach this four-wheel-drive road, which crests over Weston Pass and joins Colorado 9 south of Breckenridge, drive south of Leadville on U.S. 24 for 7.4 miles. Bear left at the Weston Pass road sign and continue to the end of the plowed section. Usually, plowing ends at the entrance to a nice valley. The western portion makes for a good out-and-back snowshoeing tour.

# Twin Lakes

Colorado Highway 82 links Leadville and the Arkansas River Valley with Aspen and the Roaring Fork Valley via Independence Pass, but in winter, snows close this narrow, winding, two-lane road hacked into the mountainside. The highway's eastern end becomes a quiet retreat for backcountry enthusiasts, who enjoy excellent snow, fantastic views of Colorado's highest string of fourteeners and very few people.

## 65. Interlaken Trail

| | |
|---|---|
| Starting elevation: | 9,210 feet |
| Highest elevation: | 9,270 feet |
| Elevation difference: | 60 feet |
| Distance: | 3 miles (one way) |
| Difficulty: | Easy |
| Avalanche hazard: | None |
| Map: | USGS 7.5 Minute, Granite |

Like its Swiss namesake, Interlaken is the name of an old resort, built in the 1870s for Leadville's carriage trade and now long abandoned. It was beautifully situated between two lakes—in this case the two sections of Twin Lakes Reservoir. To reach the trailhead, take Colorado 82 about 3 miles to the western end of the eastern lake. From the parking area, cross the bridge and follow the dam. At the intersection with the Colorado Trail, bear right (west) and follow it to the resort, which today consists of a few boarded-up cabins and outbuildings. Explore this site, imagining what it was like more than 120 years ago, and return the way you came.

## 66. South Elbert Trail

| | |
|---|---|
| Starting elevation: | 9,620 feet |
| Highest elevation: | 10,500 feet |
| Elevation difference: | 880 feet |
| Distance: | 1.8 miles (one way) |
| Difficulty: | Moderate |
| Avalanche hazard: | None |
| Maps: | USGS 7.5 Minute, Granite, Independence Pass |

To reach this trail, drive 4.2 miles west on Colorado 82 from U.S. 14 and then take Lake County Road 24, which angles off to the right. Wind up the south-facing hill for 1.3 miles to the parking area on the left. Walk across a small bridge on the main road to the South Elbert Trail, a four-wheel-drive route marked as Forest Service Road 125, which is on the left.

The trail, which heads essentially west, is especially interesting for its vegetation. As you ascend from the trailhead, you will pass through a semiarid meadow spiked with sagebrush. Soon, aspen mingles with sage, creating an attractive combination. The aspen forest stretches for a mile, intercepted by just one band of coniferous trees and a few strays here and there. If you see large animal tracks in the snow, it's most likely evidence of a hundred-head herd of elk whose main range is around the flanks of Mt. Elbert and Mt. Massive. The trail

Vegetation along the South Elbert Trail includes conifer and aspen groves, sage and other bushes. *Photo by Claire Walter.*

steepens and then flattens, and through openings in the trees are great views of Hope Mountain, Quail Mountain and the aptly named Twin Peaks.

The trail becomes steeper again, contouring around a hillside to a small rise that overlooks a willow-filled valley called Bartlett Gulch, which is moist in summer, evidence of beaver activity in the area. The steep and dramatic chutes and gullies of Elbert's eastern face are on your left. The trail dips slightly through the gulch, then climbs steeply through an evergreen forest. At 1.6 miles, it crosses Corske Creek, a good place to turn around. Corske Creek is in another valley, pocked with the Lily Ponds, which you can explore before you return, retracing your route.

## Mt. Elbert Lodge Snowshoe Clinics

Beginning in late 1998, snowshoeing guru Tom Sobal inaugurated two-day snowshoeing clinics based in this congenial lodge in tiny Twin Lakes. Initially, they are concentrated just before Christmas and shortly after New Year's. The clinic format could change in subsequent winters, but as of this writing, they begin with a program of an informational slide presentation and demonstration on snowshoeing equipment, clothing, technique, good snowshoeing places in the region and winter safety. This indoor session is followed by on-snow instruction. One level of clinic is aimed at beginners to intermediates and one at advanced snowshoers who want to refine their technique. Melissa Lee-Sobal assists with the clinics and also offers optional massages. The clinic includes two nights' accommodations in the quaint lodge or nearby cabins, as well as all meals. The remote and tranquil setting makes for a winter idyll. Mt. Elbert Lodge, P.O. Box 40, Twin Lakes, CO 81251; (800) 381-4433 or (719) 486-0594; http://colorado-bnb.com/mtelbert.

## 67. South Fork Lake Creek Road

| | |
|---|---|
| Starting elevation: | 10,130 feet |
| Highest elevation: | 10,540 feet |
| Elevation difference: | 410 feet, but numerous rises and drops adding about 250 feet |
| Distance: | 2.6 miles (one way to Sayres Gulch Road) |
| Difficulty: | Moderate |
| Avalanche hazard: | Low (to Sayres Gulch Road); high thereafter |
| Map: | USGS 7.5 Minute, Independence Pass |

The parking area is a short distance beyond the beginning part of South Fork Lake Creek Road, a summer four-wheel-drive road. Although it is also used by snowmobilers, it does not tend to get overrun and makes a fine snowshoe tour. Remember too that the snowmobile tracks do minimize the effort of breaking trail, which is not inconsequential given the cumulative feet climbed. While the elevation difference between the start of the road and its junction with Sayres Gulch Road, the recommended turnaround point, is just 410 feet, many small ups and downs produce roughly an extra 250 feet lost and regained each way if you go the entire distance.

The unplowed road is on the south side of Colorado 82, 14.5 miles from the turnoff from U.S. 24. You will snowshoe over a bridge over Lake Creek almost immediately and then follow South Fork, one of its tributaries, up a long valley. At the La Plata summer trailhead, on the left (south) after 0.3 mile, continue straight on the main road, bearing slightly to the right (southwest). After 1.5 miles, the route crosses into the San Isabel National Forest boundary, winding gently between 12,000-foot-plus mountains before opening into a generous basin below Grizzly Mountain. The junction with the Sayres Gulch Road, which branches off to the left (south), makes a good turnaround point for a safe snowshoe tour.

### If You Want a Longer Hike
The road does continue straight more than 2 miles more, first passing a four-wheel-drive trail into McNasser Gulch, to a larger fork, whose left branch continues along South Fork Lake Creek and whose branch goes into Peekaboo Gulch, but this back section is not recommended because of the potential for avalanches.

# Tennessee Pass

The Leadville regional map is dotted with place names that include states older than Colorado: California Gulch, Iowa Gulch, Missouri Creek, Missouri Mountain and Tennessee Pass, thought to have been named by prospectors from the Volunteer State. At 10,424 feet, it is not one of Colorado's highest passes, nor is it the most dramatic, but it is significant. The pass, which is 10 miles northwest of Leadville on U.S. 24, is part of the Continental Divide. It separates the Eagle River, which is part of the Colorado River system, and the Arkansas River, which eventually flows into the Mississippi. The Denver and Rio Grande Railway once traversed the pass, and its rail bed today is one of many snowshoe-friendly trails in the network that crown it. Half a dozen interlinked trails on the west side of Tennessee Pass can be combined into routes of various lengths, so that every fitness level, snowshoeing speed and energy level can be accommodated.

## 68. Mitchell Creek Loop

| | |
|---|---|
| Starting elevation: | 10,420 feet |
| Lowest elevation: | 10,040 feet |
| Highest elevation: | 10,600 feet |
| Elevation difference: | 560 feet |
| Distance: | 7.25 miles (loop) |
| Difficulty: | Easy to moderate |
| Avalanche hazard: | None |
| Maps: | USGS 7.5 Minute, Pando, Leadville North |

Beginners, or anyone who isn't comfortable climbing at these altitudes, can snowshoe out and back for about a mile on the right (northern) section of the trail or as far as 2.5 miles on the left (southern) section, which are both fairly flat. Stronger snowshoers can do the whole loop, which passes many artifacts from the past. The trailhead is at a large, well-maintained and well-marked parking lot directly off the road on the west side of Tennessee Pass.

To hike this loop counterclockwise, bear right (northwest) at the trailhead and descend gently on the Colorado Trail along an old railroad grade past some old charcoal kilns. The downhill steepens slightly as the trail descends into the valley. Keep to the left at the point where the Colorado Trail branches off to the right, and continue on the old railroad grade until it reaches its lowest point, 10,040 feet, at about the 2-mile mark. At the hairpin turn in the old railroad grade, follow the stream up the valley as the trail steepens and enters the trees. After about 2.75 miles, you'll reach the high point, which is a shade above the trailhead elevation, as you cross Wurt's Ditch and the Wurt's Ditch Road at about

4.6 miles. Stay to the left (south) at this intersection and cross through the saddle. Soon, the trail intersects the Colorado Trail. You need to bear left (east) on the Colorado Trail. After two creek crossings, you begin a gentle 2.25-mile ascent back to the trailhead.

## 69. Lily Lake Loop

| | |
|---|---|
| Starting elevation: | 10,310 feet |
| Highest elevation: | 10,620 feet |
| Elevation difference: | 385 feet of gain; 75 feet of loss |
| Distance: | 4 miles (loop) |
| Difficulty: | Moderate |
| Avalanche hazard: | None |
| Map: | USGS 7.5 Minute, Leadville North |

This trail suffered from the blowdown that afflicted the Mt. Zirkel Wilderness in 1997 (see Steamboat Springs chapter, page 219), and at this writing, the trail is still closed. However, it is such a nice route, with interesting twists and turns and offers such a fine combination of distance and moderate pitches, that it will again be worthwhile if and when it opens. Check with the U.S. Forest Service Ranger Office in Leadville.

To reach the trailhead, follow U.S. 24 north about 7 miles to the first left after the road to Sylvan Lakes Estates. If you do not have a four-wheel-drive vehicle, park in the plowed lot and add 1.3 miles each way and an additional 170 feet of elevation change to your route. Otherwise, drive up the four-wheel-drive road to the West Tennessee Pass sign.

To do this loop clockwise, bear right (west) at the trailhead onto a gently climbing section of Forest Service Road 181. Pass an old cabin and go straight, through the intersection with the Colorado Trail. At 1 mile, you will pass a culvert and soon thereafter, a Forest Service gate. This is the high point of the route. Stay left (west) while going around the lake. The trail curves to the left (south) along the lake and then begins its mild descent, turning left (east) again to parallel West Tennessee Creek and then north along an old road back to the trailhead. It can also be snowshoed in a counterclockwise direction.

## *Piney Creek Nordic Center*

This high-altitude cross-country facility shares a base area with Ski Cooper on the east side of Tennessee Pass, making it convenient for families and groups that have some members who ride the lifts to pursue their sports and some who prefer not to. The trail system backs up against the north side of the mountain on which Ski Cooper is located. Its 15.5 miles of trails are groomed and trackset, and snowshoers may use the skating lanes for a trail fee. In addition to the interlinked trails, varying from pancake flat to challenging hills, the 5.1-mile Cooper Loop starts at the Alpine ski area base, circles it on a Forest Service trail and returns via the Nordic center's groomed trails. This challenging route offers energetic snowshoers and cross-country skiers some 800 feet of elevation change, a good chunk of it between mile 3 and mile 4. Snowshoes are available at the Nordic center's shop. **Piney Creek Nordic Center, 1520 Mt. Elbert Drive, Leadville, CO 80461; (719) 486-1750.**

## Hut Access

Four of the 10th Mountain Division Hut System's 12 huts are around Leadville. Though developed for and still primarily frequented by backcountry skiers, some of them are good destinations for strong snowshoers who are familiar with the backcountry and able to hike several miles carrying heavy packs. Of the huts near Leadville, one stands out as being the most comfortable snowshoeing distance. Vance's Cabin is 3.1 miles from and 555 vertical feet above the trailhead at the base of Ski Cooper, plus an additional 200 feet of elevation loss and gain. Uncle Bud's Hut is just 3.8 miles from the trailhead at Turquoise Lake, but the elevation gain is 1,130 feet, which puts it in the realm of a difficult ascent and a steep descent. The 10th Mountain Division Hut is 4.4 miles and 1,343 vertical feet from the Crane Park trailhead near Tennessee Pass. Reservations for overnights need to be made well in advance, and someone in the group should be a good route finder. For details and reservations, contact the **10th Mountain Division Hut Association, 1280 Ute Avenue, Suite 21, Aspen, CO 81611; (970) 925-5775; www.aspen.com/huts.**

### Tennessee Pass Cookhouse

If you want to dine at the Tennessee Pass Cookhouse, you have to work for your feast, ascending 400 vertical feet above the Piney Creek Nordic Center. Snowshoeing through the forest, with moonbeams brightening the trail or snowflakes swirling around you, is a wonderful prelude to a dinner in an honestly charming yurt. If you are snowshoeing at Piney Creek, the yurt is a natural on-mountain lunch stop, but you need to make an effort to have dinner there. In addition to nightly dinners, the Cookhouse serves lunches on weekends. During the day and during the early evening late in the season, the views of Mts. Elbert and Massive are awesome.

Enter through the swinging doors into a cozy restaurant under canvas. A woodstove takes care of the physical warmth, and the candles glow softly atop wooden tables whose rich patina attests to many fine meals and good times. Melodic music, the likes of which no Mongolian ever created, and a decent wine and microbrew selection enhance the atmosphere. The carefully prepared *prix fixe* dinner consists of an elegant appetizer platter, soup or salad, a choice of entrées (elk tenderloin, rack of lamb, trout, chicken or a vegetarian selection) and dessert. A dinner of this caliber would be impressive at sea level, which makes it all the more impressive at 10,800 feet. Reservations are required and can be made by calling **(719) 486-8114** or **(719) 486-1750.**

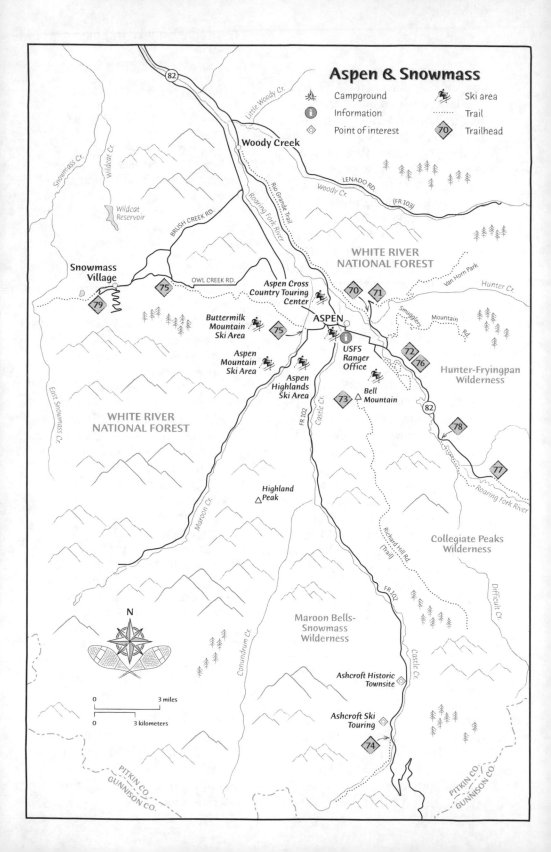

# Aspen & Snowmass

Campground
Information
Point of interest
Ski area
Trail
Trailhead

82

Little Woody Cr.
Snowmass Cr.
Wildcat Cr.

**Woody Creek**

Wildcat Reservoir

LENADO RD.
Woody Cr.
(FR 103)

BRUSH CREEK RD.

Rio Grande Trail
Roaring Fork River

OWL CREEK RD.

**Snowmass Village**

75
79

Aspen Cross
Country Touring
Center

**ASPEN**

70   71

Van Horn Park
Hunter Cr.

WHITE RIVER
NATIONAL FOREST

Smugglers
Mountain Rd.

Buttermilk
Mountain
Ski Area

75

USFS
Ranger
Office

72
76

Hunter-Fryingpan
Wilderness

Aspen
Mountain
Ski Area

Aspen
Highlands
Ski Area

73   △ Bell
Mountain

82

78

East Snowmass Cr.

WHITE RIVER
NATIONAL FOREST

Castle Cr.
FR 102

77

Roaring Fork River

Maroon Cr.

△ Highland
Peak

Collegiate Peaks
Wilderness

Richard Hill Rd.
(Trail)

Difficult Cr.

N

Conundrum Cr.

Maroon Bells-
Snowmass
Wilderness

FR 102

Castle Cr.

0        3 miles
0        3 kilometers

Ashcroft Historic
Townsite

Ashcroft Ski
Touring

74

PITKIN CO.
GUNNISON CO.

PITKIN CO.
GUNNISON CO.

# Aspen and Snowmass

Aspen was established in 1879 as one of Colorado's great silver camps, initially called Ute City. Quick riches and a burgeoning population put the town on the map, but the boom went bust after the Sherman Silver Purchase Act of 1893 shifted U.S. currency from the silver standard to gold. By the 1930s, the only thing that had spared Aspen from becoming a total ghost town was its role as Pitkin's county seat. After World War II, the first chairlift was strung up Aspen Mountain, and a new ski-fired boom began. The strikingly revitalized town has became synonymous with winter pleasures. In recent years, "pleasure" has taken on a new luster, as celebrities and the paparazzi who follow them have descended on Aspen, which is characterized by fantastic shops, restaurants, art galleries and celebrities' palatial vacation homes dotting the south-facing hillsides.

In 1967, Snowmass debuted as a built-for-skiing resort a dozen miles from Aspen. Snowmass has convenient slopeside lodging with doorstep skiing from many accommodations. It isn't as ritzy as Aspen, but keeping up with its sparkling sibling has not really been a Snowmass ambition. As built up as Aspen and Snowmass are, this consummate resort area is surrounded on three sides by wilderness: the Hunter-Fryingpan Wilderness to the east, the Collegiate Peaks Wilderness to the southeast and the Maroon Bells-Snowmass Wilderness to the west and southwest.

But you don't have to go into the wild for snowshoeing. Aspen and Snowmass boast the nation's largest free cross-country trail system—65 miles worth, linking two developed cross-country centers and more. Some are accessible directly from town centers via a free or low-cost bus. Snowshoers too are welcome on these trails, but are firmly requested to avoid walking on the set tracks. Aspen and Snowmass between them also offer more guided snowshoe tours than anyplace else, and hard-charging locals have made Aspen in general and Buttermilk Mountain in particular the state's gonzo uphill snowshoeing capital.

## Getting There

From Denver, take Interstate 70 west to Glenwood Springs. Turn right at the bottom of the ramp of Exit 116, right at the first set of stoplights and an immediate right over the bridge and onto Colorado 82 east, which is the main thoroughfare through town. Follow Colorado 82 up the Roaring Fork Valley. The turnoff to Snowmass Village is well marked, while the highway becomes Aspen's Main Street. It is also possible to fly to Aspen's Sardy Field and get around quite effectively, because the Roaring Fork Transit Authority (RFTA) has an excellent system of free or low-cost buses linking Aspen, Snowmass and many excellent snowshoeing venues.

> **Maps**
> USGS 7.5 Minute, Aspen
> Trails Illustrated #127, Aspen/Independence Pass
> USFS White River National Forest
> Eagle Eye Maps, Aspen-Carbondale Cross-Country Skier's Map (formerly Trails Illustrated)
> Aspen/Snowmass Nordic Council Cross-Country Ski Trail Map·

# Aspen

Aspen is the engine that drives the entire Roaring Fork Valley's sports and lifestyle—brassy yet tasteful, magnetically attractive to the rich and famous from the world over yet home to fiercely loyal locals living on average incomes. Urban and sophisticated yet at the doorstep of backcountry and wilderness areas of incomparable beauty, Aspen has it all. The center of town harbors a wonderful collection of Victorian commercial and residential buildings, accessorized by later in-fill additions, while the outskirts contain fabulous vacation getaways of the rich and famous—or at least the rich. Several popular snowshoeing routes offer a close-in wilderness experience in surprising proximity to someone's well-guarded mountain mansion. You'll find some wonderful trails right at the edge of town, while others are deep in the side valleys off the Roaring Fork Valley in which Aspen nestles so attractively.

For tourist information, contact the **Aspen Chamber Resort Association, 425 South Rio Grande Place, Aspen, CO 81611; (800) 262-7736** or **(970) 925-1940; www.aspen.com.**

## 70. Rio Grande Trail

| | |
|---|---|
| Starting elevation: | 7,900 feet (Puppy Smith Street trailhead) |
| Lowest elevation: | 7,770 feet (Aspen Airport Business Center) |
| Highest elevation: | 7,900 feet |
| Elevation difference: | 130 feet |
| Distance: | 4 miles (one way) |
| Difficulty: | Easy |
| Avalanche hazard: | None |

This long, flat trail, which once was the Denver & Rio Grande Railroad bed, is part of the 65 kilometers (some 40 miles) of the Aspen-Snowmass area's maintained winter trails. Snowshoers are welcome, and since dogs are too, there isn't the usual degree of caution about not stomping around on the Nordic tracks because the canines march around where they please and "predestroy" ski tracks. The most-used portion of the trail connects downtown Aspen and the Aspen Airport Business Center (AABC). The town trailhead is at the end of Puppy Smith Street, right near the post office, and the other is at the AABC. Additional short access trails are at Aspen Meadows and from the parking area near Slaughter House Bridge at Cemetery Lane, which is served by public bus every half hour.

Starting from town, you will cross two bridges, the first over the Roaring Fork River and the second over Hunter Creek, after which the trail follows the valley carved by the Roaring Fork. The first mile and a half are through the most developed area. It's truly in-town snowshoeing. The next stretch feels quite wild, as it threads through a small canyon between the steep slopes of Red Butte and Red Mountain. When the AABC comes into view to the left and down the hill, be alert for a steep trail descending toward a bridge. Bear right past the entrance to the sewage-treatment plant (not nearly as bad as it sounds), climb the hill on the left and pass through the business park, on snowshoes or on foot, and return to Colorado 82 to catch a bus either back to Aspen or on to Snowmass. The only drawbacks to this popular trail are its heavy use and the fact that it isn't as snow sure, especially early and late in the season, as mountain routes.

Though the return without a car shuttle isn't quite as convenient, the Rio Grande Trail continues another 5 miles to Upper Woody Creek, where a short, steep (and sometimes snow-free) descent leads virtually to the door of the fabled Woody Creek Tavern, a notable local hangout of considerable charm. If you cannot manage to arrange a car shuttle, return via RFTA, which runs a Woody Creek route.

# 71. Hunter Valley

| | |
|---|---|
| Starting elevation: | 8,300 feet |
| Highest elevation: | 9,000 feet |
| Elevation difference: | 700 feet |
| Distance: | 3.7 miles (one way) |
| Difficulty: | Moderate |
| Avalanche hazard: | Low |

From the center of Aspen, take Mill Street north (away from the Aspen Mountain ski area). Bear left onto Red Mountain Road at the fork just beyond the Aspen Art Museum. The road switchbacks for a mile through one of Aspen's ritziest residential neighborhoods. Be sure to take the

The Hunter Creek Trail leads to the ghost town of Van Horn Park, as well as to several backcountry huts. *Photo by Claire Walter.*

sharp left hairpin turn just before the elegant stone gate with the "Private Property" sign. The road dead-ends at a small parking area for the Hunter Creek trailhead.

To reach the trail itself, walk back down the road. You can either take a sharp left around an old wooden barn and follow an unofficial trail up over a steep little ridge, bearing right at a wooden fence on the other side of the ridge, or enter the stone gate and walk 0.25 mile up the private road. The ridge option is more difficult but offers the rare view of all four Aspen ski areas (Aspen Mountain, Aspen Highlands, the Tiehack portion of Buttermilk and the Elk Camp section of Snowmass), and even Mt. Sopris in the distance, on the far right. The two trail options meet at the official, and well-marked, beginning of the Hunter Creek Trail. This route is the access to the 10th Mountain Division Trail, so especially if you start in midmorning, your trailmates will probably be touring skiers heading for the popular McNamara, Margy's and Benedict Huts.

From the trailhead, the route bears northeast, etched into the hillside, with Hunter Creek cutting the deep valley to the right. A sturdy wooden bridge crosses the creek about 0.25 mile from the trailhead. The wide trail climbs steeply in a wide arc through lovely woods of aspen and conifers. Another option is to make a sharp right onto the Verena Mallory Park Trail, marked by a small sign on the right just after the bridge. This is a narrower, less-used trail, but with lovely views. It rejoins the main trail after about 0.25 mile, after which the grade is less steep.

About 1 mile from the trailhead, you will pass through a gate and onto White River National Forest land (marked by a sign) and cross a large, open meadow. Stay on the main trail (a trail to the right goes toward the Benedict Hut). The route crosses Hunter Creek again over another sturdy bridge—this one built by and named for the 10th Mountain Division Trail Association—into a large, open valley dotted with old cabins and outbuildings, about 2 miles from the trailhead. Some structures are tumbledown ruins, but others are quite solid, and the variety of buildings is picturesque and photogenic. You can explore this wonderful high-mountain valley, which makes a wonderful turnaround point, but before you head back, be sure to admire the glorious views of Aspen Mountain and Tiehack, with the landmark Maroon Bells above.

With time to explore and energy to keep going, you can also reach the next plateau, Van Horn Park, by following the trail northeast to the Van Horn Park sign, which is the large, tree-free basin beyond a gate. The route continues about 2 more miles from Van Horn Park to the McNamara Hut, located at 11,360 feet.

## Aspen Center for Environmental Studies (ACES)

ACES is a real treasure, a 25-acre natural preserve at the edge of this highly developed resort town, which provides a refuge for threatened wildlife and educates children and adults about the mountain environment. The organization has ample summer opportunities to carry out their mission, but in winter, snowshoeing is one of ACES' aces when it comes to introducing people to the outdoors. Their winter display even features a collection of historic snowshoes. You can take a self-guided tour on property around Hallam Lake. ACES will even lend you snowshoes if you don't have any and

ACES Naturalist-guide Rebecca Lemberg Weiss, a former snowshoe racer, explains the mysteries of mountain ecology on Richmond Ridge, at the top of Aspen Mountain. *Photo by Claire Walter.*

the trail isn't packed down enough for comfortable walking. There is no set admission fee, just a very modest suggested donation.

Naturalist Nights at Hallam Lake are scheduled every Tuesday evening from 7:30 to 9:00 P.M. during the winter season. Reservations are required for the low-cost program, which begins with a short but informative film that serves as an indoor introduction to the winter environment specifically around the lake. A guided snowshoe walk around the lake follows with hot drinks, dessert and discussion around the potbelly stove. It is especially beguiling if Tuesday happens to fall on or just before the full moon. This is not the kind of nightlife that Aspen is famous for, but it truly shows the gentler, more sensitive and concerned side of this glamorous community.

The ACES complex, which is open weekdays between 9:00 A.M. and 4:30 P.M., is worth a visit, but you don't have to go near the place to participate in Fresh Tracks. These daily guided snowshoe walks atop Aspen Mountain and at Snowmass are easy, but also enlightening even for experienced snowshoers. They are an ideal introduction for people who have never tried snowshoeing. Children eight years old and older are welcome. The thrill of a panoramic view from atop Aspen Mountain, far from the madding downhill crowd, or a quick lesson on identifying animal tracks in the snow, can convert a skeptic into a snowshoer in just two hours.

All of the ACES tours are short (less than a mile) but packed with information. The Aspen Mountain tour is a loop from the top of the gondola. At Snowmass, guides use either a loop from the top of Two Creeks or another along Government Trail, which is all downhill. Make reservations with ACES and pick up tickets at the Aspen Mountain and Two Elk Ski School Desks. The fee includes lift ride, use of snowshoes, snack and, best of all, a leisurely, two-hour tour led by a naturalist knowledgeable about the winter environment, mountain ecology, mining history and geological history of the area.

For information or program reservations, or to visit, ACES is at 100 Puppy Smith Street, Aspen, CO 81611; (970) 925-5756; www.aspen.com/aces/.

## 72. Smuggler Road

| | |
|---|---|
| Starting elevation: | 7,900 feet |
| Highest elevation: | 9,200 feet |
| Elevation difference: | 1,300 feet |
| Distance: | 1.5 miles (one way) |
| Difficulty: | Challenging |
| Avalanche hazard: | Low |

Drive east on Main Street, turn left (north) onto Mill Street for 0.25 mile. Cross the bridge and turn right onto Gibson Street. Bear left at the fork onto South Avenue and then turn right onto Park Circle. After a few hundred feet, you will come to Smuggler Road (Forest Service Road 131) on the left.

This steep road is a year-round favorite climb of legions of Aspen fitness buffs who bike, hike, powerwalk, run, snowshoe and ski it, depending on their tastes and level of fitness. Nothing else in town, except ascending a steep Alpine ski trail, can provide so much aerobic benefit in so little time—and the views are darned good too. This wide road is technically simple to snowshoe; the steep and steady grade is what makes it challenging. The elevation gain comes in the first 1.5 miles of constant switchbacks. Each one provides a different view of town, Aspen Mountain and beyond—and each one represents an uphill accomplishment. A trail at this crest, before the road circles behind the mountain, offers a viewing platform with especially wonderful scenes of town and surrounding mountains. This makes a good turnaround spot.

### If You Want a Longer Hike
The road continues for another 3.5 miles and 1,500 vertical feet, including some additional steep sections, toward Warren Lakes.

# 73. Richmond Ridge

| | |
|---|---|
| Starting elevation: | 11,212 feet |
| Highest elevation: | 11,460 feet |
| Elevation difference: | 248 feet, plus several substantial ups and downs |
| Distance: | 5 miles (one way) |
| Difficulty: | Easy to moderate |
| Avalanche hazard: | None for the first 4 miles; low thereafter |

This ridge, which is called Richmond Hill on some maps, stretches south from the top of Aspen Mountain's Silver Queen Gondola. Circle around the gondola terminal to the left and take a short footpath behind the building leading to a gate. Pass though the gate, drop down a slight incline and then follow the wide, snowcat-packed route along the spine of the ridge. This is actually a numbered road, Forest Service Road 123, so don't be surprised that you are sharing it with over-snow vehicles. Snowshoeing Richmond Ridge will cost you a "foot pass" to ride up and down on the lift. On a clear day, when you are promenading along a groomed boulevard with panorama after panorama of famous peaks and entire glorious ranges on either side, you'll feel this is the best bargain on earth. When it's windy or densely clouded—not unusual in winter at 11,000 feet or more—no one can pay you enough to endure the unpleasant weather or frustrating lack of visibility.

Sturdy bridge across Hunter Creek, a protected area close to some of Aspen's most elegant homes. *Photo by Claire Walter.*

On those brilliant, cloudless days that often grace Colorado winters, you will see the Sawatch and Collegiate Peaks Ranges and Independence Pass to the left (east), the Elk Mountains toward Crested Butte straight ahead (south) and more Elk Mountains, the Maroon Creek and Castle Creek Valleys, Mt. Sopris and eventually Hayden Peak and the Maroon Bells to the right (west). Once you have climbed the first section, you can also look behind you (north) to Aspen, set against the backdrop of Red and Smuggler Mountains. (This view is a lovely carrot dangling before the weary on the return.) Intermittent stands of trees beside the trail provide some wind shelter if you need to take a break, but they don't interfere much with the views.

The beginning of the route is a steady, gradual ascent that itself is easy to follow and easy to snowshoe. The constant high elevation escalates the difficulty rating to "moderate" for the unacclimatized. After 0.5 mile, the gradient steepens, and then the road forks into a wide route to the left and a narrower one used by snowmobilers to the right. (This is not recreational snowmobiling, but the only winter transportation—other than snowshoes or cross-country skis—for people living in cabins deep in the backcountry.)

In any case, the left option is more level and easier, offering excellent views of Independence Pass. The right fork has more up-and-down rollers but is more spectacular. The high point of the trail is about 1.3 miles from the gondola. From then on, the route evens out and passes through large open areas before dropping down into MacFarlane Gulch. Though the trail does descend into the valley to Taylor Pass/Taylor Lake Road (Forest Service Road 133), this really is the farthest recommended route for most people— and it is more than far enough for recreational snowshoers.

## Aspen Cross-Country Center

This full-service cross-country center is operated on Aspen's municipal golf course just west of downtown. You'll see it just off Colorado 82, near the intersection with snowshoe trails near the Maroon Creek Road (which accesses the high school, the hospital and Aspen Highlands). The center's flat terrain makes it a fine place for visitors from the lowlands to get acclimatized. The retail and rental shop in the lodge carries snowshoes for rent or sale. Taking a snowshoe walk on the side of the immaculately groomed skating lanes is as easy as snowshoeing gets—and for many first-timers, the heated lodge, with locker rooms, food service and lounge, is a comfort too.

There is direct access from the Nordic center's trail system to the Owl Creek Trail, the high school trail system between Maroon Creek and Castle Creek and the Marolt Property trails. The center also runs a guided, one-and-one-half-hour beginner tour along Maroon Creek, with technique tips, plus custom tours of various lengths and degree of challenge. All tours are by appointment. Rental snowshoes are also available. For information or tour reservations, call **(970) 925-2145.**

## Ashcroft Ski Touring

Ashcroft, an old ghost town deep in the Castle Creek Valley, was proposed for Alpine ski area development when Aspen Mountain was still a far-off dream, but World War II intervened, and Aspen Mountain was started first. Still, Ashcroft became a noteworthy ski area in its own right—a Nordic ski area. Established in 1971, Ashcroft Ski Touring became the first self-sustaining cross-country ski center in a national forest, and it is now a fine snowshoeing center as well.

To reach Ashcroft, take Colorado 82 west from Snowmass and turn south at the traffic light onto Maroon Creek Road, marked with signs for

Aspen Highlands and Ashcroft. Take the first left onto Castle Creek Road, and follow it about 11 miles to the end of the plowed section. The parking lot is on the left, overlooking the ghost town. The Toklat Gallery is across the street, and the King Cabin, which serves as the day lodge and rental shop, is on the right, a short walk up the road. You can get details on Ashcroft by calling **(970) 925-1971**. If you prefer not to drive the twisting valley road, a daily shuttle operates between Aspen and Ashcroft; call **High Mountain Taxi at (970) 925-TAXI** or **(970) 925-8294** for rates and schedules.

There are currently three ways to snowshoe at Ashcroft, and a fourth will probably be available if and when the Forest Service approves (and Ashcroft cuts) designated snowshoe trails. Currently, the first way to snowshoe in this spectacular part of the Castle Creek Valley is via the road (details below). The second is to take a guided evening snow-

Snowshoers can explore the ghost town of Ashcroft, deep in Castle Creek Valley, near Aspen. *Photo by Claire Walter.*

shoe tour to the Pine Creek Cookhouse, surely one of the finest excursions in Colorado. A merry procession of serious diners who are willing to shoe or ski, and cross-country skiers and snowshoers convinced that they are already working off the dinner they are about to enjoy, leave from King Cabin. Miners' lamps or perhaps moonlight illuminate the Flynn Trail, which is not open to snowshoers during the day. A sleigh ride also makes the trip on the road for those who prefer horsepower to their own power. Reservations are required; call **(970) 925-1044**.

Ashcroft Ski Touring now offers ACES-style naturalist tours, which provide the third and most enlightening opportunity to snowshoe at Ashcroft. In 1997–1998, these two-hour naturalist tours based out of the touring center were scheduled weekdays from 11:00 A.M. to 1:00 P.M. Children eight years old and older are welcome. The tours focus on the ecology and human history of the valley. To maintain such an unspoiled environment as the far reaches of Castle Creek Valley so close to Aspen requires understanding and protection, but "unspoiled" does not equate with "untouched." Ashcroft was settled in 1879, the same year as Aspen, and in its heyday, 2,500 people called it home. Today, the remnants of a handful of structures poke out of the snow, and nature has reclaimed much of the valley. The naturalist explains it all. The use of snowshoes is included in the fee. Reservations are requested; call **(970) 925-7345** or **(970) 925-1971**.

## Toklat, With These Hands Gallery

Near the end of the plowed section of Castle Creek Road, across from the remains of old Ashcroft and just downhill from the touring center's King Cabin, is Toklat. This rambling log and stone building harbors a treasure trove of exquisite artwork and crafts. It also guards the memory of Stuart Mace, one of Aspen's legendary pioneers, a climber, botanist, artist and photographer. He also served in the famous 10th Mountain Division, the U.S. Army's crack mountaineering and ski troop, where he learned to handle guard dogs and sled dogs. After World War II, he tried keeping huskies in Boulder, but they were too noisy, so in 1947 he moved to Ashcroft, whose beauty he remembered from his climbing days.

His dogs and his valley starred in the television series, "Sargeant Preston of the Yukon," and the sled dog legacy is still alive and barking at Krabloonik, the kennel established in 1974 in Snowmass with 55 of Mace's dogs. He was instrumental in establishing the Aspen Center for Environmental Studies and led naturalist tours in his beloved valley. A naturalist who guides snowshoe tours out of Ashcroft is in residence at Toklat, along with several artists. Mace died in 1994, but his legacies are the artists now nurtured at and by Toklat, the pristine environment of Castle Creek that he assiduously preserved and his own photography and art that survive him. His daughter Lynne and son Bruce now operate the gallery. When you snowshoe at Ashcroft, be sure to visit; call **(970) 925-7345.**

## Snowshoe Tours

In addition to tours put on by ACES (see page 147) and the area's cross-country centers at Ashcroft and Snowmass (see pages 150 and 159), the current boom in commercial snowshoe tours echoes the silver boom of the late nineteenth century. Some are run by long-established outfitters with expertise in many outdoor adventures; others are low-key enterprises established by men and women who love to explore the backcountry on snowshoes. Call to check fees and schedules or to make reservations. Keep in mind that as snowshoeing continues to grow in popularity, more snowshoe guides will probably surface in Aspen, a very service-oriented resort. At this writing, local outfitters with guided snowshoe trips include:

**Aspen Alpine Guides:** This mountain guide service specializes in longer tours that include the use of snowshoes, poles and a daypack, as well as transportation to the trailhead, snacks on all tours and lunch on full-day programs. Their most popular tour is to Buttermilk Meadows via Government Trail, available as a 6-mile round-trip on the full-day program and 3.5 miles on the half-day option. They also offer an almost-full-day, 5.5-mile tour along Richmond Ridge from the top of the Aspen Mountain gondola. They have a U.S. Forest Service permit. **Aspen Alpine Guides, P.O. Box 7937, Aspen, CO 81612; (970) 925-6618** or **(970) 379-1716; www.aspen.com/aspenalpine/.**

**Blazing Adventures/Elk Mountain Guides:** This outfitter and mountain guide service has a Forest Service permit and offers various scheduled and custom tours. They offer half- and three-quarter-day tours, including transportation from Aspen and Snowmass, use of equipment (snowshoes, poles, daypack), hot cocoa, snacks and lunch on the longer program. They also guide overnight excursions to nearby 10th Mountain Division huts. You can visit them at the Aspen Sports location on Snowmass Village Mall, or contact **Blazing Adventures, P.O. Box 5068, Snowmass Village, CO 81615; (970) 923-4544.**

**Environmental Snowshoe Tours:** Naturalist Gracie Oliphant's slogan is "Listen to the Quiet," which nicely sums up one of the sport's greatest appeals. She offers full- and half-day tours, with an emphasis on winter ecology, particularly what animals must do to survive in the high-country cold. She takes snowshoers to three or four off-the-beaten-track areas, on- and off-trail, accessible from Snowmass. Equipment and such snacks as tea, trail mix, homemade cookies and fresh breads are included. **Call (970) 923-3649.**

**Sun Dog Athletics:** Snowshoer, sports model and trainer Erik Skarvan specializes in customized tours of Richmond Ridge, Hunter Creek Trail, Maroon Creek, Owl Creek, the Snowmass Nature Trail, North Star Nature Preserve and other routes in the area. The emphasis can be whatever the clients wish: with or without a gourmet (or simple) lunch, with a focus on instruction, nature and fitness training or simply the services of an experienced snowshoe guide. Sun Dog also offers children's snowshoe parties. Skarvan's distinctive specialties also extend to snowshoe racing and training programs, either one-on-one or in group clinics on Buttermilk Mountain. Some workshops are for women only. **Call (970) 925-1069.**

**Aspen Snowshoe Striders:** Beginning and intermediate snowshoers, locals and visitors alike, are invited to join Snowshoe Striders' group tours every Sunday. Free, informal and fun, these weekly outings offer companionship and the occasional tip on recreational snow-shoeing in the beautiful backcountry around Aspen. For time and place, call **Sun Dog Athletics, (970) 925-1069.**

## Hut Access

Aspen is the epicenter of Colorado's backcountry huts, which increasingly are being used by snowshoers as well as touring skiers. The 10th Mountain Division Hut Association, which handles reservations both for its own huts and for others, is located in Aspen. The 10th Mountain huts are located in the high country, roughly between 10,000 and 11,500 feet, in a circle around the Holy Cross Wilderness, north of Aspen. The Alfred

Braun Huts are in the Elk Mountains, between Aspen and Crested Butte. They are most popular with touring skiers, but strong snowshoers with backcountry experience are beginning to use the routes to these huts too. 10th Mountain Division Hut Association, 1280 Ute Avenue, Suite 21, Aspen, CO 81611; (970) 925-5775; www.aspen.com/huts/.

## 74. Castle Creek Road

| | |
|---|---|
| Starting elevation: | 9,500 feet |
| Highest elevation: | 9,750 feet |
| Elevation difference: | 250 feet (to Pine Creek Cookhouse) |
| Distance: | 1.5 miles (one way) |
| Difficulty: | Easy |
| Avalanche hazard: | Low to Pine Creek Cookhouse; high beyond |

The unplowed road beyond King's Cabin as far as the Pine Creek Cookhouse, a wonderful backcountry restaurant, is safe, straightforward and free of charge. It skirts the left bank of Castle Creek, which bisects this beautiful and pristine valley, hemmed in by 13,000-foot peaks. Beyond the restaurant are three serious slide areas (the road and vulnerable Nordic trails are closed when there is avalanche danger), so don't even think about continuing by detouring around the closures.

You might share the route with some cross-country skiers, with folks heading toward the Alfred Braun hut system or with snowmobiles hauling supplies to the restaurant. Don't resent them. Instead, plan on lunch in this wonderful expanded cabin or on its deck. The Cookhouse serves gourmet food in a friendly and casual atmosphere in a million-dollar setting (actually, being Greater Aspen, make that a billion-dollar setting). Reservations are required; call (970) 925-1044.

At this writing, snowshoeing was permitted not only on the road, but also on the other side of Castle Creek and south of the groomed Nordic trails, and Ashcroft Ski Touring is hoping to add several trails just for snowshoeing, pending Forest Service approval. One trail might cross the creek, loop back and connect with the Logan Trail, which would be converted from skiing to snowshoeing and extended to the Pine Creek Cookhouse. Another could follow Green Mountain Trail, a hiking route, well up the west side of the 12,054-foot peak. For information on programs, naturalist tour reservations and the extent of the snowshoeing trail system, call (970) 925-1971.

# Up with (Snowshoeing) People

Aspen's lemmings aren't rushing to cliffs. They are snowshoeing up ski slopes—fast. On any given winter day, 300 or more of these fleet, fit athletes are cruising up Buttermilk. The real hardcore make their way up Aspen Mountain, early enough to download when the gondola starts running. Rules of this sort can change, but 1997–1998 Aspen Skiing Company policy was as follows:

**Aspen Mountain:** Uphillers must make the 3,267-foot ascent to reach the top of the gondola by 9:00 A.M. Download is free, and snowshoers are prohibited from using the ski trails once the lifts start running for regular skier traffic. Dogs are prohibited on Aspen Mountain.

**Aspen Highlands:** Snowshoers must reach the Merry-Go-Round Restaurant by 9 A.M. in order to be permitted to continue to the 11,675-foot Loge Peak summit, a total climb of 3,635 vertical feet. Hiking up to midmountain along the edges of any of the ski trails is permitted throughout the day, and downloading on the Loge Peak or Exhibition chairlift is free. Dogs are not allowed.

**Buttermilk:** Uphill-bound snowshoers are asked to follow a designated snowshoe route along the edge of one of the ski trails, starting up the Government Trail from the Main Buttermilk base. Downloading on the Summit Express chair is free all day (that is, from 8:45 A.M. to 3:45 P.M.). In addition, snowshoers using the Owl Creek Trail may cross the ski slopes along a well-marked route from the Tiehack base. Dogs are prohibited.

**Snowmass:** Upward-bound snowshoers are permitted on all trails at all times, but they are asked to keep to the edges of the trails. They may bring leashed dogs with them as long as they clean up after their pets. Snowshoers may ride up or down on any lift free of charge.

In addition to downtown shops, rental snowshoes are available at the Aspen Highlands Ski Shop, Buttermilk Sports and Two Creeks Ski Shop at the bases of the lifts at those three mountains, and also at the Snowmass Touring Center and Aspen Cross-Country Center.

## Snowshoe Races

If a serious Alpine area ascent looks like a good workout to you and you want to get the knack of doing it right, or if you are already contemplating training for a snowshoe race, check out Sun Dog Athletics' snowshoe fitness training workshops directed by snowshoe racing ace Erik Skarvan. General fitness or race-specific training is available on a one-time or ongoing basis. For rates, schedules and other details, call Erik at **(970) 925-1069.**

All that training—whether with Skarvan or independently—comes into play during the uphill snowshoe races that are held throughout the valley. The inspiration for the daddy of all snowshoe ascent competitions is America's Uphill, dedicated to a local mountaineer named Fritz Stammberger, who used to train by running up 3,267-vertical-foot Aspen Mountain with a pair of heavy skis over his shoulder in less than an hour, and who disappeared on a Himalayan expedition in 1976. Now a number of regular snowshoeing events with history behind them are on the Aspen calendar, including:

Land Rover 24 Hours of Aspen: While downhill skiers are making laps on Aspen Mountain during a grueling, twice-round-the-clock race in early December, snowshoers have their own race at Buttermilk, typically on the Saturday morning before the twice-round-the-clock downhill ski competition. For information, call the Aspen Skiing Company, (800) 525-6200 or (970) 925-1220.

Winterskol Buttermilk Uphill: During this annual winter festival held in mid-January, another uphill race takes place on Buttermilk. For details, call the Aspen Chamber Resort Association, (970) 925-1940.

Up from the Heart: A Valentine's Day fund-raising race on Buttermilk Mountain; call the Aspen Chamber Resort Association, (970) 925-1940.

Mardi Gras: Snowshoe race up Snowmass, held on the appropriate Tuesday, usually in early to mid-February. More information is available from the Snowmass Resort Association, (970) 923-2000.

America's Uphill: The oldest and most serious snowshoe and cross-country ski race in the Roaring Fork Valley, to the top of Aspen Mountain via Spar Gulch, held the third Saturday in March. The 1998 winner was a snowshoer who did the 3,267 vertical feet in 42 minutes and 58 seconds. The gondola ascends the same distance in 15 minutes. Details are available from the Aspen Skiing Company, (800) 525-6200 or (970) 923-1220.

Mother of All Ascensions, Snowmass: Competitors in this morning event, normally held late in February, climb from the Snowmass Mall to the High Alpine Restaurant. Further information is available from the Snowmass Resort Association, (970) 923-2000.

K9 Uphill: Snowshoers and their dogs (or teams of dogs) race up Buttermilk after the area has shut down for the season. For more information, call Sun Dog Athletics, (970) 925-1069.

High Country Duathlon: First held in 1997, this March race at the Aspen Cross-Country Center is a 10-kilometer, country-country freestyle ski leg followed by 5 kilometers on snowshoes. It's not an uphill, but it is a competition in which snowshoes are key. Details are available from the Aspen Cross-Country Center, (970) 925-2145.

# 75. Owl Creek Trail

| | |
|---|---|
| Starting elevation: | 8,020 feet (at Tiehack base) |
| Highest elevation: | 8,560 feet |
| Elevation difference: | 540 feet (but many additional ups and downs) |
| Distance: | 7.5 miles (one way) |
| Difficulty: | Moderate to challenging |
| Avalanche hazard: | Low |

This scenic trail between Buttermilk and Snowmass can be done in either direction, but the climbs are steeper from the Snowmass (west) end. There are two access points from the east, which is closer to Aspen. You need a four-wheel drive to get to the trailhead at West Buttermilk Road, but you can also drive or take a bus to the Tiehack base, which does require crossing additional downhill ski trails along a well-marked route. From the west, access is from the Snowmass Touring Center, also reachable by bus, via Twin Pine and Sinclair Divide, at 8,345 feet. Because it is popular with Nordic skiers, be especially respectful and stay at the edge of the trail. It is not particularly challenging, but it is long for some people, and there is no bailout in the middle.

From Tiehack, the route ascends consistently to Main Buttermilk and offers views north toward the Roaring Fork Valley. Since it also is a downhill ski trail with traffic coming toward you, keep well to the side. After crossing the main part of the ski area, the trail goes through aspen woods before joining West Buttermilk Road, which you cross shortly after reaching the route's highest point. From then on, it is a long but beautiful slog through alternating forest and open areas. When you have come out of the woods, crossed a driveway called Ross's Road and reached a picnic table, you will be at the halfway point. Owl Creek Trail passes a cabin and then crosses Sinclair Divide. The rest is a cruise, including descents of some fairly steep sections. Be alert for skiers hurtling down the Flying Kilometer. You will closely parallel Owl Creek Road and pass the new Two Creeks lift base and a real estate development of prepossessing homes on this last stretch as you approach the Snowmass Touring Center.

# 76. North Star Loop

| | |
|---|---|
| Starting elevation: | 8,010 feet |
| Highest elevation: | 8,030 feet |
| Elevation difference: | Negligible |
| Distance: | 3.2 miles (loop) |
| Difficulty: | Easy |
| Avalanche hazard: | None |

Take Main Street (Colorado 82) east to the North Star Nature Preserve's parking area on the right side of the road. This oblong trail loops along the highway on the north and the Roaring Fork River on the south, accessing riparian land and lovely woods. The 175-acre preserve also contains stands of aspen, an old quarry and a few very modest ups and downs. This easy trail is popular with beginning snowshoers, and it is also often used by naturalist-guides. Dogs are prohibited.

### If You Want a Longer Hike

The Benedict Trail leads toward the Aspen Club property from the west end of the North Star Nature Preserve loop. Take it along some gentle bends if you like. There is one sharp turn to the left, and a hairpin to the right, then it enters a potential avalanche area and should be avoided.

## 77. Independence Pass Road

| | |
|---|---|
| Starting elevation: | 8,600 feet |
| Highest elevation: | 9,600 feet |
| Elevation difference: | 1,000 feet |
| Distance: | 5.5 miles (one way) |
| Difficulty: | Moderate |
| Avalanche hazard: | Low to Lincoln Creek Road, but be aware of rockfalls on the beginning of the route |

Every autumn, when the snows begin in the high country, Colorado 82 is closed for the season at mile marker 47, just 5 miles southeast of Aspen. This takes the Independence Pass Road out of the hands of motor vehicle operators and puts it under the feet of recreational users. The first 5.5 miles are generally safe for winter travel, and cross-country skiers, snowmobilers and dogs share it with snowshoers. Under the snow is pavement, so the wide, flat road can accommodate many users, especially if they are mindful of each other. From the road closure, head generally east. The 5.5-mile out-and-back route translates into an 11-mile round-trip. This is a sprint for a snowmobiler, but for a snowshoer, it can feel like a marathon, so go as far as you feel comfortable and then return.

The ascent over the first couple of miles is so easy as to be virtually imperceptible. Just before mile marker 49, the road slices into the hillside as it skirts a very narrow, gorgelike section of the valley. The route becomes gentler as you pass the Weller Campground, and then it narrows again and follows the river's curves. Dramatic rock walls rise directly from the road on the left (north). Another mile takes you to the Grottos, a popular summer attraction of huge granite formations and river-cut caves. You can explore this area, carefully, on snowshoes and perhaps even find a good spot for a break or a picnic.

## If You Want a Longer Hike

If you decide to continue up the road (remembering that you have to return), Lincoln Creek Road on the right, just beyond mile marker 51, is a reasonable turnaround for fast and fit snowshoers.

# 78. Difficult Trail

| | |
|---|---|
| Starting elevation: | 8,160 feet |
| Highest elevation: | 9,300 feet |
| Elevation difference: | 1,140 feet |
| Distance: | 1.8 miles (one way) |
| Difficulty: | Challenging |
| Avalanche hazard: | Low on the lower part of the trail; high beyond the rock cliffs |

Access to this aptly named trail is from the Difficult Campground, just off Colorado 82, 3 miles southeast of Aspen. From the parking area, follow the road to the gated campground entrance and then continue 0.5 mile to the campground fee station. Beginners can explore the flat area where tents and RVs nest in the summer. The campground has also been the Aspen site of Winter Trails Day, an introduction-to-snowshoeing event aimed at families and first-timers. Experienced and strong snowshoers just use the campground as a launching platform for a challenging ascent.

Take the old road immediately to the right past the campground. Cross the bridge over the Roaring Fork River and bear right across a flat, exposed area where sagebrush and scrub oak poke out of the snow to Difficult Creek and the actual start of Difficult Trail. It is steep. It is narrow. It makes you grateful for snowshoes' grip. The trail climbs quickly through a dense conifer forest that has an almost magical quality. There's real avalanche danger when the trail begins slicing past rock cliffs, and only the foolhardy would think to continue.

# Snowmass

Snowmass has traditionally been lower key and more family-friendly than glamorous Aspen. Slopeside condos, a pleasant walk-through mall and low-level nightlife have characterized the resort. But that is all changing. Trophy homes are sprouting at the Alpine ski area's newest lift base, called Two Creeks, on hillsides and ridge tops, along once-isolated streams and on old grazing land. Other than the ski slopes, the Snowmass Club's golf course is the rare remaining open parcel in Snowmass Village. In winter, it becomes the Snowmass Club cross-country center, nestled in a huge bowl with grand views of both the impressive, human-made trail system and of the natural splendor of Mt. Daly.

For tourist information, contact the **Snowmass Resort Association,** P.O. Box 5566, Snowmass Village, CO 81657; **(800) SNOWMASS** or **(970) 923-2000**; www.snowmassvillage.com.

## Snowmass Touring Center

The golf-course snowshoeing available at the Snowmass Club is just a tad more difficult than the Aspen Cross-Country Center because it is hillier. The lodge, located at 8,300 feet, is in the center of the lower trail system on and near the golf course. The trail system comprises the 2.2-mile Lower Sundance Loop and the 1.5-mile Upper Sundance Loop, which hairpins around the Anderson Ranch Art Center. There are also connections to the Owl Creek Trail (see page 157), Gracie's Trail and Snowmass Village via Village Way, 1.2 miles up the mountainside. Snowshoers are welcome on the skating lanes but are asked to stay on the side of the groomed trail. In addition to renting snowshoes and giving tips on using them, the center offers guided snowshoe tours on request; call **(970) 923-3148.**

## 79. Ditch Trail

| | |
|---|---|
| Starting elevation: | 8,600 feet |
| Lowest elevation: | 8,400 feet |
| Elevation difference: | 200 feet (ascend on the return) |
| Distance: | 2 miles (one way) |
| Difficulty: | Easy |
| Avalanche hazard: | None |

To reach this mellow and lovely trail, which follows an irrigation ditch, go to the Top of the Village condominiums at the uppermost part of Snowmelt Road and continue around the buildings. Take two rights onto the trail, which crosses under the Campground chairlift and four steep Alpine ski runs (use caution while crossing here). As soon as you are out of sight and earshot of the ski area, you feel as if you are really in the distant outback. Animal tracks abound, and the trail offers lovely views of the Snowmass Creek Valley and Mt. Daly. The East Snowmass Creek Trail junction marker is a good place to turn around for the mild ascent back to the resort.

# Glenwood Springs and Carbondale

Glenwood Springs is a historic spa resort, whose healing and soothing waters have attracted visitors for more than a century and Ute Indians long before that. Located at the confluence of the Colorado and Roaring Fork Rivers and hemmed in by high hills, the town is at once scenic and accessible. It is bisected by the railroad and Interstate 70, so the famous Hot Springs Pool right in the middle of everything feels like something of a hub. It is the world's largest naturally spring-fed outdoor pool complex, and its plumes of sulfuric steam serve as a visible and olfactory winter landmark for locals and travelers alike. One of the great benefits of snowshoeing around Glenwood is the pleasure of soaking in the pool afterward.

Glenwood Springs is also a mecca for recreationalists, who come for the fishing, rafting, hiking, mountain biking, skiing and, increasingly, snowshoeing. The low-key community offers a lively little downtown and ample, economical accommodations. One of the things that makes Glenwood itself such a pleasant place to stay is its elevation (5,736 feet), which is not much higher than Denver. That means a bit of a commute to snow-covered trails, but it's worth it for the relatively benign climate. Sunlight Mountain Resort is a mid-sized ski area just 10 miles from town that offers miles of free snowshoeing and cross-country skiing trails. Carbondale, located up-valley between Glenwood Springs and Aspen, is the gateway to McClure Pass, which itself offers outstanding snow trails. For tourist information, contact the **Glenwood Springs Chamber Resort Association, 1102 Grand Avenue, Glenwood Springs, CO 81601; (800) 221-0098** or **(970) 945-6589.**

## Getting There

Take Interstate 70 west from Denver or east from Grand Junction. Get off at Exit 116 (Glenwood Springs) and turn right at the exit ramp, right again at the first set of traffic lights just after the exit ramp and right once more at the next light, crossing the high bridge into downtown Glenwood Springs. In addition to lodgings in town and along Route 82, many motels are located in West Glenwood at Exit 114. Glenwood Springs is 160 miles from Denver and 85 miles from Grand Junction. For Sunlight, follow Colorado 82 2 miles from downtown and turn right (west), cross over the bridge, turn left at the first intersection and right at the second one to the Ski Sunlight access road (also marked as Garfield County Road 117). For Carbondale and McClure Pass, stay on Colorado 82 east 7 miles and turn right (south) onto Colorado 133.

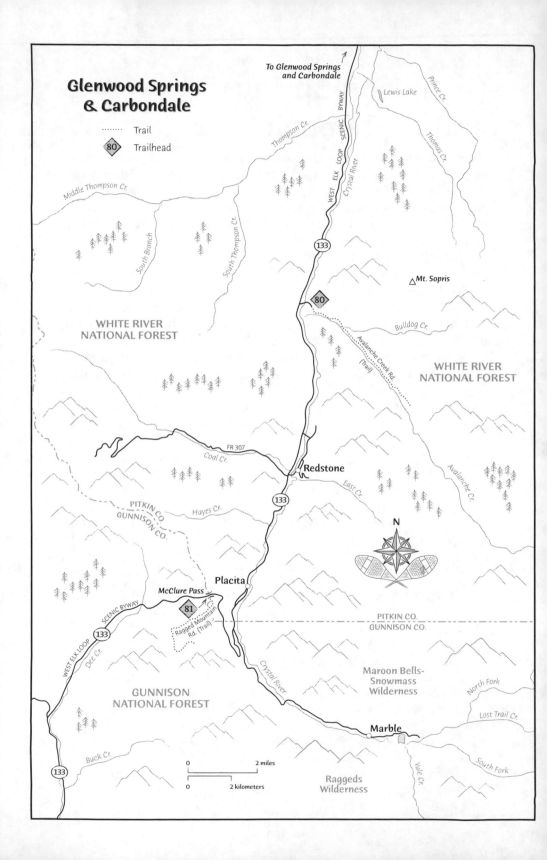

## Maps

For USGS maps, see individual trail descriptions
Trails Illustrated #123, Flattops Southeast/Glenwood Canyon; #128, Maroon Bells/Redstone/Marble
USFS White River National Forest
Eagle Eye Maps, Cross-Country Skier's Map, Aspen/Carbondale (formerly Trails Illustrated)

## *Sunlight Mountain Resort*

This mid-sized Alpine area is well known among Colorado skiers for low prices and an informal, old-fashioned ambience. Its 28 miles of free trails for snowshoeing and Nordic skiing are surprisingly unknown. From a trailhead directly at the parking lot, they wend their beautiful way up **Babbish Gulch** and through a glorious aspen forest. Most steep parts are on the lower trails, after which the trails fan out more gently. Sixteen kilometers (that is, nearly 10 miles) are pack-groomed but not track-set, so snowshoers don't have to worry about tramping down Nordic skiers' precious tracks. An additional 13 kilometers (or more than 8 miles) of trails are marked but not groomed. They lead higher on the ridge to over 9,800 feet, into a thinner forest and open meadows with fine views up into the Crystal River Valley and the surrounding mountains.

Babbish Gulch, adjacent to Sunlight Mountain Resort, is the site of the annual Day of Infamy Snowshoe Race and is also popular for recreational snowshoeing. *Photo by Roy Willey/ Sunlight Mountain Resort.*

Just 1.5 miles up the main trail, in what was once the mining town of Sunlight (from which the ski area took its name), is a rustic backcountry

### Day of Infamy Snowshoe Race

Held on a Sunday close to December 7, Pearl Harbor Day, this 8-kilometer (4.95-mile) race is a wonderful season opener. It is long enough to be challenging but not so grueling that it is too much for most participants so soon after Thanksgiving. The race starts at the cabin and each year follows a slightly different route along the trail system. The race is organized into men's and women's competitive and sport categories. For more information or to register, contact **Summit Canyon Mountaineering, 732 Grand Avenue, Glenwood Springs, CO 81601; (800) 360-6994** or **(970) 945-6994.**

cabin. Located at 8,400 feet, it is heated by a woodstove and furnished with bunks. Overnights in this easily accessible cabin are usually booked well in advance on weekends, but weeknights are generally wide open. It's a great introduction to the hut experience without a really demanding trek in. There is also a shelter high up on the trail system, at 8,960 feet. For cabin reservations or more information, contact **Sunlight Mountain Resort, 10901 Road 117, Glenwood Springs, CO 81601; (800) 445-7931** or **(970) 945-7491; www.sunlightmtn.com.**

## 80. Avalanche Creek

| | |
|---|---|
| Beginning elevation: | 6,760 feet |
| Highest elevation: | 7,400 feet |
| Elevation difference: | 640 feet |
| Distance: | 3 miles (one way) |
| Difficulty: | Moderate |
| Avalanche hazard: | Low |
| Map: | USGS 7.5 Minute, Mt. Sopris |

Skiers pay to ride Sunlight's lifts, but snowshoers hike Babbish Gulch gratis. *Photo by Claire Walter.*

From Carbondale, take Colorado 133 south past Redstone. After 12.5 miles, pull over at the Avalanche Campground sign, on the left (east), at the confluence of Avalanche Creek and the Crystal River. From the plowed-out parking area near the highway, walk around the gate and start snowshoeing up the campground road, soon passing a small mine on your left. The first portion of this unpaved road (3 miles) through the mixed forest to the Avalanche Campground is wide, long and steady enough to be a desirable snowshoeing route in its own right. It also accesses the Maroon Bells-Snowmass Wilderness, for the hardcore snowshoer.

Winter users occasionally have reported spotting an elk or even a bighorn sheep herd as they travel up this pretty valley, which is flanked by steep slopes before widening into a generous basin. The lower slopes of Mt. Sopris are on your left, but you can't see the summit of this huge 12,953-foot mountain from the route. Various species of bushes, scrub trees and tall conifers line the route but rarely block the views.

The road begins to the southeast, jogs into a sharp bend and then gentles again, following the stream all the way up to the Avalanche Campground. The middle section of the trail is the steepest part, after which you also have the option of following a small ski trail that veers off to the right.

## If You Want a Longer Hike

A trail from the campground leads 11 more miles into the Maroon Bells-Snowmass Wilderness, with Avalanche Lake as the destination of many a summer hiker or backpacker. You can take it a little way longer, but you are then getting into the serious backcountry and some potentially hazardous areas.

# 81. McClure Pass

| | |
|---|---|
| Beginning elevation: | 8,763 feet |
| Highest elevation: | 9,338 feet |
| Elevation difference: | 575 feet |
| Distance: | 2.5 miles (one way) |
| Difficulty: | Moderate |
| Avalanche hazard: | Low for 2.5 miles; higher thereafter |
| Map: | USGS 7.5 Minute, Chair Mountain |

From Carbondale, drive 22 miles south on Colorado 133 to the McClure Pass summit and park on the left (south) side of the highway. This wide and popular route is an old logging road just off the McClure Pass summit. It gets heavy use, especially on weekends, so you need to be alert for skier traffic, especially fast-moving skiers on their return to the trailhead. If it's views you want, views you'll get on clear days, because the changes in the road's course mean that, at times, you can see the Crystal River Valley, Mt. Sopris, the Elk Mountains,

The rustic cabin part-way up Babbish Gulch is available for overnight rentals. *Photo by Claire Walter.*

Chair Mountain and the peaks of the Raggeds Wilderness. The route's essentially southward course is detoured with some big bends.

Start hiking toward the south. Soon the road makes a gentle jog to the southwest. The climb is a steady one. About 1.2 miles from the trailhead, the route makes an abrupt left turn to head southeast, and then, after about 0.75 mile, a second left turn that sends the compass needle around again as you head northeast. The road also gets steeper here and passes a couple of gates. Most people turn around at about 2.5 miles, at or near the intersection with the Ragged Mountain Trail to return by the same route.

## If You Want a Longer Hike

If you do continue, be sure to stay on the road, because after the next right turn, there are some avalanche areas above to the left.

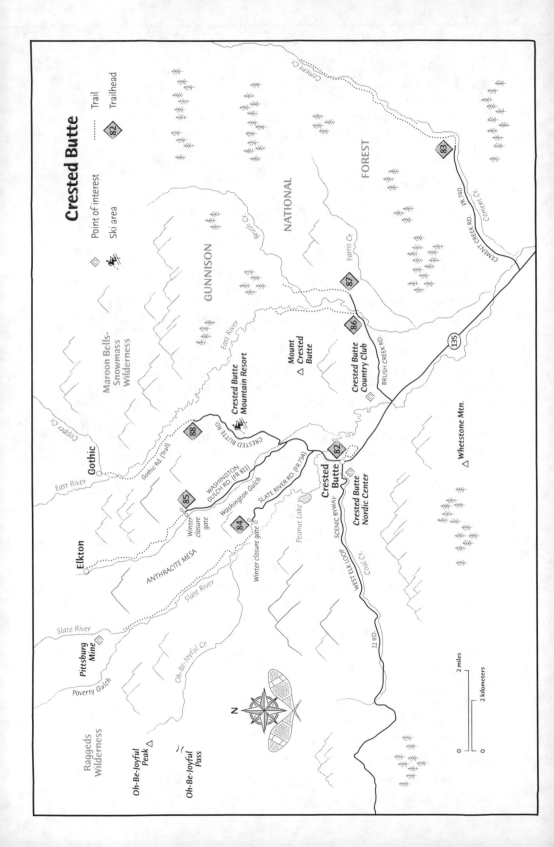

# Crested Butte

Crested Butte is both the name of a precious gem of a Victorian town and its namesake ski and mountain resort nearby. Together, they are cutting-edge outdoorsy. In addition to regular skiing and snowboarding preeminence, this is where modern telemarking was born. It is also America's unofficial capital of extreme skiing, hosted the first ESPN Winter-X Games in the Rocky Mountains in 1998 and ranks as one of the country's great mountain biking centers. The town of Crested Butte nestles alluringly in a high valley. False-front Victorian buildings house fine restaurants and nice shops along Elk Avenue, the main commercial street, while brightly painted homes trimmed with gingerbread are found on the side streets and historic outbuildings line the alleys. Heaps of plowed snow add to this idyllic Currier & Ives scene. Crested Butte Mountain Resort is the name of the ski resort just north of town. (Mt. Crested Butte, the high pinnacle above

The broad valley at the beginning of the Slate River Gulch Trail. *Photo by Claire Walter.*

the slopes, is what inspired the entire resort's name.) Alpine skiers like the base-of-the-lifts convenience of the resort's condos and hotels. Free shuttle buses connect the old town and the newer center.

Surrounded on three sides by four wilderness areas—Raggeds, West Elk, Maroon Bells-Snowmass and Collegiate Peaks—Crested Butte is the gateway to some of Colorado's prime backcountry as well. Many old mining roads provide safe routes directly into gorgeous valleys. Some are open to snowmobilers, while others are limited to nonmotorized recreational activities. For those who prefer snowshoeing in a controlled environment, the local cross-country ski center welcomes snowshoers. The mountain resort launched into snowshoeing during the 1998–1999 winter season, and guided excursions are easy to book as well.

For tourist information, contact **Crested Butte/Mt. Crested Butte Chamber of Commerce, P.O. Box 1288, Crested Butte, CO 81224; (800) 545-4505** or **(970) 349-6438.**

## Getting There

From Denver, there are two options. The first is to take Interstate 70 west to the Copper Mountain exit and then follow U.S. 91 south to Leadville, where it merges with U.S. 24, and continue through Buena Vista to Poncha

Springs. The other is to take U.S. 285 southwest over Kenosha Pass into South Park. From Colorado Springs, follow U.S. 24 west into the southern section of South Park. At Johnson Village, Highway 285 merges with U.S. 24. The combined 285/24 highway heads south to Poncha Springs, where you must turn right (west) on U.S. 50. Continue over Monarch Pass to Gunnison. Then take Colorado 135 north to Crested Butte. The distance from Denver is 200 miles and from Colorado Springs is 170 miles.

## Maps
USGS 7.5 Minute, Mt. Axtell, Gothic, Oh-Be-Joyful
Trails Illustrated #131 Crested Butte, Pearl Pass; #133 Kebler Pass, Paonia
USFS Gunnison National Forest
Gunnison Country Cross-Country Ski Map

## *Crested Butte Nordic Center*

Few mountain communities have a trail system right in town that so quickly leads away from the sights and feeling of being in the middle of everything. Located just three short blocks from Elk Avenue, the bustling main street, the Crested Butte Nordic Center is located right at the edge of all the downtown action but remains removed from it. You can snowshoe in the morning, stroll over to one of the fine Elk Avenue restaurants at midday, and return to work your lunch off with more snowshoeing in the afternoon. Or, you can pick up a picnic lunch on your way to the trails and not see civilization until you're ready to call it quits.

The Crested Butte Nordic Council, which runs the center, grooms three loop systems, totaling between 15 and 20 miles, and charges a trail access fee. Snowshoers are permitted on all skating lanes, and rental snowshoes are also available in the Nordic Center's day lodge. You'll

find two of the most popular trails nearby. You can climb up a small connector trail to the Bench, a plateau overlooking town. There you will find the 3-kilometer (1.9-mile) **Electric Loop** and the 3.5-kilometer (2.2-mile) **Big Mine Loop,** both directly accessible from the lodge. At first, when you pass the scattering of hillside homes, you feel as if you are snowshoeing in the cusp of residential development. But a curve in the trail here, a few feet of elevation difference there and you are away

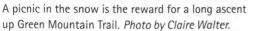
A picnic in the snow is the reward for a long ascent up Green Mountain Trail. *Photo by Claire Walter.*

from it all. The Big Mine Loop also links into the **Green Mountain Trail,** a public trail south of town. Three additional loop trails—**Red Lady, Magic Meadows** and **Keith's Revenge**—are connected to each other but not to the two other trails. The Nordic Council also grooms the 2.5-kilometer **Town Ranch Trail** (see below) and its onward connection to the Crested Butte Country Club trail system.

The Nordic Center also offers half-day, full-day and moonlight tours and puts on the popular **Alley Loop Race,** a long-established cross-country race of various lengths through Crested Butte's picturesque alleys, which now also has a snowshoeing category. It is held in early February. For information on the Nordic Center or the race, contact the **Crested Butte Nordic Council,** P.O. Box 1269, Crested Butte, CO 81224; (970) 349–1707.

# 82. Town Ranch Trail

| | |
|---|---|
| Starting elevation: | 8,910 feet |
| Highest elevation: | 8,910 feet |
| Elevation difference: | Negligible |
| Distance: | 1.6-mile loop |
| Difficulty: | Easy |
| Avalanche hazard: | None |

When locals talk about Echo Ranch, they are referring to what is now officially called the Town Ranch, bought by the Crested Butte Land Trust as open space and a recreational buffer between the old town and subdivisions now springing up nearby. To reach the trailhead for this free 2.5-kilometer snowshoeing and skiing loop, which is located in a huge meadow, turn east onto Red Lady Road at the large "Welcome to Crested Butte" sign at the entrance to town. Drive through the stop sign and around the school to the trailhead.

The Town Ranch Trail is not only short, about 1.5 miles—but there is even a bailout halfway around the loop. It is virtually flat and ideal for first-timers, timid snowshoers and even the mobility impaired. The trail is groomed by the Crested Butte Nordic Council, and snow-shoers are asked to stay off the classical tracks. Use of this easy trail may be free, but the views are priceless. Dogs are permitted on this trail, so even your pooch can enjoy the panorama.

## Crested Butte Country Club

If snowshoeing on wide open meadows and surrounding hillsides appeals to you, check out this private club. This is a golf course, so it has some of the finest fair-weather terrain you can find, with flats, rolling hills and spectacular views of Mt. Crested Butte, the Elk Mountains and down-valley. On low-visibility, high-wind days, a more sheltered trail system is a better bet. Set on a rolling plateau just south of town, the country club offers some 6 miles of groomed cross-country ski trails and permits snowshoers on the skating lanes or right next to the groomed lanes. Guided tours, with or without the addition of a gourmet picnic lunch, are available several times a week. Advance reservations are required. Another option is snowshoe workouts, which start with a warm-up, include running or fast walking, a cool-down and stretching. It's a great way to explore the potential of snowshoeing as part of a winter fitness program. Rental snowshoes are available at the pro shop. For information or reservations, call **(800) 628-5496** or **(970) 349-6127**.

## 83. Cement Creek

| | |
|---|---|
| Starting elevation: | 8,960 feet |
| Highest elevation: | 9,828 feet (Italian Creek Road junction) |
| Elevation difference: | 868 feet |
| Distance: | 5.1 miles (one way) |
| Difficulty: | Moderate |
| Avalanche hazard: | Low in lower section; moderate beyond Cement Creek Ranch |

To reach this spectacular trail, take Colorado 135 south from Crested Butte for 7 miles (or north from Gunnison for 20 miles). Turn east at the Cement Creek Road (also Gunnison County Road/Forest Service Road 740); this is a left turn from Crested Butte and a right turn from Gunnison. At the fork in the Crested Butte South subdivision, go straight onto the unpaved road. Continue 4 miles from the highway to the end of the plowed section and begin snowshoeing up the road. Snowmobiles are permitted, which results in a packed trail and smoothes the way, so it is possible for a fit snowshoer to extend his or her range.

The route starts out spectacularly as both the creek and the road thread through a narrow canyon with high rock cliffs on both sides. It is gorgeous and the ascent is steady. After about 0.6 mile, the canyon narrows still more and the creek courses down a rock-strewn ditch just at the edge of the road, as the cliffs press closer. It is a dramatic little cleft between the rock walls. At the top of the steepest section, about a mile from the trailhead, the rock walls suddenly part to reveal a picture-postcard scene of the creek flowing past Cement Creek Ranch against a wonderful mountain backdrop. The hillside to the left of the road is blanketed with aspens, while the broad valley that stretches ahead and to the right is a prototypical Western scene. Just after the ranch you will pass an open gate designating the former winter closure point. Continue along the road, being mindful of private property alongside.

After about 0.5 mile, you will notice a break in the aspens on the left. This is the only avalanche path along this portion of the road. If avalanche hazard is reported as substantial, do not cross below this path. Even with lesser danger, cross below it one person at a time, or turn back just after the ranch, a lovely destination for a shorter hike. Although most snowshoers won't go that far, Italian Creek Road, merging from the right about 5.1 miles from the trailhead, should be your turnaround point, because slide hazard becomes substantial after that. Return the way you came.

### If You Want a Longer Hike

This unpaved road reaches some 9 miles to the northeast, along the north side of Cement Creek, petering out above the timberline at a mine on the side of Mt. Tilton. This is far more than the vast majority of snowshoers would be willing or able to hike (and much farther than is pru-

The Cement Creek Trail leads through a narrow, rock-walled chasm before opening into a high valley. *Photo by Claire Walter.*

dent), but if you want to continue beyond Italian Creek, only do so late in the season when the snowpack is reported to have stabilized.

## *Crested Butte Mountain Resort*

Crested Butte Mountain Resort's new Atlas Snowshoeing Center, launched in 1998–1999, is located in the Gothic Building at the base of the lifts. Details had not been ironed out at this writing, but the resort expected to offer guided snowshoe tours, designate specific snowshoeing-only trails on the mountain, sell single-ride lift tickets and offer rental equipment for those who want to go out on their own. For a guided tour schedule and other snowshoeing information, call **(970) 349-2240**.

## *Adventures to the Edge*

Jean Pavillard, an internationally certified and licensed Swiss mountain guide, and his wife Mary Pavillard-Cain run this guiding and outfitting service. If you're so taken by the backcountry that you want to enhance your outdoor skills, check out their specialty courses, which include avalanche training, winter mountaineering or even guide training—among the best and most respected in the West. But Adventures to the Edge also has a gentler side, with customized half- and full-day snowshoe excursions and overnight tours for all levels. They have access to a private back-country A-frame and a yurt, guide hut-to-hut trips for the hardcore and also have experience in helping people with mobility impairments enjoy the winter outdoors. **Adventures to the Edge, P.O. Box 91, Crested Butte, CO 81224; (800) 349-5219** or **(970) 349-5219.**

## Alpineer Tours

This outdoor and mountaineering retail shop has been organizing free group snowshoe outings since the 1995–1996 winter season. At this writing, groups depart from the store on Sundays at 10:00 A.M. and Wednesdays at 1:00 P.M., but this is subject to change. Full-moon excursions are also occasionally scheduled. The store sells and rents snowshoes, but again as of this writing was offering free demo models for participants in these outings. All ability levels are welcome, but reservations are strongly suggested. **The Alpineer, 419 Sixth Street, Crested Butte, CO 81224; (970) 349-5210.**

## The Pioneer

The Pioneer is 2 miles east of the highway on Cement Creek Road—just 10 miles but light-years away from Crested Butte Mountain Resort. A charming main house and four quaint cabins dating back to the 1930s remain from the Pioneer Ski Area, Colorado's first ski area with chairlift service. Four more cabins were built in the 1970s, long after the ski area had closed. They now comprise a small year-round resort with direct backcountry access and special appeal for thrifty snowshoers. Nightly rates are low, and each cabin has kitchen facilities. You can snowshoe right out the door, exploring the old ski area's ghost trails leading up to an old warming cabin at the top of the original lift, which was adapted from an old mine hoist.

Michael Martin, whose family owns this small resort, has a Forest Service permit to lead snowshoe tours in winter (and mountain bike tours in summer). His tours are available both to ranch guests and outside guests seeking customized half- or full-day or overnight excursions into the Gunnison National Forest. **The Pioneer, Cement Creek Road, Crested Butte, CO 81224; (970) 349-5517.**

# 84. Slate River Gulch

| | |
|---|---|
| Starting elevation: | 8,920 feet |
| Highest elevation: | 9,100 feet (at Oh-Be-Joyful Road) |
| Elevation difference: | 180 feet |
| Distance: | 2 miles (one way) |
| Difficulty: | Easy to moderate |
| Avalanche hazard: | Low |

From the four-way intersection in Crested Butte, take Gothic Road toward the ski resort (north), but turn left (northwest) after 1 mile onto Slate River Road (Gunnison County Road 734). Drive 3.5 miles to the plowed parking area just beyond Nicholson Lake. The first 0.5 mile has virtually no history of avalanche activity. In normal years, the hazard is low, but in times of severe slide conditions, some paths do cross this road, so be wary.

From the trailhead, climb up the bank and begin snowshoeing up the road. The beginning of the route passes an open area and climbs slightly. After about 0.25 mile, you will come to a small blank signboard and fork in the trail. You can take either path, because they pass on opposite sides of a small, forested knob and meet shortly in a wide portion of the valley. As you proceed up-valley, on the left is Schuylkill Ridge and on the right is Anthracite Mesa.

Slate River Gulch offers easy-street snowshoeing and first-rate scenery. *Photo by Claire Walter.*

The road climbs gently but steadily to the northwest, always in the direction of tantalizing views of the Paradise Divide and the beautiful summits of the Raggeds Wilderness, and gradually draws closer to the river that winds sinuously through the valley bottom below. If you want to get closer to the river and perhaps take a break or have a picnic not far from the trailhead, the Gunsight Pass Road (Forest Service Road 585), to the left at about 1.1 miles, is an ideal place to do so. Otherwise, continue as far up the valley as you wish. The junction with the Oh-Be-Joyful Road (Forest Service Road 754), about 0.5 mile farther, is a good turnaround point. Return the way you came.

### If You Want a Longer Hike
The Slate River Road continues to the Pittsburg town site and mine, a total of about 5 miles and about 500 vertical feet from the trailhead. However, as you continue up-valley, you need to be concerned about slide potential, and don't even consider going past the town site.

## 85. Washington Gulch

| | |
|---|---|
| Starting elevation: | 9,400 feet |
| Highest elevation: | 9,900 feet |
| Elevation difference: | 500 feet |
| Distance: | 2.3 miles (one way) |
| Difficulty: | Moderate |
| Avalanche hazard: | Low |

From the four-way intersection in Crested Butte, drive up Gothic Road for 1.7 miles and turn left onto County Road 811 (Washington Gulch Road). Continue 2.6 miles to the end of the plowed section near the Meridian Lakes subdivision. The temporary Quonset hut on your left is a snowmobile parking shelter for one of the most-used snowmobile trails around Crested Butte. If sharing the trail troubles you, select another route, but you can avoid some of the snowmobile traffic by bearing left at the "Skiers" sign about 1 mile from the trailhead.

In the 1880s, when Crested Butte was a gold mining town, much of the $350,000 worth of gold credited to it came from Washington Gulch mines. Today, the riches are all scenic and recreational. From the parking area, begin snowshoeing up the unplowed road, which bears northwest. The trail initially drops down into a long basin, passes through a fence and then begins ascending gently up the long, sparsely treed valley. You are just one drainage north of and higher than Slate River Gulch (see page 172), so the mountain on your left is Anthracite Mesa. The one on your right is Gothic Mountain, and you should be aware that in heavy snow years, avalanches have been known to break off this mountain and occasionally reach the road. About 2.3 miles from the trailhead, you will pass through a second fence with a small hill topped by a clump of trees ahead. You can just see the top of White Rock Mountain, poking above the saddle between Gothic Mountain and Snodgrass Mountain. This spot makes both for lovely views and a reasonable turnaround point.

## If You Want a Longer Hike

The Elkton Huts are about 6 miles from the trailhead and at an elevation of 10,700 feet. A local outfitter and guide service, **Adventures to the Edge,** leads overnight tours to the huts and also handles overnight bookings for those who would like to travel independently (see page 171). If you want to continue on your own, and if the slide hazard is reported to be low, follow the road as it contours first around Gothic Mountain and then around Elkton Ridge. You will drop into a deep ravine at about 3.5 miles, and you need to factor in two fairly steep ascents when assessing your fitness for this route. The first comes at about 3 miles from the trailhead, and the second is just before the Elkton Huts. Many people are tired from a long tour when they arrive there, which is one reason the huts are popular for overnights.

Snowshoe the Ditch Road
for solitude and scenery.
*Photo by Claire Walter.*

## 86. Ditch Road

| | |
|---|---|
| Starting elevation: | 8,900 feet |
| Highest elevation: | 9,050 feet |
| Elevation difference: | 150 feet |
| Distance: | 1.75 miles (one way) |
| Difficulty: | Easy |
| Avalanche hazard: | Low |

Take Colorado 135 south from Crested Butte and turn left at the Crested Butte Country Club sign onto Brush Creek Road. Continue straight onto the unpaved section instead of turning toward the country club. This is Forest Road 738, which you will find on USFS maps, but currently it has no sign. It bends to the left (east). Park in the plowed lot to the left, 3.6 miles from the highway, as directed by the "Trailhead Parking—No Parking Beyond This Point" sign. The trailhead is at the north end of the parking area.

Begin walking north along the Ditch Road, which is flat and gentle, paralleling a fence line that marks a private property boundary. On your left is the bottom of the massif on which the Crested Butte ski area is located, and up and out of sight is the summit of Mt. Crested Butte itself. But your eyes will be drawn to the beautiful valley to your right to a Marlboro Country setting of achingly picturesque ranch buildings, grazing cattle and snow-covered pastures, through which the East River gracefully flows.

The Ditch Road's gentle grade is between the aspen-covered hillside and the beautiful valley. After about 0.75 mile, you will pass through a fence and climb slightly into mixed woods of aspen, brush and conifers, alternating with small clearings. You might have to find a snow bridge to cross the small stream flowing down from the left. Soon the road bends to the right, crosses a footbridge and peters out in a meadow of breathtaking vastness, with the Teocalli Mountain, its slopes horizontally striped in the gray and white that characterize the Maroon Bells range, as a dramatic backstop. Return the way you came.

## 87. West Brush Creek Road

| | |
|---|---|
| Starting elevation: | 8,900 feet |
| Highest elevation: | 9,200 feet |
| Elevation difference: | 300 feet |
| Distance: | 3.7 miles (one way) |
| Difficulty: | Easy to moderate |
| Avalanche hazard: | None in lower Brush Creek Valley; moderate to high beyond |

There's more than a touch of Marlboro Country to the beautiful Brush Creek Valley near Crested Butte. Several snowshoeing routes fan out from a trailhead at the bottom of Brush Creek Road. *Photo by Claire Walter.*

Follow the directions to the parking lot for the Ditch Road trailhead (see page 175), but return on foot to the vehicle road and begin walking or snowshoeing 0.7 mile east past the Cold Spring Ranch to the end of the plowed section. Respect private property on both sides of the road, which at nearly 1.5 miles round-trip makes a fine and ultra-gentle beginner snowshoe walk. The route is also used by snowmobiles and even winter horseback riders, so you will appreciate the flexibility and convenience of snowshoes on a choppy snow surface.

At the ranch, bear left (north) to stay on West Brush Creek Road (the continuation of Forest Service Road 738), which is an easy route along the valley floor. You can snowshoe for some 1.7 miles, crossing the stream, after which you will see the entire gorgeous valley, originally named the Brush Creek Cow Camp. The view of 13,208-foot Teocalli Mountain in the Maroon Bells-Snowmass Wilderness gets better with every step. The cow camp makes a good turnaround point if you want scenery without any real workout. After that, the road begins to climb very gradually. After about a mile, you will come to a fork with Middle Brush Creek Road, a second good turnaround point. Whichever way you choose and however far you go, retrace your tracks on the way back.

## If You Want a Longer Hike

You can either bear left at the fork to continue along West Brush Creek Road (this part is Forest Service Road 738-2A) or right for Middle Brush Creek Road (Forest Service Road 738). If you take the former, you will be following the West Brush Creek streambed, with Teocalli Ridge rising to your right (east). Turn around at the junction with Forest Service Road 528 on the left, because after that, potential avalanche activity increases. The latter trail follows East Brush Creek into a tighter, more slide-prone valley.

# 88. Gothic Road

| | |
|---|---|
| Starting elevation: | 9,300 feet |
| Highest elevation: | 9,640 feet |
| Elevation difference: | 340 feet (including 290 feet of gain; 280 feet of loss) |
| Distance: | 5 miles (one way) |
| Difficulty: | Moderate |
| Avalanche hazard: | High |

Located "behind" Crested Butte Mountain Resort, this is one of the most gorgeous areas around Crested Butte. It is a popular ski tour too, and at times tracks are even set across the grand valley. However, in times of avalanche danger—especially in December and January of most winters—it is also one of the most potentially hazardous areas, particularly near the northeast sides of Snodgrass and Gothic Mountains. The scenery cannot be beat and the modest elevation gain won't beat you up, but always check avalanche conditions if you plan to try it. In no case should you consider continuing past Gothic to Schofield Pass.

To reach the trailhead, drive past Mt. Crested Butte and park at the plowed area at the end of the road. Begin snowshoeing along the unplowed road, which angles up the hillside, with Snodgrass Mountain above you on the left and the East River in the valley below on the right. The route heads to the northwest and ends in the old mining town of Gothic. If you make it all the way, be sure to stay on the road as you look at the town site, as there is private property on both sides. The round-trip is a long one on snowshoes, mitigated only by the modest elevation change. One cabin in Gothic can be rented overnight; contact the Crested Butte Nordic Center for details.

A less avalanche-prone parallel route, with a trailhead behind the Crested Butte Stables, follows the right side of the river and also leads to Gothic. Skiers consider it quite a bit more difficult, but it's not so much of an issue for snowshoers. You can either do an out and back or make a loop. If there are any doubts about safety in this area, choose someplace else entirely.

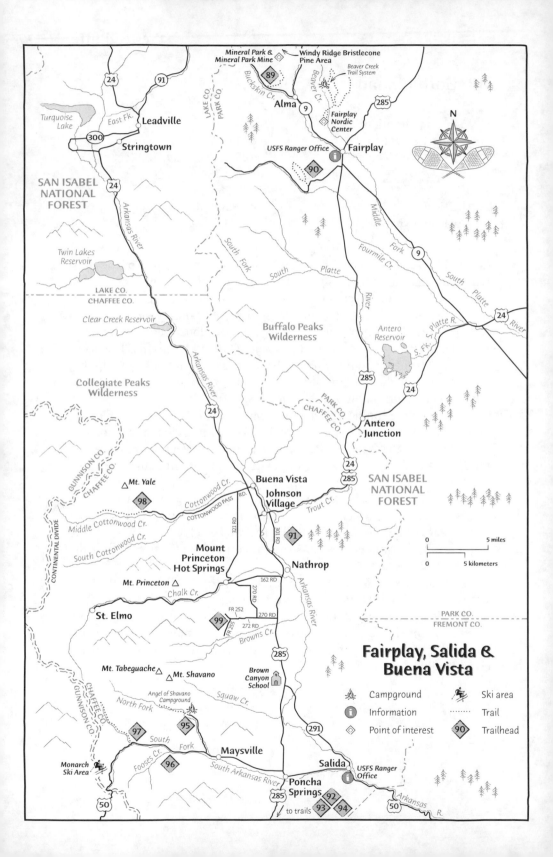

# Fairplay, Salida & Buena Vista

- **24** / **91** / **300** / **285** / **9** / **50** / **291** — (highway markers)

## Labels

- Turquoise Lake
- Leadville
- East Fk.
- Stringtown
- SAN ISABEL NATIONAL FOREST
- Twin Lakes Reservoir
- Arkansas River
- LAKE CO. / CHAFFEE CO.
- Clear Creek Reservoir
- Collegiate Peaks Wilderness
- GUNNISON CO. / CHAFFEE CO.
- CONTINENTAL DIVIDE
- △ Mt. Yale
- **98**
- Cottonwood Cr.
- COTTONWOOD PASS RD.
- Middle Cottonwood Cr.
- South Cottonwood Cr.
- Buena Vista
- Johnson Village
- Mount Princeton Hot Springs
- Mt. Princeton △
- Chalk Cr.
- 321 RD.
- 301 RD.
- **91**
- Nathrop
- 162 RD.
- 270 RD.
- FR 252
- 272 RD.
- 270 RD.
- **99**
- St. Elmo
- FR 255
- Browns Cr.
- Mt. Tabeguache △
- △ Mt. Shavano
- Angel of Shavano Campground
- North Fork
- Squaw Cr.
- Brown Canyon School
- **95**
- **97**
- South Fork
- **96**
- Fooses Cr.
- Maysville
- South Arkansas River
- Monarch Ski Area
- CHAFFEE CO. / GUNNISON CO.
- Salida
- USFS Ranger Office
- Poncha Springs
- 285
- to trails
- **92** / **93** / **94**
- Arkansas R.
- PARK CO. / FREMONT CO.
- Buckskin Cr.
- PARK CO. / LAKE CO.
- Mineral Park & Mineral Park Mine
- Windy Ridge Bristlecone Pine Area
- Beaver Creek Trail System
- Beaver Cr.
- **89**
- Alma
- Fairplay Nordic Center
- USFS Ranger Office
- Fairplay
- **90**
- South Fork
- South Platte
- Middle Fork
- Fourmile Cr.
- River
- Buffalo Peaks Wilderness
- Antero Reservoir
- S. Fk. S. Platte R.
- South Platte River
- PARK CO. / CHAFFEE CO.
- Antero Junction
- SAN ISABEL NATIONAL FOREST
- N

## Legend

- 🔥 Campground
- ℹ️ Information
- ◇ Point of interest
- 🎿 Ski area
- ⋯⋯ Trail
- **90** Trailhead

Scale:
- 0 — 5 miles
- 0 — 5 kilometers

# Fairplay

Compared to the northern part of Colorado, there is far less easily accessible public land, and therefore there are fewer trails, close to the cities of the southern part of the Front Range. This means that some of the most attractive snowshoeing trails are something of a drive. This community has access to some interesting and varied trails.

Fairplay is in South Park, which is not just a fictitious setting conjured up for the controversial TV cartoon of the same name. It is a real place. This enormous valley—40 by 30 miles, or roughly three-quarters the size of Rhode Island—is fringed by mountains and sparsely populated by ranchers and cattle. It is surrounded by newly booming counties and

Family snowshoe outings into the beautiful backcountry are the stuff of which memories are spun. *Photo courtesy Tubbs Snowshoe Company.*

is beginning to get some spillover development, yet it still has a sense of timelessness and great open space. When you drive through it on U.S. 285 or U.S. 24 between the Front Range and the central Colorado Rockies, you are overwhelmed by the sense of vast emptiness.

The South Platte River angles through the valley, but unless you are right at its banks, you are hard-pressed to spot it even from a short distance across the flat landscape. Winter is different in South Park than it is in the high country or in other, more temperate river valleys. An old-timer's saying goes: "It never snows in South Park, but a hell of a lot of snow blows through." In the winter, powerful winds often sweep across plainslike South Park, raking the ground of snow and depositing it on the lee sides of fences, ridges and barns. Such a "ground blizzard" is a curious and disorienting weather phenomenon when you're driving through it. On clear days, however, you can see South Park's beauty, a huge expanse ringed with snowy mountains and capped by a Colorado-blue sky.

Prospecting, mining, saltworks and lumbering all played their roles in the history of South Park and the nearby mountains, but today it is somnolent and rural. The Mosquito and Park Mountains to the north and the Tarryalls to the east offer not just scenic but also recreational possibilities, often without crowds. Fly fishing, hiking, camping and four-wheeling are the major attractions during the warm months, with winter a distant second in terms of popularity. Fairplay, tucked into South Park's northwest section, is the only town of note; even at that, it is more village than town, especially in winter, when tourism slows to a trickle. For tourist information, contact the **Park County Tourism Office, P.O. Box 220, Fairplay, CO 80440; (719) 836-4279.**

### Getting There

From Denver, take U.S. 285 southwest over Kenosha Pass into South Park. Fairplay is about 85 miles from the metro area and is the jumping-off point for some of the best snowshoeing venues. You can also reach South Park from Interstate 70 by driving south from Breckenridge on Colorado 9 over Hoosier Pass. From Colorado Springs, also about 85 miles, follow U.S. 24 west into the southern section of South Park. From the west, the route is via U.S. 24 through Leadville and Buena Vista.

### Maps

For USGS maps, see individual trail descriptions
Trails Illustrated #110, Leadville, Fairplay
USFS Pike National Forest
Eagle Eye Maps, Frisco-Breckenridge Cross-Country Skier's Map
(formerly Trails Illustrated)

## Beaver Creek Trail System

The Beaver Creek Trail System north of Fairplay is a near-secret network of excellent winter trails. One unplowed road on which snowmobiles are permitted (but which few snowmobilers actually use) and three adjacent loops total about 15 miles. To reach it, take Fourth Street northeast out of the center of Fairplay. After four blocks, turn left onto Bogue Street at the Fairplay Nordic Center sign. This street becomes Bear Creek Road (Park County Road 659). Pass the cross-country center, which does not permit snowshoeing, and continue to the parking area at the end of the plowed section. Begin snowshoeing up the road.

The first and shortest loop, aptly called the Short Loop, is to the left, just after the gate and cattle guard. It arcs over relatively tame terrain and rejoins the main road after 1.6 miles. On the other side of the main route (right, as you come up from the trailhead), the Crooked Creek Trail begins. It is marked with an orange diamond and the number 4. This trail leads over a ridge and down into the Crooked Creek Valley where it splits into two loops, a 5-mile trail to the right that also is marked with an orange diamond and a 4-mile trail to the left, which is marked with an orange diamond and the number 7. The only slide zone on this system under normal conditions is at the far, narrow end of the trail marked 7, so avoid it if avalanche hazards are reported. The return to the main trail is over the ridge. Farther up the last loop, which is marked with an orange diamond and the number 3, is a scenic 3-miler. It is the most challenging option along the Beaver Creek Trail System but also the most scenic. It ascends through heavy timber to a high spot on the ridge, just below treeline, which in clear weather offers views of the Mosquito, Tenmile and Sangre de Cristo Ranges, truly one of Colorado's most spectacular panoramas.

## Moonlight Tours

Forest Service rangers lead bimonthly full-moon hikes on various trails in the Fairplay district throughout the year. In winter, some of these are snowshoe hikes, while others are cross-country ski tours. All are free. You can get information on the schedule and make reservations, which are recommended, by calling the U.S. Forest Service, Fairplay Ranger Office, (719) 836-2031.

# 89. Windy Ridge Bristlecone Pine Scenic Area

| | |
|---|---|
| Starting elevation: | 11,060 feet |
| Highest elevation: | 11,400 feet (Mineral Park Mine) |
| Elevation difference: | 340 feet (to Mineral Park Mine) |
| Distance: | 3 miles (one way) |
| Difficulty: | Moderate |
| Avalanche hazard: | Low |
| Map: | USGS 7.5 Minute, Alma |

The Windy Ridge Bristlecone Pine Scenic Area is on the southeastern side of 14,172-foot Mt. Bross, Colorado's 22nd highest peak. But this trail is not about climbing this popular fourteener. It is about exploring a little-traveled winter route through one of Colorado's first mining areas to see one of the true natural wonders of the high country. The gnarled, twisted bristlecone pines, which resemble giant bonsai, are nature's oldest living things. They can survive for thousands of years in the harshest climates of aridity, high winds and lofty elevations (conditions you may find on your snowshoe hike).

From Fairplay, drive 7 miles northwest on Colorado 9, and from Breckenridge, drive south over Hoosier Pass to Alma. Turn west onto Park County Road 8, which is usually plowed for 3 miles to the old Paris Mill. Begin snowshoeing up the Dolly Varden Road (Forest Service Road 787). This is the first road on the right (north) from the parking area and is marked with a "Bristlecone Scenic Area" sign. Snowmobiles are permitted on the road, which passes many remnants of mining activities and old cabins as it ascends steadily toward the east for about a mile. It bends to the left (northeast) and, after 1.4 miles, ascends a ridge before dropping slightly to cross Sawmill Creek, where it curves to the right. If the weather is uncertain, Sawmill Creek makes a good turnaround spot. Otherwise, a couple of additional wide curves lead to Dolly Varden Gulch and the Mineral Park Mine, just below the bristlecone area. Return the way you came.

### If You Want a Longer Hike

Because you are so close to tree-line, continue up Windy Ridge for a closer view of the bristlecones only when the snowpack is reported stable and the winds are not too strong. You can figure on a total elevation gain of up to 700 feet and a one-way distance of 3.5 to 4 miles from the trailhead, depending on when you turn back. This promotes the trail rating to "Challenging" because of the distance and the elevation.

## 90. Tie Hack Trail

| | |
|---|---|
| Starting elevation: | 9,980 feet |
| Highest elevation: | 10,640 feet |
| Elevation difference: | 660 feet (plus many ups and downs) |
| Distance: | 5.5 miles (loop) |
| Difficulty: | Moderate |
| Avalanche hazard: | Low |
| Map: | USGS 7.5 Minute, Fairplay West |

From the Fairplay intersection of U.S. 285 and Colorado 9, continue south on U.S. 285 for 1.2 miles and turn right (west) onto Park County Road 18, which is also known as the Fourmile Creek Road. Bear right at the fork and continue for a total of 3.5 miles from the turnoff to a parking area on your right. This trail was named for the workers who cut timber to make the ties on which railroad tracks were laid. In this case, it commemorates the tie hacks who built the Denver, South Park & Pacific Railroad across the wide valley, but the route actually incorporates not railroad track but part of an old stagecoach road that served the old Horseshoe and Sacramento mining camps. Horseshoe is the name of a present-day Forest Service summer campground.

The trail is shaped like an elongated and slightly irregular lollipop. You snowshoe up the stick and then make your way around the sweet part in either direction. The lollipop stick heads northwest about 1 mile from the trailhead and may have iffy snow conditions, but the cover improves as you climb toward the loop, which is marked by blue diamonds. Be sure to follow these blazes, because there are several junctions with other old roads that can throw you off the trail. At the marked intersection, pick your direction. If you snowshoe clockwise, you will start with a steeper climb and descend on a gentler portion of the loop on your return—and vice versa if counterclockwise is your choice.

If you decide to go clockwise, bear left at the signs and climb up a steep section of the trail. Pass a Sheep Mountain sign after 0.5 mile to reach a fork after another 0.4 mile. The trail to the left leads to the old Horseshoe mining camp site, but to continue on the loop, bear right (north). You will soon reach the high point of the trail and the apex of the loop, where it bends sharply to the right. Bear right again at the next fork. The blue markers will lead you back down through the trees and some clearings to complete the loop. Turn left and descend via the lollipop stick by which you came up.

## 91. Bassam Park

| | |
|---|---|
| Starting elevation: | 7,800 feet |
| Highest elevation: | Varies |
| Elevation difference: | Varies |
| Distance: | Varies |
| Difficulty: | Easy to moderate |
| Avalanche hazard: | None |
| Maps: | USGS 7.5 Minute, Castle Rock, Emich |

We were in a bit of a quandary about whether to put this under "Fairplay" or "Salida and Buena Vista" Access is on the Arkansas Valley side of Trout Creek Pass, but it is also closer to Fairplay. From Fairplay, take U.S. 285 over the pass. After about 4 miles, turn left onto Chaffee County Road 187/Forest Service Road 215, which soon becomes County Road 185. From Buena Vista or Salida, take U.S. 285 north for about 6.5 miles to Chaffee County Road 187/Forest Service Road 215. Follow the road south for about 7 miles to Bassam Park.

This is not so much a trail or trail system as it is a winter playground for snowshoers, snowmobilers and cross-country skiers—and there's plenty of elbow room for all. When the snow is deep, it's a powder pig's paradise of open areas, wooded places, hills and dramatic rock formations, all ripe for free-form exploring.

# Salida and Buena Vista

Snow-covered peaks of the Sawatch Range.
*Photo by Claire Walter.*

With the Arkansas River at its feet and the fantastic mountainscape of the Sawatch Range as its western backdrop, the Upper Arkansas Valley is in a charmed location. Its two main towns, Salida and Buena Vista, enjoy excellent valley weather and mountain access. The towns' (relatively) low elevations and (relatively) mild climate dovetail beautifully with the power, beauty and pleasures of Colorado's beefiest mountains, which are a short drive away. For après-snowshoeing soaking, the region's open-to-the-public hot springs beckon, including Salida Hot Springs and Princeton Hot Springs. Salida and nearby Buena Vista combine into the West's biggest summer whitewater rafting and kayaking mecca, so winter is low season. And although snow-covered mountains and two ski areas (Monarch and Ski Cooper) are close by, this is not by any stretch a ski resort area, so prices remain reasonable. For regional tourist information, contact the **Chaffee County Visitors Bureau, P.O. Box 726, Salida, CO 81201; (800) 831-8596; www.colorado.com/ chaffee;** or call **(800) 228-7943** for the activities hotline. Another website with regional tourist information is **www.vtinet.com/14ernet.**

## Salida

Unlike many early transportation centers that are located along rivers, Salida grew up with the railroads. It was a key division point for the Denver & Rio Grande, where the Leadville line spurred off from the main line. When the railroad pulled out, Salida stagnated. That resulted in the preservation of much of the quaint old town center, mainly because no one had the money to do much modernization. As a result, the heart of Salida is a noteworthy National Historic District. Now revitalized, the downtown hums with interesting restaurants, shops and galleries. In fact, it has become something of an art community, and the combination of creativity and sporty outdoorsyness adds to its distinctive qualities.

For tourist information, contact the **Heart of the Rockies Chamber of Commerce, 406 West Rainbow Boulevard, Salida, CO 81201; (719) 539-2068.**

## Getting There

From Denver, there are two choices. The most popular is the 150-mile drive via U.S. 285 southwest to Poncha Springs, and then east 4 miles on U.S. 50 to Salida. The other is Interstate 70 west to Copper Mountain, south on U.S. 91 to Leadville, south on U.S. 24 to Poncha Springs and east on U.S. 50 to Salida. Colorado 291 angles off to the southeast from U.S. 285 north of Poncha Springs to become the main commercial thoroughfare in Salida. From Colorado Springs, take U.S. 24 west to U.S. 285 and continue as above. From Pueblo, take U.S. 50 west, which skirts the southern part of town. Each is about a 90-mile trip.

## Maps

USGS 7.5 Minute, Mount Ouray, Poncha Pass
USFS San Isabel National Forest

## *Trails South of Salida*

From downtown Salida, go west on U.S. 50 to the intersection with U.S. 285 at Poncha Springs. Turn left (south) and drive south for 5.1 miles. Turn right (southwest) onto Chaffee County Road 200. The road soon crosses the unmarked county line, where the number changes to Saguache County Road 201. It is not paved, but is plowed to several trailheads.

# 92. Old Railroad Grade

| | |
|---|---|
| Starting elevation: | 8,690 feet |
| Highest elevation: | 8,800 feet (at Forest Service Road 201B trailhead) |
| Elevation difference: | 110 feet |
| Distance: | 2.3 miles (one way) |
| Difficulty: | Easy |
| Avalanche hazard: | None |

From the turnoff, drive 2.6 miles to the Shirley Site, a large, plowed parking area on the left. From the parking area, walk 0.2 mile along the road to a bridge marked Forest Service Road 201A. Cross the bridge and bear right (southwest) onto the wide, flat old railroad bed that parallels the county road on which you drove in. Snowshoe along this pretty and gentle route as far as you like and return the way you came, or do this mellow walk as a minor car shuttle, leaving another vehicle at the Forest Service Road 201B access (see page 186).

# 93. Road 201B/C

| | |
|---|---|
| Starting elevation: | 8,800 feet |
| Highest elevation: | 9,360 feet |
| Elevation difference: | 560 feet |
| Distance: | 1.5 miles (one way) |
| Difficulty: | Moderate |
| Avalanche hazard: | None |

From mid-trail, Road 201 'C displays views of Chipeta M untain and nearby peaks. *Photo by , Sandberg.*

At the turnoff from U.S. 285, drive 4.1 miles (passing the Shirley Site at 2.6 miles) and pull as far off the road as you can when you see a bridge marked Forest Service Road 201B/C. Snowshoe across the bridge along the Old Railroad Grade (see page 185), then bear right across the open area to a wooded hillside. If you look closely, you will see an orange diamond affixed to one of the trees. This marks the start of a lovely trail along a summer road, roughly paralleling Silver Creek, which offers more bang for your buck than almost any other trail in this guide. It is accessible to snowmobiles, but you probably won't see any sledders, skiers or even other snowshoers on this little-used jewel of a trail.

The route, which is marked by occasional orange blazes, alternates moderately steep pitches with rather flat sections. As you gain elevation, you will pass through a beautiful forest of conifers and aspen as it contours around a hillside and gains elevation. The trees open up now and then for fi views of Mt. Ouray, Chipeta Mountain, Sheep Mountain and other high aks. But, as the cliché goes, "You ain't seen nothin' yet." After you pass e marked intersection with the Rainbow Trail, a summer hiking trail, and just before you reach an old fence line, turn left and bushwhack up the hill to the rounded top.

As you ascend, you may wonder why you bothered with the "summit" of a nonpeak. The answer is in the views. When you look to the north, you will see 14,229-foot Mt. Shavano leading the procession of the mighty Sawatch Range. Turn around and gaze to the south, where the magnificent Sangre de Cristo Range soars above the San Luis Valley. On a clear day, you will probably be able to see more fourteeners from this spot than any other in this guide.

## 94. Beaver Creek

| | |
|---|---|
| Starting elevation: | 8,680 feet |
| Highest elevation: | 9,600 feet (to the ridge above Poncha Creek) |
| Elevation difference: | 920 feet |
| Distance: | 2 miles (one way) |
| Difficulty: | Moderate to challenging |
| Avalanche hazard: | Low |

From the Shirley Site parking area, cross the road and snowshoe south-west along Poncha Creek for about 0.25 mile (either along the road or on the north side of the creek, avoiding any possible snowmobile traffic), to the point where Beaver Creek enters Poncha Creek from the northwest. Turn into the Beaver Creek drainage, and follow the road up-canyon and then up to the ridge that separates Beaver Creek from Poncha Creek. Snowmobiles are not permitted on Beaver Creek.

The route switchbacks through varied ecosystems, starting with meadows at the bottom of the trail near the creek and snaking up to Alpine vegetation to the left (south) and sagebrush desert flora to the north (right). As you climb, you will have increasingly excellent views of the mountain, including the Sangre de Cristo Range.

### Trails West of Salida

Salida is temperate, but just a few miles to the west and a few thousand feet higher, the snows fly early and pile up deep. Storms blow over Monarch Pass and dump onto the mountains and valleys east of the pass. Take U.S. 50 west of Salida to access several excellent trails.

### Maps

USGS 7.5 Minute, Maysville, Garfield
Trails Illustrated #130, Salida, St. Elmo, Shavano Peak
USFS San Isabel National Forest

## 95. North Fork

| | |
|---|---|
| Starting elevation: | 9,160 feet |
| Highest elevation: | 10,760 feet |
| Elevation difference: | 1,600 feet |
| Distance: | 4.5 miles (one way to Shavano) |
| Difficulty: | Moderate to challenging |
| Avalanche hazard: | Low |

From Salida, drive west on U.S. 50 through the hamlet of Maysville, for about 10 miles (7 miles from Poncha Springs). Turn right (north) on Chaffee County Road 240. If you can, continue 5 miles to the trailhead at the Angel of Shavano summer campground. If the road is not plowed past the last residences, you may add nearly a mile to your hike and subtract that much from the drive if you have to pull over sooner. Snow-mobiles also use this road, but not heavily.

Begin snowshoeing up the summer four-wheel drive road that heads northwest, paralleling the North Fork of the South Arkansas and Mt. Shavano, rising on your right. At times, the road skirts the side of a deep, forested valley. Other stretches are lined with dramatic rock walls. The views keep changing and include Shavano and Mt. Tabeguache. The road contains a few moderately steep sections, especially during the first mile, but then becomes gentler as it approaches the ghost town of Shavano, which not only provides a gonzo workout but also is the safest section. (The road does go on for another 5 miles through some dicey, avalanche-prone areas, eventually reaching the North Fork Reservoir, but it should be avoided in winter.)

## 96. Fooses Creek

| | |
|---|---|
| Starting elevation: | 8,800 feet |
| Highest elevation: | 9,580 feet |
| Elevation difference: | 780 feet |
| Distance: | 2.6 miles (one way) |
| Difficulty: | Easy to moderate |
| Avalanche hazard: | Low |
| Maps: | USGS 7.5 Minute, Maysville, Garfield |

This is everyone's favorite snowshoeing route. It's gentle enough for beginners, long enough for experienced snowshoers and wind protected during stormy days for everyone—and part of the Colorado Trail as well. To reach it, drive west on U.S. 50 approximately 9 miles from Poncha Springs. Turn left (southwest) onto Chaffee County Road 225, which is marked for Fooses Creek. At the bottom of the hill, turn left, cross the wooden bridge and continue to the plowed parking area. Snowmobiles are prohibited on this trail.

The beginning of the route is the easiest, most sheltered part—the one favored by families and beginning snowshoers and skiers. Aspen, pine, sage and juniper flank various parts of this attractive trail, which alternates forests and open areas. Follow the gently climbing route west alongside Fooses Creek, which is on your left for more than 2.5 miles. After another

0.25 mile, cross the creek and continue to a fork where the trail divides into North Fooses and South Fooses, which makes a good turnaround spot.

### If You Want a Longer Hike
The North Fooses Trail, on the right, is the flatter of the two and also the more popular, for the same reason that people like Fooses in the first place. Because of former logging activity, it leads past new-growth forest, mostly pine. There are even occasional views east to Salida. The left fork is the South Fooses Trail, which is also part of the Colorado Trail, passing first through conifers and then through willows and offering fine views of Mt. Shavano and Taylor Mountain. It is a good continuation of this lovely route—at least for the first mile, which is safe. After the trail climbs a small rise and drops into a large meadow, it enters a slide-prone area and should be avoided at any time when hazardous avalanche conditions are reported.

Signing in at the trailhead register near the Angel of Shavano Campground. *Photo by Claire Walter.*

## 97. Middle Fork

| Starting elevation: | 9,680 feet |
| --- | --- |
| Highest elevation: | 10,900 feet |
| Elevation difference: | 1,220 feet |
| Distance: | 2.5 miles (one way) |
| Difficulty: | Challenging |
| Avalanche hazard: | Low for the first 2.5 miles; higher thereafter |

The trailhead is 13 miles west of Poncha Springs and 16 miles west of Salida. Pass the Monarch Mountain Lodge and park. On the right, you will find two trailheads very close together. The second one is Middle Fork Road, marked as Chaffee County Road 230. It heads northwest toward the Continental Divide. The first half mile of this road, which is also used by snowmobiles, is the steepest. After you leave this breath-sapping stretch, you can relax and hike along as the trees become thinner, and "breathtaking" replaces "breath-sapping" as the adjective of choice. The scenery is stunning, with Mt. Etna, Taylor Mountain, Vulcan Mountain and Clover Mountain arrayed around you. After about 2.5 miles you will come to two old cabins. Turn around there, for the avalanche danger beyond can be severe.

## Snowshoe Tours

Snowshoeing guides who call Salida home take clients into favorite routes in the nearby Sawatch Range. Mountain Spirit Adventures' half- and full-day programs can be tailored for various levels and interests: beginners or families with small children, people wanting a naturalist orientation or experienced hikers looking for the day's best trail conditions. Guide Terry DuBeau has special expertise with small children, seniors, women-only groups and people with developmental or physical disabilities. She includes equipment (she likes Baldas snowshoes from France), a snack on a half-day tour and also lunch on a full-day program. Her most popular itineraries end with a stop in the tasting room of the **Mountain Spirit Winery. Mountain Spirit Adventures, P.O. Box 26, Salida, CO 81201; (719) 530-0914.**

American Adventure Expeditions, formerly Monarch Mountain Guides, offers a range of snowshoe programs, from half-day beginner tours to multiday backcountry adventures, with or without winter mountaineering or ice climbing instruction. The outfitter is located in and shares an address with **Headwaters Outdoor Equipment, 228 North F Street, Salida, CO 81201; (800) 288-0675** or **(719) 539-4680.**

## Stay Inn Style

Bed-and-breakfast inns abound in Salida's wonderful Victorian neighborhoods as well as the surrounding countryside. Some, like the **Century House (719-539-7064)** and the **Gazebo Country Inn (719-539-7806),** are picture-pretty Victorian mansions within strolling distance of the center of town. One, the **Thomas House (719-539-7104),** was a railroad boarding house. Still another, the stately **River Run Inn (800-385-6925** or **719-539-3818),** is the former county poorhouse, but what a B&B it makes, with twelve-foot ceilings, antique furnishings and million-dollar mountain views.

# Buena Vista

Buena Vista's most famous sports are whitewater rafting and kayaking on the Arkansas River, and many outfitters are located there. But it is also fourteener central, with commanding views of some of Colorado's beefiest peaks. Mt. Princeton, a compelling hulk of a mountain, lies west of town and, with its neighbors, Mt. Harvard, Mt. Columbus and Mt. Yale, comprises the Collegiate Peaks portion of the mighty Sawatch Range. The land between U.S. 24 and the mountains offers some fine gentle snowshoeing terrain, while other more demanding routes lie in high valleys between the mountains. Just east of the highway's motel and gas station strip is the funky charm of downtown Buena Vista—which, by the way, locals for some mysterious reason pronounce as "Byoonah Vista." For tourist information, contact **Greater Buena Vista Area Visitors Center, 342 South Highway 24, P.O. Box 2021, Buena Vista, CO 81211; (719) 395-6612; www.fourteenernet.com.**

### Getting There
Follow the same route as for Salida. Buena Vista is along U.S. 24, about 25 miles north of Salida. Whether you take U.S. 285 from Denver or drive via Leadville, the distance to Buena Vista is about 125 miles; it is about 100 miles from Colorado Springs.

### Maps
USGS 7.5 Minute, Mt. Yale
Trails Illustrated #129, Buena Vista, Collegiate Peaks; #130, Salida, St. Elmo, Shavano Peak
USFS San Isabel National Forest

## 98. Collegiate Peaks Campground

| | |
|---|---|
| Starting elevation: | 9,000 feet |
| Highest elevation: | 9,000 feet |
| Elevation difference: | Negligible |
| Distance: | Varies |
| Difficulty: | Easy |
| Avalanche hazard: | None |

From U.S. 24 directly in the center of Buena Vista, drive west on Cottonwood Pass Road (Chaffee County Road 306) for 10.6 miles. Pull out at the sign to the Collegiate Peaks Campground, which is unplowed. The road for the campground and the flat areas to and around the campsites and picnic areas are excellent for those first steps on snowshoes or for exploring with small children on big feet.

## 99. Evans-Rush Trail Area

| | |
|---|---|
| Starting elevation: | 8,560 feet |
| Highest elevation: | Varies |
| Elevation difference: | Varies |
| Distance: | Varies |
| Difficulty: | Easy |
| Avalanche hazard: | None |

From U.S. 24 between Buena Vista and Salida (via Colorado 291), drive west on Forest Service Road 270, which shoots arrow-straight toward the mountains. Proceed straight at the four-way stop sign, passing through

Mount Princeton dominates the scenery at the Evans-Rush Trail Area, a scenic and appealing venue for families and novice snowshoers. *Photo by Ral Sandberg.*

widely spaced pines, to the intersection with Forest Service Roads 272 and 274, where you will see a sign for Evans-Rush Cross-Country Ski Trail on the south side of the parking area. This popular trail was named for local skiers Art Evans and Keith Rush, who were killed in an avalanche on January 14, 1975.

We are not going to suggest snowshoeing along this trail, which includes a demanding climb and descent of Mt. Antero's eastern flank that is taxing enough for skiers without the distraction of snowshoers. We are going to suggest an exploration, within sight of the parking area, of the area around the skiers' trailhead as an ideal place for first-time snowshoers or young children. You can prowl around among the trees, climb a small roll a few hundred feet north of the parking area or go west a short way on Forest Service Road 274, continuing a mile or more along Raspberry Gulch Road (Forest Service Road 273) or Eddy Creek Road (Forest Service Roads 274 and 274A). These roads are level, flat and easy to follow, yet they offer incredible mountain views. Return the way you came.

# 4

# NORTHERN COLORADO

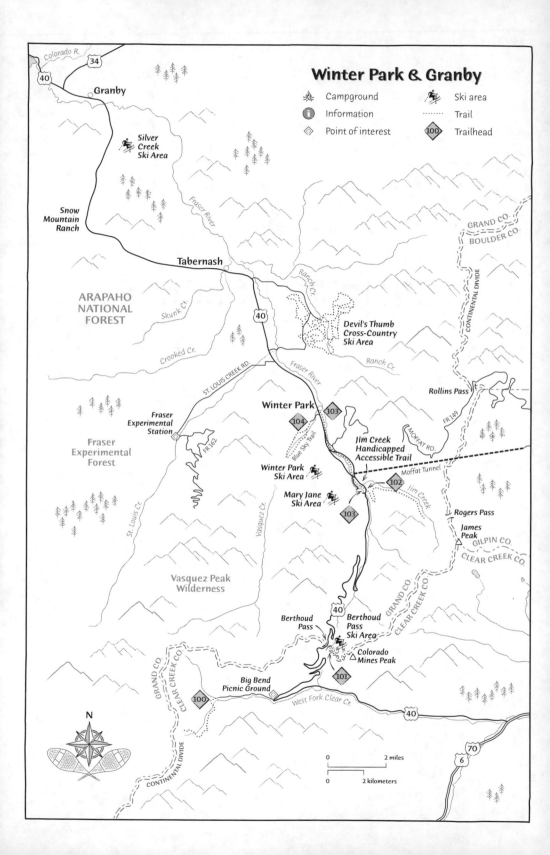

# Winter Park and Granby ━━

This vast valley, just a crow's flight from the busy Front Range, has an amorphous image. Locals think Middle Park when they consider the huge basin reaching from Berthoud Pass north to Granby and west to Hot Sulphur Springs. Alpine skiers think of it as Winter Park and not much more. Grand County is the governmental entity that administers Middle Park and environs. However you think of it, consider that this area, so close to metro Denver yet separated from it, is a winter recreationist's paradise of rugged, snow-blessed mountains and pastoral valleys. It offers a rare combination of full resort amenities, uncrowded backcountry routes and wide open spaces.

Berthoud Pass, an 11,315-foot mountain pass, is the southern gateway into Middle Park. It is also the name of Colorado's first lift-served ski area, built in 1938 at the crest of the pass, on the Continental Divide. Later on, larger resorts, including neighboring Winter Park, eclipsed it. Little Berthoud Pass foundered and even closed for six years. During this period, Berthoud Pass became a backcountry skier's and snowboarder's haven, and so it has remained, even when the lift service returned in early 1998. The Winter Park resort, at the bottom of Berthoud Pass, is one of Colorado's most popular ski areas and a summer mountain biking mecca as well. It introduced on-mountain snowshoe tours before the activity really caught on. Many of the bike trails translate perfectly to snowshoeing, and the local mountain bike map is therefore an excellent winter resource too. The resort is now poised for major real estate development at the base of the lifts.

Middle Park is a scenic wonder. The Indian Peaks and Never Summer Ranges comprise its eastern wall, the Gore Range is to the west and the Rabbit Ears Range to the north and the Colorado River runs through it. Most of Middle Park is controlled by either the U.S. Forest Service (Arapaho National Forest) or the Bureau of Land Management, so development will occur just in limited areas. Amid all these soaring peaks are lots of open space and a sprinkling of small towns. Winter Park, which is still little more than a commercial strip along U.S. 40 rather than a town or village with a definable center, caters to skiers and other visitors, and Fraser is getting a bit touristy too, but Granby and Hot Sulphur Springs remain unspoiled and laid-back hamlets that haven't yet put on resort airs. Grand Lake (see Rocky Mountain National Park—West Side chapter, page 209) is part of Grand County too and a winter sports center in its own right. For overall Grand County visitor information, contact **Grand County Tourism Board, P.O. Box 36, Winter Park, CO 80402; (800) 729-5821, (800) 247-2636, (970) 726-5387;** or check the website at **www.grand-county.com.**

### Getting There
U.S. 40 is Middle Park's main street, with Winter Park, Fraser, Tabernash, Granby and Hot Sulphur Springs strung out along it. To reach it, take Interstate 70 west to Exit 232. Drive though Empire (slowly, for this is a well-known speed trap) and over Berthoud Pass. Winter Park is 67 miles from Denver. Continue along Highway 40 to the other towns, or turn right (east) onto U.S. 34 for Grand Lake.

### Maps
For USGS maps, see individual trail descriptions
Trails Illustrated #103, Winter Park, Central City, Rollins Pass
USFS Arapaho National Forest

# Empire and Berthoud Pass

Empire, a tiny hamlet on U.S. 40, is only one place between Interstate 70 and Winter Park where you can get a tank of gas, a cup of espresso or a speeding ticket. Local businesses are geared to fuel travelers, and the local constabulary is alert for drivers who try to pass through too fast. Empire is not in Middle Park, but it is at the southern gateway.

## 100. Butler Gulch

| | |
|---|---|
| Starting elevation: | 10,320 feet |
| Highest elevation: | 11,350 feet (timberline) |
| Elevation difference: | 1,030 feet |
| Distance: | 2 miles (one way) to timberline |
| Difficulty: | Challenging |
| Avalanche hazard: | Low to moderate, including some easily avoided slide paths |
| Map: | USGS 7.5 Minute, Berthoud Pass |

You can reach this trailhead and route before driving over Berthoud Pass (from Denver), which many people consider a good thing, plain and simple. Locals know the pass can be slick, and it is also closed periodically for avalanche control work. To reach Butler Gulch, take U.S. 40 through Empire and make a sharp left at the first hairpin turn at 7.3 miles, exiting just as the road starts steeply up toward the pass. Follow the plowed road paralleling the west fork of Clear Creek to the parking area across from the large Henderson Mine complex.

Begin snowshoeing up a heavily used, unplowed road. At 0.25 mile, take the left (south) fork and climb for about 0.5 mile. Cross the creek as it cuts through a meadowed area before beginning an even steeper ascent to and through the trees. The route hairpins to the left and then bends to the right to head south, and the gully widens into a huge basin enfolded in a panorama of high ridges and peaks. The left side (east) is the safest route into this basin, because there are slide run-outs on the right. Telemark skiers and snow-boarders often continue hiking past the treeline to make a few powder runs. Stay to the side when you are snowshoeing on a narrow part of the route, because skiers move fast on the downhill.

The best time for snowshoeing here is on a nonholiday midweek day, because the route is also very popular with snowmobilers and cross-country skiers. The right fork soon after the trailhead leads to Jones Pass Road, which is more difficult, has more snowmobile traffic and has significantly more avalanche hazard areas and is therefore not recommended—except perhaps in midweek and only when snow conditions are reported to be stable.

## 101. Colorado Mines Peak

| | |
|---|---|
| Starting elevation: | 11,315 feet |
| Highest elevation: | 12,934 feet |
| Elevation difference: | 1,619 feet |
| Distance: | 1.3 miles (one way) |
| Difficulty: | Moderate to challenging |
| Avalanche hazard: | Low to moderate |
| Maps: | USGS 7.5 Minute, Berthoud Pass, Empire |

Many people who drive over Berthoud Pass have looked up at the distinctive communications towers high above the east side of the road without a clue as to the name of the rounded mountain on which they perch. It is the Colorado Mines Peak, undramatic and undistinguished as Colorado mountains go, but a worthy destination that offers more altitude than attitude. An unpaved service road from just beside the Berthoud Pass parking area to these towers makes a good snowshoe route. If avalanche hazards are reported to be low, you can ascend well above the treeline on a route whose challenge comes from a high elevation and often rough winds.

Now that the Berthoud Pass ski area is operating again, you can get a hot drink, make a pit stop, buy a tube of sunscreen or even rent snowshoes at the ski area lodge. The traditional way to begin your hike is by snowshoeing up the road to the right of the chairlift, but you can save yourself the first 400 vertical feet by buying a single-ride ticket and hiking over to the nearby trail when you get off the lift.

The service road's switchbacks on the south side of the lift make long loops through the woods. Shortly after the chairlift's unloading station, the switchbacks are farther apart. As you climb above the timberline, the views get better and better, first on the left, then on the right. But even as the views improve, the stronger winds may get. The slope here is steep but steady, so when the snowpack is stable, you can short-cut the hairpins and climb as straight up or down as you wish. If you make it to (or even near) the Colorado Mines Peak's 12,934-foot summit, you'll be astonished at how different the communications paraphernalia looks up close from what you might have expected just looking up at it from the pass road below. If you reach the top, you'll be astride the Continental Divide.

# Winter Park and Fraser

Winter Park, on the north side of Berthoud Pass, is Middle Park's winter sports centerpiece. It is well named, for it is one of Colorado's oldest continuously operating ski areas. It has grown from a small winter get-away by the railroad tracks into a huge Alpine skiing and snowboarding center beloved by generations of Coloradans, and now it is poised to develop into a full-fledged resort with lodging at the base. Winter Park's Alpine skiing pedigree is secure, and it has also been a pioneer in embracing snowshoeing as a way to help nonskiers to appreciate the beauty of the mountains. For tourist information, contact **Winter Park/Fraser Valley Chamber of Commerce, P.O. Box 3236, Winter Park, CO 80482; (800) 903-7275, (970) 726-4118** or **(303) 422-0666 (metro Denver); www.winterpark-infocom/wpfv.**

## 102. Jim Creek

| | |
|---|---|
| Starting elevation: | 9,220 feet |
| Highest elevation: | 10,060 feet (end of road) |
| Elevation difference: | 840 feet |
| Distance: | 2.5 miles (one way) |
| Difficulty: | Moderate |
| Avalanche hazard: | Moderate in places but avoidable |
| Maps: | USGS 7.5 Minute, Fraser, East Portal |

This is the first fine snowshoeing route on the north side of Berthoud Pass. It is easy to reach from the Front Range, as well as for Winter Park visitors. Not surprisingly, it is therefore very popular. The trailhead is at the parking area marked "Bonfils-Stanton Foundation Nature Trail," on the right (north) side of U.S. 40, directly across from the first Winter Park entrance, the next one past the Mary Jane access road as you are driving north. On weekends, the Bonfils/Jim Creek parking lot is often filled up and you may have to park on the road.

The Jim Creek trail starts on a wide, smooth four-wheel-drive road that connects to the official trailhead via a short connector on the south side of the plowed parking area. On the map, it looks like a straightforward trail, heading east and paralleling Jim Creek, but despite its popularity and its deceptively easy configuration, stream crossings and clearings sometimes make it tricky to follow, especially after a midweek snowfall when there has not been much traffic. The first section of the trail follows the south side of the creek, where you will see many signs of human activity, as it passes close to a summer campground, under a large green aqueduct that is part of the Denver water system and a junction with a road to a dam. Novices or anyone looking just for a shorter, or at least flatter, hike can simply follow this aqueduct road out and back as far as they like. Turning right (southwest) leads back to U.S. 40, 1.5 miles from the intersection. Turning left (east) takes you out of the Jim Creek drainage and leads to a junction with the (also) unplowed Rollins Pass Road, 3.5 miles farther.

However, continuing straight through the aqueduct intersection is the main route for this hike. After the junction, the steadily climbing Jim Creek road narrows and makes one short, sharp bend to the left, about a mile from the trailhead, and then straightens out again, continuing east past creekside willow thickets and into a thick forest of spruce and fir away from the stream. The trees periodically open up into clearings with tantalizing views. About 1.3 miles later, you will enter an open meadow, the last on the most popular part of the route, where you can see an avalanche chute across the creek. Stay on the right (south) side of the creek to avoid this chute. Soon after that, a large snowbank usually builds up, blocking the right side of the trail.

## If You Want a Longer Hike

Most snowshoers and skiers turn around here, but if you climb up the bank and continue heading east, still following the stream, you will ascend steadily until you reach a large clearing with a great view of James Peak dead ahead. This extension is as much as 4 miles from the trailhead and 600 feet higher, which is a far more spectacular end to a hike.

## 103. Fraser River Trail

| | |
|---|---|
| Starting elevation: | 8,574 feet |
| Highest elevation: | 9,000 feet |
| Elevation difference: | 426 feet |
| Distance: | 2 miles (one way) |
| Difficulty: | Easy |
| Avalanche hazard: | None |
| Maps: | USGS 7.5 Minute Fraser, West Portal |

### Ski Train

The Winter Park Ski Train, which operates Fridays, Saturdays and Sundays from mid-December until early April, is a Colorado tradition. For decades, it has ferried skiers between Union Station in downtown Denver and Winter Park. In recent years, it has become popular with cross-country skiers, sightseers and, increasingly, snowshoers. The ride is a two-hour show-stopper through 29 tunnels, including the 6.21-mile Moffat Tunnel under the Continental Divide. Just as you enter the tunnel at East Portal, you'll even see the parking area where skiers and snowshoers get set for their treks in that area. You detrain directly at Winter Park's slopes, with additional access to other snowshoeing areas by free shuttle buses. For Ski Train details and reservations, call **(303) 296-4754.**

The Fraser River Trail is a paved multi-use recreational trail that totals 5 miles in length and stretches down-valley as far as Fraser, but the 2 miles between the town of Winter Park and the base of the Winter Park ski area generally offer the best conditions for snowshoeing. There are several access points in Winter Park, including a crossing of U.S. 40. From the town end, the trail is just east of the highway and west of the Fraser River. The trail closely parallels the road and leads through stands of trees and intermittent meadows before crossing the river. At the intersection with the Corona Pass Road, it traverses the highway to the west side for its final gentle climb, paralleling the railroad tracks directly to the ski area base. You can do the Fraser River Trail out and back from either direction, or under good snow conditions, follow it to Fraser. If you want to do it one way, Winter Park's free buses can take you back to your starting point.

## 104. Blue Sky Trail

| | |
|---|---|
| Starting elevation: | 8,790 feet |
| Highest elevation: | 9,290 feet |
| Elevation difference: | 500 feet |
| Distance: | 1.6 miles (one way) |
| Difficulty: | Moderate |
| Avalanche hazard: | Low |
| Maps: | USGS 7.5 Minute, Fraser; Winter Park-Fraser Mountain Bike Map |

This trail, a key part of Winter Park's summer mountain bike system, is used by cross-country skiers and snowmobilers as well as snow-shoers. Its popularity is understandable, given its easy access, for its start is less than a mile north of downtown Winter Park. From U.S. 40 west, turn left (southwest) on Vasquez Road for 0.4 mile, crossing the railroad tracks, and then left again onto Arapaho Road for another 0.4 mile to the Little Vasquez trailhead.

Start up Little Vasquez Trail, staying on the trail and passing two intersecting trails that come in on the left. After just 200 yards, cross the bridge over the creek and then take the next trail, which is Blue Sky. It begins climbing steadily south through the trees. The trail ends 1.4 miles from the bridge at an intersection with the Denver Water Board road that is part Vasquez Cut Trail system (straight and to the left) and the Vasquez Ford Trail (right). Return the way you came.

### If You Want a Longer Hike
It is also possible to make a loop by continuing straight ahead until you reach a T-intersection. Turn right onto Big Vasquez Road and descend to the next intersection, where you turn left onto Grand County Road 159 to return to Winter Park. The total distance is 7 miles, with additional vertical to be considered too.

## Winter Park Ski Area

Snowshoers are permitted on all trails within the resort's boundaries at no charge, but several stand out. If you snowshoe up the Corridor, a connector trail from the southern end of the 9,000-foot Winter Park base to the northern end of the 9,450-foot Mary Jane base, it is safest to stay on the far left side of the trail to give fast-moving skiers plenty of room for their descent. Take a free shuttle bus back to your starting point instead of snowshoeing down with your back to descending skier and snowboarder traffic. Another nice route is a loop combining Turnpike

### Winter Park Snowshoe Race

The Winter Park Snowshoe Race is held each January. It is cosponsored by the Town of Winter Park and Beaver Village Lodge, which is at the edge of downtown Winter Park. The event includes 5- and 10-kilometer races for men and women, and a 1-kilometer kids' category. For information, contact **Beaver Village Lodge, P.O. Box 43, Winter Park, CO 80482; (970) 726-5741.**

and 300 Yard Walk, two of the several novice ski trails on the north end of the Winter Park section of the ski area. The same caution applies here, especially on much-used Turnpike: Keep to the edge of the trail. The legions of beginning skiers who use it may have a hard time steering around upward-bound snowshoers. 300 Yard Walk, which passes the top of Winter Park's ski jumps, is so flat that it's little used by skiers and presents few problems for snowshoers.

For a high-mountain experience without a major climb, consider a guided snowshoe tour. Groups leave the base area at 10:30 A.M. and 1:00 P.M. daily for a two-hour trek through the woods on summer mountain-biking trails and game trails near Discovery Park. The fee includes use of Redfeather snowshoes and poles, as well as a one-ride lift ticket. Information and reservations are available at the Tour Center desk in Balcony House at the Winter Park base or by calling **(970) 727-5514, Ext. 1727.**

## Fraser Experimental Forest

This vast tract of land snugs beneath the Continental Divide in the Vasquez Mountains. There is just one road entry, Grand County Road 73, which is a spur off U.S. 40 in Fraser, but it offers some 25 miles of unplowed roadways that become winter recreational trails. Snowmobiles are permitted on the east side of this access road, while only nonmotorized activities are permitted on the west side. You'll find a medley of short loops, long one-way trails, flats and steeps, but rarely will you encounter crowds. **Spruce Creek Trail, Deadhorse Trail** and **West St. Louis Creek** rank among the best snowshoeing trails. The Fraser Experimental Forest is tucked in behind the vast Winter Park Ski Area, but in winter it feels remote and isolated.

## Devil's Thumb Ranch

Known as one of America's premier cross-country ski centers, Devil's Thumb Ranch is gaining a reputation as an extraordinary snowshoeing center as well. Snowshoers are permitted on more than 100 kilometers (that is, more than 60 miles) of cross-country ski trails, just as long as they stay off the classical tracks. But the best part are three truly wonderful snowshoeing trails, flagged so that snowshoers can wind their way through the forest, studying the animal tracks in the snow, traversing the meadows among the trees and enjoying the unsurpassed tranquillity without becoming disoriented or concerned about getting lost.

If you are a beginner, you can't find a better trail than the **Creekside Trail,** a gentle route connecting two mellow Nordic trails with a crossing of Ranch Creek. If you are experienced and like a little climbing, you have two more challenging options. **Blackhawk,** which Devil's Thumb's pros nickname **Black Five** because of its length, is 5 kilometers (3.1 miles). It has everything: steady climbs, welcome descents, sinewy sections snaking through a beautiful ponderosa pine forest, straightaways across open meadows and those wonderful views for which Devil's Thumb is known. **Moose Stomp** is the longest of the three snowshoeing trails, a languorous loop of nearly 7 kilometers (almost 5 miles) that offers a matchless assortment of everything a

Devil's Thumb Ranch is a well-known cross-country center whose version of a red carpet is dedicated snowshoe trails. *Photo by Claire Walter.*

trail in this area can have: ponderosa pines, willows along a creek and glorious stands of aspen. A spur trail adds 0.5 mile and a climb to Vista Point at the 9,075-foot summit of Marker Hill, the highest point on the trail system.

Devil's Thumb can be a day trip for Front Range snowshoers, a change of pace from nearby Winter Park's Alpine slopes or a vacation destination in its own right. The resort component comprises a handful of small and charming cabins and a few lodge rooms that accommodate a small number of guests in a relaxing setting, and the Ranch House Restaurant & Saloon is gaining a reputation for fine food. The ranch operates a free weekend shuttle to Winter Park and Fraser, including connections to the Ski Train. The shuttle runs on demand at other times, so staying there does not mean mandatory isolation. Contact **Devil's Thumb, P.O. Box 750, Tabernash, CO 80578; (970) 726-8231** for snowshoeing information. Call **(800) 933-4339** or **(970) 726-5632** for lodging reservations. For **Ranch House Restaurant** reservations, call **(970) 726-5633**

A couple of special events regularly appear on Devil's Thumb's calendar. The center traditionally hosts the first of the season's Salomon Race Series and its accompanying 5-kilometer **Sherpa Snowshoe Race.** Information and registration materials are available by calling **(970) 726-8231.** The **Wild Hare Snowshoe Race** for women is an annual benefit for the Colorado Coalition Against Sexual Assault, generally in late February. For registration materials, contact **The Sporting Woman, 2902 East Third Avenue, Denver, CO 80206; (303) 316-8392.**

# Granby Area

Granby's town center epitomizes small-town Colorado. It was built on ranching and railroading in what urbanites used to dismiss as the boondocks. Only recently have people begun to value the wide-open-spaces valleys on the northern end of Middle Park. Two of this region's most snowshoer-friendly facilities—Snow Mountain Ranch and Silver Creek Resort—are just off U.S. 40, shortly before you get to the center of Granby.

Snow Mountain Ranch staffer introduces snowshoeing to a school group. *Photo by Claire Walter.*

## Snow Mountain Ranch/YMCA

This huge spread—3,500 acres of forests, meadows and private mountains—is a distinctive resort that isn't a resort, a retreat that isn't tranquil or retreatlike, an educational place that is fun. Church and school groups, families and Elderhostel travelers come to experience winter sports and the winter environment. If you know a teenager on the Front Range, the chances are that he or she has visited Snow Mountain Ranch on such a winter school trip. This is also an excellent cross-country ski center.

Snow Mountain Ranch was one of the first places in the country to commit to snowshoeing. That happened back in the mid-1980s, before snowshoeing was hot, when one of the Y's hiking guides introduced a snowshoeing program to keep his type of activity going in the winter. Now, when school and Elderhostel groups come to Snow Mountain Ranch, an interpretive snowshoeing tour is invariably offered.

Snowshoers are not permitted on cross-country ski trails, but a 300-acre dedicated snowshoe area and three trails totaling nearly 12.5 miles are only for snowshoers and cross-country skiers with dogs. In addition to the trails, the ranch invites—in fact, encourages—people to explore the dense lodgepole forest. If you wander through the woods, look for evidence of wildlife. Just poking around, you can go in any way that seems interesting. It's easy to find your way back to a trail just by going straight in any direction.

Both **Peter's Trail** and the **Dirt Camp Trail** are 3.1-mile loops, and the lower portion of 9 Mile Trail, in combination with the Aspen Grove, makes an even longer route. Peter's is a flat loop through the woods, while Dirt Camp Trail adds a long descent into a shallow creek drainage and a gentle ascent on the other side, plus some open areas with fine views to the north. Capping this snowshoeing network is the **9 Mile**

**Trail,** which is not 9 miles long but ascends to 9 Mile Mountain's 9,681-foot summit. The trail winds west along the edge of the dedicated snowshoe area, before ascending a steep hill called Clint's Climb. When you stop to catch your breath, you can look across the valley, over the crown of aspen trees, to Devil's Thumb and the ragged profile of the Indian Peaks Wilderness's highest summits. And speaking of summits and views, your reward, after another steep climb to the top of 9 Mile Mountain, is a 360-degree panorama.

Rentals are available on-site at Flanagan's Ski Rentals on the ground floor of the Program Building. Trail use is free for overnight guests. A very modest fee, officially a "one-day membership" to the Y, for everyone else includes use of such facilities as the indoor pool and sauna, skating rink and gym. **Snow Mountain Ranch/YMCA, P.O. Box 169, Winter Park, CO 80482; (970) 887-2152 or (303) 443-4743 (Denver line).**

Snow Mountain Ranch was one of Colorado's first to designate a special snowshoeing area. *Photo by Claire Walter.*

## Silver Creek

This small resort is right off U.S. 40, 78 miles from Denver and 13 miles beyond Winter Park. Located on the side of a broad valley surrounded by rounded ridges and gentle hills, Silver Creek isn't so much in the mountains as it is near the mountains. Self-contained, compact and safe, it appeals mainly to skiing families. It's less known as a sweet spot for snowshoers as well. The 40 kilometers (nearly 25 miles) of Nordic trails are groomed but not track-set, so snowshoers are welcome and needn't exercise their usual keep-out-of-the-classical-tracks cautions.

The Alpine skiing is on two modest mountains, with the Nordic trails flared out behind them. You can access them by snowshoeing about 200 vertical feet up Lone Pine Bowl, the gully between these two mountains, by ascending along the sides of any of the 33 ski trails or by purchasing a foot pass, good for two lift rides per day. Most of the trails are laid out as elongated ovals that stretch through the aspen and conifer forest and are linked with short connectors, which provides a great variety of routes. The layout resembles a layer cake. The easiest—Low Road, Middle Road and Long Hill Loop—are on the bottom, stacked one over the other in the open area above Lone Pine Bowl. Enjoy these now, because these gorgeous, sage-studded meadows are slated for development in the next few years. The next layer is composed of the hillier ones—High Road, Silver Spur and Silver Ridge Trails—

and above that is the steeper Cabin Trail, named for the old cabins it passes. The upper trails lace through gorgeous aspen and conifer woods.

You can get a good workout by ascending from Silver Creek's 8,202-foot base to the upper reaches of the trail system, but if you prefer a mellow walk, hop on the Expedition chairlift to save 1,000 feet of climbing. The views from the Silver Ridge Trail at the top of the Expedition chairlift are fabulous, reaching across sagebrush-covered slopes to the Fraser River Valley and the spine of the Continental Divide beyond. The lift ride also saves a lot of time and energy for exploring the lovely trail system and working your way down. Even if you ride up the hill, Cabin Trail crests above the highest lift-served elevation and includes a short, steep section.

The rental shop at the base of the lifts carries snowshoes. Silver Creek periodically puts on snowshoe races and other special events. Women's Workshops every weekend include a morning cross-country ski lesson, an afternoon snowshoeing walk, rental equipment for both activities, lunch and an afternoon social. Reservations are required. **Silver Creek Resort, P.O. Box 1110, Silver Creek, CO 80446; (800) SKI-SILVer Creek (800 754-7458) or (970) 887-3384; www.silvercreek-resort.com.**

## C Lazy U Ranch

Trivia buffs know that the C Lazy U is the nation's highest-rated dude ranch, annually garnering five diamonds from AAA and five stars from the Mobil Travel Guide. But fewer people think of it as a winter haven that sprawls over 2,000 acres of rolling countryside. Ranch guests enjoy about 13 miles of groomed cross-country ski trails, which snowshoers may use. They range from a short half-miler called **Coyote** to the 3.6-mile **Wilson Trail**, which offers gorgeous views of the Willow Creek Reservoir. Some routes cross open meadows, and others slice through thick woods. There are also longer, more challenging backcountry routes, including the demanding Hogback, which may be done only with a ranch guide. Snowshoes are available at the Nordic Nook.

Accommodations are stylish and spacious, as befits so highly honored a property, and the meals are abundant and delicious. Activities and facilities included in package rates include Nordic trail use, winter trail rides, equestrian activities in the ranch's indoor riding arena, outdoor heated swimming pool, ice skating, sledding, tubing, horsedrawn sleighrides, racquetball and even a modest workout facility. Winter is low season at the C Lazy U, as it is at all guest ranches,

The C Lazy U Ranch offers splendid facilities—and scenery to match. *Photo by Claire Walter.*

so a stay in such classy surroundings is a relative bargain. That does not make it inexpensive, but still, when you sit in the main lodge to watch the sunset and see an elk herd coming down the mesa, you'll feel as if you are living a *National Geographic* special, and that you've gotten the best value in the world. **C Lazy U Ranch, P.O. Box 379, Granby, CO 80446; (970) 887-3344.**

# Kremmling Area

Kremmling resembles Granby in that both are small, laid-back commercial centers serving vast rural areas for miles around. It's tall-hat, high-on-a-horse, elbow-stretching country, where you just want to be on the move.

## *Latigo Ranch*

Kremmling is as near to Granby as it is to any other town, and Latigo is as near to Kremmling as it is to any town, which is a way of saying that it is way out in the country. Situated at 9,000 feet on the eastern slope of the Gore Range and with views of the Indian Peaks and Never Summer Ranges, Latigo Ranch is one of Colorado's fine dude and guest ranches that now operate year-round. It has developed a quiet reputation as a Nordic and snowshoeing retreat, both for overnight guests (22 maximum) and for day visitors, who pay a modest trail use fee.

More than 30 miles of groomed track across rolling pastureland and through the woods beckon cross-country skiers and snowshoers. Snowshoers are encouraged to stay on the skating lanes, right next to but not interfering with the classical tracks. In addition, there is a half-mile snowshoe loop right near the lodge for beginners who want to practice snowshoeing before they head out on longer routes, and several snowshoeing trails to scenic points beyond the groomed trail system. Snowshoes are available at the ranch. In addition to the ranch's own 450 acres, snowshoers can explore the adjacent Arapaho and Routt National Forests.

Accommodations are in cozy cabins with wood-burning stoves and separate sitting areas. Packages include all meals, which are traditionally hearty all-American fare, use of such facilities as the hot tub and recreation building and gratuities. For details, contact **Latigo Ranch, P.O. Box 237, Kremmling, CO 80459; (800) 227-9655** or **(970) 724-9008; www.dude_ranch.com.**

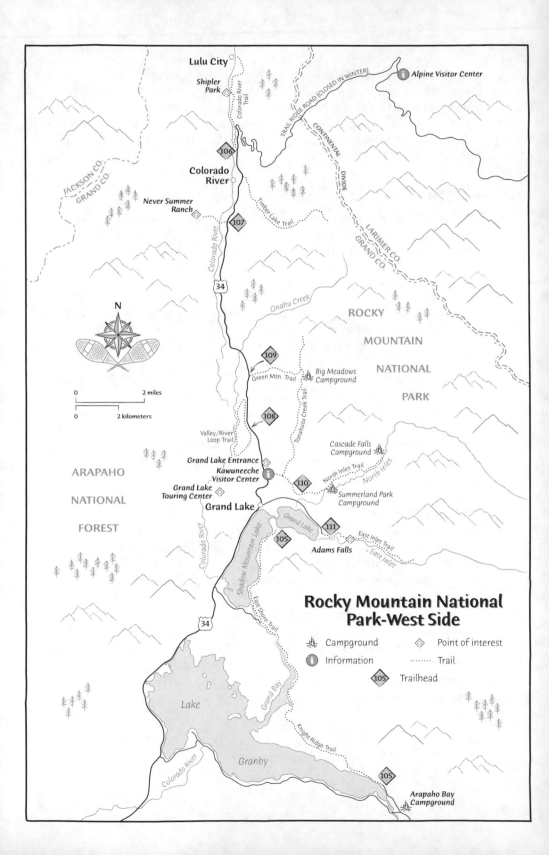

Lulu City

Shipler Park

Colorado River Trail

Trail Ridge Road (closed in winter)

Continental Divide

Alpine Visitor Center

106

Colorado River

JACKSON CO.
GRAND CO.

Never Summer Ranch

107

Timber Lake Trail

LARIMER CO.
GRAND CO.

34

Onahu Creek

ROCKY

MOUNTAIN

NATIONAL

PARK

N

109

Green Mtn. Trail

Big Meadows Campground

Tonahutu Creek Trail

0        2 miles

0        2 kilometers

108

Valley/River Loop Trail

Cascade Falls Campground

North Inlet Trail

North Inlet

ARAPAHO

NATIONAL

FOREST

Grand Lake Entrance
Kawuneeche Visitor Center

Grand Lake Touring Center

Grand Lake

110

Summerland Park Campground

Grand Lake

111

East Inlet Trail

Colorado River

Shadow Mountain Lake

105

Adams Falls

East Inlet

# Rocky Mountain National Park-West Side

East Shore Trail

Campground        Point of interest

Information        ........ Trail

105    Trailhead

Lake

Grand Bay

Knight Ridge Trail

Colorado River

Granby

105

Arapaho Bay Campground

# Rocky Mountain National Park—West Side

The town of Grand Lake and the west side of Rocky Mountain National Park rank among Colorado's best-kept winter secrets. Just two hours and change from metro Denver, Grand Lake remains a low-key charmer, with a casually paved main street, board sidewalks and a dose of uncontrived, laid-back quirkiness. The summer population is 5,000. In winter, fewer than 500 people call Grand Lake

Photo by Claire Walter.

home, and if you spend a few days around town while exploring the nearby trails, you'll quickly begin spotting familiar faces and feeling at home yourself. Grand Lake boasts tourist cabins and inns rather than chain motels, a real downtown instead of strip malls and one-of-a-kind shops and restaurants instead of cloned fast-food joints. As such, it would be a refreshing and appealing place even without the excellent snowshoeing.

In summer, Grand Lake is full of sightseers who drive over Trail Ridge Road (see Rocky Mountain National Park—East Side, page 49) and boaters who come for Colorado's largest natural lake (also called Grand Lake). In winter, the area is a haven for snowshoers, skiers and snowmobilers, but it rarely gets so crowded that these activities are in serious conflict. The Kawuneeche Visitors Center, just inside the park boundary, is open all winter and can provide maps and advice on good snowshoeing routes. If you want trail information, snow conditions or other information on the west side of the park before you arrive, call **(970) 627-3471**. Park rangers lead snowshoe tours on weekends (see page 217). Most of the park is a fee area (a few areas are accessible without charge), and the Grand Lake Entrance Station is just north of the visitors center.

Snowmobilers have discovered Grand Lake, but there's gratifyingly little conflict between motorized and nonmotorized recreation. Many snowmobilers go on organized tours, whose guides know the trails that are best for them. In addition, the park's stringent controls mean that snowmobiles are only permitted on Trail Ridge Road between the winter closure and Milner Pass. Everything else is restricted to nonmotorized activities.

For resort information, contact the **Grand Lake Area Chamber of Commerce, P.O. Box 57, Grand Lake, CO 80447; (800) 531-1019** or **(970) 627-3402; www.grandlakecolorado.com**.

## Getting There

From Denver, take Interstate 70 west to U.S. 40 west (Exit 232) through Empire, over Berthoud Pass through Winter Park and Fraser and past Silver Creek. Turn right (east) on U.S. 34 for 14 miles, which leads north into Grand Lake Village and the western entrance to Rocky Mountain National Park. The total distance from Denver is 102 miles.

## Maps

USGS 7.5 Minute, Grand Lake
Trails Illustrated #200, Rocky Mountain National Park
USFS Arapaho National Forest
USPS Rocky Mountain National Park (free at the visitors center)

# 105. Knight Ridge Trail/East Shore Trail

| | |
|---|---|
| Starting elevation: | 8,280 feet |
| Highest elevation: | 9,070 feet (on Knight Ridge) |
| Elevation difference: | 790-feet, plus many mild ups and downs |
| Distance: | 10.8 miles |
| Difficulty: | Easy to moderate; challenging for entire length |
| Avalanche hazard: | None, except for directly under Shadow Mountain |

This long trail follows the eastern shores of Lake Granby and Shadow Mountain Lake from Arapaho Bay to the village of Grand Lake. Some parts of it fall under the jurisdiction of the U.S. Forest Service, while others are under the U.S. Park Service, so regulations technically vary. For snowshoers, the bottom line is that dogs are prohibited on any but the southern portion of the trail, which is administered by the Forest Service. The route has several access points, so it can be done in segments, either as out-and-back or car-shuttle hikes. Most people don't do the whole route, summer or winter, but it certainly does provide an excellent workout for anyone in training for a snowshoe race or using snowshoeing for serious conditioning.

To reach the southeast end of the trail, take U.S. 34 west 8.9 miles from Grand Lake or east 5.4 miles from Granby. Turn left from Grand Lake or right from Granby onto unpaved Grand County Road 6. Follow it

8.6 miles along the south shore of Lake Granby to the Arapaho Bay Campground entrance and continue for another mile to the parking lot at the Forest Service cabin. The Shadow Mountain Dam access at about two-thirds of the way along the route (from the southeastern end) is closer to town and enables you to avoid the longest, and steepest, section. It is 3 miles from Grand Lake and 11 miles from Granby, with a parking lot just off U.S. 34, on the east side of the highway.

The northern trailhead, just outside the village center of Grand Lake, is the most complicated to reach. From U.S. 34, turn east toward Grand Lake Village. Take the first right and continue down the fill on an unpaved road called Center Drive. Pass the post office and a school. Go straight at the first stop sign, where Center Drive becomes Elk Lane. Bear right at the first "Yield" sign onto Lakeside Drive. At the Hilltop boat launch sign, turn right again and cross a bridge. The parking area and trailhead are 0.4 mile farther on the left. The roads described here lead through residential areas and are confusing, so don't hesitate to get directions while looking for this trailhead.

When you hike the trail from the southeast, the water is always to your left (until you reach the small isthmus between Shadow Mountain Lake and Lake Granby at the far end of the route). From the Arapaho Bay trailhead, cross the Roaring Fork over a wooden footbridge and continue north over a small dike alongside frozen beaver ponds. Enter a lodgepole forest and emerge from the trees as the trail begins ascending the steep and treeless slope above Lake Granby's eastern shore. Above McDonald Cove, the trail steepens as it climbs up Knight Ridge, with switchbacks to ease the climb. This is the highest part of the trail, and the views from the top are excellent. The 1.5-mile ridge-top section leads through fine aspen groves. You will probably see elk and deer tracks, and perhaps also some herds. On the descent from the ridge, you will reenter the lodge-poles. The next Forest Service cabin is 3.9 miles along the trail at Grand Bay, where the Colorado River flows into Lake Granby from Shadow Mountain Lake.

To continue north to Grand Lake, follow the trail along Grand Bay's east shore and cross over Twin Creek on another log foot bridge, past a couple of cabins and over the boundary between the National Forest and Rocky Mountain National Park. This fairly level and easy section is very pretty as it flirts with the lakeshore, riverbank and forest. Pass the junction with the Columbine Creek Trail and continue north to the Shadow Mountain Dam, which controls the outflow from Shadow Mountain Reservoir. North of the dam, the trail changes names and is called East Shore Trail. It follows a still-level path 3.5 miles through more lodgepole forest along Shadow Mountain Lake to the northern trailhead.

## 106. Colorado River Trail/Lulu City

| | |
|---|---|
| Starting elevation: | 9,080 feet (Colorado River trailhead) |
| Highest elevation: | 9,200 feet at upper end of Shipler Cabins; 9,400 feet at Lulu City |
| Elevation difference: | 120 feet to Shipler Cabins; 320 feet to Lulu City |
| Distance: | 2.4 miles (one way) to Shipler Cabins; 3 miles (one way) to Lulu City |
| Difficulty: | Easy to moderate |
| Avalanche hazard: | Low (one avalanche-prone area, 1.2 miles from the trailhead) |

Snowshoers enjoy free as well as fee trails on the west side of Rocky Mountain National Park. *Photo by Claire Walter.*

The most popular and, after the Valley/River Trail Loop (described on page 214), the easiest section of the Colorado River Trail begins at the Colorado River trailhead, which is at the end of the plowed road. Shipler Cabins, a pair of ruins 1.8 miles (one way) and 200 vertical feet from the trailhead, makes an excellent destination.

At the beginning of the hike, you snowshoe through the summer parking area to the trailhead, soon crossing four bridges in fairly rapid succession. The trail curves to the right (north) and follows the river through such varied terrain as open meadows and woods, beneath rock walls and open talus slopes. About 1.9 miles from the trailhead and 0.5 mile before Shipler Park, you will pass by a west-facing slope with avalanche potential, so shorten your hike if danger is reported. Although the cabin site is not high, it is an open area called Shipler Park boasting wonderful views of the Never Summer Mountains. Retrace your steps on the way back.

Lulu City, a mining town that thrived for four short years around 1880, is another 1.2 miles up the trail, and 200 feet higher than Shipler Park. Foundations of the few remaining Lulu City buildings are visible in summer, but in winter you'll have to rely on the sign because the snow usually buries these remnants of this briefly booming settlement. In either case, retrace your route to return to the trailhead.

### If You Want a Longer Hike

In most cases, you need to keep going higher and farther if you want to extend any of the hikes in this guide. Here, however, lengthening the hike means starting lower and closer to town. In winter, when the ground is frozen, it is often possible to snowshoe parallel to the Colorado River for nearly 10 miles north from the boundary of Rocky Mountain National Park all the way up to Lulu City. It is a mix-and-match route, with numerous places to park along the road before the end-of-road trailhead.

If you drive any farther up Trail Ridge Road than the entrance station just beyond the Kawuneeche Visitors Center, you will have to pay the park fee. Below the fee station, you can access the river trail just off U.S. 34 at the park boundary. Alternatively, access is possible from the road bridge leading to the Winding River Resort Village, just across from the visitors center. This section of the marked trail rejoins Trail Ridge Road at the Green Mountain trailhead. However, in winter, when the ground is frozen and snows lie deep, you can continue along the river, which here becomes the park boundary, to the Bowen-Baker trailhead. Beyond are the Never Summer Ranch road, the Timber Creek Campground and the Colorado River trailhead. All provide parking opportunities. So does the Colorado River trailhead, 9.6 miles from the Grand Lake Entrance Station.

## 107. Never Summer Ranch Road

| | |
|---|---|
| Starting elevation: | 8,903 feet |
| Highest elevation: | 8,920 feet |
| Elevation difference: | Negligible |
| Distance: | 0.5 mile (one way) |
| Difficulty: | Easy |
| Avalanche hazard: | None |

This is the shortest, easiest snowshoeing trail in the park. It is the one rangers use for their beginner guided snowshoe walks. Drive 7.2 miles from the entrance station to the parking and summer picnic area on your left. The flat access road to this historic ranch, which was once a noteworthy taxidermy business and then operated as a guest ranch until well into the 1970s, passes through open meadows and crosses the Colorado River. It is an ideal little stretch for small children, who also have the ranch buildings as a goal.

## 108. Valley/River Trail Loop

| | |
|---|---|
| Starting elevation: | 8,720 feet |
| Highest elevation: | 8,720 feet |
| Elevation difference: | Negligible |
| Distance: | 2.5 miles (loop) |
| Difficulty: | Easy |
| Avalanche hazard: | None |

The trailhead is at the marked Harbison Picnic Area, 1 mile north of the visitors center on the left (west) side of Trail Ridge Road. Well designated with orange markers, it combines the Valley Trail and the River Trail into one long, skinny loop that runs between the Colorado River and the highway. The Valley Trail portion rolls gently through the woods, while the River Trail section is more open and provides fine views. It is more an amble than a hike, though for real beginners or young children on their first snowshoe outing, it is adventure enough. You can do this route in either direction.

## 109. Green Mountain Trail

| | |
|---|---|
| Starting elevation: | 8,790 feet |
| Highest elevation: | 9,470 feet |
| Elevation difference: | 680 feet of gain; 60 feet of loss |
| Distance: | 1.8 miles (one way) |
| Difficulty: | Moderate to challenging |
| Avalanche hazard: | Low |

The Green Mountain trailhead is on the right (east), 2.8 miles north of the Grand Lake Entrance Station. The trail is relatively short, but can be a haul for some snowshoers as there are two challenging sections, one each at the beginning and near the end of the trail. Though steep, it is satisfying, as it leads from a sheltering forest to a grandiose open area that clearly merits the name "Big Meadows." (The nearby Tonahutu Trail, which is very popular in summer, is Ute for "big meadow.") The hardest part of the snowshoe hike is in the beginning, as the trail follows a creek bed and climbs sharply through the forest of mixed conifers and aspens. After about a mile, the grade becomes milder and the view opens up, as the trail crosses through a marshy area and over several small foot-bridges. The eastern end of the trail has a few rolling ascents and descents before climbing to reach the Big Meadows, with a fine display of the dramatic mountains and the Continental Divide. Return the way you came.

# 110. North Inlet Trail

| | |
|---|---|
| Starting elevation: | 8,540 feet |
| Highest elevation: | 8,600 feet at Summerland Park; 8,760 feet at Cascade Falls |
| Elevation difference: | 60 feet to Summerland Park; 220 feet to Cascade Falls |
| Distance: | 1.4 miles (one way) to Summerland Park; 3.4 miles (one way) to Cascade Falls |
| Difficulty: | Easy to Summerland Park; moderate to Cascade Falls |
| Avalanche hazard: | Low |

This route is not within the park's fee area. To reach the trailhead, take U.S. 34 east and turn right (south) on Colorado 278 toward Grand Lake Village. After 0.3 mile, you will come to a fork before you reach the village's commercial area. Bear left onto West Portal Road (locally known as the "tunnel road") and continue 0.7 mile until you reach the intersection with an unpaved road on the left, at a "North Inlet and Tonahutu Trails" sign. Park at the small plowed area at the bottom of the road. Walk up the hill

North Inlet's initial 1.5 miles are virtually flat, before the trail begins its ascent toward Cascade Falls. *Photo by Claire Walter.*

about 0.3 mile to the water plant and proceed to the right over the stone bridge to the summer parking lot and trailhead.

Continue by descending to the level of the stream. While the stream itself meanders through a broad, marshy meadow with thick willow growth, the trail—actually an old road—is fairly straight and easy to follow as it trends east, and then angles toward the northeast. Snowmobiles are permitted on the first 1.4 miles, but actually few riders use it. For much of the way on this early part of the route, you will be hiking along a fence to your right. Cross over a bridge into Summerland Park, a valley whose incongruous landmark is a small, rustic house on the left side of the trail. The park has acquired this formerly private residence, and though it is shuttered in winter, it is surely one of the most unusual and attractive buildings in Rocky Mountain National Park. If all you want is an easy hike into a gentle and scenic valley, this is a good turnaround.

For different scenery and a longer route, stay on the trail as it narrows into a footpath and begins ascending through a thickening forest of lodgepoles. It continues in basically the same northeasterly direction, contouring along the hillside on the north side of the valley. There are also open areas with nice views, tight woods with no views at all and sections of the trail that run beside huge granite boulders and cliffs. The trail steepens somewhat as it approaches the base of Cascade Falls, which even at full power in late spring and early summer, is considered more picturesque from below. Return by the same route you came.

## 111. East Inlet Trail

| | |
|---|---|
| Starting elevation: | 8,390 feet |
| Highest elevation: | 8,600 feet |
| Elevation difference: | 80 feet to the top of Adams Falls; 210 feet to the end of the first meadow |
| Distance: | 0.5 mile (one way) to Adams Falls; 2 miles (one way) to the first meadow |
| Difficulty: | Easy to Adams Falls; easy to moderate to the meadow |
| Avalanche hazard: | None (until beyond the meadow) |

Follow the directions to the North Inlet trailhead (above), but keep going for a total of 2.4 miles along the tunnel road to the end of the plowed section at the East Inlet trailhead, which is down to the left (east). This trail, which is also outside of the park's fee area, offers something for every level of snowshoer. The short hike to the bottom of Adams Falls is virtually flat and extremely easy, yet the cascade is a nice goal. Along the main trail are two meadows, one after the other, that are not quite as defined a goal as a single waterfall for the mid-level snowshoer. Still, it is an attractive route of a good length. If you set the meadows as a destination, you can explore the flat, open area without a demanding elevation gain.

The trail begins by paralleling a fence line as it crosses a broad open area, before climbing ever so slightly up a rise forested with conifers and aspens. In the summer, both the up- and downhills, gentle as they are, are equipped with steps. In winter, snow covers them. Past the falls, the trail enters an area of lodgepoles, beaver meadows and a couple of frozen streams, first climbing gently and then alternating up- and downhill segments, with ever-improving views of Ptarmigan Mountain, Andrews Peak and Mt. Craig. After 2 miles, the trail becomes significantly more challenging, switchbacking up the steep valley. Regardless of how far you go, return the same way you came.

### If You Want a Longer Hike

If you are among the fleet and the hardy, and the snow is reported to be extremely stable, you can continue to Lone Pine Lake. This adds 3.5 miles of far steeper and more avalanche-prone terrain to reach Lone Pine Lake, the first of a string of five mountain lakes along the stream called East Inlet. It is nearly 1,500 vertical feet from the trailhead and therefore is not only longer and more hazardous but also far more challenging than the earlier sections of the route.

The view from the Grand Lake Touring Center. *Photo by Claire Walter.*

## Grand Lake Touring Center

Situated on a combination of public golf course and public lands, this beautiful cross-country ski center, just outside of Grand Lake Village, grooms 18.3 miles of trails that cross open areas, wind through wonderful forests and offer occasional drop-dead views of the Never Summer Range. Snowshoers are welcome on the skating lanes. Fourteen additional one-way trails and loops, which can be combined into many variations, range from the very easiest sections to those with up-and-down steeps to keep the heart pumping. **River Run,** one of the more challenging trails, leads to the North Fork of the Colorado River.

Because the day lodge is a golf pro shop and clubhouse in the summer, there is restaurant and bar service. Full-moon spaghetti dinners on the appropriate Saturday nights in December and March are very popular. The day lodge also has equipment and clothing sales and rentals. The modest trail fee is suspended for youngsters 16 and under on Mondays, and a use of a 0.6-mile "dog loop" is free at all times. To reach the touring center, take U.S. 34 east out of town and, after 0.4 mile, turn left onto Grand County Road 48. Follow it about 2 miles to the end. For details, contact the **Grand Lake Touring Center, P.O. Box 590, Grand Lake, CO 80447; (970) 627-8008.**

## Ranger Tours

In 1997–1998, Rocky Mountain National Park rangers led two-hour snowshoeing and cross-country skiing tours at 1:30 P.M. on alternate Saturdays from late December through the middle of March. With the growing popularity of the snowshoeing program, there is a distinct possibility that future tours will take place every weekend. The tours are free, but reservations were advisable at this writing (and may, in the future, be required). No rental equipment is available in the park, but sporting goods shops in Grand Lake carry it. For details and reservations, call **(970) 627-3471.**

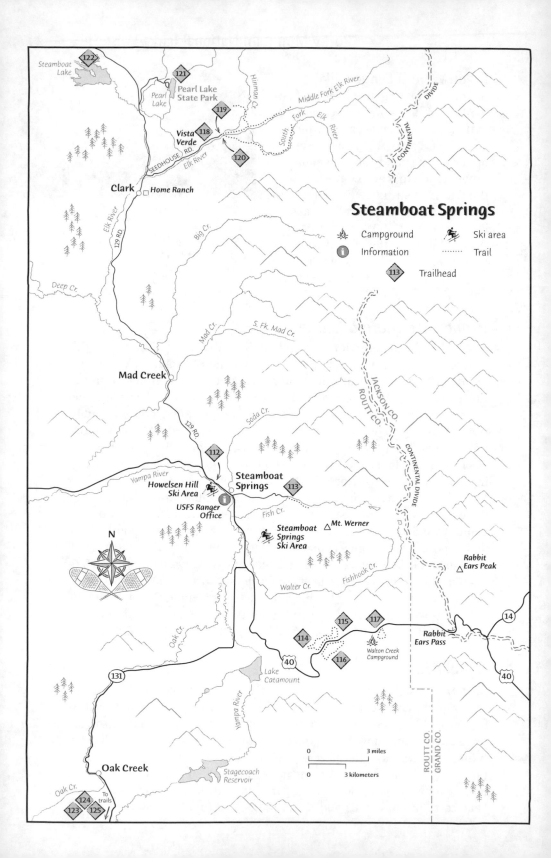

# Steamboat Springs

Campground     Ski area

Information     ....... Trail

113   Trailhead

Steamboat Lake

121

122

Pearl Lake

Pearl Lake State Park

119

Hinman Cr.

Middle Fork Elk River

South Fork Elk River

CONTINENTAL DIVIDE

118   Vista Verde

SEEDHOUSE RD.

120

Elk River

Clark   Home Ranch

Elk River

129 RD.

Big Cr.

Deep Cr.

Mad Cr.

S. Fk. Mad Cr.

Mad Creek

Soda Cr.

129 RD.

JACKSON CO

ROUTT CO.

CONTINENTAL DIVIDE

112

Yampa River

Howelsen Hill Ski Area

Steamboat Springs

113

USFS Ranger Office

Fish Cr.

N

Steamboat Springs Ski Area

△ Mt. Werner

Rabbit Ears Peak △

Fishhook Cr.

Walter Cr.

Oak Cr.

131

115   117

114   116

40

Walton Creek Campground

Rabbit Ears Pass

14

40

Lake Catamount

Yampa River

ROUTT CO.
GRAND CO.

0    3 miles

0    3 kilometers

Oak Creek

Stagecoach Reservoir

Oak Cr.

To trails

124

123   125

# Steamboat Springs

Coal miners and ranchers first settled in and around Steamboat Springs, so named because the hissing of the hot springs reminded early settlers of a steamboat. Unlike many such communities, this boomtown along the Yampa River never truly went bust. Coal didn't have precious metals' get-rich-quick allure, and the hardy ranch families who settled in northwestern Colorado proved to have staying power. Many, in fact, are still considered the region's first families. Despite lower elevations than in some of the central Rockies, northern Colorado winters are long and persistent. A town tale, related in Jean Wren's small historical book, *Steamboat Springs and the Treacherous & Speedy Skee,* tells of a visitor who approached a local rancher and asked "what the summers are like around here?" The rancher thought for a while and finally said, "Well, to tell the truth, I don't really know. I've only lived here 10, 12 years."

Like many of his counterparts elsewhere in Colorado's high country, this rancher—apocryphal or not—and his neighbors knew that the only way to get through a long winter was to learn how to play through the season. Snowshoeing has been part of the scene since the early days for utilitarian purposes and for fun, and just about the first artifact you come across at the Tread of the Pioneers Museum's winter exhibition is a 5-foot-high snowshoe of wood and rawhide. Not just snowshoes, but also skates and skis provided diversion, and they still do. Residents' passion for winter activities put the town on the international map and kept it there. The vast ski area just southeast of downtown, called simply Steamboat (no "Springs" when referring to the ski resort) has become synonymous with champagne powder, and the broad Yampa River Valley is also the centerpiece of some the most extraordinary backcountry areas in the state.

From Rabbit Ears Pass east of town to Elk River Valley on the west are miles of old logging roads, summer hiking and mountain biking trails and acres of powder-kissed meadows that invite exploration on snowshoes. By and large, this is not an area of dramatic peaks and soaring summits. Rather, the topography is of friendly looking, rounded mountains, broad valleys and appealing meadows blanketed in white. When a peak "explodes" high above the surrounding mountains—as Elk Mountain, Hahn's Peak and Mt. Zirkel, deep in the nearby wilderness—the sight can make your heart leap.

For tourist information, contact the **Steamboat Springs Chamber Resort Association, P.O. Box 774408, Steamboat Springs, CO 80477; (800) 922-2722** or **(970) 879-0880;** www.steamboat-chamber.com.

## Getting There

From Denver, take Interstate 70 west about 70 miles to the Dillon/ Silverthorne exit. Turn right and follow Colorado 9 north about 40 miles to Kremmling. At the traffic light, turn left (west) onto U.S. 40 and go over Rabbit Ears Pass to Steamboat Springs. (Parking areas for Rabbit Ears Pass trails are well marked and obvious, directly off the highway.) Steamboat Springs is 160 miles from Denver.

To reach the Elk River Valley (Clark and Hahn's Peak areas), drive 1.5 miles past town and turn right (north) onto Routt County Road 129. Clark is about 18 miles from that intersection. From the Clark Store, the entrance road to The Home Ranch is approximately 0.5 mile on the right. Seedhouse Road, which also accesses Vista Verde Ranch, is 2.5 miles, also on the right. The road to Pearl Lake State Park is 6 miles, and Trilby Flats is 11.2 miles.

It is also feasible to fly to Steamboat Springs. The town's small municipal airport is currently without commercial air service, but major and commuter airlines service Yampa Valley Regional Airport near Hayden, 27 miles west of Steamboat Springs.

## Maps

USGS 7.5 Minute, Steamboat Springs
Trails Illustrated, #118, Steamboat Springs/Rabbit Ears Pass; #116 Hahn's Peak/Steamboat Lake/Mt. Zirkel Wilderness
USFS Routt National Forest

Running through the aspens along a summer nature trail that becomes a winter snowshoeing route. *Photo by Larry Pierce/ Steamboat Ski and Resort Corporation.*

## Steamboat Springs

In Steamboat Springs, which has sent more of its sons and daughters to the Winter Olympics than any other town in America, people simply love winter. The community offers more winter sports facilities than any other in Colorado—not contrived by a corporation seeking to extract dollars from tourists but for its own citizens. Visitors, of course, are welcome to dip into the lode. Winter sports enthusiasts all know about the world-renowned and powder-blessed Steamboat ski resort, with unsurpassed Alpine skiing, telemarking and snowboarding. Steamboat Springs' dynamite municipal recreation facility at Howelsen Hill offers venues for Alpine skiing, race training, recreational and competitive snowboarding, day and night Nordic skiing, ski jumping, ice skating and yes, snowshoeing—free or at bargain rates. Other snowshoeing trails are located right on the outskirts of town, as well as in the surrounding mountains.

# 112. Howelsen Hill/Emerald Mountain

| | |
|---|---|
| Starting elevation: | 6,696 feet |
| Highest elevation: | 7,656 feet (quarry); 8,239 feet (top of Emerald Mountain) |
| Elevation difference: | 960 feet to the quarry; 1,543 feet to the top of Emerald Mountain |
| Distance: | 1.5 miles (one way) to the quarry; 2 miles (one way) to the top of Emerald Mountain |
| Difficulty: | Moderate to challenging |
| Avalanche hazard: | Low |

To reach Howelsen Hill, located virtually in downtown Steamboat Springs, take Fifth Street one block south of Lincoln Avenue (U.S. 40) and cross Yampa Avenue and the bridge. Turn right onto River Road and then left into the Howelsen Hill ski area parking area. Snowshoeing in cross-country ski tracks is a no-no and annoying to skiers anywhere, but at the Howelsen sports complex, where many of America's top Nordic competitors and hopefuls train, it can create a real problem.

To access the free trails where snowshoeing is permitted, follow the trail on the left of the ski area day lodge. Cross under the chairlift and take the trail up the left (south) side of the ski area. The first quarter-mile or so is steep, offering a fine aerobic workout. Several scenic overlook areas provide popular respites—respectively about two-thirds of the way up, halfway and at the plateau, at an old quarry—and fine views of town, the Steamboat ski area and the surrounding mountains. These overlooks offer the best vantage points of a massif to the northwest called Sleeping Giant Ridge.

The trail—which local old-timers might still call Stone Quarry Road—hugs the edge of the hill up to a rolling plateau above the top station of the chairlift. On weekends, when the chairlift operates, you can avoid the steepest portions of the lower mountain by buying a single-ride ticket, and save yourself several hundred feet of climbing. Many snowshoers find the plateau area to be the most fun anyway. There are two marked but ungroomed Nordic and snowshoeing trails on the contoured mountainside behind the ski area. The **Orton Loop** is about 1.3 miles and the **Emerald Meadows Loop** is a little under a mile, and both are easily followed and popular.

## If You Want a Longer Hike

Additional routes through the pine forest and open meadows on that plateau generally lie above and southeast from the ski area. Strong snowshoers can continue to the top of Emerald Mountain, which was once the top of the lift-served ski area. Many local snowshoer runners like to kick up the powder by running down the arrow-straight old lift line.

The summit of Emerald Mountain (called Agate Mountain or Quarry Mountain on some maps) is at 8,239 feet.

## 113. Fish Creek Falls

| | |
|---|---|
| Starting elevation: | 7,530 feet |
| Lowest elevation: | 7,470 feet |
| Elevation difference: | 60 feet (ascend on the return) |
| Distance: | 0.25 mile (one way) |
| Difficulty: | Easy |
| Avalanche hazard: | Low |

### Steamboat Snowshoe Sundays

Sometimes it seems as if Steamboaters can't do anything without making a competition of it, so it's no surprise that Steamboat Snowshoe Sundays were launched in 1995. Within a few years, this race series had attracted up to 100 competitors, some racing seriously and some just there for the fun of it (and perhaps for the prizes). Monthly races are held on a 5-kilometer loop starting at the bottom of the mountain and winding around on the plateau. Entrants in the 10-kilometer category do it twice. Categories are youngsters 17 and under, men and women aged 18 to 30 and aged 31 to 39, veteran men and women aged 40 to 49 and masters men and women 50 and older.

Snowshoeing is also a component of the annual Steamboat Pentathlon, which includes Alpine skiing, cross-country skiing, mountain biking and running as well as what is described as an "intermediate" snowshoeing course of 3.5 miles. Three- to five-member teams compete in various age groups and other combinations. For further information on either competition, contact the City of Steamboat Recreational Services, P.O. Box 775088, Steamboat Springs, CO 80477; (970) 879-4300.

Fish Creek got its name from the huge brook trout and whitefish populations that allowed early settlers to easily snag enough fish to tide them through a long winter. From Lincoln Avenue (U.S. 40), drive west on Third Street. Go one block and turn right onto Fish Creek Road, which winds 4 miles through residential neighborhoods to a parking area at the end of the plowed road. The short but dramatic route down to the base of the falls is a favorite of Steamboat locals, who use it for a quick run or snowshoe through magnificent high cliffs whenever they have time just for a short getaway. The route threads downhill through a steep-walled canyon to the foot of Fish Creek Falls, which plunge 285 feet from a hanging valley. In winter, falling water freezes into glistening free-form sculptures. No wonder this jewel is the highlight of a route that has been designated as a National Recreation Trail.

### If You Want a Longer Hike

For a longer route and a workout as well, continue to the top of the falls. Four switchbacks make up the steepest part of the ascent from the canyon, and after a short straight section, two more switchbacks complete the climb, which is about 850 feet from the base of the falls. Here, the trail becomes more exposed, so it might be a good idea to turn back. Branches of the trail continue to Fish Creek Reservoir and Long Lake, but these cross through some hazard areas and are not recommended for casual snowshoeing excursions.

## Steamboat Ski Area

All snowshoers are permitted to strike off on their own on Steamboat's ski trails without charge, though management asks that they stop at the Ski Patrol station at the base of the Christie lifts for guidance to the best snowshoe-ing routes, as well as safety tips for sharing runs with downhill skiers and snowboarders. Base area to midmountain provides a daunting 3,180-foot vertical, but out-and-back snowshoers can climb as much or as little as they wish.

Wide open powder fields abound at Steamboat, a ski area that permits snowshoers on all Alpine Trails. Free guided tours are also available. *Photo by Cynthia Hunter/Steamboat Ski and Resort Corporation.*

Mountain hosts also guide midweek snowshoe tours (currently Wednesdays, Thursdays and Sundays, which could change). Steamboat sells "foot passenger" tickets for gondola transport both up- and downhill. While the tours are complimentary, they require a lift ticket. All tours depart from Thunderhead at the top of the gondola, where snowshoes may also be rented. The beginner tour, currently at 1:00 P.M., is about a little more than a mile on flat terrain along a loop that is a summer nature trail. Intermediate and advanced tours begin at 9:00 A.M. The intermediate tour to Rendezvous Saddle is about 4 miles round-trip, with a 250-foot elevation gain, along a route called Duster. The advanced tour is shorter in length but involves a greater elevation gain (640 feet) to Four Points Hut, located at 9,080 feet. The resort's Information Center at the base of the gondola is the place to get current scheduling information or sign up, or call **(970) 879-6111, Ext. 515 or 516.**

## Steamboat Ski Touring Center

Tucked in behind the Alpine ski area is the cross-country center. The center is located at about 7,000 feet, and the 5-mile dedicated snowshoe trail has virtually no climbs or descents. With an optional cutoff that cuts the distance in half, this is a perfect first outing for a small child or beginning adult snowshoer who might be fearful, out of shape or affected by altitude. The trail is easy to follow, and the touring center patrols it. Rental snowshoes are available, as is a warming hut with snack service. There is a modest trail use fee. For details, contact the **Steamboat**

Ski Touring Center, P.O. Box 775401, Steamboat Springs, CO 80477; (970) 879-8180; www.nordicski.com.

# Rabbit Ears Pass

This pass was named for a pair of 100-foot rock pinnacles that to the surveyors resembled a rabbit's ears. At 9,300 feet and more above sea level, this is not Colorado's highest mountain pass, but it is among the biggest and broadest. Rather than being a relatively low spot threaded between summits, Rabbit Ears Pass is actually a huge, rolling tableland that sprawls between two high spots, known as the West Pass and East Pass. The whole area is a winter playground of unsurpassed proportions, with ample space for motorized and nonmotorized recreationists. They rarely need to cross either others' tracks, because snowmobiles prevail on the East Summit but are barred from West Summit routes. The area is far north, quite high and wild. You might find weather conditions there sublime or terrible, sometimes on the same day. As you hike you may encounter an area that feels like a wind tunnel or may find a treasured hidden powder pocket that has been untouched by wind or traffic. You may find a no-visibility whiteout or blue skies and sunshine. Rabbit Ears Pass epitomizes the ever-changing conditions in Colorado's high country.

While it would seem that Rabbit Ears Pass presents snowshoers with an ideal, go-anywhere playground, it is advisable for most people to stick to marked and well-traveled routes through this sprawling area, where landmarks are few and the chances of backcountry disorientation are not to be trivialized. A trail map, a compass and the skills to use both are especially useful here, and many locals, in fact, save Rabbit Ears Pass for their springtime excursions because midwinter can be so severe.

## 114. West Summit Loop A

| | |
|---|---|
| Starting elevation: | 9,350 feet |
| Highest elevation: | 9,700 feet |
| Elevation difference: | 350 feet, plus many small ups and downs |
| Distance: | 3.6 miles (loop) |
| Difficulty: | Moderate |
| Avalanche hazard: | Low |

This trail, accessed from the West Summit parking lot on the north side of U.S. 40 just 12 miles from Steamboat Springs, is both one of the most popular and one of the easiest routes on Rabbit Ears Pass. Scramble up the embankment, a high mound of plowed snow, and bear left (west) just past the trail sign onto Loop A. Amble through the gentle initial section, where the trail crosses open meadows and lovely woods.

At the farthest reach, about 1.75 miles, where a telephone line crosses high over the trail, the route doubles back sharply to the right through an open field to the highest point. On good days, this knoll provides gorgeous views of Hahn's Peak, the Sleeping Giant and the Flat Tops. All that remains are a couple of bends, a sharp descent and an intersection with West Summit Loop B on the left, and you're back at the parking lot, climbing for a short distance. It's always courteous to avoid ski tracks, but on this trail's well-known downhill, stay as far off the cross-country routes as you can, because Nordies can pick up quite a head of speed on the descent. Skiers normally do this route clockwise, but snowshoes provide the flexibility to do it in either direction with equal comfort.

## 115. West Summit Loop B

| | |
|---|---|
| Starting elevation: | 9,350 feet |
| Lowest elevation: | 9,180 feet |
| Highest elevation: | 9,520 feet |
| Elevation difference: | 340 feet difference, many small ups and downs |
| Distance: | 4.4 miles (loop) |
| Difficulty: | Moderate |
| Avalanche hazard: | Low |

Drive, park and begin snowshoeing as above, but at the trail sign, bear right (northeast) onto a stretch that serves both as the end of Loop A and the beginning of Loop B. After a little more than 0.1 mile, take a second right fork and drop down into a broad drainage along the trail, marked by blue diamonds. Continue along the trail, which skirts a broad meadow and roughly parallels U.S. 40. When you come to a third fork after about 0.6 mile, stay left. Loop B arcs to the left, continues north and offers spectacular panoramic views. At the farthest point from the trailhead, the route curves left, first south and eventually west, back toward the intersection with Loop A. As on its twin, skiers on this trail move in a customary direction (this time counterclockwise), but snowshoes give you the freedom to do Loop B in either direction.

## 116. South Summit Loop

| | |
|---|---|
| Starting elevation: | 9,320 feet |
| Highest elevation: | 9,550 feet |
| Elevation difference: | 230 feet, plus many small ups and downs |
| Distance: | 3 miles (loop) |
| Difficulty: | Moderate to challenging |
| Avalanche hazard: | Low |

For the South Summit Loop, which on some maps and in some books is called West Summit Loop C, drive to and park at the West Summit as above, but cross to the south side of the highway to begin your trek. To follow this loop counterclockwise, begin with a short, sharp climb. Continue south-southeast, following an unplowed road. The trail curves to the left, turning east to parallel, at some distance, U.S. 40. Walton Peak is the landmark looming to the southeast. The trail horseshoes around the Meadows Campground, which means that it is easy to do a car shuttle for a short hike. The campground is on your left, about 1.5 miles from the trailhead, and you can cross through it to cut off the tail (or is it the tip?) of the route at the farthest point from the West Summit trailhead, where the Par-a-lel Route continues on to the east toward Walton Creek. South Summit Loop doubles back toward the trailhead, closely paralleling the highway. The trail can be done in either direction.

### If You Want a Longer Hike

You can also take the 2-mile-long Par-a-lel Route to combine the South Summit Loop and Walton Creek Loop into one longer route.

## 117. Walton Creek Loop

| | |
|---|---|
| Starting elevation: | 9,470 feet |
| Highest elevation: | 9,630 feet |
| Lowest elevation: | 9,380 feet |
| Elevation difference: | 250 feet, plus many ups and downs |
| Distance: | 1.7 miles (loop) |
| Difficulty: | Moderate to challenging |
| Avalanche hazard: | Low |

From Steamboat Springs, drive past the West Summit parking area to the Walton Creek parking area, on the south side of the highway just over 18 miles from town. The trail divides right after the trailhead. Take the right fork, which heads south and first drops into the drainage, then goes across a relatively flat section. After about 0.6 mile, where the Par-a-lel Route merges from the right (west), the Walton Creek Loop bends to the left (east). Climb a short rise, traverse a small plateau and then drop into the Walton Creek drainage. The trail crosses the creek, where the North Walton Peak Road merges from the right. This part of the route, which often is used by snowmobilers, then curves left (north) to ascend back to the trailhead, following a power line at the very end. You can also do this route clockwise by taking the left option at the trailhead.

### If You Want a Longer Hike

Follow the 2-mile Par-a-lel Route to combine it with the South Summit Loop, with or without a car shuttle, if time and stamina permit. The east-to-west direction is more challenging because there are more uphills.

# Elk River Valley

This beautiful valley northwest of Steamboat Springs boasts a strong ranching heritage and absolutely incredible scenery. In summer, the valley's dude and guest ranches put up the "no vacancy" sign, the three Forest Service and four state park campgrounds are filled and significant numbers of sightseers pass through. In winter, two of the ranches have committed heavily to snowshoeing, the closed campgrounds are the gateways to some terrific backcountry snowshoeing areas and hardly anyone simply drives by.

## Clark Store

For all intents and purposes, the Clark Store and the town of Clark are one and the same. Behind the green false-front facade are Clark's convenience store, grocery store, liquor store, neighborhood cafe, local deli, post office, library and video store. It's a great place to pick up sandwiches for the trail, have your Thermos topped off with homemade soup or buy a dynamite cookie for later. The store is owned by The Home Ranch, which does the cooking and baking, so the vittles are really, really good. **Clark, CO 80428; (970) 879-3849.**

## Maps

USGS 7.5 Minute, Farwell Mountain
Trails Illustrated #116, Hahn's Peak, Steamboat Lake
USFS Routt National Forest

## The Home Ranch

The Home Ranch is a member of the international luxury resort consortium called Relais et Chateaux, one of only two dude and guest ranches in the country and one of only two resorts of any type in Colorado to be so honored. When it comes to meeting the highest international standards of hospitality, it just doesn't get any better than Relais et Chateaux. Antique furniture, firm mattresses, woodstoves set and ready to light, down feather beds, private hot tubs right outside the door and

Snowshoeing along the fenceline at The Home Ranch. *Photo by Claire Walter.*

even a cookie jar that is restocked daily are the stuff of winter escape dreams.

The ranch's 1,500 acres are accessible only to overnight guests—and even at capacity, which is unlikely in winter, that still means only about 50 people. You can snowshoe right from the door, on your own or on twice-daily guided snowshoe walks and hikes around the property or into the nearby Routt National Forest. The Home Ranch offers 80 kilometers of

## Hey Dude! Let's Snowshoe

For a romantic winter getaway, you can't do any better than The Home Ranch and Vista Verde. These two warm and wonderful guest ranches on the Elk River, roughly half an hour from Steamboat Springs, epitomize "new Western deluxe," which combines the horse-and-bridle atmosphere of a classic dude ranch with the exceptional cuisine and fine service of a classy resort. Both ranches have been stalwarts in the cross-country community, grooming miles of trails, setting track and offering instruction and guide services. They both also were quick to latch onto the snowshoeing boom, providing equipment, tips and guided snowshoe walks and hikes to guests, included in the rate. The snowshoeing along the ranches' rolling acreage is easy and safe (no slide zones on the ranches), and it's also exceptionally lovely, with trails threading through stands of aspen and conifers. Both also adjoin the Routt National Forest for easy-access, off-ranch tours.

The ranches have much in common. Each one sits on a broad, sunny plateau, surrounded by wooded hillsides and national forest lands. Accommodations are lodge rooms and log cabins that define rustic comfort. The Home Ranch's cabins are tucked into aspen woods; Vista Verde's nestle amid pines. The food is a country mile from the old chuckwagon. Both ranches offer three opulent meals a day: breakfast and lunch buffets and multicourse gourmet dinners with choice of entrée. The luxury ranch experience is not inexpensive, but when you are celebrating a special occasion with a special someone, you can't put a price tag on the atmosphere, scenery, cuisine and rare tranquillity offered by such fine places.

immaculately laid-out cross-country skiing and snowshoeing trails on its own property and the adjacent Whitmer Ranch. Track skiers and skaters have groomed trails, which snowshoers are asked to walk beside. More than a dozen routes, which The Home Ranch calls "powder trails," are left ungroomed, wholly or in part, for snowshoers and only those skiers who like to venture off the manicured path. The trails come in various steepnesses, but the difference in elevation from the lowest point of the lowest trail to the highest section of the highest is about 400 feet. The verticals may be moderate, but the variety and quality are first-rate. It's hard to find a prettier snowshoeing trail in the state than The Home Ranch's Aspen Arches, and if you like to snowshoe to a destination, you can go about 1.4 miles to the Clark Store for a latte and pastry break.

A gate on the north end of the ranch accesses Routt National Forest land, where you can follow a trail along the Elk River for miles. For an additional challenge, you can bushwhack along the ridge that forms the eastern backdrop to The Home Ranch and continue to the top of Home Mountain, an elevation gain of close to 1,000 feet. **The Home Ranch, P.O. Box 822, Clark, CO 80428; (970) 879-1780 or (970) 879-9044.**

## Vista Verde

Vista Verde is smaller, covering "only" 500 acres, but you'd never know it from the grandiose views. Its commitment to winter activities is indicated by its full name, Vista Verde Guest Ranch & Ski Touring Center, and who knows but it may metamorphose into Vista Verde Guest Ranch & Snowshoeing Center, given its enthusiasm for the booming sport on big feet. Vista Verde also welcomes day visitors who pay a trail use fee or buy a package that includes lunch for a wonderful, civilized snowshoeing experience. The ranch's winter season is from just before Christmas through mid-March.

Steamboat's notable guest ranches abound in Routt National Forest, offering backcountry as well as on-ranch snowshoeing possibilities. Guides and meals are included in the cost of a dude-on-snow getaway. *Photo courtesy Vista Verde.*

Snowshoers who prefer a gentle meander across open fields love to follow beside Vista Verde's 30 kilometers of marked and groomed cross-country trails. You can make lovely and easy loops where it's difficult to get lost, or blaze your own trail past stands of conifers and the frozen-over bed of Hinman Creek. Marked but ungroomed trails up the scrubby south-facing hillsides climb some 200 feet above the meadows and are accessible both to snowshoers and skiers.

If you're of a mind, and in shape, for a challenge, you can ascend sharply a marked trail up a ridge fittingly nicknamed Heartbreak Hill and follow a horse trail along the crest to Hinman Lake, where you can skirt the south shore and make a loop of it by descending via the Forest Service trail until you return to an outlying trail on ranch property. This dramatic route is a virtual naturalists' tour through several ecosystems, first through beautiful aspen stands, then through conifers on shaded north slopes, next back into the aspens and finally even through desertlike scrub on the final descent to the ranch. The initial climb is so steep that the 600-foot vertical feels like more, but the experience of being alone at this beautiful lake is worth every puff.

Vista Verde's amenities include a small fitness center with hot tubs on the deck (some cabins also have their own), winter horseback riding and weekly guided night tours on snowshoes or Nordic skis. There's après-ski/après-snowshoe every afternoon at Bob's Bar at Sweetheart's, the original main building and now a congenial recreation room. But the outdoor fun doesn't need to end when the sun sets. The trails are groomed first thing in the morning, so it is often all right to snowshoe them in the moonlight. A moon that is full or nearly so is bright enough to cast shadows on the glistening snow. **Vista Verde, P.O. Box 465, Steamboat Springs, CO 80477; (800) 526-7433** or **(970) 879-7433.**

## 118. Seedhouse Road

| | |
|---|---|
| Starting elevation: | 7,680 feet |
| Highest elevation: | 8,450 feet |
| Elevation difference: | 770 feet |
| Distance: | 6.5 miles (one way) |
| Difficulty: | Easy |
| Avalanche hazard: | None |

To reach the snowshoeable portion of Seedhouse Road, continue on County Road 129 north of Clark and turn right onto Seedhouse Road (Forest Service Road 400), passing the Glen Eden Resort on the left. Continue for about 6 miles to the end of the plowed section and park. The unplowed road provides a leisurely place to snowshoe as far as you like. You will be stepping through a portion of northern Colorado history. The road was cut in 1912 by the Forest Service to allow the collection and drying of spruce and pine cones. After 1933, the facility itself was used as a ranger station and summer camp.

Now snowshoers, skiers and snowmobilers share the wide road, which heads in a nearly straight, steady northeasterly direction, ascending gradually toward Slavonia and the Mt. Zirkel Wilderness. The road lies close to the Elk River and (farther upstream) the Elk's Middle Fork, providing an ever-changing picture of frozen and unfrozen stretches. From the winter road closure, it is about 3 miles to Seedhouse and another 3.5 to Slavonia, named for the Eastern Europeans who settled there in the nineteenth century.

## 119. Hinman Creek Trail

| | |
|---|---|
| Starting elevation: | 7,680 feet |
| Highest elevation: | 8,240 feet |
| Elevation difference: | 560 feet |
| Distance: | 2.6 miles (one way) |
| Difficulty: | Moderate |
| Avalanche hazard: | Low |

Hinman Peak, Hinman Meadows, Hinman Lake and all the other features that share that name owe their name to a trapper who first settled there in 1870. The mountain lake that bears his name is a fitting destination for a half-day snowshoe excursion. To reach the lake, drive to the winter closure (see above) and begin snowshoeing along the north side of the road. Turn left onto the first road, which is marked as Forest Service Road 430, across an open meadow and then through beautiful stands of aspen. At the end of the road, at the Hinman Creek crossing, the route narrows into a trail that veers to the left (north), where it connects with the maintained Vista Verde guest ranch system. Stay on the unmaintained trail, climbing steadily through a ravine deep in the woods. Some sections are rather steep. Where the ravine narrows, the trail hugs the hillside and continues its climb. At a fork, bear left (west) on an unmarked but usually somewhat packed-down auxiliary trail. When you crest a rise overlooking Hinman Lake's frozen surface, you are at your beautiful destination. Beyond the lake to the north is Farwell Mountain, whose rounded summit is a local landmark.

To see the lake from another vantage point, descend to the lake and skirt the south shore. You can make your own route up a hill on the western end for another nice view and also a quick lesson in the trees of northern Colorado. The south-facing slope that you climb is a lovely pine forest. At the top of the ridge, nature has virtually drawn a line, with aspens and firs on the north-facing side of the hill. When you turn around to retrace your steps, you can have great fun loping down the deep and usually unmarked snow blanketing the steep hill.

## If You Want a Longer Hike

Return to the junction with the main trail, which will now be on your left. The main Hinman Trail now bears toward the northeast. Stay to the right at the first trail intersection (about 0.5 mile) and, if you

### Routt Divide Blowdown

On October 25, 1997, an early-season blizzard dumped 2 feet of snow on Denver, causing accidents, road closures and other well-televised urban and air-travel woes. What few people realized at the time was that another storm was stalled over northern Colorado, a storm of high and persistent winds that ultimately affected 20,000 acres of pristine landscape on the west side of the Continental Divide. The event, now called simply "the Routt Divide blowdown," felled millions of trees on the west side of the Mt. Zirkel Wilderness and adjacent nonwilderness sections of the Routt National Forest. In the months that followed, experts deduced what had occurred. Prevailing winds in this part of Colorado are from the west and north, and the trees set their roots to withstand winds from those directions. Because the blizzard was caused by a storm system that stalled over the Front Range, a secondary dry storm backed up behind it and whipped ferocious and sustained winds from the east, a direction that the trees have less fortitude to withstand. Toppled trees destroyed trails and trailheads, perhaps unleashing new slide zones. At this writing, rangers had not finished damage assessment but were proposing several projects, including some salvage logging that may also impact recreational use, so be especially conscious of posted signs warning backcountry users of safety issues in effected areas.

want some lovely views, turn right at the second intersection (0.25 mile) to a side trail that provides excellent views to the west. If you wish to continue up Hinman Creek Trail, return to the main trail and cross an upper section of Hinman Creek, where the trail peters out, roughly 4.75 miles and 1,400 vertical feet from the trailhead (and about 5 miles from the road).

## 120. South Fork Trail

| | |
|---|---|
| Starting elevation: | 7,680 feet |
| Highest elevation: | 8,220 feet |
| Elevation difference: | 540 feet |
| Distance: | 3 miles (one way) |
| Difficulty: | Moderate |
| Avalanche hazard: | Low |

The South Fork Trail is one of the most popular snowshoeing routes in the Elk River Valley. *Photo by Claire Walter.*

Take Seedhouse Road (Forest Service Road 400) as above, but just after the Vista Verde Ranch turnoff, turn right to the Hinman Campground. The trailhead is at the signs on the south side of the parking area. Bear left (east) and ascend gradually through an open meadow. The trail steepens somewhat as it enters the trees. Though it has some curves, it heads primarily in a southeasterly direction, paralleling a small creek that is later visible as the South Fork of the Elk River. The trail is pleasantly contoured, with a series of alternating small pitches and gentle climbs. Stay alert, and stick to the side of the trail, for skiers can pick up quite a head of speed on the downhills. This is especially important to remember when you yourself are descending, and the skiers are coming down behind you.

As you approach the high spot on the trail, the trees get a little sparser but the aspens become more imposing, displaying beefy trunks with the girth of low-altitude maples. The route arcs gently to the right until it overlooks the South Fork, which here lies in a wide, marshy valley. In summer, hikers can pick their way through this damp area and rejoin the trail, which then continues northwest to a road junction just west of Seedhouse; however, in winter, snow and ice over flowing water can make crossing the area tricky.

### If You Want a Longer Hike

A map and a compass are strongly recommended if you decide to bushwhack through the dryer, higher ground north of the marshy section and make a loop by returning on Seedhouse Road. That would make for a hike of 3 miles along the South Fork Trail, plus about 1.75 miles down the unplowed road back to your starting point.

# 121. Pearl Lake State Park Road

| | |
|---|---|
| Starting elevation: | 8,000 feet |
| Highest elevation: | 8,080 feet |
| Elevation difference: | 90 feet |
| Distance: | 0.6 mile (one way) |
| Difficulty: | Easy |
| Avalanche hazard: | None |

If you don't have much snowshoeing time or energy and want a short, sweet tour to a pretty destination, Pearl Lake State Park fits the bill. Turn right from County Road 129 onto County Road 209, bearing right at the Y-junction with 209A. The road is plowed only as far as a small parking area at the fee station. The snow-shoeing route follows the paved road to the campground and boat ramp, respectively the left and right options at a fork about two-thirds of the way along the trail. The easy trail cuts a broad swath though tranquil woods of lodgepole, fir and spruce. Snowmobiles are permitted but uncommon, so the trail might be snowmobile packed but not groomed. The road provides a gentle, steady uphill through the luxuriant pine forest. You will experience a sense of peace and protection as you snowshoe up this sheltering trail. Once you are close to the shore of the frozen lake, the woods open to a lovely, but undramatic, view. The occasional ice angler fishing for cut-throat trout or grayling is a picturesque addition to the scene. Turn around and retrace your steps.

## If You Want a Longer Hike
When the ice is solid, you can make a loop by following the shore and rounding the peninsula that separates the campground and boat ramp trails, or you can even follow the lakeshore around to the south to the dam, but take a map if you are going off-trail.

# 122. Trilby Flats

| | |
|---|---|
| Starting elevation: | 8,400 feet |
| Highest elevation: | Varies |
| Elevation difference: | Varies |
| Distance: | Varies |
| Difficulty: | Easy to moderate |
| Avalanche hazard: | None |

A few yards of Forest Service Road 486, on the left (west) of the highway, 11.2 miles from the Clark Store, are plowed out to create a small parking

A snowshoer breaks trail for her dog at Trilby Flats.
Photo by Claire Walter.

pullout. The road sign is often buried in snow, but look for the parking area immediately after the second Hahn's Peak Recreation Area sign. Spread generally to the north is Trilby Flats, several hundred acres of rolling meadows punctuated with stands of bronze-barked aspens and soaring pines that are grouped into clusters, punctuating the pure snow. Even days after a storm, you can find untracked powder if you're in a mood to break trail or follow the tracks etched into the powder by previous snowshoers and skiers. The Flats, an excellent playground for snowshoers, can provide the comfort of trail-free exploration within sight of your car. This wide open area is ideal on a sunny, windless day, when a bonus reward is 10,800-foot Hahn's Peak spiring into the sky to the east. You will, however, want to avoid this open area if it's blustery or if the light is really flat.

## If You Want a Longer Hike

On the other side is a hilly area to the right (east) of the road, which locals refer to simply as "across from Trilby Flats." This area has more vertical and is more challenging. You can make a nice loop by bearing left around the most prominent stands of trees, climb as far as you like, loop back behind the gladed areas and return to your starting point. You're likely to see the tracks of others who have taken these routes.

## Stagecoach

The Stagecoach Ski Area, about 20 miles southeast of Steamboat Springs, was launched with great expectations during the 1971–1972 season. It quickly succumbed to the first OPEC crisis and oil embargo and has not operated within memory of many of today's snowshoers. Like Rip Van Winkle, it emerged in early 1998 from a long slumber. Its new incarnation, however, is not as a lift-served Alpine area, but rather as a free-heelers paradise where snowshoers, cross-country skiers and telemarkers take guided excursions on a private mountain.

The base camp is a yurt set in an open field at about 7,400 feet. It directly accesses lower-mountain loop trails that wind through a wonderful forest of aspens and ponderosa pines, and even a stark, dry hillside studded with sagebrush poking eerily above the snow. A 5.5-mile road winds to a summit cabin and another trail network. Hardy snowshoers on the overnight excursion have the option of trudging up the mountain or taking a ride on a snowcat or snowmobile. The summit trails run along the ridge top through lodgepole pines, topping out at 9,350 feet. Every opening provides a view—toward Steamboat Springs, over to the Flat Tops Wilderness or even as far as the Gore Range—and a trio of old cabins here, a radio tower there add interest and dimension to these trails.

The log cabin at the summit accommodates a group of overnighters. It seem like an expensive adventure for a low-key activity such as snowshoeing, but the opportunity to enjoy a private mountain is priceless. Transportation from Steamboat Springs, meals and the service of guides are included in the rates. For information and reservations, contact **Bucking Rainbow Outfitters, Fourth and Lincoln Streets, Steamboat Springs, CO 80477; (888) 810-8747** or **(970) 879-8747; www.buckingrainbow.com.**

# Dunckley Pass

Dunckley Pass resembles Rabbit Ears Pass, only it's a smaller area off a state rather than a federal highway and consequently gets a lot less usage. The recreational options include eight recommended trails and loops for snowshoeing and Nordic skiing, some of which are also shared with snowmobiles. To reach the pass, take U.S. 40 east from Steamboat Springs. Turn right (south) onto Colorado 131, then right again onto County Road 15 at Phippsburg. At the junction of County Road 132, bear right once more to Dunckley Pass Road (Forest Service Road 16), which is plowed for about a mile to the trailhead. The distance from Steamboat Springs is 32 miles.

## Maps
USGS 7.5 Minute, Sand Point
USFS Routt National Forest

## 123. Aspen Flats Loop

| | |
|---|---|
| Starting elevation: | 8,610 feet |
| Highest elevation: | 8,710 feet |
| Elevation difference: | 100 feet |
| Distance: | 1.5 miles (loop) |
| Difficulty: | Easy |
| Avalanche hazard: | None |

This is the shortest, easiest trail at Dunckley Pass. The name "Aspen Flats" says it all. It passes through lovely stands of aspen, and it is rather flat. From the trailhead, proceed south on an unplowed four-wheel-drive road. Bear left on the Aspen Flats Trail, which merges with the inbound Spronks Creek Trail and immediately joins the road. Bear right to return to the trailhead and complete the loop, which is equally pleasant in either direction.

## 124. Spronks Creek Trail/Crosho Lakes Trail

| | |
|---|---|
| Starting elevation: | 8,610 feet |
| Highest elevation: | 9,000 feet |
| Elevation difference: | 390 feet |
| Distance: | 6 miles (loop) |
| Difficulty: | Moderate |
| Avalanche hazard: | Low |

From the main trailhead, proceed south and either take the Aspen Flats Trail (slightly longer) or stay on the road. At the next trail intersection, bear right (east) onto the Spronks Creek Trail, which is fairly level and passes through open meadows. The trail follows the creek through the valley. After about 0.75 mile, the trail makes a sharp turn to the right (south) and the grade steepens. Continue about 0.25 mile more along the hillside to the next sharp bend. At the Crosho Lake Trail junction, take another right and continue west, returning via the Crosho Lakes Trail, which hugs the hillside. Bear right at each of the next two forks to return to the trailhead. You can also do this loop in the other direction.

### If You Want a Longer Hike

If you have time, energy and inclination, you can continue more or less straight (south) at the Crosho Lakes Trail, which is 0.75 mile one way. Remember that you have to return again, which adds about 1.5 miles to the total hiking distance.

## 125. Wildcat Alley

| | |
|---|---|
| Starting elevation: | 8,610 feet |
| Highest elevation: | 8,890 feet |
| Elevation difference: | 280 feet |
| Distance: | 3.6 miles (loop) |
| Difficulty: | Easy to moderate |
| Avalanche hazard: | Low |

Drive a few hundred feet past the Aspen Flats trailhead to the end of the plowed road to a parking area that is also used by snowmobilers. You will be sharing the Dunckley Pass Road with sleds, so keep to the side of the trail. Snowshoe straight (west) along the road, making a long steady climb through the woods. After about 0.75 mile, take the right fork to Wildcat Alley. This summer jeep road makes a long loop around a modest hill, which is covered by aspens and conifers. Along the way, you will see remnants of oil and gas strikes, including a couple of drill holes and an oil well close to the trail. Wildcat Alley rejoins the Dunckley Pass Road, which you then take east to return to the trailhead. You can also do the loop in the other direction.

# 5

# WESTERN COLORADO

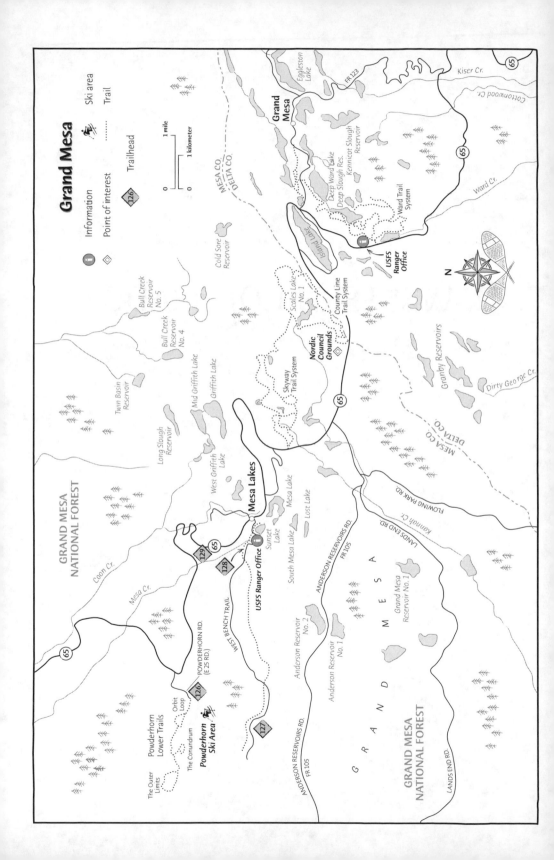

# Grand Mesa

The Grand Mesa emerges from the near-desert like a marvelous mirage, appearing as a whitecap erupting from a rocky sea of beige, taupe and sand. At 350,000 acres, it is the world's largest flat-top mountain, and it has rightly been called "an island in the sky." The Colorado River and its tributaries have sliced through this high tableland for millennia, carving canyons to give the land its character and sustain its life. In this stark and beautiful setting is the Grand Mesa, a unique topographic wonder that combines the features of canyon country with a high-Alpine environment. The top of the Grand Mesa and the distant San Juan Mountains are snow-capped eruptions out of western Colorado's canyon country, a region whose landscape otherwise relates more to Utah's deserts than to the Rockies. You can snowshoe on rolling Alpine meadows with great stands of conifers, mountain lakes and deep snows, which often last well into June, and look out at a very different scene.

The maps and guidebooks say "Grand Mesa," but people on the Western Slope simply call it "the Mesa." This year-round recreational paradise boasts hiking, camping and fishing in summer, and easy access to some of Colorado's least-known, yet best and most snow-sure, winter trails. Cross-country ski and snowshoeing trails and snowmobile routes lace the Mesa's sprawling top. The Alpine runs of Powderhorn Resort cling to its north side like a sparkling white Gumby. No wonder outdoor enthusiasts from Grand Junction, Montrose, Delta and other Western Slope communities feel that paradise is at their doorstep.

Colorado 65, officially named the Grand Mesa National Scenic and Historic Byway, snakes across the Mesa, cresting at over 10,600 feet. It passes dozens of frozen lakes and, most important, separates the trails where snowmobiles are permitted from those where only such nonmotorized sports as snowshoeing and cross-country skiing are allowed. Skating lanes, ungroomed trails within these networks, many additional miles of backcountry trails and acres and acres of open areas beckon snowshoers. When the moon is full and the sky is clear, the snow-covered landscape glows day-bright, and there's simply no place better for moonlight snowshoeing.

On weekends, legions of snowmobilers roar around their designated snow-covered trails, meadows and roads on the west side of the highway, but during the week, even these are uncrowded and are therefore fine for snowshoers to explore. When Front Range residents look at a map of Colorado, it seems as if Grand Mesa is really far away, but it's just four hours from Denver.

For tourist information, contact the **Grand Junction Visitor and Convention Bureau, 740 Horizon Drive, Grand Junction, CO 81506; (800) 962-2547** or **(970) 244-1480.**

## Getting There

Grand Mesa is 40 miles east of Grand Junction. Take Interstate 70 east, get off at Exit 49 and continue on Colorado 65 south. From the east, drive west on I-70. If the weather is good and the roads are clear, get off at Exit 62, 200 miles from Denver. Turn left, cross over the highway and continue for about 10 miles on a winding and hilly road known as the DeBeque Cut-Off. At the T-intersection, turn left onto Colorado 65 south. If the road conditions are dicey, continue on I-70 another 13 miles to Exit 49. Cross the highway to Colorado 65 south.

Whatever your routing to this point, drive through the center of the village of Mesa. The Powderhorn access road is on the right (south), about 6 miles farther up the road. The highway then continues winding up the side of the Mesa and leads to myriad trailheads and ultimately down the other side toward Cedaredge. Three winter trail systems top the Mesa: Skyway at the highway's mile marker 32.5, County Line at mile marker 30 and Ward Creek at mile marker 25.

## Maps

USGS 7.5 Minute, Skyway
Trails Illustrated, #136 Grand Mesa
USFS Grand Mesa National Forest

## *Powderhorn Resort*

As Colorado ski resorts go, Powderhorn is a minor-league player. As far as snowshoeing is concerned, Powderhorn is a pioneer. While other ski resorts have added snowshoeing as an afterthought to other snow sports offerings, at Powderhorn, it has real first-rate status. Powderhorn's Crescent Moon Snowshoe Center is not a cross-country venue that also offers snowshoeing, but rather a facility developed for and dedicated to snowshoeing. This is the first in the state. It occupies a prime parcel directly at the ski area's base, and offers easy access to an ambitious network of snowshoeing trails. The initial 8 kilometers (nearly 5 miles) are the beginning of what is planned as an extensive system of marked trails. Beyond these, plans are afoot at this writing to develop more mileage on 2,000 acres of adjacent private land and perhaps, with Forest Service approval, eventually on ad-

Three loops comprise Powderhorn's lower snowshoeing trails, a short walk from the ski area base lodge. *Photo by Claire Walter.*

jacent public land. An additional 3.1-mile trail along the Mesa's West Bench connects the upper terminals of Powderhorn's two main chairlifts.

During lift operation hours, snowshoers are permitted on two of Powderhorn's downhill ski trails, Bill's Run and Red Eye. Snowshoers are asked to stay on the right side of the trail, both while climbing and descending. If you want to snow-shoe these ski trails or the West Bench Trail at the top but aren't in-terested in climbing 1,650 vertical feet, you can buy a one-ride lift ticket, which is good either just for a one-way uphill or a round-trip. This lift ticket is complimentary with rentals at the snowshoe cen-ter and inexpensive if you have your own gear. Races, moonlight snowshoe tours, races and rental snowshoes complete the program di-rected by racer Robb Reese. For details, call **Powderhorn Resort, P.O. Box 370, Mesa, CO 81643; (970) 268-5700, www.powderhorn.com.**

> ### Crescent Moon Snowshoe Series
>
> The shorter two of Powderhorn's first three loops are used for the Crescent Moon Snowshoe Series. A 5-kilometer running category and a 2-kilometer hik-ing category appeal to serious and rec-reational snowshoers. If the series proves popular, snowshoe running continues to grow and the trail system is developed further, additional distances and catego-ries could be added, and a snowshoe festival will probably be part of the fes-tivities too. Stay tuned. For race infor-mation and applications, write to **Crescent Moon Snowshoe Series, P.O. Box 3572, Grand Junction, CO 81582.**

## Mesa Lakes Resort

This rustic resort, composed of a group of log cabins on Grand Mesa's scenic north side, is just off the highway, making it a hideaway that's not really off the beaten path. Several miles of snowshoeing and cross-country skiing trails are right beyond the doors of the 21 winterized cabins. These trails—some pack groomed and some left natural—adjoin the resort, which is located at 9,870 feet. These trails wind around several lakes (Jumbo, Sunset, Beaver and Mesa) and through a summer camp-ground area. Most are fairly flat, short and easy—excellent for beginners or for anyone just looking to warm up, after a long drive, for the longer trails on the nearby Mesa top.

There is also access to the West Bench Trail to Powderhorn, as well as to the Old Grand Mesa Road, and full-moon tours were popular from the evening they were introduced. This traditional Western Slope fishing retreat opened for the first winter during 1997–1998. Its cozy restaurant serves breakfast, lunch and dinner, the only place on the Mesa to do so at this time of year. Limited snowshoe rentals are available in the small shop adjacent to the restaurant. **Mesa Lakes Resort, P.O. Box 230, Mesa, CO 81643; (970) 268-5467.**

## Moon Over the Mesa

In 1997, retired forester Joe Colwell began organizing informal group walks on the Mesa the night before the full moon each month. During the 1997–1998 winter, cross-country skiers dominated, but snowshoers took part too. In the future seasons, there may be separate programs for snowshoers and skiers, and Colwell invited snowshoe groups to request special walks to be set up just for them. The programs are informal but informative. A local speaker with special expertise in history, wildlife, geology or some other subject gives a brief presentation about halfway through the tour, which can be anywhere from 1 to 3 miles in length and from one to two hours in duration. Participation is free. No reservations are needed, but information on meeting time and place is available from the **Western Colorado Interpretive Association, (970) 874-6695.**

## 126. Lower Trails

| | |
|---|---|
| Starting elevation: | 8,200 feet |
| Lowest elevation: | 8,150 Feet |
| Highest elevation: | 8,400 feet |
| Elevation difference: | 250 feet |
| Distance: | 4.9 miles (loop) |
| Difficulty: | Easy to moderate |
| Avalanche hazard: | None |

The start of a snowshoeing hike here is uninspiring, leading from the main base area through a parking lot and along a service road almost to the bottom of Lift 2. But a few hundred yards from the base, you come to the true trailhead sign on the right, and the entry to a marked and magical trail network that threads delicately through the woods and fields in areas that are narrower and more tranquil than those that are groomed for cross-country. You won't have to worry about tromping on classical tracks or being eclipsed by flashy skate-skiers. The area is habitat for red fox, deer, elk, wild turkey and coyote. You may hear coyotes howling in the distance, their sounds echoing off the rocky cliffs as you snowshoe, and you will definitely see tracks during your hike.

The snowshoeing trail begins south, dropping slightly into the Big Beaver Creek drainage, and then turns sharply to the left. (The way straight ahead leads to the 8,000 Foot Road, which in turn contours along lower down the hill and is expected to be incorporated into the snowshoeing trail system, possibly in 1999 or 2000.) The recommended direction is counterclockwise, because that's the most interesting direction.

Almost immediately into the system, beginners may prefer to take the **Orbit Loop,** just 1.2 miles in all along a flat area of beaver ponds and meadows. The most popular snowshoe tour is to continue along the 3.1-mile **Conundrum** or **C-Loop,** whose interesting features make the miles fly, even if you are just meandering along. Valley View is at the low point of the trail, but it provides the best views. You can look north and see more than just the valley. You can see the Book Cliff's enormous rock walls, banded with multihued strata, resembling neighboring Utah, and also Chalk Mountain, an 8,092-foot volcanic plug, rising nearly 3,000 feet above the Colorado River Valley.

From Valley View, the route continues west past Beaver Pond and an abundance of aspens, oak brush and salt cedars. Just when the Salt Shack, an old log hut, comes into view, look back over your left shoulder toward the last group of aspen trees. Wood carving is never a good thing along a trail, but one practitioner at least showed a sense of humor, engraving a curvaceous woman's outline into the bark of one tree. Take the right trail at the fork after the artistic aspen and the Salt Shack. Here, the trail turns south again. If you want to continue onto **The Outer Limits** and perhaps to some of the newer trails that will be added in years subsequent to the publication of this book, bear right. The Outer Limits extends your route to the full distance as of this writing and is a relatively level route.

If you stay on the C-Loop, that is, to the left, you will begin ascending through the Enchanted Forest portion of the trail. Be sure to take a look at the bear claw marks on aspens on both sides of the trail at its highest point. It's one thing to hear coyotes in the distance in broad daylight, but it's another to see such sign of bear. Then again, it's also comforting to know that the bears who decorated those trees, if still around, are hibernating. Pass through the Crossroads, where several trails intersect, and wind down the Flume, where you quickly loose all the elevation you gained earlier. the Flume resembles a snowy waterslide. Some snowshoers skip down it; others sit down and slide it, with less glory but still a lot of fun. At the bottom of the Flume is Beaver Pond and the end of the circuit. Continue your return by retracing your steps to the start of the trail and back to the intersection of the service road.

## 127. West Bench Trail (West)

| | |
|---|---|
| Starting elevation: | 9,850 feet |
| Highest elevation: | 10,050 feet |
| Elevation difference: | 200 feet, plus some ups and downs |
| Distance: | 2.8 miles (one way) |
| Difficulty: | Moderate |
| Avalanche hazard: | None |

Ride Lift 1 to the top of the ski area. Cross the Maverick ski trail and amble through a small stand of trees past the patrol building and across

Snowshoers can hike up one of Powderhorn's lower snowshoeing trails, a short walk from the ski area base lodge. *Photo by Claire Walter.*

the open meadow (there may be snowmobile or other tracks to follow). You will see a blue stake on the far right (southwest) corner of the field, marking the start of the West Bench Trail, which is marked with blue diamonds. The trail follows a fairly steady contour, with a few curves and a few ups and downs to keep it from being simply a snowy highway linking two lift stations. Several clearings located a few steps from the right (north) side of the trail provide an opportunity for sensational views. They are unmarked, but you can usually spot them by tracks left by other snowshoers and skiers. You'll have to climb up a small snow-covered rise to get the views and the photo opportunity, and it's worth every step.

The high point of the trail is roughly halfway between the two lift unloading areas. As you climb toward this point, notice that "normal" Colorado-sized conifers and aspens suddenly approach the dimensions of the Pacific Northwest's mammoth Douglas firs. As you snowshoe through these enormous trees, in a silent world, you may feel as if you are walking through a nave in nature's cathedral. Ride Lift 2 back down. You can also do the trip from west to east, riding up Lift 2 and down Lift 1.

### If You Want a Longer Hike

You can start your hike directly at the resort's base and ascend Bill's Run if you want to add a big aerobic component to this scenic hike, or end it by snowshoeing back down to the base via the Flume Run and get those quadriceps into gear on the downhill.

## 128. West Bench Trail (East)

| | |
|---|---|
| Starting elevation: | 9,850 feet |
| Highest elevation: | 10,000 feet, plus ups and downs |
| Elevation difference: | 150 feet |
| Distance: | 4.5 miles (one way) |
| Difficulty: | Moderate |
| Avalanche hazard: | None |

This lovely wooded trail connects the top of Powderhorn's Lift 1 with the Mesa Lakes Resort, a quaint and homey resort complex (see page 241).

You can make a very respectable round-trip of this route or do it with a car shuttle. If you snowshoe up Bill's Run for a 1,650-foot elevation gain before beginning this hike, you're in great shape and have ambition to match. Most snowshoers take the lift up. In either case, proceed as above across the open meadow, but then look for the blue stake on the left. The trail to Mesa Lakes Resort climbs steadily—even steeply at times—to the south through a mixed forest of aspens and conifers. It enters the resort's trail system near a summer ranger station and just to the west of Sunset Lake. Grand Mesa's more open upper areas can get windy, and when they do, either section of the heavily treed West Bench Trail provides relief from the gusts.

## 129. Old Grand Mesa Road

| | |
|---|---|
| Starting elevation: | 9,920 feet |
| Highest elevation: | 10,440 feet |
| Elevation difference: | 520 feet |
| Distance: | 2.3 miles (one way) |
| Difficulty: | Moderate |
| Avalanche hazard: | Low |

The road designated as Colorado Highway 65 over the Grand Mesa is known by locals as the new road. Portions of the old road—narrower, less hospitable to modern traffic, yet even more scenic—today are used as a recreation trail and are not plowed. To get a nice workout, begin your hike at the west end of the Mesa Lakes Resort trails. The old road first heads south, then east and, after one large switchback and a series of small curves, joins Highway 65. You can also park here and snowshoe down to the resort. In either case, you can do the trail as an out-and-back hike or with a car shuttle.

# Grand Mesa's Three Grand Trail Systems

In addition to numerous official and unofficial trailheads right off Highway 65, three trail systems, all in very low avalanche areas, are available for nonmotorized recreation. Volunteers from the community-based Grand Mesa Nordic Council maintain all three. Of course, they especially plead with snowshoers to stay off the classical tracks. For membership information, contact the **Grand Mesa Nordic Council, P.O. Box 266, Cory, CO 81414; (970) 434-9753.** If you want a basic trail map, a stamped, self-addressed, letter-sized envelope would be appreciated by this not-for-profit organization.

## Skyway

This is the only one of the trio of trail systems that approaches commercial status, yet infrastructure-wise, this is far from a conventional, contemporary cross-country center. Certainly there are excellent groomed and track-set trails—and very good ones at that—but the warming hut, snack bar and rental shop are all in trailers, and the portable john is set up on a platform to keep it out of the snow. The plowed parking area of this superlatively funky facility is just off Colorado 65 at 10,660 feet. Five groomed loop trails vary in length from 3 kilometers (just under 2 miles) to 9.3 kilometers (about 6 miles). They can be combined into longer or shorter routes as well. Snowshoers are welcome on the skating lanes of all the trails. They are all quite gentle, and the entire trail network has a maximum 150-foot elevation change.

There is currently no fee, but a donation box to help cover grooming expenses is affixed to a fence post at the trailhead. Make your way to the overlook at the northeastern end of the trail system for an incredible view of the Book Cliffs. A 1.55-mile marked connector trail to the County Line Nordic Trails is used surprisingly little, but it makes a particularly nice one-way hike with a car shuttle. **Skyway Nordic Ski Area, P.O. Box 63, Grand Mesa, CO 81413; (970) 872-2872.**

## County Line

Skyway's minimal infrastructure seems like a big development when compared with County Line, where a plowed parking area and a trailhead is about all you get. Tailgate picnics or trailside stops are the rule at this web of easy routes at the gorgeous crest of the Grand Mesa. The trails are laid out in four loops, ranging from 0.7 mile to 4.6 miles in length, and they are generally not groomed. Even gentler than Skyway, they measure out to a mere 53-foot elevation difference from the lowest to the highest. Still, the scenery equals the best in the state. For one of the finest views, bear right (east) at the first two junctions from the trailhead, and at about 1.3 miles, look south toward the San Juan Mountains.

## Ward Creek

Of the Grand Mesa's three trail systems, Ward Creek is the most extensive. The groomed and ungroomed trails range in length from 1.5 miles to nearly 10 miles, and in elevation between 9,760 and 10,290 feet. There are two main parking areas and major trailheads, located respectively at the Grand Mesa Visitors Center, which is staffed by park rangers on most winter weekends, and also along Highway 65, 29 miles north of Cedaredge. Because Ward Creek is the largest of the three systems and is also farthest from Grand Junction, it tends to get the fewest crowds. However, it is also the lowest and southernmost of the three trail networks, meaning that its season of good snow is somewhat shorter than its higher neighbors'. Unlike the other two, a few of Ward Creek's most outlying trails are also used by snowmobilers.

# Ouray and Ridgway

Cartographers plot Ouray County at 542 square miles. This is modest by Colorado standards, but if you ironed it out, the county set deep in the heart of the San Juan Mountains would probably be the size of Texas. It has just two towns, the county seat of Ouray, where the north-flowing Uncompahgre River tumbles down from the high country, and Ridgway, where the valley opens up slightly. The towns' residents and the few people who live in the surrounding mountains and valleys approach a total population of about 3,500. Outsiders think that they live in a beautiful but remote area, but there were not always so few residents and the country did not always seem so remote. In the heyday of mining, Ouray was a major mining center, and Ridgway was developed as a significant rail junction of southwestern Colorado. But that was then and this is now. Old wagon roads, mining camps and ghost towns are found throughout the region, but in winter, much of it is buried or inaccessible.

When the San Juans lie under a deep mantle of snow, even the two populated towns feel somnolent. The mass of summer tourists is absent, and the locals themselves are probably playing in the snow. Their games are not without risk. These mountains are among the steepest of all the Colorado Rockies ranges, and they often snare the state's highest snowfalls too. Added to the natural terrain and snowfall patterns is the fact that mining activities denuded many of the slopes and increased avalanche danger. Still, for the cautious snowshoer, opportunities to explore this gorgeous area do present themselves. Both towns boast wonderful natural hot springs pools to unwind in after a day of trekking around the mountains. Check out the **Orvis Hot Springs** in Ridgway or the **Ouray Hot Springs,** or check in at the Ouray's **Wiesbaden Hot Springs Spa and Lodge.**

For tourist information, contact the **Southwest Colorado Travel Region, 195-A Girard Street, Durango, CO 81301; (800) 933-4340; www.swcolotravel.org,** or **Ouray Chamber Resort Association, P.O. Box 145, Ouray, CO 81429; (800) 228-1876** or **(970) 325-4746.**

## Getting There

From Denver, take Interstate 70 west to Grand Junction and then U.S. 50/550 south, which in Montrose continues as U.S. 550. Or make your way via U.S. 285 and U.S. 50 via Gunnison and Montrose to U.S. 550 South. Either way, the drive is about 330 miles, which in winter can take an eternity. Another option is to fly to Montrose.

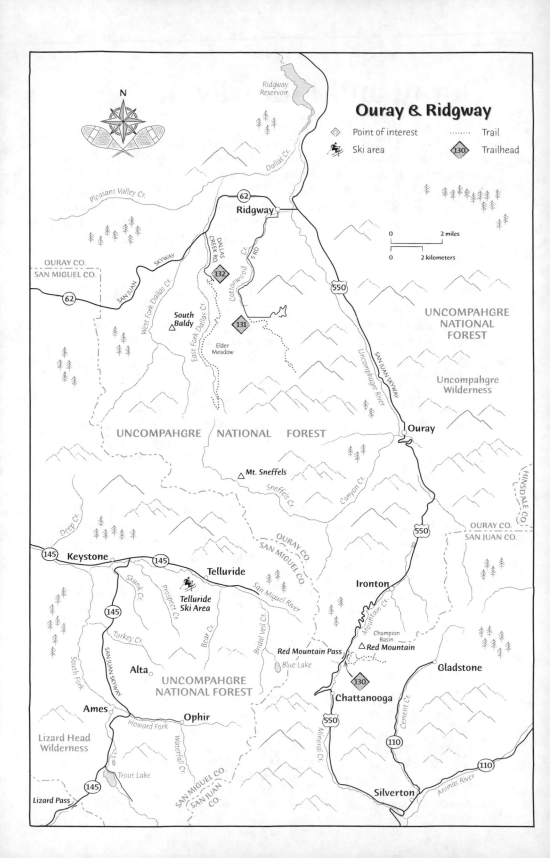

# Ouray & Ridgway

◇ Point of interest
🎿 Ski area
⬦130 Trailhead
········ Trail

Ridgway Reservoir

N

Dallas Cr.

Pleasant Valley Cr.

62
Ridgway

0 ——— 2 miles
0 ——— 2 kilometers

DALLAS CREEK RD.
Cottonwood Cr.
S RD.

SAN JUAN SKYWAY

OURAY CO.
SAN MIGUEL CO.

62

⬦132

West Fork Dallas Cr.

East Fork Dallas Cr.

South Baldy △

⬦131

Elder Meadow

550

UNCOMPAHGRE NATIONAL FOREST

Uncompahgre Wilderness

Uncompahgre River

SAN JUAN SKYWAY

UNCOMPAHGRE   NATIONAL   FOREST

△ Mt. Sneffels

Sneffels Cr.

Canyon Cr.

Ouray

HINSDALE CO.

Deep Cr.

145
Keystone

145

145
Telluride

🎿
Telluride Ski Area

Skunk Cr.

Prospect Cr.

Bear Cr.

Bridal Veil Cr.

San Miguel River

OURAY CO.
SAN MIGUEL CO.

OURAY CO.
SAN JUAN CO.

550

Ironton

Mountain Cr.

Champion Basin
△ Red Mountain

Gladstone

Turkey Cr.

SAN JUAN SKYWAY

Alta

UNCOMPAHGRE NATIONAL FOREST

Red Mountain Pass
Blue Lake

⬦130

South Fork

Ames

Howard Fork

Ophir

Waterfall Cr.

Chattanooga

550

Cement Cr.

Lizard Head Wilderness

Trout Lake

SAN MIGUEL CO.
SAN JUAN CO.

Mineral Cr.

110

110

145

Lizard Pass

Silverton

Animas River

**Maps**
USGS 7.5 Minute, Ouray, Ironton, Dallas, Ridgway
Trails Illustrated #141, Silverton, Ouray, Telluride, Lake City
USFS San Juan National Forest
Map of the Mountains of Silverton, Telluride and Ouray,
Drake Mountain Maps

# Ouray

Even among Colorado's beautiful Victorian villages, Ouray stands out. It is tucked into a canyonlike valley sliced into 13,000- and 14,000-foot mountains by the Uncompahgre River. Ouray (locally pronounced "Your-Ray") is on a major highway—its main street is, after all, U.S. 550. But it also has an end-of-the-earth quality. The San Juan Mountains press in on it from both sides, and like Telluride, Aspen, Breckenridge and other towns from that era, its wealth came from mining.

Telluride is just a few miles to the west, but as the cliché goes, "you can't get there from here." Not easily, anyway. The only more or less direct routes are either by harrowing four-wheel-drive roads that are closed in winter because they pass through severe avalanche territory or by an old mine tunnel, a historic curiosity, that bores under the mountains. People must go the long way around, some 50 miles though Ridgway. Vast tracts of rugged backcountry east of Ouray separate it from Lake City, also tucked into a deep mountain valley, but the "long way" to Lake City is even longer.

South of Ouray is Red Mountain Pass, at 11,018 feet one of the highest to be plowed and kept open in the winter. It is Colorado's snowiest pass road and also the hairiest to drive. In summer, the surrounding mountains boast many of the state's finest four-wheel-drive roads, and some are winter snowshoeing and ski trails. It's worth your life to explore others, which lead deep into slide-prone high basins. Some people, of course, think that it's worth your life to navigate Red Mountain Pass too.

Still, skiers and snowshoers drive the pass, scary or not, to reach high trails. On the south side of the pass is Silverton, another more-or-less neighboring community that is also awash with Victorian atmosphere and mining history. U.S. 550 may be the map name, Red Mountain Pass may mark it geographically, but Million Dollar Highway is what this Ouray-Silverton road is called. It got its name either because the roadbed was made of gold-bearing mine tailings or because it was so expensive to build ($40,000 per mile back in the early 1880s), but everyone who drives it today agrees that it proffers million-dollar views at every switchback.

## Ironton Park

This small cross-country trail system, directly off U.S. 550 9 miles south of Ouray, is operated by Ouray Nordic Council volunteers. They groom several old mining roads, which make rather gentle winter trails away from avalanche zones. Snowshoers are welcome on these trails but are asked not to stomp on cross-country skiers' tracks. Use of these trails is free, but there is a donation box for anyone who wants to help defray the cost of grooming. For a map, send a stamped, self-addressed envelope to the **Ouray Nordic Council, P.O. Box 468, Ouray, CO 81427.**

# 130. St. Paul Lodge

| | |
|---|---|
| Starting elevation: | 11,060 feet |
| Highest elevation: | 11,400 feet |
| Elevation difference: | 340 feet |
| Distance: | 1 mile (one way) |
| Difficulty: | Moderate |
| Avalanche hazard: | Low to moderate |

### Ouray Ice Park

Snowshoeing and ice climbing have only one thing in common: They are both practiced on some form of frozen water. If you are snowshoeing around the Ouray-Red Mountain Pass area, don't miss visiting the Ouray Ice Park, the world's first dedicated public ice-climbing facility, located in the spectacular Uncompahgre Gorge, just south of town. Ice climbers are a rare and rugged breed who combine the risks of rock climbing with the uncertainty of climbing as fragile and unpredictable a medium as ice. Watching them dance up the frozen waters plastered against the canyon walls is a thrilling spectator sport. The ice park is generally open from early winter until mid-March. For information, contact the **Ouray Chamber Resort Association** (see page 247).

Drive south from Ouray on U.S. 550 for 22 miles of gut-gripping switchbacks, sheer drop-offs and magnificent scenery to the summit of Red Mountain Pass. The unpaved, unplowed road to the lodge is on the left (east) side of the pass. Begin snowshoeing past old mine buildings. The route then bends south and southeast around a snow-covered knob and up a small valley that contours around Red Mountain itself. Its steep climb of about 160 feet at this elevation may seem more like 1,600 feet! Catch your breath, cross the creek and climb more gently to the lodge. As you come over the last rise to a broad clearing where the lodge is located, you'll feel as if you were hit between the eyes by a mirage.

The St. Paul Lodge is so rustic that it makes other mountain huts look like the Ritz. It began life as the tipple house of an old mine but was "developed" with scabbed-together timbers, windows, roofing, doors, windows and fixtures salvaged from old buildings that broaden the meaning of the adjective "quirky." It is operated by an eccentric Englishman named Chris George who runs it dorm-style, serves hearty meals and even puts together groups to explore the nearby backcountry. Following someone who knows the way is a very good idea up here, because avalanche hazards can be severe in this region of heavy snow and steep mountains. For some people, overnighting at a place where the "facilities" consist of commodes built over a deep mineshaft is just too, too much. For others, that's part of the charm. You don't have to overnight at the St. Paul Lodge, but if you wish to, contact Chris at **P.O. Box 463, Silverton, CO 81433; (970) 387-5367.**

### If You Want a Longer Hike

The St. Paul Lodge is a good launching pad for treks back toward U.S. Basin, an area favored by telemark skiers, and accessed by a trail with fantastic views. You can also return to the Red Mountain Pass trailhead by a longer, roundabout way, via Champion Gulch to the north, and then doubling back southwest on another old mining road.

# Ridgway

Ridgway is 10 miles north of Ouray. In contrast to the drama of Red Mountain Pass, the Ouray-Ridgway stretch is a piece of cake. The two towns are a real study in contrasts. Less Victorian and far more eclectic, Ridgway is a down-home sort of place at the crossroads of routes to Telluride, Ouray and the regional airport and commercial center of Montrose, which is still farther to the north. Ouray is a Colorado mountain community, pure and simple. Ridgway would be described as a mountain town in any other context, but within the tight framework of the sky-high San Juan Mountains, locals think of it as a valley community. It spreads (relatively) in a (relatively) broad basin in a place where the Uncompahgre River has created a wider valley than that in which its nearest neighbor, Ouray, is located.

## Chipeta Sun Lodge

This charming, 12-room B&B and new adjacent suite accommodations are made all the more congenial by innkeepers Lyle and Shari Braund, avid outdoorsfolk who not only snowshoe, ski and hike, but more often than not accompany guests on complimentary excursions from Ridgway to Red Mountain Pass and other routes. They love their region, and they love to show it off. The original solar adobe inn was designed and decorated in southwestern trendy style but with attention to environmental friendliness.

The Braunds serve an opulent daily breakfast in a bright, three-story atrium overlooking a huge, free-form ice sculpture and a fine mountain view. In late 1997, the Chipeta Sun Lodge added eight one- and two-bedroom suites that are ideal for families, as well as a 2,700-square-foot health and fitness center. The inn offers a lot of comfort and luxury (as well as convenient access to excellent snowshoeing trails and Ridgway's restaurants and shops) at moderate rates. As one of the main stops on the San Juan Skyway scenic auto loop, the Chipeta Sun Lodge considers summer to be high season, so winter offers additional value. **Chipeta Sun Lodge, 304 South Lena, Ridgway, CO 81432; (800) 633-5868** or **(970) 626-3737; www.independence.net/chipeta.**

## Come and See

Come and See is a Ridgway-based "activities broker" that customizes packages that include snowshoeing tours, lodging, meals and other components. San Juan Mountain Guides is the Forest Service–licensed guide service that handles the backcountry component, which can include everything from an easy tour to a rousing winter adventure. The San Juan Mountains can be as treacherous as they are gorgeous. They often snare Colorado's biggest snowfalls and harbor significant avalanche hazards in many spots, so it's smart to go guided. **Come and See, P.O. Box 321, Ridgway, CO 81432; (970) 626-3926; www.montrose.net/comeandsee/.**

## 131. Miller Mesa Road

| | |
|---|---|
| Starting elevation: | 8,650 feet |
| Highest elevation: | 9,200 feet |
| Elevation difference: | 550 feet |
| Distance: | 4 miles (one way) |
| Difficulty: | Easy |
| Avalanche hazard: | None |

Million-dollar view from the top of Miller Mesa. *Photo by Ral Sandberg.*

Drive west out of Ridgway on Colorado 62 and turn left onto Ouray County Road 5. After 0.25 mile turn right onto the Elk Meadows Road. Park near the cluster of mailboxes at the Elk Meadows subdivision sign and hike up the unplowed road. The road first heads south and then east, very gently ascending the Mesa, and a couple of small, unpaved side roads merge into it. Gratification is immediate, with views down toward the town of Ridgway and up at the jagged peaks of the Mt. Sneffels Wilderness, one of Colorado's most spectacular mountain ranges. You can amble along this beautiful stretch as far as you wish and return the way you came.

## 132. East Fork Dallas Creek

| | |
|---|---|
| Starting elevation: | 7,760 feet |
| Highest elevation: | 9,050 feet |
| Elevation change: | 1,290 feet |
| Distance: | About 5 miles (one way, to start of Willow Swamp) |
| Difficulty: | Moderate to challenging |
| Avalanche hazard: | Low |

From Ridgway drive west on Colorado 62 for nearly 5 miles. Turn left (south) onto Ouray County Road 7 to the junction with Forest Service Road 851, which forks off to the right about 4 miles from the highway turnoff. Begin snowshoeing up the unplowed road, which crosses Beaver Creek and then begins winding up the ridge between Beaver Creek and the East Fork of Dallas Creek. It is flanked by private property. The road roughly follows the ridge, passing through dense scrub forests, aspen groves and stands of conifers. South Baldy, which is crisscrossed by a web of old roads, rises to the west, while Miller Mesa is the valley is more distant eastern wall. The valley opens up into a large willowy area, aptly known as Willow Swamp. In winter, it makes for good snowshoeing and a good turnaround spot too. The head of Willow Swamp is a good place to turn back, though you can explore the frozen marsh and should certainly pause to admire the craggy splendor of 14,150-foot Mt. Sneffels to the southeast.

### If You Want a Longer Hike

Or you can explore the Willow Swamp. The road crosses Dallas Creek on a wooden bridge at the southern end of this frozen-over marsh, just below the confluence of Wilson Creek and then makes a sharp turn climbing to the northwest and soon narrows down into a trail and passes Cocan Flats. Eventually, it leads to the Blue Lakes Hut, part of the San Juan Hut System (see Telluride and Lizard Head Pass chapter, page 255).

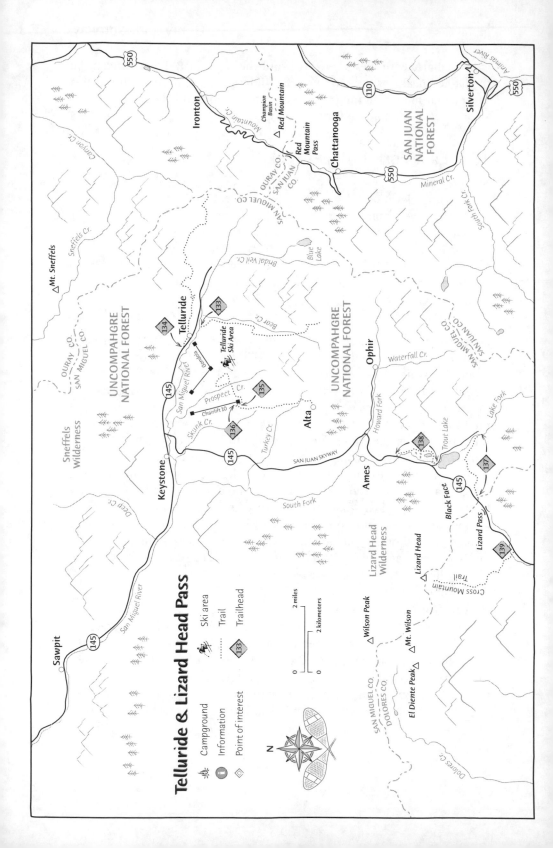

# Telluride & Lizard Head Pass

**Legend:**
- Campground
- Information
- Point of Interest
- Ski area
- Trail
- Trailhead 133

**Map labels:**

550
110
550
550

SAN JUAN NATIONAL FOREST

Silverton

Animas River

Mineral Cr.

South Fork Cr.

Chattanooga

Red Mountain Pass

△ Red Mountain

Champion Basin

Mountain Cr.

Ironton

Canyon Cr.

OURAY CO.
SAN JUAN CO.

SAN MIGUEL CO.

Sneffels Cr.

△ Mt. Sneffels

UNCOMPAHGRE NATIONAL FOREST

Sneffels Wilderness

OURAY CO.
SAN MIGUEL CO.

Blue Lake

Bridal Veil Cr.

Bear Cr.

Telluride 134
133
Telluride Ski Area

Gondola

San Miguel River

145

Prospect Cr. 135

Chairlift 10

Skunk Cr. 136

Turkey Cr.

Alta

145

SAN JUAN SKYWAY

Keystone

Deep Cr.

South Fork

UNCOMPAHGRE NATIONAL FOREST

Ophir

Waterfall Cr.

Howard Fork

Lake Fork

SAN MIGUEL CO.
SAN JUAN CO.

Trout Lake

138

137

145

Black Face

Lizard Pass

Ames

Lizard Head Wilderness

Lizard Head

△ Lizard Head

Cross Mountain Trail

139

San Miguel River

Sawpit

145

△ Wilson Peak

△ Mt. Wilson

△ El Diente Peak

SAN MIGUEL CO.
DOLORES CO.

Dolores Cr.

2 miles
2 kilometers
0
0

N

# Telluride and Lizard Head Pass

Telluride is a gorgeous Victorian town wedged into a steep-sided box canyon, carved by the San Miguel River and its cascading little tributaries. This long, skinny town has an enchanted location, with mountains soaring from the edge of town, literally where the sidewalks end. Its scenic beauty is matched only by the abundance of doorstep recreational opportunities. The original Telluride, once one of the West's richest mining towns, is awash with authentic Victorian charm of the sort that will melt your heart, while Telluride Mountain Village is a new resort that can dent your wallet. Mountain Village is an exquisite, elegant, expensive and exclusive new resort enclave built in a large bowl into which most of the Alpine ski trails feed. Mountain Village also provides lift access to several outstanding snowshoeing areas, where you can enjoy some of the best views and least precarious terrain, without having to climb up to it.

If you are trying snowshoeing for the first time, or if you want to extend your snowshoeing activities, Telluride is a fine place to do both. Pleasant trails become workouts if you run them. Guided tours add a dose of history to your snowshoe trip. Routes in high bowls offer fantastic scenery, and lift access puts them within the range of casual snowshoers. However, the high, steep-sided mountains, frequent and abundant snowfalls and even deforestation from long-ago mining activities make for real avalanche hazards, not only in the distant backcountry but along some easily accessible trails. Let "caution" and "conservatism" be your watchwords when you explore this magnificent region.

For tourist information, contact the **Telluride Resort Chamber, 666 West Colorado Avenue, P.O. Box 653, Telluride, CO 81453; (800) 525-3455** or **(970) 728-4434; www.telluridemm.com.**

## Getting There

Telluride is a long drive from Denver, no doubt about it. One option is to take U.S. 285 south to Salida, then turn right (west) onto U.S. 50 and follow it over Monarch Pass to Montrose, then turn left (south) onto U.S. 550. Another option is to take Interstate 70 west to Glenwood Springs, then Colorado 82 south to Carbondale, turning right onto Colorado 141 over McClure Pass and left (south) onto U.S. 50/U.S. 550. In either case, the last stretch is on U.S. 550 south to Ridgway, where you turn right at the traffic light onto Colorado 62 over Dallas Divide. Turn left onto Colorado 145 and follow it to Telluride. Whichever you select, it is more than 300 hard winter miles, which translates to at least a seven- to eight-hour drive.

For Lizard Head Pass, take Colorado 145, which connects Telluride and Cortez. Drive west out of Telluride (the only direction possible), and stay on Highway 145 as it makes a left (south) on the outskirts. You will pass the Telluride Mountain Village access road on the left as you climb toward Lizard Head Pass.

It is also possible to fly directly to Telluride or to Montrose, 65 miles away. Rental cars and van transfers are available from both airports. Once at the resort, you don't need a car. Use of the gondola, which connects the historic town of Telluride and Telluride Mountain Village over a shoulder of the main ski mountain, is free unless you have skis or a snowboard. Chair 10, which accesses groomed trails high on a secondary ski mountain, requires a "Nordic ticket" for snowshoeing or cross-country skiing.

### Maps
USGS 7.5 Minute, Telluride, Mt. Sneffels
Trails Illustrated #141, Silverton, Ouray, Telluride, Lake City
USFS San Juan National Forest
Map of the Mountains of Silverton, Telluride and Ouray,
Drake Mountain Maps

## Trails from the Town of Telluride

Very good and exceptionally convenient snowshoeing routes are the winter incarnation of popular summer hiking, mountain biking and even four-wheel-drive routes right at the end of town. Out-and-back routes prevail, which is a kindness, given both Telluride's lofty elevation and its steep mountains. This is a place to be especially mindful of avalanche condition reports, even when you are snowshoeing within sight of the town's Victorian rooftops.

# 133. St. Miguel River Trail

| | |
|---|---|
| Starting elevation: | 8,700 feet |
| Lowest elevation: | 8,530 feet |
| Elevation difference: | 170 feet |
| Distance: | 5 miles (one way) |
| Difficulty: | Easy |
| Avalanche hazard: | Low |

This riverside boulevard is Telluride's easiest route, used (depending on snow conditions) by snowshoers, cross-country skiers, joggers, winter hikers and dog walkers. It follows the San Miguel River from Telluride's eastern reaches, skirts the south side of town, darts beneath the downhill ski runs, crosses the river and continues west through the open valley that so far remains undeveloped. The (for Telluride) low elevation and such aggressive multi-use can make for unpredictable snow conditions, but that's where snowshoes really shine. Even as they offer flotation in powder, they smooth out the lumps and bumps on well-used snow, and the claws grip on the boilerplate hardpack.

### If You Want a Longer Hike

There is also a challenging option, a side trail that angles off to the left roughly 0.5 mile from the edge of town and climbs to the lower part of Telluride Mountain Village, a steep ascent of some 600 vertical feet. In addition to getting a good workout, you'll probably find good snow, because this is a north-facing slope.

## 134. Bear Creek Trail

| | |
|---|---|
| Starting elevation: | 8,760 feet |
| Highest elevation: | 9,800 feet |
| Elevation difference: | 1,040 feet |
| Distance: | 2 miles (one way) |
| Difficulty: | Moderate |
| Avalanche hazard: | Moderate in some sections below the falls. |

Popular Bear Creek Trail, culminating at a lovely waterfall, is an all-time, year-round favorite excursion for locals and visitors alike. From the trailhead at the foot of Pine Street, it begins with a short steep section. This is quickly followed by a languorous uphill, roughly paralleling, but angling northeast and away from, the San Miguel River. A handful of narrow chutes on the right could funnel slide debris onto the trail, so if you stop to rest, sip some water or wait for a companion, don't do so directly at these outlets. After about 0.3 mile, the trail curves to the right (south) and continues straight to the waterfall. En route to the falls, you will pass a few trail junctions and the remnants of old mining activity tucked into the woods—easy to explore on snowshoes. Don't go above the falls, for the avalanche danger there is substantial, from both natural releases and slides set off by backcountry skiers and snowboarders above.

Photo by Claire Walter.

# 135. Tomboy Road

| | |
|---|---|
| Starting elevation: | 8,700 feet |
| Highest elevation: | 9,537 feet |
| Elevation difference: | 837 feet |
| Distance: | 1 mile (one way) |
| Difficulty: | Moderate to challenging |
| Avalanche hazard: | Low at beginning of trail (moderate to high at Owl Gulch, at 0.75 mile); moderate to high on upper portions of the road |

The trailhead on the north end of Oak Street accesses an old wagon road leading to Tomboy, once the Telluride area's largest mining camp, located high in a cirque that was aptly named Savage Basin. Where miners and mule trains once slogged, Telluridians now come to play. No other route offers such a combination of easy access, aerobic benefit and gratifying views of the town and mountains. The lower sections of the road provide an excellent snowshoeing opportunity for the fit and ambitious, but the upper sections should be approached only under the most snow-sure conditions—and even then with caution, because mining activities thinned the trees well below the natural timberline.

The Tomboy Road (Forest Service Road 869) is wide and technically easy, but the grade ratchets it up in challenge. It angles from town, heading due east and climbing surprisingly steeply and steadily for the first mile before making two hairpin turns and angling more toward the northeast. Step lively as you cross Owl Gulch about 0.75 mile from the trailhead. For many casual snowshoers, the demanding first mile is more than enough. In addition to safety issues, one benefit of turning around at the first hairpin is that you get to enjoy the views of town and the San Miguel River Valley all the sooner.

## If You Want a Longer Hike

If conditions—yours and especially the snow's—warrant continuing, you will pass Royer Gulch (again, keep moving) and through the Social Tunnel, blasted into the rock. On your left are the Bullion Tunnel and the Cimarron Mine, major landmarks along the Tomboy Road, as is the Marshall Creek crossing, which is about 2 miles and 2,000 vertical feet from the trailhead. It provides another goal, and yet another very sensible opportunity to turn back before reaching the treacherous (and, yes, savage) precincts of Savage Basin and the Tomboy ghost town itself. Even assuming that you've gotten this far, continue with caution. If, and only if, the snowpack is reported secure should you consider ascending past Marshall Creek. The other drawback to this route—and this is more one of snowshoeability than snow safety—is that this might not be a good early-season choice or in a dry spell, because the sun can fry the snow off of the south-facing slope into which Tomboy Road is etched.

## Trails from the Telluride Ski Area

Since snowshoeing began taking off, the Telluride Resort has been hospitable to the sport. Guided excursions once were offered deep in the basin where Telluride Mountain Village and the golf course are now located. The Peaks at Telluride, the development's largest and fanciest accommodation, still offers snowshoe tours around the golf course as part of its activities program, but most of the snowshoeing is now high on the ski mountains. Good lift access, especially the gondola (which does not require a lift ticket for snowshoers, who are considered foot passengers), makes safe, high-mountain snowshoeing a reality, whether on a tour or hiking independently.

# 136. Prospect Basin

| | |
|---|---|
| Starting elevation: | 10,800 feet (top of Chair 10) |
| Highest elevation: | 11,000 feet |
| Elevation difference: | Varies, but maximum is 200 feet |
| Distance: | 3.75 to 5 miles (loop or out and back, depending on route) |
| Difficulty: | Easy |
| Avalanche hazard: | None |

Prospect Basin and its companion trail system, Magic Meadows (see page 260), are accessible from the top of Telluride's Chair 10. To reach the snowshoeing trails, cut across the broad ski run to a groomed trail through the woods. A few steps will take you to an intersection, at which you take the trail to the left. It is groomed wide for skate skiing, which enables three or four snowshoers to walk abreast, but do step aside quickly when skiers come up behind you.

The white pine forest provides shelter from the wind and definition even on flat-light days. After about 1.25 miles, the trail breaks open into a glorious bowl called Prospect Basin. As you look down on this huge cirque, you may wonder why a power line runs through this pristine landscape. Do not think of it as blight. Think of it as history, for it was strung from the world's first power plant transmitting

A guided snowshoe tour on Prospect Basin's broad, groomed trail. *Photo by Claire Walter.*

alternating current in Ames over the mountains to Telluride, and it became the first in the nation to deliver AC electricity to a community.

The grooming follows a rough figure eight. If you decide to do the entire groomed route, you can take either the left or right fork and know that you'll come back to the same spot. The entire route is about 5 miles, but many people are so enchanted by the jagged ridgeline of Gold Hill, Palmyra Peak and Silver Mountain that they just spread out a picnic and admire the view. You can return to the top of Chair 10 by retracing your steps or bearing left at a trail intersection where the basin meets the woods. If you take the latter option, also completing the figure eight, you will have the odd sensation of descending farther than you ascended on the way to the Basin. It is one of the most curious illusions of all of Colorado's main snowshoeing routes. At the next trail intersection, turn right to return to the top of Chair 10 or left to add Magic Meadows to your day's itinerary.

A reasonably priced Nordic ticket is available for those who only want to ride Chair 10 to access the high country, and the lift, a high-speed, detachable quad chairlift, also permits downloading. Prospect Basin is slated for direct lift service, which will change the ambience even if snowshoeing is still encouraged there. For now, however, it is the playground of snowshoers and cross-country skiers, who can experience true high altitude without having to work for it.

## 137. Magic Meadows

| | |
|---|---|
| Starting elevation: | 10,800 feet (top of Chair 10) |
| Highest elevation: | 10,800 feet |
| Lowest elevation: | 10,500 feet |
| Elevation difference: | Varies, but maximum is 300 feet (ascend on the return) |
| Distance: | Up to 4 to 5 miles (one way), depending on the route |
| Difficulty: | Easy to moderate |
| Avalanche hazard: | Low |

Take Chair 10 and cross the ski run, as if you were going to Prospect Basin, but continue through the first trail intersection and take the trail straight ahead. Go mostly downhill for about a mile and a half. You will pass through white pine woods on a wide, groomed trail (see Prospect Basin description, page 259) until you reach expansive Magic Meadows. On some maps, this area is broadly identified as Turkey Creek Mesa, but Magic Meadows is a suitable name, because the views seem to have been conjured up by a wizard of a scene painter. The Meadows provide an incredible panorama of 14,017-foot Wilson Peak, the Lizard Head formation and the San Sophia Ridge.

You can bear left and snowshoe around Bald Mountain, the humpy knob to the south, or continue straight into the heart of the Magic Meadows trails. Continue straight at the intersection of the groomed trails to make a pleasant loop through the open meadow. Take a hard right (north) to explore the mesa top or a left toward Alta and Alta Lakes (see below). The Magic Meadows loop alone is 4 to 5 miles, depending on your precise route, and when you are heading out, remember that the return route to Chair 10 is mostly uphill.

### If You Want a Longer Hike

If the weather is fine (and promising to stay so) and you are feeling frisky, you can continue across Magic Meadows to Alta Lakes. Cross the Meadows on the groomed trail to a well-marked intersection with Boomerang Road. You will pass around Bald Mountain, which will be on your left, to the ghost town of Alta, a distance of about 1.5 miles. In "town," bear left (east) and left again, following Forest Service Road 632A (from the intersection with Forest Service Road 632B) roughly 1 mile to the trio of Alta Lakes, which are frozen over in winter. The terrain is rolling and rather flat, but keep in mind that the hike to Alta adds a 3-mile round-trip, and the add-on to Alta Lakes a total of 5 miles round-trip to your tour, which is not insignificant at altitudes that top 10,000 feet—substantially so, for Alta Lakes are at about 11,300 feet. Another possible option would be to make the steep descent of nearly 1.5 miles to Skyline Ranch, a guest ranch off Colorado 145, and have a car waiting (or call a taxi from Telluride).

## San Juan Hut System

Five spartan eight-bunk huts tucked under the soaring Sneffels Range between Telluride and Ouray make up the San Juan Hut System, Colorado's southwesternmost system. It is known for spectacular scenery, a rustic ambience and backcountry immersion. It takes stamina and winter wilderness knowledge to snowshoe there, but an increasing number of people are doing so, particularly snowboarders, who prefer snowshoes to skis for the approach. The "easiest" to reach is the Blue Lakes Hut, 5.2 miles and 1,180 vertical feet from the trailhead (see the East Fork Dallas Creek trail description in the Ouray and Ridgway chapter, page 253). Guide services and vehicle shuttle services are available and are recommended for users inexperienced in the backcountry. **San Juan Hut System, P.O. Box 1663, Telluride, CO 81435; (970) 728-6935; www.telluridegateway.com/sjhuts/.**

## Mountain Adventure Snowshoe Tours

These three-hour guided tours into Prospect Basin and Magic Meadows debuted during the 1997–1998 winter, providing an excellent and safe introduction to high-country snowshoeing. The package includes snowshoe rentals, lift ride on Chair 10, guided tour and on-trail snack. In their inaugural season, they were scheduled every Wednesday and Saturday, from 8:45 to 11:45 A.M. These tours provide a fine example of the benefits of layering. Because you will be riding a shady lift early in the morning, you need to dress for the ride, but you'll probably warm up and start peeling as soon as you begin snowshoeing through the sheltering trees on either route. For details, pricing, schedule and other routes that may have been added after the initial season, check at the Mountain Village Ski & Snowboard School desk or call **(970) 728-7533.**

### Ranger Tours

A U.S. Forest Service ranger leads a free tour of one and one-half to two hours along Coonskin Ridge and down to Mountain Village. Schedules might change, but at this writing, the tours departed at 1:00 P.M. every day except Saturday from the large trail map sign at the bottom of Lift 3, near the San Sophia station of the gondola. Since you are not skiing or snowboarding, the lift ride is free too. From the gondola, the trail bears northwest into Mountain Village. There are two marked options: one a summer foot trail that essentially goes straight down the nose of the ridge, the other a single-track mountain bike trail. The ranger usually takes the foot trail, which is about 1 mile to Mountain Village, imparting information about the U.S. Forest Service and its role in outdoor recreation, conservation issues and the flora and fauna of the region. You can also do these routes on your own, either descending from the gondola for a pleasant excursion through the woods or ascending for a good aerobic workout.

### Backcountry Tours

Although it is primarily a mountaineering and climbing guide service, Ryder-Walker Alpine Adventures can also customize snowshoeing tours in the area for various levels of snowshoeing skills and different interests. **Ryder-Walker Alpine Adventures, P.O. Box 947, Telluride, CO 81435; (970) 728-6481.**

# Lizard Head Pass

It is but 60 miles—and light-years—between Cortez/Dolores with their wide mesas, piñon-juniper forests and Native American-Hispanic cultural accents (see the Mesa Verde Country chapter, page 267) and Telluride, a fashionable oasis in the heart of the high, snow-capped peaks of the San Juan Range. As you drive north on Colorado 145 from balmy 6,200-foot Cortez toward Lizard Head Pass, winter gets more—well—wintry. The landscape changes dramatically, becoming absolutely Alpine at 10,450-foot Lizard Head Pass, named after the dramatic rock formation that—from some angles and to some observers—resembles a reptile's head. Peaking at 13,113 feet, the Lizard Head is as much a symbol of southwestern Colorado as the Matterhorn is of Switzerland, and many people who have gazed at both find them equally compelling. As you approach Lizard Head Pass from Telluride to the north, civilization—especially the fancy resort brand of civilization—recedes and the sense of wildness prevails. The pass area itself is Telluride's favorite winter back-country playground, with less ultrasteep (and therefore less slide-prone) slopes than the daunting territory between Telluride and Ouray.

Lizard Head Pass in the heart of the dramatic San Juan Range has knockout scenery and excellent, uncrowded trails. *Photo by Claire Walter.*

## Maps

USGS 7.5 Minute, Mt. Wilson
Trails Illustrated #141, Silverton, Ouray, Telluride, Lake City
USFS San Juan National Forest
Map of the Mountains of Silverton, Telluride and Ouray,
Drake Mountain Maps

# 138. Railroad Grade

| | |
|---|---|
| Starting elevation: | 9,900 feet |
| Highest elevation: | 10,200 feet |
| Elevation difference: | 300 feet |
| Distance: | 3 miles (one way) |
| Difficulty: | Easy |
| Avalanche hazard: | None |

In the midst of the awesome, intimidating San Juan Mountains is one of Colorado's most congenial and comfortable snowshoeing routes. A portion of the historic Denver Rio Grande & Southern Railroad rail bed provides a gentle, continuous grade plus close-to-the-highway security. You can either do the railroad grade as an out-and-back route from either the northern end at North Trout Lake Road or the southern end atop Lizard Head Pass, or as a car shuttle. This much-used, much-loved road is wide enough for snowshoers and skiers.

The historic narrow gauge railroad trestle is a landmark on the north end of the mellow trail known as Railroad Grade. *Photo by Claire Walter.*

Starting from the northern end, park at the small pullout and cross over the Lake Fork Bridge. To your right is a historic trestle bridge, the last survivor of the old rail line. The snowshoeing route is the un-paved and unplowed Forest Service Road 636, a languorous uphill through widely spaced pines, across a pretty, snow-covered stream (you'll know it by the sign prohibiting vehicular traffic across a bridge that may be buried so deeply you won't even know you're on it) and eventually to an area of grandiose open fields. Most of the route is westerly, but when you approach Colorado 145, the trail orientation is more to the southwest, paralleling the highway. You can turn around near the old corrals and retrace your route to the railroad trestle bridge or stay and play in the great powderfields. If you start from the south, you'll simply reverse the route—though sometimes romping through the snow atop the pass is so much fun that you'll never want to hit the trail.

## 139. Priest Lakes Road

| | |
|---|---|
| Starting elevation: | 9,500 feet |
| Highest elevation: | 9,700 feet |
| Elevation difference: | 200 feet |
| Distance: | 2 miles (one way) |
| Difficulty: | Easy |
| Avalanche hazard: | Low |

This unplowed road paralleling the highway on the north side of Lizard Head Pass makes a short and sheltered snowshoe tour. Like the Railroad Grade, if can be snowshoed out and back from either end or done with a very short car shuttle. If you start at the north end, you can park at the Matterhorn Campground. The parking at the south end is limited, because it is in a subdivision at the first left on North Trout Lake Road, just 0.2 mile from Colorado 145. It is therefore better to start at the north end of Priest Lakes Road. If you are driving from Telluride, take the first "real" left off Colorado 145 at Matterhorn Campground and the large Quonset hut; if you see Telluride Helitrax's base on the right side of the highway, you've gone too far.

The route is carved out of the hillside, roughly paralleling the highway, which is to your right. You cross one stream directly after the campground, a second shortly thereafter and finally a third, the inlet to Priest Lake, near the southern end. The basically north-south route hugs the hillside and passes along the east side of the lake, terminating just off Route 145.

# 140. Cross Mountain Trail

| | |
|---|---|
| Starting elevation: | 10,050 feet |
| Highest elevation: | 11,250 feet |
| Elevation difference: | 1,200 feet |
| Distance: | 4 miles (one way) |
| Difficulty: | Challenging |
| Avalanche hazard: | Low in the trees at the beginning; high above timberline |

From the parking area and trailhead on the west side of Colorado 145, about 2 miles south of the Lizard Head Pass summit, head down into the gully until the trail sign is in sight. Bear right at the fork at about 0.4 mile, following the trail, which is an old four-wheel-drive road, as it contours up the mountainside. Watch the highway recede and the mountains draw in as you climb northward, virtually toward the Lizard Head formation that shares its name with the pass, a small creek (which the beginning of the trail briefly follows) and the dramatic wilderness area it symbolizes.

The first several miles of the road are safe, but do not succumb to the temptation of continuing above the treeline to Black Face, a looming, near-perpendicular wall that is a notorious slide zone. Also, don't stray into the high open country beyond that is dominated by such skyscraping peaks as Mt. Wilson and El Diente.

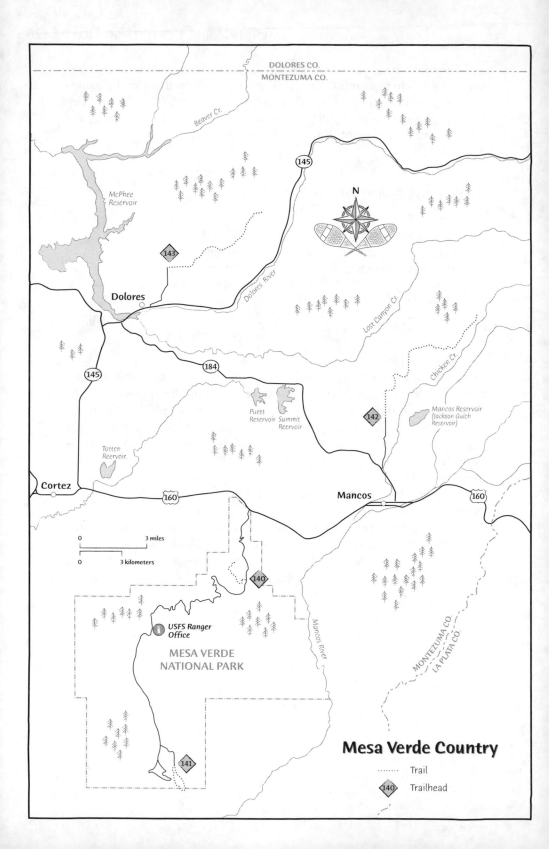

## Mesa Verde Country

········· Trail

◆140◆ Trailhead

# Mesa Verde Country

The Four Corners, the only point in the United States where four right-angled state lines meet, is a geographical anomaly. Its nickname has spread over a starkly beautiful landscape of mesas and canyons of exposed rock walls and desert plants. It does not appear, on the surface, to be prime snowshoeing country and, in fact, it isn't. Snowfall is more erratic here than in the state's mountain regions, and snowshoeing is peripheral to the Four Corners experience. Yet, because one of the sport's real pluses is that it doesn't require deep or consistent cover, you can gain a different perspective on a place when you see and experience it in such an unusual way—which is to say, a winter way. The Colorado portion of the Four Corners, often called Mesa Verde Country, does provide some decent snowshoeing, and as you gain elevation into the San Juan Mountains, winter becomes more predictable, virtually guaranteeing good snowshoeing. The state's sunny southwestern corner is not a place to put on your must-do snowshoeing list, but rather a region to put on a winter itinerary, when crowds are absent, and to take your snowshoes along and hope for snow.

For tourist information, contact the **Mesa Verde Country Visitor Information Bureau,** P.O. Box HH, Cortez, CO 81321; (800) 253-1616; www.swcolo.org, or Montezuma County Development Council, 925 South Broadway, Suite 259, P.O. Box FF, Cortez, CO 81321; (800) 253-1616.

## Getting There
U.S. 160 is southern Colorado's main drag, from the Kansas border through Walsenburg on the southern end of the Front Range to Cortez and the Four Corners itself. From Durango, drive west to Mancos, Cortez and the entrance station to Mesa Verde National Park. For the Chicken Creek Cross-Country Area or Mancos State Park, go north on Colorado 184 and follow the directions that accompany each of the descriptions below. The Four Corners are a long way—eight hours or more by car—from Denver and other northern Front Range cities and not much less from the southern Front Range, but you can also fly to Durango or Cortez.
   For maps, see individual sections.

## Mesa Verde National Park

The jewel of the Four Corners region is Mesa Verde National Park, one of the West's most extraordinary places and one of the world's true

A ranger bundles up for her presentation of spruce Tree House, one of Mesa Verde National Park's most compelling sites. *Photo by Caire Walter.*

archaeological treasures. Picture it in summer: museum, lines for the rest rooms, lines of cars waiting to get into overflowing parking areas and an often scorching midday temperature. Think of the same place in winter: tranquillity, purity, quiet and stark beauty unmarred by crowds, with a benign climate that invites exploration. Snowshoeing across a mesa on ground covered in winter white, just as the ancient people saw it, or being virtually alone in a PJ woodland, as locals call the piñon and juniper growth of southwestern Colorado, is indeed a special experience.

This World Heritage Cultural Site, one of two full-fledged national parks in Colorado, is the rare national park whose renown does not come from its scenic splendor or outdoor recreational opportunities. It is world famous for its ancient cliff dwellings and other archaeological wonders. The overwhelming majority of people visit in the warm months, and while the park itself remains open in winter, the accommodations, one of the two visitors centers and some of the Anasazi sites are closed. However, some of the sites aren't closed, and they aren't crowded, either. Ranger-led interpretive tours of Spruce Tree House are given daily at 10:00 A.M., 1:00 P.M. and 3:30 P.M., weather and trail conditions permitting. Unlike summer, there probably won't be a waiting line, and you'll be missing something really special if you don't take the tour.

The park is not a snowshoeing mecca, but it provides one of the most fantastic days you can ever spend, combining snowshoeing with the unique cultural experience of seeing these impressive sites in a pristine and uncrowded way. The park's single unplowed loop road makes an unusual and rewarding snowshoe tour. Consider it a bonus if the snow is good.

While part of snowshoeing's appeal is the ability to go off-trail and bushwhack, Mesa Verde National Park is not the place to do that. You will get a park map at the entrance station, and because your options are so limited, you won't really need a topo map. Stop at the ranger's office, or call **(970) 529-4461** or **(970) 529-4475** in advance to check on road, weather and snow conditions before you hit the trail. Interestingly, snowshoeing provides a small footnote to the rich but still mysterious Anasazi story, for the park's archaeological collection includes one wooden snowshoe. Unfortunately, it is not on display. Be sure also to visit the Chapin Mesa Museum (it's warm as well as educational). Limited cafeteria service is available at the Spruce Tree Terrace concession building.

## Getting There

Take U.S. 160, 35 miles west from Durango or 9 miles east from Cortez. Go south on the well-marked entrance road. This is a fee area, payable at the park entrance station. The road is paved, but it is steep and can be slick, so snow tires or chains are required. You can stop at Morefield Village and snowshoe the campground area in this valley, or continue about 20 miles to the Spruce Tree House parking area.

## Maps

USGS 7.5 Minute, Point Lookout, Moccasin Mesa
Park Service map given at the entrance station

# 141. Morefield Village

| | |
|---|---|
| Starting elevation: | 7,600 feet |
| Highest elevation: | 7,800 feet |
| Elevation difference: | 200 feet |
| Distance: | 1 mile (loop) |
| Difficulty: | Easy |
| Avalanche hazard: | Low |

Morefield Village is nestled in a valley that had been homesteaded and is now a May to October campground. After the RVs leave, the deer return to the beautiful valley at the base of the mesa's looming sidewalls. The paved road, which is unplowed, makes a very nice easy route of only about 1 mile. It winds past the park's store, filling station, campsites and picnic areas, which feel almost as unused and ghostly as the mesa-top and canyon sites that the Anasazi abandoned hundreds of years ago. The hillsides may look tempting, and there are, in fact, summer hiking trails to the ridges, but they are not recommended for winter travel. However, with enough snow, the entire valley floor is snowshoeable, and it's neat to wander around, search for animal tracks and simply enjoy the solitude.

# 142. Cliff Palace Loop

| | |
|---|---|
| Starting elevation: | 7,040 feet |
| Highest elevation: | 7,240 feet |
| Elevation difference: | 200 feet |
| Distance: | 6 miles (loop) |
| Difficulty: | Easy |
| Avalanche hazard: | None |

A full moon over Mesa Verde from Flagstone Meadows Ranch, a B&B with doorstep snowshoeing as well as grandiose views. *Photo by Claire Walter.*

It is 0.3 mile from the Spruce Tree House parking area to the Ruins Road-Cliff Palace Road four-way stop, the beginning of the mesa-top road that provides summer access to the Cliff Palace and Balcony House, two of Mesa Verde's best-known sites. The unplowed road begins to the southeast and then bends south. About 2.5 miles from the road closure, you will come to a fork. It seems natural to take the right fork to do the loop portion counterclockwise, which is the direction cars use in the summer. There are no mesa-top ruins along Cliff Palace Road, and the famous cliff dwellings are closed in winter, but you should stop at two fine viewpoints. Both are on the western leg of the loop, which is another reason to bear right at the fork if you aren't interested in, or can't do, the entire loop. The first viewpoint is just before Cliff Palace, about 0.23 mile from the fork, and the second is a mile farther. If you have the stamina, the time and the interest, you can also follow a hiking trail to the Soda Canyon Overlook, on the eastern leg of the loop, for a view of Balcony House. If going nearly all the way around to this side trail seems too much, take the left option at the fork, hike about 0.45 mile and then return the way you came.

# Mancos State Park

Mancos State Park is a small recreational area that butts up against the huge San Juan National Forest. Pristine and quiet in winter, the park offers ice fishing on Jackson Gulch Reservoir and a short snowshoeing and skiing trail around the lake. This is a fee area.

## Getting There

From the center of Mancos, turn north on Colorado 184. After 0.25 mile, turn right (east) on Montezuma County Road 42 (also Forest Service Road 561). Continue north for 4 miles to Montezuma County Road N. Then turn left (west) to the marked park entrance.

## Maps

USGS 7.5 Minute, Millwood, Dolores West

# 143. Jackson Reservoir Trail

| | |
|---|---|
| Starting elevation: | 7,800 feet |
| Highest Elevation: | 7,800 feet |
| Elevation difference: | Negligible |
| Distance: | 3.5 miles (loop); 1.25 miles (connector trail to Chicken Creek, one way) |
| Difficulty: | Easy |
| Avalanche hazard: | None |

Jackson Gulch Reservoir is shaped somewhat like an arrowhead, not inappropriate for a human-made lake overlooking the Mancos Valley and Colorado's densest concentration of tribal lands and native heritage sites. The "arrow" points northeast, and the road entrance is from the east. You can snowshoe around the reservoir clockwise or counterclockwise, passing the dam on the south end as well as two campgrounds.

## If You Want a Longer Hike

A trail on the northwestern portion of the lake links Jackson Reservoir with the Chicken Creek Cross-Country Area, 1.25 miles to the west. This enables the intrepid to mix and match trails for hikes of various lengths.

## *Chicken Creek Cross-Country Area*

This tight trail system provides down-home snowshoeing, and when the snow is good, offers pleasing routes of various lengths. It combines the ambience of rural ranch country with the ecosystem that locals call "PJ woodland" country—that is, congenial woods of piñon pine and juniper. You'll mingle with outdoor-loving locals if you set off to discover Chicken Creek Cross-Country Area on a weekend, but if you go on a weekday, you might have it all to yourself. Volunteers from the Mancos Recreation Association groom more than 9 miles of trails for track skiing and skating, leaving ample room for snowshoers too. Unlike many Nordic areas, Chicken Creek not only permits but welcomes snowshoers and even encourages them to use the skating lanes.

From the traffic light in the center of Mancos, take Colorado 184 north for 2 miles. Turn right onto County Road 40 (Forest Service Access-Millwood Road 559), and drive 3 miles to the parking area and trailhead. (Note that you will pass Montezuma County Road 39, marked "Chicken Creek," which is not the road to this ski and snowshoeing center.)

The trail system comprises three loops, one strung behind the other from the trailhead, weaving between small reservoirs. It offers undulating uphills and gradual downhills. All the trails are easy, so the challenge really comes from the distance you choose to snowshoe. Because the 7,500-foot base elevation is no guarantee of winter-long snow cover, this is not an area to count on. Views of the Mancos Valley and Mesa Verde National Park to the south and La Plata Mountains to the northeast add to the enjoyment. Bring everything you need when you snowshoe here, for there are no concessions or rentals. There is no use fee, but the volunteers who maintain the system would appreciate a trailhead donation. They would also appreciate your leaving your dogs at home, because they do damage groomed trails.

All three loops are both double-tracked and groomed for skating. The area is especially well marked, which is useful because traffic on the two inner loops is counterclockwise and on the last one is clockwise, making it possible for first-timers to forget where they are. To parry confusion, all trails are marked, and all junctions feature posted trail maps with "you are here" indicators. The 3.2-mile **Little Bauer Loop,** the one directly at the trailhead, makes an easy excursion. Add the second, the 4-mile **Dolph Kuss Loop,** and you'll use up the best part of a day. The third is the shortest. Continuing on the 2.3-mile **Hamlin Loop,** with or without the addition of some of the 9 ungroomed miles, is only for strong snowshoers or runners. One kilometer along, the Hamlin Loop's eastern leg skirts the edge of Chicken Creek Canyon, with great views of the La Plata Range.

In addition, there are 9 more miles of marked but ungroomed trails— **Rush Creek Spur** off the northwest leg of the Dolph Kuss Loop, the trail down to Chicken Creek off the southeast bend of the Hamlin Loop and the **Turkey Creek Loop** off the northwest corner of the Hamlin Loop. The right fork of the Turkey Creek Loop continues toward the unplowed Ditches Road, a popular snowmobile route, 4 miles away.

## *Flagstone Meadows Ranch Bed & Breakfast*

It's worth staying at this spacious, antique- and artifact-filled log home just for the views, which take in Mesa Verde National Park and Sleeping Ute in one magnificent panorama. All of the eight rooms have private baths, and most have balconies also. In addition to the charming and romantic double rooms, there is also a downstairs four-bunk room for families, making Flagstone Meadows the rare B&B that welcomes families with children. In midwinter, when the hills, meadows and woods on the north side of the Mancos Valley are buried in white, you can stoke up on a hearty breakfast, prepared by host Harris Court, and snowshoe from the front door.

Flagstone Meadows' 40 acres are available, as is the little-traveled road. Cheyenne, the resident Siberian husky, is usually available to accompany you. The inn is also convenient to the Mesa Verde National Park gate, Chicken Creek Cross-Country Area and the Mancos Hill Area.

Innkeeper Harris Court, a former rodeo rider and lone-eagle securities and insurance broker, whips up dynamite breakfasts. On-site amenities include an entertainment room with the only television in the house, a workout station and a gorgeous antique pool table. Outside is a large hot tub. When the full moon is illuminating the mesa and the valley, there's no better place on earth to be. **Flagstone Meadows Ranch Bed & Breakfast**, P.O. Box 11377, Mancos, CO 81328; (800) 664-0719 or (970) 533-9838; www.ipxnet.com/home/flagstone/.

## 144. Boggy Draw

| | |
|---|---|
| Starting elevation: | 7,750 feet |
| Highest elevation: | 8,600 feet |
| Elevation difference: | 850 feet |
| Distance: | Varies |
| Difficulty: | Easy to moderate |
| Avalanche hazard: | Low |
| Map: | USGS 7.5 Minute, Boggy Draw |

Take Colorado 145 10 miles north from Cortez to Dolores. Turn left at the large McPhee Reservoir sign onto Forest Service Road 526 (also known as the Dolores-Norwood Road) to the junction with Forest Service Road 527. There are parking areas at the plowed sections of both roads, with parking lots at the National Forest Boundary.

This sizable area can be a gentle playground of rolling terrain, unplowed roads and open fields not far from the parking lot—or it can be a gonzo workout of up to 20 miles for the fanatical, fit, long-distance snowshoer far up the snowed-over road. The degree of difficulty depends on how far and how fast you choose to go. Sections of Forest Service Roads 526 and 527, which form a loop, are popular snowmobile routes. Mushers also occasionally share this road, so you never know what the huskies have deposited on the trail. Road 526 skirts the nonmotorized area on the east side of McPhee Reservoir, so it is a better choice than 527. In any case, this is a place where you might prefer off-road snowshoeing, but if you do, be sure to take a good topo map and a compass.

# Appendix A:
# Touching Other Bases

The preceding chapters include some of the best, most readily accessible snowshoeing venues in Colorado, but they barely scratch the surface of what's available in the state. Following are some other areas that you might want to try, although these represent just a deeper scratch.

## Black Canyon of the Gunnison

Just as Mesa Verde National Park's Cliff Palace loop road is unplowed in winter and available to snowshoers and cross-country skiers, so is the main road in the Black Canyon of the Gunnison National Monument. It offers great views and a unique winter perspective on one of Colorado's natural wonders.

## Blue Lake Trail and
## Long Draw Reservoir Road

Located a dozen miles northwest of Fort Collins, these neighboring trails accommodate every level of snowshoer. Beginners and casual snowshoers seeking just a pleasant outing tend to prefer the gentle Long Draw Reservoir Road, while those looking for a workout like to muscle up the steep and steady road to Blue Lake. Excellent views toward Rocky Mountain National Park reward those who have made the climb.

## Camp Hale

Located just north of Tennessee Pass right off U.S. 24, Camp Hale is set in a huge, open valley that was the site of the 10th Mountain Division's training camp during World War II. From the plowed winter trailhead directly off the highway, you can explore this snow-safe valley, following the marked East Fork Valley, South Fork or Resolution Creek Trails, or simply roam around. The Camp Hale area accesses the Colorado Trail and the steep route to the 10th Mountain Division Hut Association's Jackal Hut.

# Colorado State Forest

The Colorado State Forest takes up a huge tract of land in North Park, on the western slope of the Medicine Bow Mountains. Many of its 110 miles of summer hiking and mountain trails are reasonably accessible for winter recreation too. The main entrance to the forest, which functions as a state park, is 20 miles from Walden. The **Never Summer Nordic Yurts** **(970-482-9411)** are popular for overnights. Weekends and holidays are booked far in advance, but Sunday and especially weeknight reservations are usually available even at the last minute.

# Cottonwood Pass

At 12,126 feet, Cottonwood Pass is as high as many significant mountains, but because it runs through the state's thickest stand of fourteeners, its rank isn't anywhere near the top. From 9,218-foot Rainbow Lake, the unplowed road climbs 10 miles to the trail's crest on the Continental Divide, a greater distance than most snowshoers would even dream of. The road passes from a thick conifer forest into the tundra, offering a dramatic ascent at breath-sapping elevations but good access from Buena Vista and Salida.

# The Crags and Horsethief Park

This beautiful and isolated area on the backside of Pikes Peak offers spectacular snowshoeing. The Crags are a forest of rocky pinnacles and superfine scenery. You can follow the Colorado Springs crowd along popular trails and routes, and explore the huge granite formations that snare the snow. Nearby Horsethief Park offers flat terrain on the valley floor and a ridge trail if you are seeking an elevation gain.

# Cuchara

A network of old roads, including the Cordova Pass Road and the Old La Veta Pass Road, draw backcountry enthusiasts from Pueblo, Walsenburg and elsewhere to this pretty part of southern Colorado. Wahatoya Base Camp **(719-742-3163)**, an excellent sporting goods store at the base of the Cuchara ski resort, offers a series of scheduled snowshoe tours and custom hikes.

# Flat Tops Wilderness

This is Colorado's second-largest wilderness area, but there are few approach roads and few of those are plowed. Yet the entire region, even that on the fringes of the wilderness, is spectacular. The wide-open spaces and big skies high on the White River Plateau inspired the concept of protected wilderness. Several winter trails flank West Elk Creek Road, roughly 20 miles northwest of Glenwood Springs. Trappers Lake (on the northern edge of the Flat Tops Wilderness) and the rustic lodge of the same name (970-878-3336) are an off-the-beaten-path destination for snowshoers, cross-country skiers and snowmobilers. Located about 40 miles from Meeker, Trappers Lake is hard for many people to reach but worth the effort for its beauty and the quality of the snow.

# Great Sand Dunes National Monument

You don't need winter to snowshoe. Heck, you don't even need snow. Climbing up and around these enormous shifting hills of sand that rise as high as 700 feet is a unique thrill, and on a moonlit night, there's no place better. You can even sign up for a snowshoe race. The aptly named Extreme Heat 5K Snowshoe Race takes place each October, and the Park Service has felt compelled to limit the event to 250 competitors. The health threats here are more along the lines of sunburn and dehydration than of frostbite and hypothermia—and avalanches are not a problem.

# Havilland Lake Campground

This summer campground between Durango and the Purgatory Resort offers easy and scenic snowshoeing on its roads, as well as access to an adjacent road that is both unpaved and unplowed. An old wagon road makes a 3-mile loop for anyone wishing for a longer and more interesting hike.

# Kenosha Pass

This 10,000-foot pass separates the mountains of Jefferson County southwest of Denver from the grandiose expanse of South Park. On the pass you'll find a section of the Colorado Trail, a summer campground that perches on top of it and a couple of old logging roads, all of which provide fine winter recreation trails not far from metro Denver.

# Lime Creek

From a trailhead 2 miles north of the Purgatory Resort near Durango, the Lime Creek Road is prime snowshoeing territory. This popular route is a former stagecoach road up to Silverton and is also used by snowmobilers to access high cabins. Snowshoers hike along this forested route to the bases of Spud Mountain and, even better, the Needle Mountains, which tower dramatically above a spectacular gorge and soar to 13,000 feet.

# Mill Creek

More than 12 miles of winter trails paralleling Mill Creek and surrounding the Cunningham Park Reservoir are easily accessible from Gunnison.

They can be combined into out-and-back and loop trails of various lengths. The main section to avoid in winter is avalanche-prone Little Mill Creek.

## Molas Pass

This dramatic 10,910-foot pass between Silverton and Purgatory offers incredible views of Engineer Mountain, the Grand Turk and the Grenadier Range. Additional benefits are acres and acres of sparsely wooded rolling terrain and little avalanche danger. You can take Andrew Lake Road on the west side of U.S. 550 to the frozen lake, just 0.5 mile off the highway, or bushwhack around the sparse stands of new-growth pine.

## Mt. Falcon Park

This 1,400-acre preserve is the crown jewel of Jefferson County's fantastic Open Space program. There's not always snow on the ground in the park, which is just outside of Morrison and some 20 miles from Denver, but after a storm, snowshoers and skiers are legion on 10 miles of trails and there are plenty of off-trail places to explore as well.

## Mueller State Park

Mueller is one of the few Colorado state parks that does not owe its existence to an artificial reservoir. This 12,100-acre preserve 30 miles from Colorado Springs, just off Colorado 67 between Cripple Creek and Divide, offers the best and closest winter trails to Colorado's second-largest city. Ninety miles of trails lace through pine woods, over hills, across meadows and between wondrous granite rock formations. The park is known for its abundant wildlife, and winter is a good time to spot it. The views of Pikes Peak and the Sangre de Cristo Range can't be beat, either.

## Peaceful Valley

The Peak to Peak Highway runs through this serene valley, which does live up to its name. The **Peaceful Valley Ranch Resort (303-747-2881)** makes a terrific snowshoeing getaway. The ranch's extensive acreage includes excellent snowshoeing terrain. You can snowshoe the unplowed road to the Camp Dick Campground, with its access to the Indian Peaks Wilderness, which is just across the highway, or explore nearby Rocky Mountain National Park.

## Powderhorn Wilderness

Remote and magnificent, this wilderness area in the northern San Juan Mountains comprises high plateaus, deep forests and incredible views that stretch all the way to the Sawatch Range. Slumgullion Pass, south of Lake City, accesses a tiny section of the wilderness. Mesa Seco, just west of the protected wilderness, is also accessible in winter, with snowshoers, skiers and snowmobilers sharing the terrain.

## Red Feather Lakes

Fourteen lakes sprinkled in a basin north of the Cache la Poudre Canyon 50 miles from Fort Collins are a northern Colorado recreational haven. The winter centerpiece is the **Beaver Meadows Ranch Resort and Nordic Center (970-881-2450),** which has developed four or five dedicated snowshoe trails. Numerous trails also reach into national forest land.

## Roxborough State Park

With a low elevation, this beautiful park 20 miles southwest of Denver does not offer guaranteed snow cover, but after a storm, when the sandstone cliffs and canyons are blanketed in white, it is a dramatic, beautiful and convenient snowshoeing destination. The 18 miles of trails include both flat routes along the valley floor and ascents up the park's hillsides.

## Sarvis Creek Wilderness

The Sarvis Creek Wilderness, just a dozen miles southwest of Steamboat Springs, is more pristine than dramatic. Plowed winter access roads enable snowshoers and skiers to reach several lovely trails through the quiet forest that characterizes this little-known preserve in north-central Colorado.

## Saylor Park

This lovely and gentle part of the Rampart Range was designated as a ski touring area back in 1970, and now it ranks as an excellent snowshoeing venue too. Various trails lead through this basin, which includes forests, flatland and ridges. It is located just north of Woodland Park and a short drive from Colorado Springs.

## Spring Peak Pass

A plowed highway, Colorado 149, threads between the Powderhorn and La Garita Wilderness areas. Squaw Creek Pass, on the Continental Divide at 10,900 feet, skirts La Garita's western boundary. It also accesses the Colorado Trail and Snow Mesa, which just sounds as if it needs to be on everyone's to-be-snowshoed list.

## Taylor Park

The Taylor Park Reservoir nestles in this huge and high basin between the Gunnison and Arkansas River drainages. Winter access is from Gunnison (the west side). Taylor Park's numerous side valleys offer exceptional winter recreation opportunities, but be alert to avalanche conditions. Doctor Park Trail, South Lottis Creek, Stagestop Meadows, Summerville Trail leading into the Fossil Ridge Wilderness, Union Canyon and Union Park are among the most popular sections with skiers and increasingly with snowshoers as well.

## Tincup Pass

You must be willing to share your pleasure with snowmobilers in order to really appreciate this route, which starts in the old mining town of St. Elmo and ascends to 12,154 feet. The first part is the steepest, so even the most tolerant skiers and snowshoers are frequently put off by the ease with which snowmobilers power up the unplowed road. The top of the pass is 8.5 miles from St. Elmo, much farther than most snowshoers can go. Buena Vista and Salida are the nearest towns.

## Wet Mountain Valley

Located on the east side of the magnificent Sangre de Cristo Range in southern Colorado, this is one of the state's most gorgeous valleys. However, it also has a relatively poor snow record. The best bet for snowshoeing is to go there after a storm, when chances of snow are greatest. Drive to the end of the plowed roads accessing routes like Hermit Pass Road, South Colony Road or the Rainbow Trail and begin hiking west.

# Appendix B: Media Sources

## Books

### Snowshoeing Books

*The Essential Snowshoer,* by Marianne Zwosta, 1998. Camden, ME: Ragged Mountain Press.

*Snowshoeing,* by Sally Edwards and Melissa McKenzie, 1995. Champaign, IL: Human Kinetics.

*Snowshoeing,* fourth edition, by Gene Prater, edited by Dave Felkley, 1997. Seattle, WA: The Mountaineers.

*Snowshoeing: A Trailside Guide,* by Larry Olmsted, 1997. New York: W. W. Norton.

### Trail Guides

#### Current Trail Guides

*Aspen-Snowmass Cross-Country Ski Trails,* by Warren Ohlrich, 1989. Aspen, CO: WHO Press.

*Colorado Mountain Ski Tours & Hikes,* by Dave Muller, 1993. Denver, CO: Quality Press.

*The Complete Guide to Colorado's Wilderness Areas,* by John Fielder and Mark Pearson, 1994. Englewood, CO: Westcliffe Publishers.

*Cross-Country Ski Trails Near Steamboat Springs,* by Geri Anderson, 1993. Oak Creek, CO: Trail Finders Press.

*The New Summit Hiker and Ski Touring Guide,* by Mary Ellen Gilliland, 1996. Silverthorne, CO: Alpenrose Press.

*Peak to Peak: Colorado Front Range Ski Tours,* by Harlan N. Barton, 1995. Boulder, CO: Front Range Publishing.

*Poudre Canyon Cross-Country Ski and Snowshoe Trails,* by Mary Hagen, 1996. Fort Collins, CO: Azure Publishing.

*Skiing Colorado's Backcountry,* by Brian Litz and Kurt Lankford, 1989. Golden, CO: Fulcrum Publishing.

*Vail Hiker and Ski Touring Guide,* by Mary Ellen Gilliland, 1997. Silverthorne, CO: Alpenrose Press.

#### Out-of-Print Trail Guides (Still Useful If You Can Find Them)

*Central Colorado Ski Tours,* by Tom and Sanse Sudduth, 1976. Boulder, CO: Pruett Publishing.

*Colorado Front Range Ski Tours,* by Tom and Sanse Sudduth, 1975. Beaverton, OR: Touchstone Press.

*50 Colorado Ski Tours,* by Richard DuMais, 1983. Boulder, CO: High Peak Publishing.

*Northern Colorado Ski Tours,* by Tom and Sanse Sudduth, 1976. Beaverton, OR: Touchstone Press.

## Related Reference Books

*Exploring Colorado State Parks,* by Martin G. Kleinsorge, 1992. Niwot, CO: University Press of Colorado.

*Field Guide to Tracking Animals in the Snow,* by Louise R. Forrest, 1988. Harrisburg, PA: Stackpole Books.

*Mystery Tracks in the Snow,* by Hap Gilliland, 1990. Happy Camp, CA: Naturegraph Publishers.

*Snow,* by Nolan J. Dockson and Arthur Judson, 1995. Fort Collins, CO: Colorado State University.

*Winter Adventure: A Trailside Guide,* by Peter Stark and Steven M. Kauzer, 1995. New York: W. W. Norton.

## Periodicals

*Rocky Mountain Sports,* monthly publication distributed free at Front Range sporting goods stores and elsewhere in the state; it claims that 45 percent of its readers snowshoe, and covers the Colorado snowshoe racing and recreation scene aggressively; (303) 861-9229.

*The Snowshoer,* magazine published five times between October and March; P.O. Box 458, Washburn, WI 54891; (715) 373-5556; www.thesnowhoer.com.

## Maps

Colorado Mountain Club, 710 Tenth Street, #200, Golden, CO 80401; (800) 633-4417 in Colorado only or (303) 279-3080; www.cmc.org/cmc/ or www.earthnet.net/~cmc/, or from the CMC's local groups statewide.

Drake Mountain Maps, 433 Apodaca Hill, Santa Fe, NM 87501; (505) 988-8929.

Eagle Eye Maps, P.O. Box 1457, Glenwood Springs, CO 81602.

Trails Illustrated, P.O. Box 4357, Evergreen, CO 80437; (800) 962-1643 or (303) 670-3457; www.colorado.com/trails.

U.S. Forest Service maps are available from all District Offices and Ranger Stations (see information in Appendix C).

U.S. Geological Service, Denver Federal Center, Lakewood, CO 80225; (303) 236-7477.

Wildflower Productions (interactive computer maps), 375 Alabama Street, Suite 230, San Francisco, CA 94110; (415) 558-8700; www.topo.com.

## Videos

"How to Get Started in Snowshoeing," a 10-minute video from Tubbs; (800) 882-2748 or (802) 253-7398.

"Snowshoeing 101," an instructional video available for $19.95 from Sun Dog Athletics; (970) 925-1069.

# Appendix C: Government Agencies

## U.S. Forest Service

U.S. Forest Service
Rocky Mountain Region
740 Simms Street
Golden, CO 80401
(303) 275-5350

### Administrative Offices

Arapaho National Forest
240 West Prospect
Fort Collins, CO 80526
(970) 498-1100

Grand Mesa National Forest
2250 U.S. Highway 50
Delta, CO 81416
(970) 874-6600

Gunnison National Forest
2250 U.S. Highway 50
Delta, CO 81416
(970) 874-7691

Pike National Forest
1920 Valley Drive
Pueblo, CO 81008
(719) 545-8737

Roosevelt National Forest
240 West Prospect
Fort Collins, CO 80526
(970) 498-1100

### Ranger Districts (and Locations If Different from Name of District)

Clear Creek (Idaho Springs)
Dillon (Silverthorne)
Middle Park (Kremmling)
Pawnee National Grasslands
(Greeley)
Sulphur (Granby)

Colbran
Grand Junction

Cebolla (Gunnison)
Paonia
Taylor River (Gunnison)

Pikes Peak (Colorado Springs)
South Park (Fairplay)
South Platte (Morrison)

Boulder
Estes/Poudre (Fort Collins)
Estes Park

Routt National Forest
925 Weiss Drive
Steamboat Springs,
CO 80487-9315
(970) 879-1870

Bears Ear (Craig)
Hahns Peak/Bears Ear
(Steamboat Springs)
North Park (Walden)
Parks (Kremmling)
Yampa

San Isabel National Forest
1920 Valley Drive
Pueblo, CO 81008
(719) 545-8737

Leadville
Salida
San Carlos (Cañon City)

San Juan/Rio Grande
National Forest
1803 West Highway 160
Monte Vista, CO 81144
(719) 852-5941

Conejos Peak (La Jara)
Creede
Del Norte
Saguache

San Juan National Forest
701 Camino del Rio
Durango, CO 81301
(970) 247-4874

Columbine East (Bayfield)
Columbine West (Durango)
Dolores
Mancos
Pagosa Springs

Uncompahgre National Forest
2250 U.S. Highway 50
Delta, CO 81416
(970) 874-7691

Norwood
Ouray (Montrose)

White River National Forest
P.O. Box 948
Glenwood Springs, CO 81602
(970) 945-2521

Aspen
Blanca (Meeker)
Dillon (Silverthorn)
Eagle
Holy Cross (Minturn)
Rifle
Sopris (Carbondale)

# State Agencies

Colorado Division of Wildlife, 6060 Broadway, Denver, CO 80203; (303) 297-1192

Colorado State Forest, Star Route, Box 91, Walden, CO 80480; (970) 723-8366

Colorado State Parks and Recreation, 1313 Sherman Street, #618, Denver, CO 80203; (303) 866-3437

# Appendix D: Equipment

## Snowshoe Manufacturers

(*Indicates major suppliers of contemporary aluminum frame snowshoes)

*Atlas Snowshoe Company, 1830 Harrison Street, San Francisco, CA 94103; (888) 48-ATLAS or (415) 703-0414; www.atlasworld.com

Baldas Snowshoes, imported by Vanguard Development International, 1900 Wazee Street, Suite 310, Denver, CO 80202; (303) 607-9498; www.baldas.com

*Crescent Moon, 1199 Crestmoor Drive, Boulder, CO 80303; (800) 587-7655 or (303) 494-5506

Elfman Snowshoes, Accessory Productions, 245 Tank Farm Road, #K, San Luis Obispo, CA 93401; (805) 543-9463

Faber & Company, 180 Boulevard de Rivière, Loretteville, Quebec G2B 3W6; (418) 842-8476

Great Bear Enterprises (traditional wood frame snowshoes), P.O. Box 428, Kila, MT 59920; (406) 257-6992; www.shopworks.com/greatbear

Great Canadian Canoe Co. (traditional wood frame snowshoes), Route 146, Sutton, MA 01590; (800) 98-CANOE or (518) 865-0010; www.greatcanadian.com

Havlick Snowshoe Company, 2513 State Highway 30, Mayfield, NY 12117; (800) TOP-SHOE or (518) 661-6447

Iverson Snowshoe Company (traditional wood frame snowshoes), P.O. Box 85, Maple Street, Shingleton, MI 49884; (906) 452-6370; www.seekwilderness.com

K2 Back Country (snowshoes designed for compatibility with Clicker snowboard boot/binding system), 19215 Vashon Highway SW, Vashon Island, WA 98070; (800) 972-4038; www.k2snowboards.com

Little Bear Snowshoes (children's models), 2477 I Road, Grand Junction, CO 81505; (800) 655-8984 or (970) 241-8546

Mountain Safety Research (Denali snowshoes for adults, Little Llama for children), P.O. Box 24547, Seattle, WA 98124; (800) 877-9677 or (206) 624-8573; www.msrcorp.com

Northern Lites, 1300 Cleveland, Wausau, WI 54401; (800) 360-LITE; www.northernlites.com

PowderWings (snowboard-compatible snowshoes), 1325 West Industrial Circle, Springville, UT 84663; (800) 453-1192 or (801) 489-3864; www.powderwings.com

*Redfeather Design, Inc., 4955-D Peoria Street, Denver, CO 80239; (800) 525-0081 (product info: 888-669-SNOW); www.redfeather.com

*Sherpa, 444 South Pine Street, Burlington WI 53105; (800) 621-2277; www.sherpasnowshoes.com

TSL Snowshoes, 925 NW, Suite A, Portland OR 97209; (503) 241-9380; www.tsl-snowshoes.com

*Tubbs Snowshoes (modern aluminum and traditional wood frame snowshoes), 52 River Road, Stowe, VT 05672; (800) 882-2748 or (802) 253-7398; www.tubbssnowshoes.com

Winterstick, 435 West 400 South, Suite 201, Salt Lake City, UT 84101; (801) 974-0939; www.winterstick.com

*YubaShoes, 161 Main Avenue, Sacramento, CA 95838; (800) 598-YUBA; www.yubashoes.com

# Selected Manufacturers and Distributors of Adjustable Poles

Atlas Snowshoe Company, 1830 Harrison Street, San Francisco, CA 94103; (888) 48-ATLAS or (415) 703-0414; www.atlasworld.com

Avi Probe Poles, Backcountry Access, 4949 North Broadway, #139, Boulder, CO 80304; (800) 670-8735 or (303) 417-1345; www.bcaccess.com/bca

Black Diamond Equipment, Ltd., 2084 East 39th South, Salt Lake City, UT 84124; (801) 278-5552; www.bdel.com

Leki USA, 356 Sonwil Drive, Buffalo, NY 14225; (800) 255-9982 or (716) 683-1022; www.leki.com

Life-Link Backcountry Products, 1240 Huff Lane, P.O. Box 2913, Jackson Hole, WY 83001; (800) 443-8620 or (307) 733-2266; www.life-link.com

Redfeather Design, Inc., 4955-D Peoria Street, Denver, CO 80239; (800) 525-0081, (product info: 888-669-SNOW); www.redfeather.com

# Selected Footwear Manufacturers

New England OverShoe (NEOS), 823-B Ferry Road, P.O. Box 540, Charlotte, VT 05445; (800) 335-0184 or (802) 425-4848; www.overshoe.com

Salomon North America, 400 East Main Street, Georgetown, MA 01833; (800) 225-6850 or (508) 352-7600; www.salomonsports.com

Sorel, Kaufman Footwear, 700 Ellicott Street, Batavia, NY 14020; (800) 265-2760 or (519) 576-1500; www.kaufman.com

Stegers Mukluks, 100 Miners Drive, Ely, MN 55731; (800) MUK-LUKS or (218) 365-6553

Taiga, 1160 Labrant Road, P.O. Box 2227, Bigfork, MT 59911; (888) WARM-FEET or (406) 837-0177

Tecnica USA, 19 Technology Drive, West Lebanon, NH 03784; (800) 258-3897 or (603) 298-8032; www.tecnicausa.com

Trukke Winter Sports Products, Inc., P.O. Box 347001, Truckee, CA 96160; (888) 837-8553 or (916) 587-1001

# Selected Outdoor and Backcountry Instruments

Avocet, Inc., P.O. Box 180, Palo Alto, CA 94302; (800) 227-8346 or (650) 321-8501; www.avocet.com

Backcountry Access, Tracker GPS, 2820 Wilderness Place, Unit H, Boulder, CO 80301; (800) 670-8735 or (303) 417-1345; www.bcaccess.com/bca

Garmin International (GPS units), 1200 East 151st Street, Olathe, KS 66062; (913) 397-8200

Kestrel, Nielsen Kellerman, 104 West 15th Street, Chester, PA 19013; (800) 784-4221 or (610) 447-1555; www.nkelectronics.com

Magellan Systems (GPS units), 960 Overland Court, San Dimas, CA 91773; (909) 394-5000; www.mgln.com

Pieps, Life-Link Backcountry Products, 1240 Huff Lane, P.O. Box 2913, Jackson Hole, WY 83001; (800) 443-8620 or (307) 733-2266; www.life-link.com

Ramer Products, Ltd., 1803 South Foothills Highway, Boulder, CO 80303; (303) 499-4466

Trimble Navigation Limited (GPS units), 645 North Mary Lane, Sunnyvale, CA 91772; (408) 481-8000; www.trimble.com

# Snowshoe Retail Sales and Rentals

In addition to the independent shops or small local chains below, Breeze (www.breezeski.com), Christy Sports, which also includes SportStalker and Inside Edge stores, and Gart Sports (www.gartsports.com) carry inventory of snowshoes in their dozens of outlets in Front Range metropolitan areas and mountain communities. Breeze specializes in rentals, Gart's in sales, and the Christy Sports chains and affiliates have both rental and sales at select locations.

## Aspen

Ajax Bike & Sport, 635 East Hyman, Aspen, CO 81611; (970) 925-7662

Aspen Sports, 408 East Cooper Avenue, Aspen, CO 81611, (970) 925-6331; 303 East Durant Avenue, (970) 925-6332; Aspen Club Lodge, (970) 925-6333; The Hotel Jerome, (970) 925-4523

Gorsuch Limited, 601 East Dean Street, Aspen, CO 81611; (970) 925-3203

The Hub of Aspen, 315 East Hyman, Aspen, CO 81611; (970) 925-7970

Ute Mountaineer, 308 South Mill Street, Aspen, CO 81611; (970) 925-2849; www.aspenonline.com/ute

## Avon

Base Mountain Sports, 10 West Beaver Creek Boulevard, Century 21 Building, Suite 100, Avon, CO 81620; (970) 845-9773

Gorsuch Limited, Hyatt Regency Promenade, Avon, CO 81620; (970) 949-7115

Venture Sports, 51 Beaver Creek Place, P.O. Box 3268, Avon, CO 81620; (888) 825-8245 or (970) 949-1318; vail.net/shops/venture/index.html

## Basalt

Bristlecone Mountain Sports, 123 Emma Road, Basalt, CO 81631; (970) 927-1492

## Beaver Creek

Aalta Sports, 268 Beaver Creek Plaza, Beaver Creek, CO 81620; (970) 845-7627

Base Mountain Sports, Poste Montane Lodge, Beaver Creek, CO 81620; (970) 949-4327; http://vail.net/shops/base/index.html

Rec Sports, Beaver Creek Lodge, 26 Avondale Lane, Avon, CO 81620; (800) 525-9624 or (970) 949-5576; www.recsports.com

## Boulder

Active Imprints, Table Mesa Shopping Center, 629 South Broadway, Boulder, CO 80303; (303) 494-0321

Boulder Army Store, 1545 Pearl Street, Boulder CO 80302; (303) 442-7616; www.pearlstreetmall.com/bas/index.html

Boulder Mountaineer, 1335 Broadway, Boulder, CO 80302; (303) 442-8355

Boulder Outdoor Center, 2510 North 47th Street, Boulder, CO 80301; (303) 444-8420; www.boc123.com

Boulder Ski Deals, 2404 Pearl Street, Boulder, CO 80302; (800) 920-3325 or (303) 938-8799; www.boulderskideals.com

Cutting Edge Sports, 2516 North Broadway, Boulder, CO 80304; (303) 413-0228

Doc's Ski & Sports, 627 South Broadway, Boulder, CO 80303; (303) 499-0963

Eastern Mountain Sports (EMS), 2520 Arapahoe Avenue, Boulder, CO 80302; (303) 442-7566; www.emsonline.com

Little Mountain Outdoor Gear for Kids (kids' snowshoes, sales and rentals), 1136 Spruce Street, Boulder, CO 80302; (303) 443-1757

McGuckin's, Arapahoe Village Shopping Center, 2525 Arapahoe Avenue, Boulder, CO 80302; (303) 443-1822

Mountain Sports, 821 Pearl Street, Boulder, CO 80302; (303) 443-6770

Neptune Mountaineering, Table Mesa Shopping Center, 633 South Broadway, #A, Boulder, CO 80303; (303) 499-8866

Play It Again Sports, Table Mesa Shopping Center, 653 South Broadway, Boulder, CO 80303; (303) 499-2011; www.henge.com/~sues

Runners Roost, 1129 Pearl Street, Boulder, CO 80302; (303) 443-9868; www.runnersroost.com

## Breckenridge

AMR Ski Rentals, City Market Plaza, #9A, Breckenridge, CO 80424; (800) 999-3045 or (970) 453-6921

Great Adventure Sports Center, 400 North Park Street, Breckenridge, CO 80424; (888) 453-0333 or (970) 453-0333; www.greatadventuresports.com

The Knorr House, 303 South Main, Breckenridge, CO 80424; (970) 453-2631

Lone Star Sports, 200 Washington Street, Breckenridge, CO 80424; (970) 453-2009 or (800) 621-9733; www.colorado.net/lonestar

Mountain Outfitters, 112 South Ridge Street, Breckenridge, CO 80424; (970) 453-2201

MountainWave, 600 South Park, Breckenridge, CO 80424; (970) 453-8305

Norway Haus Ski Shop, 127 South Main, Breckenridge, CO 80424; (800) 843-6674 or (970) 453-2375

Racer's Edge, 114 North Main Street, Breckenridge, CO 80424; (800) 451-5363 or (970) 453-0995; and Peak 9 Demo Center at the Village at Breckenridge, (970) 453-6584

Rec Sports (four in Breckenridge), P.O. Box 7037, Breckenridge , CO 80424; (800) 525-9624 or (970) 453-2194; www.recsports.com

## Buena Vista

The Trailhead, 707 U.S. Highway 24 North, P.O. Box 2023, Buena Vista, CO 81211; (719) 395-8001

## Carbondale

Ajax Bike & Sport, 419 Main Street, Carbondale, CO 81623; (970) 963-0128
Life Cycles, 902 Highway 133, Carbondale, CO 81623; (970) 963-1149

## Colorado Springs

Blick's Sporting Goods, 119 North Tejon Street, Colorado Springs, CO 80903; (719) 636-3348
Eastern Mountain Sports, 750 Citadel Mall, #2142, Colorado Springs, CO 80909; (719) 574-8207; www.emsonline.com
Glenn's Army Surplus (military surplus snowshoes), 114 East Mill, Colorado Springs, CO 80903; (719) 634-9828
Grand West Outfitters, 3250 North Academy Boulevard, CO 80917; (719) 596-3031
Jumbosports, 4285 North Academy Boulevard, Colorado Springs, CO 80918; (719) 594-4998; www.jumbosports.com
Mountain Chalet, 226 North Tejon Street, Colorado Springs, CO 80903; (719) 633-0732
Play It Again Sports, 1033 North Academy Boulevard, Colorado Springs, CO 80809, (719) 574-4849; and 5338 Montebello Lane, Colorado Springs, CO 80918, (719) 528-5840
Runners Roost, 107 East Bijou, Colorado Springs, CO 80903; (719) 632-2633; www.runnersroost.com
Sports Replay, 3650 Austin Bluffs Parkway, Colorado Springs, CO 80918; (719) 531-0888
Surplus City! Outdoors, 2732 West Colorado Avenue, Colorado Springs, CO 80904; (719) 634-1264

## Copper Mountain

AB Ski Rentals, Snowbridge Square Mall, Copper Mountain, CO 80443; (800) 423-SKIS or (970) 968-2908; www.toski.com/summit/skishops.htm
Copper Mountain Cross-Country Ski Center, Copper Mountain, CO 80443; (970) 668-1385
Rec Sports, 760 Copper Road, Copper Mountain, CO 80443; (800) 525-9624 or (970) 968-2919; www.recsports.com

## Cortez

Slaven's, 237 West Main Street, Cortez, CO 81321; (970) 565-8571

## Crested Butte

The Alpineer, 419 Sixth Street, Crested Butte, CO 81224; (800) 223-4655 or (970) 349-5210; www.alpineer.com
Alternative Sports Company, 309 Sixth Street, P.O. Box 245, Crested Butte, CO 81224; (970) 349-1320; www.alternativesports.com

Cliffhangers, The Mall at Mt. Crested Butte, Crested Butte, CO 81225; (970) 349-9122

Crested Butte Ski & Kayak, 313 Elk Avenue, Crested Butte, CO 81224; (970) 349-1323

Crested Butte Sports, 35 Emmons Road, Mt. Crested Butte, CO 81225; (800) 301-9169 or (970) 349-7516; www.cbinteractive.com

Gene Taylor's, #19 Emmons Loop, Mt. Crested Butte, CO 81225; (970) 349-5386; www.genetaylors.com

Troutfitter Sports, 114 Elk Avenue, Crested Butte, CO 81224; (970) 349-1323

## Denver Metro Area

### Denver

Bevans' Sports, 5002 East Hampden Avenue, Denver 80222; (303) 756-0304

Confluence Kayaks, 1537 Platte Street, Denver, CO 80202; (303) 433-3676

Eastern Mountain Sports (EMS), 1616 Welton Street, Denver, CO 80202; (303) 446-8338; www.emsonline.com

The Edgeworks, 860 Broadway, Denver, CO 80203; (303) 831-7228

Grand West Outfitters, 801 Broadway, Denver, CO 80203; (303) 825-0300

Recreational Equipment Inc. (REI), 4100 East Mexico Avenue, Building C, Denver, CO 80222; (303) 756-3100; www.rei.com

Runners Roost, 1001 16th Street, Denver, CO 80265, (303) 694-5757; 1685 South Colorado Boulevard, Denver, CO 80222, (303) 759-8455; 6554 South Parker Road, Denver, CO 80231, (303) 766-3411; www.runnersroost.com

The Sporting Woman, 2902 East Third Avenue, Cherry Creek North, Denver, CO 80206; (303) 316-8392

Sports Plus, 1055 South Gaylord, Denver, CO 80209; (303) 777-6613

### Arvada

Sports Rent, 8761 Wadsworth Boulevard, Arvada, CO 80005; (303) 467-0200; www.sportsrent.com

### Aurora

Supreme Ski Rental, 2601 Parker Road, Aurora, CO 80014; (303) 369-5900

### Englewood

Army & Navy Surplus Store (military surplus snowshoes), 3524 South Broadway, Englewood, CO 80110; (303) 789-1827

Eskimo Ski & Snowboard, 131 East Belleview Avenue, Englewood, CO 80110; (303) 761-1101

Mountain Miser, 209 West Hampden Avenue, Englewood, CO 80110; (303) 761-7070; www.mountainmiser.com

Recreational Equipment, Inc. (REI), 9637 East County Line Road, Englewood, CO 80110; (303) 858-1726; www.rei.com

### Highlands Ranch

Runners Roost, 1970 East County Line Road, #C, Highlands Ranch, CO 80126; (303) 738-9446; www.runnersroost.com

### Lakewood

Recreational Equipment, Inc. (REI), 5375 South Wadsworth Boulevard, Lakewood, CO 80123; (303) 932-0600; www.rei.com

Rocky Mountain Sports, 790 Kipling Street, Lakewood, CO 80215; (303) 232-6834

## Littleton

Eastern Mountain Sports, Park Meadows Mall, 8405 Park Meadows Center Drive, Suite 1006, Littleton, CO 80124; (303) 790-0760; www.emsonline.com

Chap's, 8209 South Holly, Littleton, CO 80122, (303) 740-2226; and 760 South University, Littleton, CO 80122, (303) 221-8977

Colorado Recycled Sports, 133 West County Line Road, Littleton, CO 80126; (303) 797-1825

Colorado Ski & Golf, 9086 West Bowles Avenue, Littleton, CO 80123; (303) 948-7550

Custom Ski Care, 9966 West Bowles Avenue, Littleton, CO 80127; (303) 979-3400

Jumbosports, 7848 County Line Road, Littleton, CO 80124; (303) 792-3374; www.jumbosports.com

## Westminster

Eastern Mountain Sports (EMS), 8971 North Harlan, Westminster Mall Plaza, Westminster, CO 80030; (303) 650-9843; www.emsonline.com

Jumbosports, 9219 Sheridan Boulevard, Westminster, CO 80030; (303) 426-0202; www.jumbosports.com

Recreational Equipment, Inc. (REI), 8991-B Harlan Street, Westminster, CO 80030; (303) 429-1800; www.rei.com

## Wheatridge

Larson's Ski & Sport, 4715 Kipling Street, Wheatridge, CO 80033; (303) 423-0654

# Dillon

Columbine Ski & Sport, 149 Tenderfoot, Dillon, CO 80435; (970) 468-5165

Uwanna Ski, 100 Labonte, Dillon, CO 80435; (800) 988-9266 or (970) 468-5506

WildernesSports, 266 Summit Place, Dillon, CO 80435; (970) 468-5687

# Durango

Pine Needle Mountaineering, 835 Main Avenue, Durango, CO 81301; (970) 247-8728

# Estes Park

Colorado Wilderness Sports, 358 East Elkhorn Avenue, P.O. Box 4079, Estes Park, CO 80517; (800) 504-6642 or (970) 586-6548; www.cowsports.com

Outdoor World, 156 East Elkhorn Avenue, P.O. 2800, Estes Park, CO 80517; (970) 586-2114; www.rmconnection.com

Rocky Mountain Connection, 141 East Elkhorn Avenue, P.O. Box 2800, Estes Park, CO 80517; (970) 586-3361; www.rmconnection.com

# Fort Collins

Eastern Mountain Sports (EMS), Foothills Fashion Mall, 215 East Parkway, Fort Collins, CO 80525; (970) 223-6511; www.emsonline.com

Recreational Equipment, Inc. (REI), 4025 South College Avenue, Fort Collins, CO 80525; (970) 223-0123; www.rei.com

Runners Roost, 1669 South College Avenue, Fort Collins, CO 80525; (970) 224-9114; www.runnersroost.com

## Fraser

Ski Broker, P.O. Box 716, Fraser, CO 80442; (800) 544-2431 or (970) 726-8882

## Frisco

AB Ski Rentals, 829 North Summit Boulevard, Frisco, CO 80443; (800) 423-SKIS or (970) 668-5267; www.toski.com/summit/skishops.htm

All Season's Sports, Boardwalk Center, 720 Granite, P.O. Box 1281, Frisco, CO 80443; (970) 668-5599

Antler's, 908 North Summit Boulevard, Frisco, CO 80443; (970) 668-3152; www.antlerstradingpost.com

CycleSmiths, 418 Main Street, Frisco, CO 80443; (970) 668-1385

Pioneer Sports, Ltd., 842 North Summit Boulevard, Frisco, CO 80443; (800) 888-3688 or (970) 668-3668; www.colorado.net/pioneer

## Glenwood Springs

Summit Canyon Mountaineering, 732 Grand Avenue, Glenwood Springs, CO 81601; (800) 360-6994 or (970) 945-6994; www.summitcanyon.com

## Golden

Alpenglow Mountainsports, 885 Lupine, #B, Golden, CO 80401; (800) 274-0133 or (303) 277-0133

Foothills Ski & Bike, 25948 Genesee Trail Road, Golden, CO 80401; (303) 526-2036

Runners Roost, 3294 Youngfield, Golden, CO 80401; (303) 232-5000; www.runnersroost.com

## Granby

Great Divide Sports, 250 East Agate Avenue, P.O. Box 1636, Granby 80446; (970) 887-9449

## Grand Junction

Gene Taylor's, 445 West Gunnison Avenue, Grand Junction, CO 81501; (970) 242-8165; www.genetaylors.com

Over The Edge, 202 East Aspen Avenue, Fruita, CO 81521; (970) 858-7220

Powderhorn Sports, Powderhorn Ski Resort, Grand Mesa, CO 81643; (970) 268-5700, Ext. 2094

Summit Canyon Mountaineering, 461 Main Street, Grand Junction, CO 81501; (800) CLIMB-IT or (970) 243-2847; www.summitcanyon.com

## Grand Lake

Never Summer Mountain Products, 919 Grand Avenue, P.O. Box 929, Grand Lake, CO, 80447; (970) 627-3642

Rocky Mountain Sports, 830-A Grand Avenue, Grand Lake, CO 80447; (970) 627-8124

## Gunnison

Gene Taylor's, 201 Tomichi, Gunnison, CO 81230; (970) 641-1845; www.-genetaylors.com

## Idaho Springs

Outback Outfitters, 1319 Miner Street, Idaho Springs, CO 80452; (303) 567-0850

## Keystone

River Run Sports, River Run Village, Keystone, CO 80435; (970) 496-4619; www.snow.com

Mountain View Sports, Mountain View Plaza, Keystone, P.O. Box 97, Dillon CO 80435; (800) 530-3836 or (970) 468-0396; www.colorado.net/mvs

Rec Sports, 23114 U.S. Highway 6, Keystone, CO 80435; (800) 525-9624 or (970) 468-5775; www.recsports.com

## Leadville

Bill's Sport Shop, 225 Harrison Avenue, P.O. Box 588, Leadville, CO 80461; (719) 486-0739

Leadville Ski Country, 116 East Ninth Street, Leadville, CO 80461; (800) 500-5323 or (719) 486-3836

10th Mountain Sports, 500 East Seventh, Leadville, CO 80461; (719) 486-2202

## Louisville

Cutting Edge Sports, 1387 South Boulder Road, Unit D, Louisville, CO 80027; (303) 666-4550

## Ouray

Ouray Mountain Sports, 722 Main Street, Ouray, CO 81427; (970) 325-4284

## Poncha Springs

Homestead Sport & Ski, 11238 West U.S. Highway 50, Poncha Springs, CO 81242; (800) 539-7507 or (719) 539-7507; www.homesteadsports.com

Wilderness Ski Shop, 10015 U.S. Highway 50, Poncha Springs, CO 81242; (888) 639-3747 or (719) 539-3747; www.peaksnewsnet.com/wilderness

## Ridgway

Ridgway Outdoor Experience, 102 Campbell Lane, Ridgway, CO 81432; (970) 626-3608

## Salida

Headwaters Outdoor Equipment, 228 North F Street, Salida, CO 81201; (800) 288-0675 or (719) 539-4506; www.americanadventure.com

Mt. Shavano Ski Rental, 16101 West Highway 50, Salida, CO 81201; (800) 678-0341 or (719) 539-3240

## Silverthorne

WildernesSports, 171 Blue River Parkway, Silverthorne, CO 80498; (970) 468-8519
Wildernest Sports, 14 Fawn Court, Silverthorne, CO 80498; (970) 468-5970

## Silverton

The French Bakery at the Teller House, 1250 Greene Street, Silverton, CO 81433;
(970) 387-5423

## Snowmass

Aspen Sports, Snowmass Village Center, (970) 923-3566; 6268 Snowmass Village Mall, (970) 923-6111; Silvertree Hotel, (970) 923-6504, all Snowmass Village, CO 81615
Gene Taylor's, Snowmass Village Mall, Building 54, P.O. Box 5115, Snowmass Village, CO 81615; (970) 923-4336; www.genetaylors.com

## Steamboat Springs

Backdoor Sport, Ltd., 811 Yampa Avenue, Steamboat Springs, CO 80477; (970) 879-6249; www.cmn.net/~backdoor
Good Times Sports, 730 Lincoln Avenue, Steamboat Springs, CO 80477, (970) 879-7818; and Clock Tower, Ski Time Square, Steamboat Springs, CO 80477, (970) 871-0511
Helly Hanson Store, 2305 Mt. Werner Circle, Steamboat Springs, CO 80488; (970) 871-1541
Inside Edge Sports, 1835 Central Park Drive, Steamboat Springs, CO 80477; rental reservations (800) 525-5520, shop (970) 879-1250; www.skichristy.com
Lahaina Ski & Sport, 2305 Mt. Werner Circle, Steamboat Springs, CO 80487; (970) 879-8989
One Stop Ski Shop, 729 Yampa Avenue, Steamboat Springs, CO 80477; (970) 879-4916; www.steamboat.com/1stop/
Ski Haus, 1450 South Lincoln Avenue, Steamboat Springs, CO 80477; (800) 932-3019 or (970) 879-0385; www.skihaussteamboat.com
Sore Saddle Cyclery, 1136 Yampa Avenue, Steamboat Springs, CO 80477; (970) 879-1675
Steamboat Ski Rentals, 2305 Mt. Werner Circle, Gondola Square, Steamboat Springs, CO 80487; (800) 859-9959 or (970) 879-6111, Ext. 345; www.steamboat-ski.com
Straightline Outdoor Sports, 744 Lincoln Avenue, Steamboat Springs, CO 80477; (800) 354-5463 or (970) 879-7568; www.straightlinesports.com

## Telluride

Paragon Ski & Sport, 217 West Colorado Avenue, Telluride, CO 81435, (970) 728-4525; 236 South Oak, (970) 728-4581; 560 Mountain Village, (970) 728-0992
Telluride Mountaineer, 219 East Colorado Avenue, Telluride, CO 81435; (970) 728-6736
Telluride Sports, six locations in town (on Colorado Avenue at the base of the Coonskin lift and in Camel's Garden Hotel at the base of the gondola; in Moun-

tain Village, at the Franz Klammer Lodge, the Peaks at Telluride Hotel and at the base of the gondola), all Telluride, CO 81435; (800) 828-SKIS or (970) 728-4477

## Toponas

Toponas Country Store, 10000 U.S. Highway 131, Toponas, CO 80479; (970) 638-4483

## Vail

American Ski Exchange, 225 Wall Street, Vail, CO 81657; (800) 327-1137 or (970) 476-1477; www.vail.net/shops/ase

Bag & Pack Shop, 122 East Meadow Drive, Vail, CO 81657; (970) 476-1027

Base Mountain Sports, Landmark, Lionshead Square, Vail, CO 81361, (970) 476-4875; Vail 21, Lionshead, (970) 476-3600; Vail Village Inn, (970) 476-4515; Evergreen Lodge, (970) 476-6609; http://vail.net/shops/base/index.html

Colorado Bike Service, 41149 U.S. Highway 6/24, Eagle-Vail, CO 81620; (970) 949-4641; http://vail.net/shops/cbs/index.html

Curtin-Hill Sports, 254 Bridge Street, Vail, CO 81657; (970) 476-5337; http://vail.net/shopping/curtin/index.html

Double Diamond Ski Shop, 520 Lionshead Mall, Vail, CO 81657; (800) 466-2704 or (970) 476-5500; www.kennys.com

Gore Range Mountainworks, 201 Gore Creek Drive, Vail, CO 81657; (970) 476-7625

Gorsuch Limited, Vail Village, 263 East Gore Creek Drive, Vail, CO 81657; (970) 476-2294

KidSport (children's snowshoes, sales), 122 East Meadow Drive, Vail, CO 81657; (800) 833-1729 or (970) 476-1666; vail.net/shopping/kidsport/index.html

Vail Boarder Service, 450 East Lionshead Circle, Vail, CO 81657; (970) 476-1233

Vail Mountaineering, 500 Lionshead Mall, Vail, CO 81657; (970) 476-4223

## Winter Park

Alpine Sun, Crestview Place Mall, P.O. Box 3320, Winter Park, CO 80482; (800) 752-3424 or (970) 726-5107

Black Dog Mountaineering and Flanagan's Ski Rentals, 78902 U.S. Highway 40, P.O. Box 13, Winter Park, CO 80482; (800) 544-1523 or (970) 726-4412; www.blkdog.com/mountain

Ski Depot Sports, (800) 525-6484 or (970) 726-8055; Hi Country Haus, (970) 726-8700; Beaver Village, (970) 726-1100; Iron Horse Resort Retreat, (970) 726-4703; all Winter Park, CO 80482; www.skidepot.com

Viking Ski Shop, 78966 U.S. Highway 40, P.O. Box 89, Winter Park, CO 80442; (800) 421-4013 or (970) 726-8885; www.skiwp.com

# Mail-Order Sources for Snowshoes and Outdoor Activewear

(*Indicates sizable selection of snowshoes, footwear and winter activewear)

Akers Ski, P.O. Box 280, Andover, ME 04216-0280; (207) 392-4582; www.-megalink.net/~akers

*Cabela's, One Cabela Drive, Sidney, NE 69160; (800) 237-4444 or (308) 254-5505

Campmor, P.O. Box 700-G, Saddle River, NJ 07458-0700; (800) CAMP-MOR; www.campmor.com

Eagle River Nordic, 15035 Crossover Road, Three Lakes, WI 54562; (800) 423-9730 or (715) 479-7285; www.enordic.com

Early Winters, P.O. Box 4333, Portland, OR 97208-4333; (800) 458-4438

*Eastern Mountain Sports (EMS), One Vose Farm Road, Peterborough, NH 03458; (603) 924-9571; www.emsonline.com

*L. L. Bean, Inc., Casco Street, Freeport, ME 04033; (800) 221-4221 or (207) 865-4761; www.llbean.com

*Nordic Equipment, Inc., P.O. Box 980250, Park City, UT 84098; (800) 321-1671 or (435) 649-1806; www.nordicequipment.com

Peak Ski & Sport, 230 South Hale Avenue, Suite 200, Escondido, CA 92029; (800) 550-SNOW or (760) 738-8285; www.imall.com/stores/peakski

*Recreational Equipment, Inc. (REI), P.O. Box 1938, Sumner, WA 98390-0800; (800) 426-4840 or (253) 395-3780; www.rei.com

Sierra Trading Post, 5025 Campstool Road, Cheyenne, WY 82007-1802; (800) 713-4534 or (307) 775-8050; www.sierra-trading.com

*Sports Gear Direct, 1803 South Foothills Highway, Suite 100, Boulder, CO 80303; (800) 353-7432; www.geardirect.com/sportsgear

Title Nine Sports (women's sports clothing and equipment), 5743 Landregan Street, Emeryville, CA 94608; (800) 609-0092; www.title9sports.com

## Outdoor Clothing and Pack Repair

All-Sew, 2040 30th Street, Suite E, Boulder, CO 80301; (303) 444-7397

Boulder Mountain Repair, Table Mesa Shopping Center, 641 South Broadway, Boulder, CO 80303; (303) 499-3634

Needle Mountain Design Sewing, 28261 Main Street, P.O. Box 3578, Evergreen, CO 80439; (800) 795-2941 or (303) 674-2941

## Boot Repair

Rocky Mountain Resole (formerly Morin Boot Repair), 211 Oak Street, Salida, CO 81201; (800) 228-BOOT; www.rmresole.com (Drop-off locations at The Bent Gate, Golden, CO; and at Front Range Outdoor Gear, Idaho Springs, CO.)

# Appendix E:
# Other Resources

## Road and Weather Reports

Avalanche Condition Hotlines: Aspen, (970) 920-1664; Denver and Boulder, (303) 275-5360; Durango, (970) 247-8187; Colorado Springs, (719) 520-0020; Fort Collins, (970) 482-0457; Summit County, (970) 668-0600; Vail/Minturn, (970) 827-5687

Colorado Avalanche Information Center, 10230 Smith Road, Denver, CO 80239; general number, (303) 371-1080; recorded avalanche conditions, (303) 275-5364 or (303) 275-5360; www.netway.net/caic

Colorado Road Conditions, recorded road conditions, (303) 639-1111 for roads within two hours of Denver, (303) 639-1234 for roads more than two hours from Denver

U.S. Forest Service (recorded) information: (303) 275-5350

Weather and Road Conditions website, www.faceshot.com/html/weather.html

## Organizations

American Alpine Club, 710 Tenth Street, Golden, CO 80401; (303) 384-0110; www.americanalpineclub.org

American Hiking Society, P.O. Box 20160, Washington DC 20041-2160; (888) 766-HIKE or (301) 565-6704; www.ahs.simplenet.com

Backcountry Skiers Alliance, P.O. Box 134, Boulder, CO 80306; (303) 444-6476; bsaco@ibm.net

Colorado Cross Country Ski Association (trade association of Colorado Nordic centers), P.O. Box 1336, Winter Park, CO 80482; (800) 869-4560; www.AdventureNet.com/go4it/cccsa.htm/

Colorado Mountain Club, 710 Tenth Street, #200, Golden, CO 80401; (800) 633-4417 or (303) 279-3080; www.cmc.org/cmc/ or www.earthnet.net/~cmc/

Mosaic Outdoor Mountain Club (Jewish club), P.O. Box 24772, Denver, CO 80224; hotline, (303) 836-6662; www.mosaics.org/colorado

National Forest Recreation Association, 325 Pennsylvania Avenue SE, Suite 271, Washington, DC, 20003; (202) 546-8527; www.nfra.org

SnowSports Industries America (trade association of winter sporting goods manufacturers), 8377-B Greensboro Drive, McLean, VA 22102; (703) 556-9020; www.snowlink.com

United States Snowshoe Association, Route 25, Box 94, Corinth, NY 12822; (518) 654-7648

# Multiday, Guided Backcountry Tours

Adventures Afoot, P.O. Box 1565, Estes Park, CO 80517; (800) 294-8218 or (970) 586-3194; www.afoot.com

American Wilderness Experience, 2820-A Wilderness Place, Boulder, CO 80301-5454; (800) 444-0099 or (303) 444-2622; www.gorp.com/awe/

Backroads, 801 Cedar Street, Berkeley, CA 94710-1800; (800) 462-2848 or (510) 527-1555; www.backroads.com

Paragon Guides, P.O. Box 130, Vail, CO 81658; (970) 926-5299; www.vail.net/paragonguides

Roads Less Traveled, 2840 Wilderness Place, Boulder, CO 80301; (800) 488-8483 or (303) 413-0938; www.roadslesstraveled.com

Wilderness Women, Inc., P.O. Box 19777, Denver, CO 80219-9920; (303) 922-7700

# Appendix F:
# Trails Rated by Difficulty

## Easy

Pingree Park Road, 43
Upper Michigan Ditch, 46
Sprague Lake from Bear Lake Road, 54
Bear Lake, 58
Wild Basin Road, 60
Brainard Lake Road, 68
Hessie Road, 84
Echo Lake, 93
Lily Pad Lake, 107
Bemrose Ski Circus Road, 112
Interlaken Trail, 136
Rio Grande Trail, 144
Castle Creek Road, 154
North Star Loop, 157
Ditch Trail, 160
Town Ranch Trail, 169
Ditch Road, 175
Old Railroad Grade, 185
Collegiate Peaks Campground, 191
Evans-Rush Trail Area, 191
Fraser River Trail, 200
Colorado River Trail to Shipler Cabins, 211
Never Summer Ranch Road, 213
Valley/River Trail Loop, 214
North Inlet Trail to Summerland Park, 215
East Inlet Trail to Adams Falls, 216
Fish Creek Falls, 222
Seedhouse Road, 230
Pearl Lake State Park Road, 233
Aspen Flats Loop, 235
Miller Mesa Road, 252
St. Miguel River Trail, 256
Prospect Basin, 259
Railroad Grade, 263
Priest Lakes Road, 264
Morefield Village, 269

Cliff Palace Loop, 269
Jackson Reservoir Trail, 271

## Easy to Moderate

Beaver Meadows, 51
Hollowell Park, 53
Long Lake/Jean Lunning Trail, 76
Mitchell Lake, 78
Bakerville-Loveland Trail, 97–98
Sally Barber Mine, 114
Mitchell Creek Loop, 139
Richmond Ridge, 149
Slate River Gulch, 172
West Brush Creek Road, 175
Bassam Park, 183
Fooses Creek, 188
Knight Ridge Trail/East Shore Trail
    (sections of trails), 210
Colorado River Trail/Lulu City, 212
North Inlet Trail to Cascade Falls, 215
East Inlet Trail to the meadow, 216
Trilby Flats, 233
Wildcat Alley, 236
Lower Trails, 242
Magic Meadows, 260
Boggy Draw, 273

## Moderate

Zimmerman Lake, 44
Bierstadt Lake from Bear Lake, 54
Sprague Lake from Glacier Basin
    Parking Area, 54
Bierstadt Lake from Glacier Basin
    Parking Area, 56
Mills Lake, 57
Nymph, Dream and Emerald Lakes, 58

# Challenging

# Moderate to Challenging

# Glossary

**Alaskan:** Oblong snowshoes, usually measuring between 4 and 5 feet long; also called Pickerel or Yukon

**Algonquin:** Wide, teardrop-shaped snowshoe; also called beavertail, Huron, Maine or Michigan

**Anorak:** Insulated ski jacket that is pulled over the head and has a zipper from the neck to partway down the chest

**Bare-booting:** Walking on hard snow just using boot soles instead of snowshoes

**Bearpaw:** Wide and round-shaped snowshoe

**Beavertail:** Snowshoe with a wide, teardrop-shaped frame; also known as an Algonquin, Maine or Michigan

**Binding:** Snowshoe component that holds the boot to the snowshoe

**Blaze:** Originally a small nick hacked out of a tree trunk to mark a backcountry snowshoeing and skiing route; now more commonly a small colored marker attached to a tree for the same purpose

**Breaking trail:** To be the lead snowshoer through fresh powder

**Bushwhack:** To go off-trail, usually through bushes and undergrowth

**Car shuttle:** Tactic used by groups to avoid making an out-and-back hike. At least two vehicles are needed. The first vehicle is left at the end of the proposed route, and the entire group goes in a second vehicle to the trailhead for the start of the hike. At the end of the excursion, the driver of the first car takes the driver of the second car back to the vehicle.

**Carrying surface:** Surface area or deck of a snowshoe, which provides flotation

**Classical skiing:** Traditional kick-and-glide cross-country skiing in tracks etched into the snow

**Claw:** Metal talon affixed to the bottom of the snowshoe at an angle or perpendicular to the direction of travel, to provide traction

**Cleat:** Another name for claw or talon

**Corn:** Typical spring conditions, in which snow forms small balls that to some people resemble small frozen kernels

**Crampon:** Metal talon attached to a snowshoe's pivot point to provide auxiliary traction on icy or steep terrain

**Cross-country ski center:** Commercial facility for cross-country skiing and, increasingly, snowshoeing, generally featuring marked and groomed trails, warming shelter with food service, retail and rental shops instruction and patrol; also called Nordic center

**Cross-country skiing:** Skiing on flat or rolling terrain using specialized cross-country equipment; see also Classical skiing and Skating

**Deck:** Solid panel of Hypalon, urethane-coated nylon or other material within the snowshoe frame to provide flotation on the snow

**Fall line:** Most direct path down a slope; the track a ball would take if rolled down the slope

**Flotation:** Property of the deck or webbing that prevents the user from sinking deep into the snow

**Forest Service:** United States Forest Service, an agency under the Department of Agriculture, which administers national forests

**Frame:** Metal structural support for the decking and binding mechanism

**Gaiters:** Lower-leg protectors of treated nylon, Gore-Tex or other waterproof fabric, worn over boots to keep feet dry and free of snow by preventing snow from seeping into the boot tops

**Geometry:** Shape and size of a snowshoe frame

**Glissade:** Controlled downhill glide; also called snowshoe sliding

**Gore-Tex:** Brand name of a waterproof, breathable fabric that is very popular for winter active outerwear

**Harness:** Another name for binding

**Heel lift:** Removable accessory designed to keep heel from extending down to the snow and to prevent the calf muscles from overstretching and ultimately aching on steep climbs, such as in running uphill

**Heel strap:** Section of the strap that is snugged around to the back of the boot

**Huron:** Wide, teardrop-shaped snowshoe; also called Algonquin, beavertail, Maine or Michigan

**Kick step:** Technique for steep uphills in loose snow, in which the snowshoer kicks the front of the snowshoe horizontally into the slope

**Lacing:** Another name for webbing on traditional wood frame snowshoes

**Maine:** Wide, teardrop-shaped snowshoe; also called Algonquin, beavertail, Huron or Michigan

**Mashed potatoes:** Nickname for very wet, heavy snow

**Michigan:** Wide, teardrop-shaped snowshoe; also called Algonquin, beavertail, Huron or Maine

**Modified bearpaw:** Similar to a bearpaw snowshoe but with the addition of a tail

**Neoprene:** Synthetic rubberized insulation, sometimes used for gaiters or socks

**Ojibwa:** Streamlined snowshoe design characterized by an upturned toe and long tail

**Park Service:** United States Park Service, an agency under the Department of the Interior, which administers national parks and national monuments

**Parka:** Insulated ski jacket with a full front zipper

**Pickerel:** Oblong snowshoes, usually measuring between 4 and 5 feet long; also called Alaskan or Yukon

**Pivot bar:** An aluminum or other solid bar attached to the snowshoe frame that enables the binding (and therefore the foot) to rotate; also called pivot rod or simply rod

**Points:** Sharp teeth of a claw or crampon that provide traction

**Post holing:** Sinking into deep snow, usually when not wearing snowshoes

**Pulk:** Small sled to be towed over the snow; in this country, usually used to take small children on the trail

**Skating:** New form of cross-country skiing that involves pushing off the inside edge of the free ski for propulsion and done on a wide, smooth snow lane with no set tracks

**Tail:** Back of the snowshoe

**Toe cord:** Pivot system on traditional wood frame snowshoes

**Toe hole:** Aperture in the decking on the front of the snowshoe that allows the binding and foot to rotate

**Trail fee:** Use fee for the trails at a cross-country/snowshoeing area

**Traverse:** To cross a slope, rather than ascend or descend directly

**Treeline:** Elevation above which trees do not grow; also called timberline; in Colorado, the treeline is at about 11,500 feet above sea level

**Vertical:** Difference in elevation between the lowest and highest points of a route

**Webbing:** Webbed decking of rawhide, Neoprene or other material used in traditional snowshoes; also called lacing

**Yukon:** Oblong snowshoes, usually measuring between 4 and 5 feet long; also called Alaskan or Pickerel

# Index

# About the Author

Photo by Ral Sandberg.

Claire Walter was born and raised in Connecticut. A graduate of Boston University, she lived in the New York area for more years than necessary before moving to Colorado in 1988. An avid skier, hiker, scuba diver and, of course, snowshoer, she combines such avocations with a career as a freelance writer and editor. She has written a dozen books about outdoor sports, travel and other subjects, including *Rocky Mountain Skiing, Skiing on a Budget* and *The Complete Idiot's Guide to Skiing*. She is also *Skiing* magazine's travel editor and a contributor to many national and regional publications.

She has been honored with a Lowell Thomas Award for Excellence in Guidebook Writing and a Harold Hirsch Award for Books, and was named Colorado Freelance Writer of the Year by Colorado Ski Country USA. She is a member of the American Society of Journalists and Authors, Colorado Authors' League, North American SnowSports Journalists Association and Society of American Travel Writers. She lives in Boulder with her husband, Ral Sandberg, and her son, Andrew Cameron-Walter.